WILD FRENCHMEN AND FRENCHIFIED INDIANS

EARLY AMERICAN STUDIES

Series editors:

Daniel K. Richter, Kathleen M. Brown, Max
Cavitch, and David Waldstreicher

Exploring neglected aspects of our colonial, revolutionary,
and early national history and culture, Early American
Studies reinterprets familiar themes and events in
fresh ways. Interdisciplinary in character, and with
a special emphasis on the period from about 1600
to 1850, the series is published in partnership with
the McNeil Center for Early American Studies.

A complete list of books in the series is
available from the publisher.

WILD FRENCHMEN AND FRENCHIFIED INDIANS

Material Culture and Race
in Colonial Louisiana

SOPHIE WHITE

UNIVERSITY OF PENNSYLVANIA PRESS

PHILADELPHIA

For Charlie, Cleome, and Josephine

Published by
University of Pennsylvania Press
Philadelphia, Pennsylvania 19104-4112
www.upenn.edu/pennpress

Printed in the United States of America on acid-free paper
10 9 8 7 6 5 4 3 2 1

Library of Congress Cataloging-in-Publication Data
White, Sophie.
  Wild Frenchmen and Frenchified Indians : material culture
and race in colonial Louisiana / Sophie White. — 1st ed.
    p. cm. — (Early American studies)
  ISBN 978-0-8122-4437-3 (hardcover: alk. paper)
  1. French—Louisiana—History—18th century. 2. Indians
of North America—Louisiana—History—18th century.
3. Louisiana—Race relations—History—18th century. 4. Race
awareness—Louisiana—History—18th century. 5. Material
culture—Louisiana—History—18th century. 6. Clothing and
dress—Social aspects—Louisiana—History—18th century. I.
Title. II. Series: Early American studies.
F380.F8W55   2012
976.3'02—dc23   2012014401

CONTENTS

Contents

ILLUSTRATIONS

FIGURES

PLATES FOLLOWING PAGE 142

WILD FRENCHMEN AND
FRENCHIFIED INDIANS

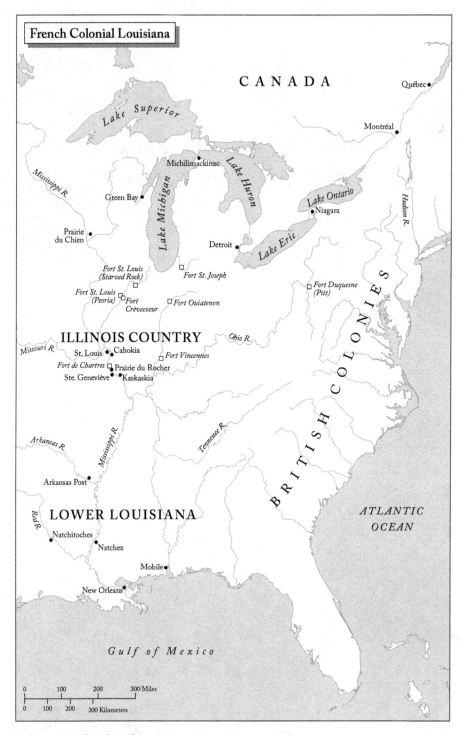

Figure 1. French Colonial Louisiana.

Introduction

In eighteenth-century French colonial Louisiana, Marie Catherine Illinoise, an Illinois Indian woman convert who was legally and sacramentally married to a Frenchman in the Upper Mississippi Valley, could be found dressed in one of her silk taffeta gowns as she sat in an armchair in her home built in the French colonial architectural style. Born Illinois, she was now "Frenchified" and was categorized in official records as French. This woman's material culture testifies to the transformations engineered by French and Indians as a result of colonization, conversion, and *métissage* (the mixing of peoples).[1] For there were numerous other instances of French-Indian exchanges and cross-cultural dressing in Louisiana.

In fulfilling her wish to take her vows as a Catholic nun in New Orleans, Marie Turpin, born from a French-Indian union, would cement her acquisition of a new identity and name through the wearing of special religious attire. A *voyageur* (canoeman or fur trader) of mixed French-Indian heritage, Jean Saguingouara, would enter into a formal agreement to go to New Orleans and back; other than his wages, he negotiated for his linens to be laundered on arrival in that town. In the same year that this trader traveled down the Mississippi River, Antoine Philippe de Marigny, Sieur de Mandeville, a French military cadet of noble origin, underwent a reverse transformation, donning Indian garb to traverse the hinterlands. In each of these anecdotes, clothing offered an especially elastic, protean means of expression. Through the act of dressing, indigenous peoples and settlers found the means to consciously express themselves even as they bought into, or were forced into, colonization's material underpinnings. For colonization in early America was built on encounters mediated by appearance, placing clothing at the center of cross-cultural relations and speaking to the vitality of cultural exchanges made visible on the body.

Analyzing the contours of French-Indian cultural cross-dressing I use identity as a category of analysis to shed light on how the French in America viewed the "savages" and formulated Frenchness.[2] The appearance of the

Indian wife, the nun, the trader, and the cadet provides insights into their consumption of material goods, specifically dress, and their skill in donning and wearing the clothes. But how these people lived and how they looked also influenced the way they were perceived. That colonial authorities could classify an Indian-born woman as French, for example, raises the question whether her manipulation of goods determined her credentials (in the eyes of the French) as "French" or "sauvage." Such sartorial exchanges raise fundamental questions about how subjectivity was defined and constructed. They also problematize the process whereby identity was explained during a period when French conceptions of difference were in transition, in a colony where policies toward Indians were colored by preoccupations with religion and acculturation, and inflected by the establishment of African slavery.

While this book illuminates the agency of Native Americans and Europeans as they encountered and absorbed each other's goods, it foregrounds colonists' rather than Indians' conceptions of difference. I argue that appearance influenced the ways the French understood and theorized ethnic, and later racial, identity. Dress was never simply a matter of self-expression but a cultural act subject to interpretation by onlookers. Over the course of the French regime, from 1673 to 1769, there was a transition from a conception of identity as fluid and mutable, to an essentialist conception based on protobiological assumptions.[3] How individual Indians living in French settlements dressed, I aver, had an impact on whether colonists hung on to older views of ethnicity as mutable, or subscribed to new models of a fixed and inborn racial identity for Indians. My book recognizes the complex geopolitical factors that paved the way for racialism. But it also underlines that there was no smooth transition to racialization, and that material culture served to complicate the ascendancy of a hegemonic protobiological model of difference in the colony as applied to Indians. For, as a genre of cultural expression, material culture did not simply reflect difference. It also helped to produce it. My analysis thus offers an innovative reading of the contours and the chronology of racialization in early America.

*   *   *

This book foregrounds the role of culture, especially dress, in explaining the process of racialization in colonial Louisiana over the course of the late seventeenth and eighteenth centuries, a key period for the study of transformations in conceptions of difference against the backdrop of religious conversion. Louisiana, originally a province of New France, was a vast colony, sparsely populated by colonists and encompassing the central two-thirds of the present-day United States (see Figure 1). As a focus of study, it has the advantage of lying at the intersection of two distinct models of French imperialism that were in tension with each other in this period. Upper Louisiana (or Illinois Country) grew out of colonization oriented toward missionary activity and the fur trade in New France. Lower Louisiana would be influenced by the development of slave plantation societies in the Caribbean and structured by slave codes.[4] Settlement practices in Upper or Lower Louisiana corresponded to their respective models but with the additional factor that African slavery would be established in Upper Louisiana on a scale never found in New France.[5] As my study reveals, each model determined how the French interacted with indigenous populations, with implications for our interpretation of the trajectory of racialism in the two areas.

In trying to understand the process of racialization in French America, historians have focused on language, legal, economic, and religious practices, sexual mores, and other usually abstract intellectual frameworks and discourses of representation.[6] My book shows that we must also contend with the material signs of culture and the concrete expressions of identity and subjectivity. As in the study of the English colonies, the body was a key site for the inscription of difference in French America.[7] This lens has provided historians of Louisiana with a way to frame the emergence of racial discourses, especially pertaining to sexuality and skin color.[8] But my research reveals that the *clothed* body—and the spatial context in which the act of dressing took place—played a specially nuanced role, for clothing itself was deployed both to signal and to construct identity. The function of clothing was not simply to insulate the body according to a given society's mores (in the colonial period, clothing was even required to clean the body). Rather, the process and rituals of dressing—the performative sequence of clothing, undressing, reclothing in convincing ways with the requisite undergarments and deportment—served another purpose, that of creating, affirming, and upholding identity on a daily basis.

In colonial Louisiana, objects framed and mediated social, political, religious, and economic interactions. Material objects both channeled and constructed ways of thinking about "race," lending themselves to cultural expressions that provide a primary means of explaining colonization. Cloth, clothing, and items of adornment were ubiquitous and dominant media of trade in the New World and testify to the economic and political role of these quotidian goods. Textiles and apparel were the major categories of commodities imported into the American colonies, and these types of merchandise far outnumbered metal implements, tools, and guns in French-Indian exchanges in the Great Lakes.[9] These were goods that played a pivotal role in colonization, attesting to the special appeal of aesthetic and tactile commodities that could be infused with meaning when applied to the body. These means of expression were deployed, sometimes simultaneously, to facilitate and to disrupt social and power relations in early America. Here, the process of cultural cross-dressing was foundational to the initially fluid ethnic, class, and gender elaborations of French colonial Louisiana. Conversely, dress might also be used to assert strict social and ethnic delineations within French and Indian populations.

Material culture was available for manipulation by all parties, not simply those who have left us documentary sources for writing the history of French America. The analysis of dress and material culture is therefore especially valuable in illuminating the lives of the nonliterate.[10] But this approach also enriches our understanding of the lives of the literate, by providing an alternative method of evaluating their responses to colonization.

My approach to this form of analysis is clearly indebted to the existing literature on cultural cross-dressing and on dress in cross-cultural contexts.[11] But I am particularly interested in attending to the actual objects adopted (or adapted) in the course of cultural cross-dressing. My interpretation rests on the analysis of the physical characteristics of clothing and textiles, whether their tactile and visual qualities, their three-dimensional embodiment based on weave, cut, and construction methods (as these intersected with bodily constructions), their cost and quality based on workmanship and materials. This methodical analysis relies on contemporary visual and documentary representations of dress in the absence of surviving objects and is necessarily grounded in the close textual reading of French documents pertaining to objects. When subjected to a detailed material culture analysis, the aesthetic qualities of shared objects of exchange, and the spaces in which they were worn, bring into focus the more subtle ways in which social status, regional affiliation, and difference were communicated in the cross-cultural performances of Indians and Frenchmen.

My emphasis on the materiality of clothing thus requires due regard for temporal and spatial factors. I pay close attention to the environment in which specific items of dress were worn and by whom. Other signs of assimilation, or the perception of assimilation, such as religious conversion for

Indians might be seen as peripheral to the subject. Yet these contexts were all the more necessary to project meaning through appearance precisely because of the protean nature of dress and its instability as a repository of meaning for disparate wearers and onlookers. For a member of the French nobility, wearing Indian garb while traversing the hinterlands had a functional justification that wearing the same garb in New Orleans could not have. For an Indian woman, wearing a French style gown was a defining act when the woman in question was an Illinois convert to Catholicism, sacramentally married to a French husband and living within a French colonial village. The spatial and situational frameworks in which each of these episodes of dressing took place reflected particular, not generalized circumstances. They also signaled the attempt to communicate an identity specific to that time, place, and circumstance, one that might be temporary and reversible rather than permanent. Indeed, just as sartorial identities were not fixed but malleable, so too was space ideological, subjective, and variable rather than neutral. The very premise of colonization depended on altering definitions or identifications of land. At the same time, acts of dressing deployed concrete three-dimensional artifacts and took place in physical environments. Space (environmental, architectural, interior), in conjunction with appearance, literally and physically mediated cultural interactions between Indians and Europeans.

The terms "French" and "Indian" (or "African") defy simplistic categorization, for these were heterogeneous groups of peoples in terms of religion, social organization, inheritance practices, and gender rules. The identifiers are, however, useful in framing a discussion of encounters between colonists and indigenous populations in early America, and I use the terms gingerly. Notwithstanding differences among and between French and Indians, the two populations shared a view (at least initially) that material markers were unstable, their meaning dependent on place and context. For example, indigenous captive adoption practices were premised on the role of dress in delineating identity. In these rituals, enemy individuals captured during warfare might have their lives saved if chosen to "cover the dead," in other words, to assume the identity of a deceased member of the tribe as his or her reincarnation. In these rituals, sartorial transformation rendered the symbolic change in tribal, clan, kin, and personal identity concrete.[12]

The French also looked to dress to define and establish rather than simply mirror identity. This was a concept crystallized in the practice of having royal brides stripped of their national fashion and changed into French dress upon crossing the border into France and into their new identity as French, a material affirmation of the renunciation of past identity and assumption of a new one.[13] More pertinent yet for this study of Louisiana, the French Crown's plans for colonization in mainland North America envisioned a role for cultural imperialism that included dress among other tools of colonization. A book centered on dress needs a textile metaphor. If religion and racialization represent the warp of this book, stripping and redressing form a thematic weft linking the stories told in each chapter.

The premise of my book is the potential of dress to unpack the process and evolution of racialization in French America. The French colonial and missionary venture in North America focused on culture (in parallel with conversion) as a means of achieving control of the region. Cross-cultural transformations in New France took place in the context of the official policy of Frenchification ("la francisation") that was at the heart of France's plans for colonizing North America and asserting demographic and religious control over the region.[14] Originally crafted for New France, the intent behind this formal policy was to turn the Indians there into French subjects of the king: not only Catholic but also linguistically, culturally, and legally "French."

Frenchification policies, with their emphasis on mutability and a cultural basis for identity, emerged from a confluence of secular and religious factors linked both to Catholic missionary goals and to the development of French nationalism, during a period when the idea of the French nation-state was still crystallizing.[15] But Frenchification was mapped onto a concept of identity that was not exclusive to the French. Rather, Frenchification policies were one manifestation of a worldview at the core of European-wide understandings of the new peoples they encountered and colonized in America. For the theory of monogenesis (that all mankind shared a common origin) framed Europeans' encounters with Indians, with its premise that identity, like skin color, was not fixed but malleable.[16] For colonists, the premise that Indians' identity was mutable carried the distinct possibility and risk of the reverse: a descent from a cultured to a wild ("sauvage") state. Where Indians had the potential to be converted and "civilized," the French could themselves be transformed as a result of their physical presence in the territory they sought to colonize, with a corresponding effect on their skin color. As my analysis shows, dress offered one way to resolve this conundrum, with implications for our understanding of colonization in French America and beyond.

In terms of conceptions of difference in the seventeenth and eighteenth centuries, monogenesis also meant that Indians were placed above Africans (but below Europeans) in the hierarchy of world peoples, privileging their aptitude and potential for being civilized and Frenchified over that of Africans.[17] Frenchification policies reflected this hierarchical framework, for this mandate was exclusively reserved for New France's Indian population. It was never intended for Africans in New France, or African populations of France's Caribbean islands. While there was limited leeway for allowing French and Africans to intermarry in the Caribbean (as seen in Article 9 of the 1685 Code Noir), the increasing association of Africans with slavery resulted in a swifter racialization of Africans than Indians.[18] In Louisiana, founded in 1682 as a province of New France, the goal of Frenchifying Indians was modulated by the eventual presence of a large-scale African slave population, also destined for conversion and also subject to degrees of assimilation yet denied the right to become French.

The French did come to enslave Indians in New France, including Louisiana (both before and after the official recognition of Indian slavery in 1709), but this was a piecemeal process focused on certain small nations and enemy tribes rather than a sustained commitment to the large-scale enslavement of all Indians.[19] For the majority of Indians there, the Crown could foresee, at least in theory, another outcome. Based on the principle of Indians' potential for transmutation (and "improvement"), Frenchification theories were clearly premised on the malleability rather than the fixedness of Indians' identity.

New France had been founded on this principle of assimilation of Indians into subjects of the king ("subjection").[20] But Frenchification was not devoid of racial or protoracial elements, as Guillaume Aubert has argued, since it simultaneously "extoll[ed] the cultural malleability of Indians while expressing concern for their possibly inherent difference."[21] But while officials and religious figures in New France continued to engage intellectually with the broader question of Frenchification throughout the seventeenth century, they were for the most part faced with the failure to achieve large-scale or lasting changes among indigenous populations, changes that could be recognized as, and attributed to, Frenchification. By the latter years of the seventeenth century, having failed to achieve substantial or lasting conversion and assimilation of Indians in New France, the Crown virtually admitted defeat in its Frenchification project. Ironically, at this precise point missionaries and officials in one part of French America, the Illinois Country, finally claimed some success in turning Indians into French by virtue of conversion and intermarriage. My analysis of the evidence for these Indians' daily lives supports this claim that Frenchification had been achieved. This finding forces us to rethink our interpretation of French attitudes toward Frenchification in the eighteenth century. It also suggests one resolution for historians' differing views of the chronology of racialization in French America.

The area in the Mississippi Valley known by the French as the Illinois Country (*le pays des Illinois*) had been populated since at least the mid-seventeenth century by groups of Algonquin people known as the Illinois or Illiniwek (see Plate 1, third man from left, standing).[22] Among the Illinois who had converged in the Upper Mississippi Valley in this period, the most important were the Kaskaskia, Cahokia, Tamaroa, Michigamia, and Peoria. Numbering around 10,000 in the 1670s when the French first encountered and quantified them, their numbers were to decline drastically over the course of the next century. Sometimes described as a "confederation," this composite group actually had few features of a confederacy beyond similar origin traditions and geographic, linguistic, and cultural ties.[23]

From 1673 onward, French explorers, missionaries, and fur traders from New France had been establishing missions and settlements in the Upper Mississippi Valley with a view to expanding the reach of France to the Gulf of Mexico (achieved in 1699 with the founding of Louisiana). Claiming this land for New France, the French found a region in flux, due to disease and prolonged incursions into the territory by members of the Iroquois Confederacy, and a people already invested in trade and eager to interact as regional middlemen with new potential military and trading allies. Starting with missionary activity at Peoria in 1673 (which also launched French farming methods among Illinois nations), the French established the first permanent settlement at Cahokia in 1699, followed by Kaskaskia in 1703, Fort de Chartres in 1719, Prairie du Rocher in 1722, Ste. Genevieve in the early 1750s, and St. Louis in 1764. After decades of intermittent French activity in the region, primarily by missionaries and fur traders—the first responsible for conversion to Catholicism, the latter drawn in to intermarriages with Indian women—in 1717, the *pays des Illinois* was removed from New France's direct jurisdiction and granted to the French colonial province of Louisiana.[24]

Beginning in the 1690s, missionaries in the Illinois Country, whose own superiors in France and America no longer promoted intermarriage, began to celebrate sacramental marriages between French men and Illinois Indian women converts (later with non-Illinois converts as well). In doing so, these priests laid the foundation for the only apparently successful model of Frenchification in French America, one that was initiated by an Illinois Indian woman, Marie Rouensa-8canic8e or just Rouensa, daughter of the chief of the Kaskaskia (the phoneme "8" or "ꝸ" was shorthand for the sound "ou"

Figure 2. Fr. Louis Nicolas, "Capitaine de la nation des Illinois," *Codex canadensis*, ca. 1674–1680. Gilcrease Museum, Acc. 4726.7.022. 5. Courtesy of the Gilcrease Museum, Tulsa, Oklahoma.

in French or "w" in English, so that the letter combination "8a" in her name was pronounced "wa").[25] Rouensa serves as a thread in this book, especially in the first part, on Upper Louisiana. This is partly because the sources pertaining to her life and that of her family members are so rich and diverse. But it is primarily because Rouensa and her descendants set up the model of intermarriage in the Illinois Country, and their stories help propel the analysis of key themes in French-Indian relations there.

Illinois Indian women had their own reasons to convert to Catholicism and partake in intermarriage and *métissage* with Frenchmen. This agency stemmed from their struggle for authority within their communities, which found an outlet in the Catholic missionary project.[26] One further result of these struggles, I suggest, was a unique pattern of cultural Frenchification in the context of the fur trade in the Illinois Country. Recent scholarship that deploys intermarriage as a lens through which to view conceptions of difference in colonial Louisiana has downplayed the distinctions between French and native forms of marriage, yet the differences between these had an impact on how French missionaries and officials viewed the Indian wives of Frenchmen.[27] The norm in Indian communities of the Great Lakes region was for Frenchmen to marry Indian women according to local marriage customs (marriage "à la façon du pays") paving the way for Métis communities.[28] In contrast, in the Illinois Country, Indian wives of Frenchmen (and their progeny, for generations to come) who lived in colonial villages were glorified for their adherence to Catholicism; married in the Church and/or according to French law; had their children baptized; were identified in official records as French; and were in essence granted the same legal rights as French men and women. In other words, they had to all intents and purposes acquired the attributes of Frenchness envisaged by the policy of "francisation." My analysis suggests that the material culture of "Frenchified Indians" in the Illinois Country, including their dress, played a key role in signaling their apparent switch of identity to French onlookers. The challenge lies in deciphering this evidence. That settlers, officials and missionaries in the Illinois Country could even conceive of Indians becoming French is all the more perplexing because this occurred in the eighteenth century, well after colonists, officials, and missionaries elsewhere around North America had begun to reject the underlying premise of Frenchification policies—that identity was mutable, and that Indians could become French.

The question of when and how the shift to racial views of Indians occurred is a crucial one for understanding the evolving contours of colonization in

French America. But scholars are still debating how far back into the seventeenth century and beyond racialism can be detected.[29] Certainly, both in France and in America, official, religious, and informal support for Frenchification was on the wane at the very moment when Louisiana began to be colonized. By then, even the belief in the potential for Indians to become French was no longer either universal or consistent, replaced by increasingly racial views and an emphasis on skin color. But well into the mid-eighteenth century some in the colony continued to support Frenchification and to assert a fluid model of difference with respect to Indians.

Enslaved Africans serve as a foil in this study of French-Indian relations and of the racialization of Indians. The first slave trade ships arrived from Africa in 1719, the year after New Orleans's founding. Within twelve years, by January 1731, all but one of the twenty-three slave ships from Africa destined for French colonial Louisiana had arrived (there was a gap of twelve years before the arrival of the final trade ship in 1743). Some Africans were present in Louisiana beginning in 1709, prior to the slave trade to that colony, but only ten were present in 1712, for example (none of them in the Illinois Country, which had not yet been transferred to Louisiana). After 1719, enslaved Africans would quickly become a majority of the colonial population of Lower Louisiana (outnumbering Europeans by four to one in 1731 and by two to one in 1760) and a significant segment of the population of the Illinois Country (25.2 percent in 1726 and 32.2 percent in 1752). They were primarily employed in commercial agriculture in both regions.[30]

Africans inflected every aspect of society even if individual lives only become visible at random points and in miscellaneous ways. In the Illinois Country, the very same missionaries who celebrated French-Indian intermarriages would become some of the largest holders of African slaves. In New Orleans, Ursuline nuns had to grapple with the distinctions between Indian girls and African ones (whether their students or their slaves) as they determined who could join their ranks. African rowers working alongside Frenchmen and Indians manned even the convoys that brought people and goods throughout the colony. And always where clothing was involved, we find enslaved African women, as well as men, laundering, sewing, repairing, cleaning and maintaining articles of dress, sometimes, in the Illinois, in households where the mistress was Indian.[31] Once enslaved Africans were brought into the colony, no space in Louisiana remained free of their influence for long. French conceptions of Africans' identity would come to provide an essential counterpoint to their understanding of the identity of

Indians. But here too there was a distinction between Upper and Lower Louisiana. First because attitudes in New France toward Frenchification policies ebbed and flowed without reference to Africans since that colony did not develop a population of enslaved (or free) Africans. Second because the unique pattern of intermarriage and *métissage* that evolved in the Illinois Country was established without reference to Africans, since it predated their arrival in the area by at least fifteen years. The eventual arrival of Africans, none of them married to Frenchmen, identified by their permanent and hereditary status as chattel, exacerbated their difference from Frenchified Indians who lived with their French families in French settlements.

Rather than seek to establish a clear, linear chronology for the emergence of racial thinking in French America, my book recognizes that alternative conceptions of difference coexisted in parallel over a lengthy period of time.[32] It is a given that geopolitical and socioeconomic factors (the system of slavery, for example) contributed to the development of racialization. My book introduces another influence, and one that is particularly relevant to understanding the shifting contours of racialization at the local and colonial levels: that of material culture. While bodily markers such as skin color were seen as permanent and binding for Africans from the onset of colonization in Louisiana, other official and religious authorities in the colony—those with first-hand exposure to "Frenchified" Indians in the Illinois Country—continued to assert the potential for the identity of Indian converts to be manipulated. My analysis shows that Indians' external manifestations of religion and culture were central to this debate. Material culture interfered with the seemingly inexorable rise of racialism in Louisiana, creating its own chronology. How Indian wives of Frenchmen and children of Frenchmen in the Illinois Country practiced Catholicism, how they furnished their homes, and how they deployed dress, I propose, influenced how colonists in Upper Louisiana interpreted ethnicity and race, highlighting the uneven development and fractured character of the process of racialization in North America.

Accounts of conversion, intermarriage, and *métissage* in the Illinois Country have provided historians of Lower Louisiana and of the Great Lakes with rich material for the study of French-Indian interactions in the region, and my work builds on sophisticated accounts by historians and ethnohistorians such as Guillaume Aubert, Kathleen DuVal, Gilles Havard, Eric Hinderaker, Susan Sleeper-Smith, Jennifer M. Spear, and Richard White. In much of this scholarship, official and religious documents relating to intermarriage in the *pays des Illinois* have been incorporated precisely because so many contemporary commentators invoked the example of the Illinois Country when discussing intermarriage, conversion, and Frenchification in Louisiana.[33] However, scholars of Lower Louisiana or the Great Lakes have taken only a selective interest in the Illinois Country, although Kathleen DuVal has offered a refreshing comparative perspective on different Indian nations' strategies toward intermarriage across Louisiana.[34] Beyond its incorporation of the full panoply of sources produced by officials and missionaries, my book introduces an extraordinary body of archival evidence drawn especially from probate records and that pertains to the everyday life of French-Indian couples in the Illinois Country. This is material these historians (as opposed to historians of the Illinois Country) have overlooked.[35]

My interpretation of this source material supports claims by missionaries and officials in the Illinois Country that some Indians did not simply convert and intermarry. Rather, these Indians—and they were primarily women, though not exclusively Illinois, and sometimes former captives—became, to all intents and purposes, "Frenchified."[36] In other words, and irrespective of any ambiguity in how they themselves viewed their immersion in French colonial culture, these women and their progeny presented evidence of having attained Frenchness. Those French missionaries and officials still arguing in favor of Frenchification policies, whether they were in Upper or Lower Louisiana, or the metropole, seized on the evidence of the women's immersion in French colonial life to bolster their claims that conversion and intermarriage could lead to the metamorphosis of Indians. For them the proof of the mutability of identity was seen in the material culture expressions of these converted and "Frenchified" Indians. Their response to evidence of Frenchification highlights the concrete role of sartorial appearance in influencing French conceptions of difference, and in marking the contrasts in views in Upper and Lower Louisiana of what it meant to be French, especially when faced with "Frenchified" Indians.

Everywhere in Louisiana, colonization was conditioned by the heterogeneous response of local indigenous groups to the arrival of settlers, missionaries, and soldiers (each of whom had their own agenda and priorities). My book frames the analysis of dress and culture in terms of the spatial and environmental contexts that structured the perceptions of individual actors. Indian wives of Frenchmen, and their children, were treated as French in the Illinois Country, with its unique pattern of conversion and sacramental intermarriages. When "Frenchified Indians" left the confines of Upper Louisiana, they were subjected to a different hegemonic view of difference that reflected the colony's place at the crossroads of New France and the French Caribbean. Their reception in Lower Louisiana provides another framework for this book's narrative structure. The concept of Frenchification also opens up French ways of thinking about skin color, as affected, for example, by the cultural practices of "Frenchified Indians," juxtaposed with the analysis of how Frenchmen, in turn, negotiated Indianness.

*   *   *

The interplay of dress, culture, and racialization is made manifest through an interdisciplinary approach that draws on primary source material pulled from every corner of the Province of Louisiana, from first exploration in 1673 to the final handover of Louisiana's territory from France to England and Spain by 1769. I deploy archaeological and visual evidence as available, but my study concentrates on an exhaustive array of archival sources. Unfortunately, visual evidence is relatively sparse. Louisiana under the French regime differed substantially from English and Spanish America with respect to artistic output by colonists. Most extant images were produced by official draftsmen or royal engineers who, like those few colonists who dabbled in amateur renditions intended to illustrate their adventures in the colony, produced maps, architectural drawings, and images of flora and fauna (see Figure 12, Plates 16, 25, 28, 33). A number of these images, which portrayed indigenous populations, can be mined for their ethnographic content, even if these depictions were infused with Europeans' stereotypes (see Figure 15 and Plates 1, 19, 20, 22, 32).[37] For example, Alexandre de Batz depicted the widow, child, and brother of Tunica Chief Cahura-Joligo in Indian dress. But Cahura-Joligo, described as "baptized and almost frenchified," had liked to dress "à la française." One may therefore speculate as to whether his wife and child wore elements of French dress on a regular basis, even if de Batz chose to stress instead their Indianness.[38] No figurative artwork by Africans is known to survive and very rarely do any images depict figures of Africans or colonists (but see Plates 1, 20 respectively).[39] Given this, it is ironic that one of the few images of *colonists* produced in the French colonial period is found on a buffalo robe pictograph likely produced by a mixed French-Quapaw artist (see Plate 24, which is a detail of Plate 23).[40]

Visual depictions of daily life are rare, and few garments are known to survive from the French colonial period; archaeological excavations have unearthed fragmentary remains of textiles and apparel including buttons, jewelry, metal braid, and leather, as well as lead seals from (nonextant) bales of cloth.[41] But written records from the period were prolific and include legal records, probate documents, court records, criminal investigations, religious correspondence, parish registers, missionary and monastic records, official and personal correspondence, published and unpublished travel and missionary accounts, mercantile papers, and records of formal and informal business activities and agreements.[42] There are inevitably complications with using such one-sided source material. But this evidence (even the literary license taken by authors) can in fact be especially useful, for example, in revealing colonists' hopes and fears about colonization and about Indians.

These sources, drawn from archival and artifact repositories throughout the Mississippi Valley—from Natchitoches, New Orleans, and its environs, to Kaskaskia in Illinois and Ste. Genevieve and St. Louis in present-day Missouri, remain underused, due in part to the language barrier, but also to the fact that repositories of material pertaining to Louisiana are scattered, seldom organized or indexed (let alone transcribed or translated), and often in poor or neglected condition. I have also mined extensive materials extracted from beyond colonial Louisiana's original territorial limits, for example, the records of the Archives of the Seminary of Quebec and the Archives of the Ursulines of Quebec, as well as source material at the Huntington Library, Newberry Library, Library of Congress, and numerous repositories of manuscripts and objects in official and private archives and museums in France (Aix-en-Provence, Bordeaux, La Rochelle, Paris) and England. Unless noted otherwise, all translations are my own.

My analysis of the source material offers the broad vantage point needed to understand a colony, and a people, at the intersection of New France and the Caribbean. The geographical span of my study stretches from the settlements in the Lower Mississippi Valley (anchored by New Orleans), to the Illinois Country in the Upper Mississippi Valley. Though it has been the focus of regional studies, the Illinois Country is absent from recent studies of French colonial Louisiana that have tended to replicate the modern limits of the state of Louisiana.[43] Yet this area was formally integrated within the official jurisdiction of the province of Louisiana from 1717 onward. More significant, examination of the main archival records relating to the daily life and economy of the Illinois Country reveals that settlers there looked increasingly to Lower Louisiana and especially to New Orleans (rather than to New France) as the primary source for their consumer goods and the primary market for their furs and agricultural products.[44]

At the same time, settlements in Louisiana depended increasingly for their staples on the large-scale import of wheat flour and other agricultural products from the Illinois Country.[45] Settlements in the Upper and Lower Mississippi Valley shared other distinguishing features, such as architectural styles and large-scale ownership of African slaves.[46] Yet the Upper Mississippi Valley has been marginalized within studies of French America (in part due to a lack of familiarity with the local records from the Illinois Country), resulting in a rigid and artificial split between histories of Lower and Upper Louisiana. Within the field of early American studies, Lower Louisiana has emerged spectacularly from its historical marginalization, as heralded by important monographs by Daniel H. Usner, Gwendolyn Midlo Hall, and Thomas N. Ingersoll.[47] The Illinois Country is following suit as it breaks free from its history of regional (ir)relevance; yet the split between Upper and Lower Louisiana has been retained in these studies.[48] My study integrates these areas, asserting that the history of French-Indian encounters in Louisiana cannot be understood in isolation and without incorporating analysis of the source material from both subregions of the Mississippi Valley.

While the colony of Louisiana was only claimed for France in 1682 (and settled from 1699), French explorers, missionaries, and fur traders from New France had settled the Illinois Country beginning in 1673, and this is when my study begins. This formative period in the development of cultural and religious interactions between colonist and Indian populations had a lasting impact on the settlements of the Illinois Country long after its 1717 cession from New France to Louisiana. Following its defeat in the Seven Years' War (1756–63) and the loss of New France, France's interest in Louisiana waned. In 1762, the area to the west of the Mississippi including New Orleans was ceded to Spain. It was this half of the territory, representing nearly one-third of the present continental United States, that was to become the basis for the 1803 Louisiana Purchase, three years after Spain had ceded Louisiana back to France. The other half, the area to the east of the Mississippi River, was ceded to Britain in 1763. Although the British were swift in their occupation of this new possession, the Spanish did not formally take control until 1769, the end date for this study. Within this vast, expansive territory, by the end of the French regime, the colonial population amounted to only about 10,000, more than half of them slaves of African descent. As a point of comparison, the Anglo-American colonial population by 1760 had reached 1,500,000, climbing to 2,210,000 by 1770.[49]

In such a sparse society, the qualitative analysis of face-to-face interactions gains in importance over quantification, allowing us to make sense of the wealth of details that enriches, and complicates, sartorial expression.[50] It is in the minutiae, in the disorderliness of material culture that we find evidence of the more subtle and suggestive aspects of sartorial identities. Objects played a key role in assertions of identity displayed through the body, for the process of colonization and experience of diaspora depended on intercultural (as well as religious, economic, and military) interactions that were not always forced. Adopting another group's material culture, and learning how to use and display it, was not only reactive or even emulative. It was also often proactive, confounding binary assumptions that reduce cross-cultural exchanges to questions of tradition or change, appropriation or persistence, authenticity or assimilation. This point is especially important in the context of romanticized and Euro-centric views of "authentic" and "pure" Native American visual and material cultures as having been "corrupted" by European influences.[51]

Cross-cultural exchange that incorporated the consumption of novelty, exotic, or prestige goods was a long-standing practice among Native Americans prior to, and after, contact with Europeans.[52] Similarly, my analysis shows that cultural cross-dressing was a dynamic form of consumerism through which appearance could be manipulated to reflect divergent values. Indian slaves turned utilitarian (French) thimbles into body ornaments. A French-Indian voyageur cleaned his skin by simply changing into a laundered shirt, rather than washing it with water, thereby opening a vista onto French ideas about skin and skin color. French settlers in the Illinois Country modified the function of the buffalo robe; in doing so, they shifted its meaning, from an item of dress—a mantle—meant for public display, to a utilitarian object—bedding—relegated to the semiprivate confines of the bedstead. A mixed French-Indian heritage woman adorned her neckline with a handkerchief, like her French neighbors. That the handkerchiefs themselves were made in India further situates this exchange in the early modern global economy.[53] These examples underline the appeal of novelty goods; and they evoke the malleability and instability of objects of exchange and of the meanings imputed to these. They also showcase how consumer objects travel across cultural boundaries, where, as they acquire different meanings in different cultural contexts, they become part of distinctive performances. This analysis thus highlights the variability of meanings (symbolic, aesthetic, economic) attached to the same material objects by diverse individuals or groups of individuals. As such, it complicates the terms of reference for the analysis of cross-cultural consumer acts.

My book explores the experience of colonization and hybridization from the viewpoint of colonizers, and as a way of understanding French concepts of identity and the process of racialization in French America. While I consider how and why some Indians might dress like the French and some French dress like Indians, my focus remains on understanding French interpretations of this practice. There are two parts that examine cultural cross-dressing in Upper Louisiana, Lower Louisiana, or in-between. Together, they illuminate the ways in which those on site in Louisiana, as distinct from metropolitan theorists, understood and deployed the evidence from concrete sartorial and material markers of identity in the face of shifting definitions of ethnic, class, and gender difference.

Part I opens the discussion by foregrounding the unusual material culture expressions of Amerindian women converts to Catholicism, sacramentally married to Canadian traders in the Illinois Country beginning in 1694. As I show from an analysis of their probate documents and other records of daily life, these women converts and their children appear to have become "Frenchified." The methodical, qualitative analysis in the opening chapter provides the necessary preparation for the interpretation that is developed in the following two chapters.

In Chapter 2, I interpret this evidence of Frenchification not simply as a sign of acculturation, but as an indication of the persistence of native social and gender frameworks, rather than their elision, an outcome facilitated by missionaries. Yet my emphasis here is on explaining how this evidence informed and bolstered proponents of Frenchification policies, as addressed in Chapter 3. For the French, the terms of the discussion for and against intermarriage and *métissage* revolved around the question of whether it was the Indian women, or the French men, who integrated into the other's culture, becoming either "Frenchified" or "Indianized." Evidence of successful Frenchification was thus crucial to officials' continued support for legal and sacramental intermarriage in the Illinois Country, seen in the legal and religious rights granted to Indian wives and their children. This was notwithstanding the increasing rejection, founded on emerging racial principles, of Frenchification policies by figures of authority in Lower Louisiana and in France. My analysis in Part I thus speaks directly to the larger question, as well as the geography and uneven chronology, of the shift in conceptualizations of difference and the emergence of racial discourse in America.

Part II shifts the focus to Lower Louisiana. The religious and legal dimensions of Frenchification coalesced in the experience of one French-Indian girl from the Illinois Country, Marie Turpin. In 1751, she became "the first creole" to become an Ursuline nun in New Orleans, though only as a converse (a lay or domestic) nun. Turpin's difficult trajectory encapsulated the conflict between the competing models of ethnicity evoked in Part I. For it highlights the ways that this difference manifested itself spatially, not in the Illinois Country but in 1750s New Orleans, the seat of the colonial government. One model, derived from New France, had allowed for Frenchification. The other model, influenced by the Caribbean, was premised on the rigidity and fixedness of racial categories, and imposed limitations on those considered inferior. Marie Turpin's experience embodied this tension and reveals how colonists in New Orleans, personally faced with evidence of Frenchification in the person of Turpin, rationalized the question of difference by inscribing it on her clothed body.

In a further case study, my focus shifts to the male experience of Frenchification and in so doing uses the lens of cleanliness to explore European beliefs about skin color. I do so through my analysis of a 1739 voyageur contract for a trip from the Illinois Country to New Orleans and back. This voyageur, Jean Saguingouara, had negotiated that his laundry costs be covered on arrival in New Orleans, an unusual clause made more significant by the fact that he was of mixed French-Indian descent and Catholic, and that he had been brought up in the Illinois Country by a French officer of noble origin married to an Indian woman. His insistence on a laundry clause signaled his adhesion to European standards of cleanliness that were compatible with his elite French guardian's notions of washing. As such, it hinted, materially, at his "Frenchness." Saguingouara's notion of cleanliness was predicated on the display of laundered *clothing*. In Europe in this period, it was the act of changing into laundered linen, rather than washing the body, that was understood to clean the body by absorbing any grime. This concept of cleanliness, I suggest, is crucial for understanding how colonists apprehended indigenous bodies, and how they rationalized differences in skin color. French-Indian notions of ethnicity were (literally) embodied in cultural practices such as washing.

A final chapter locates the hinterlands as a primary site of male sartorial exchange and examines the ways that clothing mediated Europeans' relationship with the colonial environment. I examine cultural cross-dressing by Frenchmen, a practice that allowed them temporarily to belong to the hinterlands, and to defuse anxieties about venturing into alien territory. These intermittent instances of sartorial transgression were justified because they were impermanent since dress allowed colonists to revert back from a state of dress that might otherwise progressively cause Frenchmen to turn into "sauvages." This temporary yielding to a cross-cultural identity was rationalized on the basis of its reversibility, as upheld through rank-based sartorial distinctions, and as signaled concretely through a change of dress when in Louisiana's urbanized environments. French and Indian may have temporarily merged identities as they switched clothes and traded looks, but changing their clothes also ensured that Frenchmen did not become Indian.

Taken individually, each chapter presents a discrete facet of cultural cross-dressing. Read in sequence, this narrative interprets the process of how racialization unfolded in practice in Louisiana in the context of geography, culture, and religion. My study, then, presents a fresh account of one marginalized French-American colony, arguing that the conceptions of difference that aimed at delineating, and later fixing, identities depended upon encounters mediated by appearance. In this mixed-language environment, dress—in its role as a nonverbal means of communication, its visual and tactile potency, its alternating familiarity and novelty—mediated between cultures that shared space in early America. Material artifacts did not simply reflect discourses about difference and race in the context of conversion; rather, as my analysis shows, they helped to produce them. The immediacy of sartorial display, together with its economic and symbolic importance as an object of trade exchange, suggests that clothing lay at the core of negotiations over the meaning of ethnicity and race in early America. This volume thus opens up new avenues for the interpretation of colonial projects, and the cultural and material exchanges that were fundamental to the establishment of these. Indeed, even if this book is foremost a study of one region, its methodological model aims to suggest that objects can profitably take center stage in the investigation of nascent colonial societies.

PART I

Frenchification in the
Illinois Country

In a memorandum written at Dauphine Island in Lower Louisiana in 1715, the highest-ranking administrator in the colony took up the question of intermarriage between Indian women and Frenchmen. The report produced by Commissaire-Ordonnateur Jean-Baptiste du Bois Duclos was in response to a renewed proposal by seminarian Father Henri Roulleaux de La Vente to populate Louisiana by promoting marriages between French men and Catholic Indian women.[1] Though the commissaire-ordonnateur staunchly opposed La Vente's proposal, like him, Duclos honed in on the Illinois Country, in the Upper Mississippi Valley, to make one of his key points. Citing existing intermarriage practices there, Duclos made the following assertion in support of his argument that French-Indian unions should be prohibited:

> Although there are several examples of Indian women who have contracted such marriages especially at the Illinois, it is not because they have become Frenchified, if one may use that term, but it is because those who have married them have themselves become almost Indians, residing among them and living in their manner, so that these Indian women have changed nothing or at least very little in their manner of living.[2]

Duclos's use of the term "marriage" was a narrow one limited to French definitions of the practice. He was not referring to the marriages consecrated according to indigenous rites (the marriages "in the manner of the country" that had become common among Canadian fur traders in the Great Lakes region). He was alluding to the sanctified marriages that French missionaries had been celebrating in the Illinois Country since the late seventeenth century between French men and Indian women converts to Catholicism.

Duclos's language and tone in this passage betrayed the anxieties felt by those who saw intermarriage as an impediment to colonization, even when the marriages involved Catholic converts and were conducted according to French law and Catholic rites. In this view, intermarriage led to the absorption of colonists within native society rather than their dominance of indigenous populations; it was clearly nonconducive to the establishment of social order in the colony. Given the French imperial goals of intermarriage in New France, discussions about the practice were inherently related to ideas about identity.

Among his chief concerns about intermarriage, Duclos had highlighted the

> adulteration that such marriages will cause in the whiteness and pu-
> rity of the blood in the children, for whatever Mr. De La Vente may
> say, experience shows every day that the children that come from
> such marriages are of an extremely dark complexion, so that in the
> course of time, if no Frenchmen come to Louisiana, the colony would
> become a colony of mulattoes who are naturally idlers, libertines and
> even more rascals as those of Peru, Mexico and the other Spanish
> colonies give evidence.[3]

In alluding to skin color and blood, Duclos echoed La Vente who, beginning in 1708, had argued that "the blood of the sauvages" did not prejudice that of the French.[4] Though their assessments of intermarriage and *métissage* were polar opposites, both Duclos and La Vente were grappling with the emergence of racial concepts of identity.[5]

The commissaire-ordonnateur's condemnation of intermarriage was to hold sway with the Council of the Ministry of the Colonies in France, who reiterated Duclos's argument almost word for word and added in a marginal notation that "Marriages of this sort must be prevented as much as possible and [French] girls will be sent from [France] when it will be possible to do so." While siding with Duclos, the Council had stopped short of enacting a formal prohibition on French-Indian intermarriage, only requiring that the governor and the new commissaire-ordonnateur "prevent this kind of mar-riages *insofar as it shall be in their powers*" (my emphasis).[6] As suggested by this careful choice of words, and implicit in La Vente and Duclos's opposing views, the rejection of French-Indian intermarriage in 1715 was not yet a set-tled question, and the practice would remain a contentious matter for debate in France and in the different settlements of New France.

Nor did official prohibition mean that intermarriage ceased, for French-men, including members of the elite, would continue to enter into their own legal and/or sacramental marriages with Indian women converts in the very same settlements of the Illinois Country that Duclos had alluded to. Their marriages extended a practice that had begun there by 1694 and remained concentrated in the Illinois Country, and they stood in contrast to the in-termarriages common around the Great Lakes area, which were consecrated according to indigenous rather than French and Catholic rituals. Indeed, it is only when we evaluate the effects of a concentration of mixed marriages in terms of the colonial population of the Illinois Country as a whole that we can account for the particularity of that region and that we can contextualize the expressions of identity of Indian wives and families of Frenchmen. In effect, their material culture allows us to understand why the Illinois Country was seen as central to debates about intermarriage, with implications far beyond that specific region.

Unions between European men and Indian women had taken place throughout French colonial Louisiana in the early stages of colonization. But, as asserted repeatedly by French commentators, the Illinois Country was the primary site for *legal* marriages between Frenchmen and Indian women converts, beginning with Illinois Indian women (Marie Rouensa first among them) and later extending to former captives from beyond the Illinois nation. I have identified fifty-seven legitimate French-Indian intermarriages (that is, legitimate according to the French definition of marriage), with further marriages between French men and French-Indian daughters. While these numbers may seem modest, in fact, sacramental marriages between French men and Indian women constituted approximately 20 percent of known marriages in the Illinois Country, compared to below 1 percent for French America (New France and Louisiana combined) as a whole. These figures are especially meaningful when evaluated in terms of the sparse colonial population of the Illinois Country. The entire colonial population of the Illinois Country in 1726—incorporating legitimate Indian wives of Frenchmen—stood at 307 (including 96 children), plus 189 Indian and African slaves, a total of 496.[7] In the 1752 census, the colonial population of this area was 1,360, including 445 enslaved Africans and 147 enslaved Indians.[8]

The statistical importance of French-Indian marriage applies to the number of children issued from mixed unions as well. A majority of children baptized in the parish of Kaskaskia during the formative years of French settlement (prior to 1719), totaling forty-three out of forty-eight baptisms, were born to Canadian fur traders and women from neighboring tribes. The majority of these births were identified as legitimate, meaning that both parents declared themselves Christian and had married according to Catholic rites. A religious imperative was therefore present even during the period from 1696 to 1714 when the Crown outlawed, and drove underground, unlicensed French fur traders—the very type of men who had married Indian women and bore children with them.[9] Marriages with full-blooded Indian women and baptisms of their mixed parentage children gradually waned, yet these formative practices were to have lasting effects on the population of the colonial settlements of the Illinois Country, including the continuing integration of Indian widows and their children within French villages. It sputtered on even as the demographic makeup of the French colonies changed.[10]

These were distinctive marriages that involved Indian converts and that were recognized by French religious and legal authorities. In these aspects, the pattern of intermarriage in the Illinois Country stands out from the sexual and marital unions of French and Indians across North America. However, historians have not always recognized how distinctive and unusual this pattern of intermarriage in the Illinois Country was compared to that found elsewhere in North America, and this has had the effect of obscuring the influence of the Illinois Country on French colonial conceptions of difference.

The general practice of intermarriage between Europeans and indigenous peoples fits within a geographically and historically broad compass that stretches beyond the eighteenth century and beyond the French colonies.[11] My use of the term "intermarriage" is intended to recognize Indian conventions of cross-cultural (and cross-clan) marriage alliances, and the interplay between French and Indian models of alliance through ritualized unions of individual men and women. Concomitant with the ubiquity of intermarriage practices in Atlantic societies across time and place, the actual features of the relationships reveal some common traits as well as wide variations. These variations were the result more often than not of the different marital and political strategies and diverse spiritual beliefs of the Indian nations encountered by the French.[12] Chief among these variations was the difference between forms and meanings applied to cross-cultural sexual and marital unions. Yet analyses of *métissage* in French colonial America tend to conflate the distinctive experience of sacramental intermarriage in the Illinois Country with the better known pattern of intermarriage typical of the early to mid-nineteenth century (identified especially with Métis fur-trading communities). The latter, typically, were marriages à la façon du pays (marriages in the custom of the country—according to Indian rituals that were sometimes simultaneous with sacramental marriages contracted with white women) rather than the sanctified, legal marriages described in this study.[13] Recent scholarship that deploys intermarriage as a lens into conceptions of difference in colonial Louisiana have similarly blurred or downplayed the distinctions between French and Native forms of marriage.[14] In so doing, they have sidelined the different meanings and implications of marriages that were legally contracted and/or consecrated (a feature of intermarriage in the

Illinois Country) as opposed to the marriages "à la façon du pays" characteristic of the majority of long-term mixed unions in French colonial America.[15]

This conflation of distinct Indian and European laws and rituals of marriage is made more complicated by the evidence of sexual contact and *métissage* occurring through temporary or nonritualized sexual relations.[16] In
Louisiana outside the Illinois Country a recurring pattern was for Frenchmen
to provide support for their Indian concubines and their children without explicitly acknowledging the relationship, seldom recognizing their offspring
or having them baptized. Further, European-Indian *métissage*, when it occurred in Lower Louisiana, tended to involve relations between colonists
and Indian slaves rather than marriages (whether Christian or "à la façon
du pays") with free Indian women.[17] Some of these involved members of the
elite, highlighting the risk of race, class, and religious transgressions implicit
in these *concubinages*.[18]

Those unions were often masked under the guise of a "need" for wom-
en's labor, highlighting Frenchmen's conviction that only the female sex (any
woman, whatever her cultural background) were capable of or naturally
suited to providing food preparation, housekeeping or laundry services to
Frenchmen. Officials also pointed to Frenchmen's "need" for sexual services
as justified by an uneven sex ratio in the colony between French men and
women, and colonists discussed the ease of finding indigenous women whom
they could pay to look after their households while also serving as sexual
partners.[19] In his 1713 report on the state of the colony, Governor Antoine de
La Mothe, sieur de Cadillac highlighted the demographic shortage of eligible
women in the colony by requesting that the Crown send over French women,
though preferably not "ugly or misshapen ones" since the men would choose
Indian women over them. Cadillac sarcastically noted the claims of men
whose motives were sexual but who "pretended not to be able to do without
women for their laundry and their meals and *sagamité* [a dish of seasoned
cornmeal], and to look after their huts"[20] In spite of his sarcasm, Cadillac
knew whereof he spoke: he himself is believed to have sired a mixed heritage
offspring while at Michilimackinac.[21] Such statements that foreground demography have tended to be taken at face value, but scholars now refute the
assumption that it was the uneven sex ratio of French men to French women
in the colonies that led French men to put aside their "natural" preference for
European women and engage in *concubinage* with Indian women; instead
they emphasize the strategic advantages of unions with Indian women as the
key factor in Frenchmen's intermarriage alliances, especially in the context of

the fur trade.[22] We should add another motivation for continuing such marriages once the new French settlements were well established: the benefits to French male newcomers (including members of the elite) of marriage as a means of social and economic integration. In this case, it was not so much the strategic importance of marrying Indian women that counted, as the advantages of marrying daughters of local families, irrespective of whether their mothers were French or Indian. Together, these factors help explain why only one consecrated union between a full-blooded Indian man and a European woman is known in this area.[23]

The pattern of intermarriage in the Illinois Country holds implications for our understanding of how the French there perceived these Indian wives and their offspring. But the pattern itself must be contextualized in terms of the spatial framework in which the distinctive intermarriages of the Illinois Country took place. Arriving in the last decades of the seventeenth century, the first French settlers in the Illinois Country resided within Indian villages and the new missions. Their dependency on indigenous communities was exacerbated from 1696 to 1714 during the ban on unlicensed French fur traders. As a result of their marginalization, illegal fur traders initially became dependent on their Indian wives' kin networks; in so doing they conformed to the matrilocal practices of the Illinois, though offspring continued to be baptized.[24] But in 1719, shortly after the transfer of the Illinois Country from New France to the Province of Louisiana, the French, how holding the balance of power in the area, carried out a far-reaching policy of removing those Indians who were not spouses, offspring, or slaves of Frenchmen from French settlements and creating separate French and Indian villages.[25] Though this policy could not have prevented contact and trade or relational exchanges between members of the two villages, it did alter the population dynamics and the religious, social, economic and architectural frameworks of the French colonial villages. Kaskaskia chief Mamantouensa acknowledged as much in 1725 when he spoke of having had to consent to leaving his village to "the French, my brothers and my sons-in-law."[26] As seen in Thomas Hutchins's 1771 map of the Illinois Country, which shows the continuing separation of colonial and Indian villages at Kaskaskia and Cahokia, this division remained intact through the colonial period (see Figure 3).

Among other consequences for French-Indian interactions in the region, this physical demarcation put stress on the matrilocal organization of Illinois-French settlements and created a spatial rift for Indian wives who remained with their French husbands in settlements now reserved for the

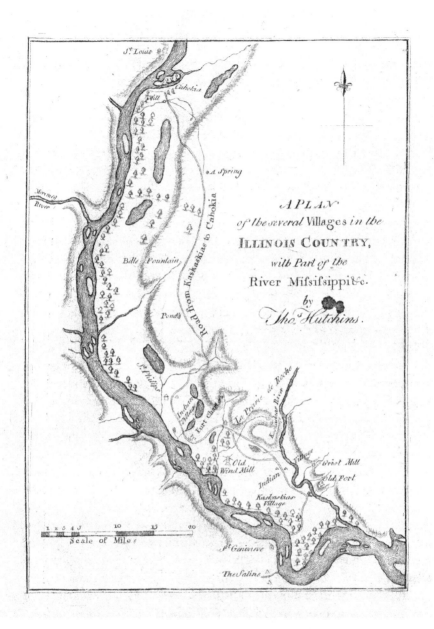

Figure 3. Thomas Hutchins, "A plan of the several villages in the Illinois country, with part of the River Mississippi &c," in *A topographical description of Virginia, Pennsylvania, Maryland and North Carolina* (London: J. Almon, 1778). Courtesy of the American Philosophical Society, Philadelphia. Note the separation of Indian from French villages, as begun by the French in 1719 and signaled here by the distinction between the French colonial "Kaskaskia village" and the Kaskaskia "Indian village" just north of it.

French (even as they and their husbands might continue to travel intermittently for fur trade purposes). In April 1723, Inspector-General Bernard Diron D'Artaguiette confirmed that Frenchmen's Indian wives now lived with their husbands in French colonial houses, within villages "composed entirely of farmers who live there very comfortably."[27] These villages were now organized according to French agrarian models, even if Illinois women had likely carried out the original clearing of the horticultural land.[28] The division of French and Indian also helped usher in the establishment of French patriarchal conventions in terms of property division and other aspects of family life within the new colonial settlements.

These women's conversion to Catholicism, their marriage with Frenchmen, and their incorporation in new French colonial settlements combined to create an unusual scenario for intermarriage, one that differs from the more usual pattern found in French America. The material culture of these Franco-Indian households reflected this distinctiveness and helped establish the possibility that Indian women could become French. In essence then, if Duclos's report and the Crown's response to it were key moments in the process of racializing Indians in French America, how can the establishment of this obvious pattern of Catholic intermarriage in the Illinois Country be explained and how was it justified by the religious and administrative officials who presided over the marriage ceremonies? Furthermore, how do we explain that the official French census records of the Illinois Country in 1724, 1732, and 1752 classified the Catholic and legitimate Indian spouses of Frenchmen, and their children, as French? Surely these instances point to a more nuanced and inconsistent view by officials of intermarriage and of its effects on the identity of Indian converts, their French husbands, and their offspring.

In fact, Duclos's authority in the matter of intermarriage practices can be impugned. His was not an eyewitness account since he had never set foot in the Illinois Country, while his views were colored by firsthand knowledge of *mestizaje* in the Spanish colonies.[29] Accordingly, his description cannot tell us much about the actual outline of intermarriage. Yet, while denying in his 1715 report that Indian women had become "Frenchified," Duclos's comments had also raised one of the key concerns in the debate for and against intermarriage. Namely, whether it was the Indian women, or the French men, who had integrated into the other's culture as a result of intermarriage, becoming either "Frenchified" or "becom[ing] almost Indian" in the process. In alluding to this question, Duclos entered squarely into the debate about how the

French defined and constructed ethnicity. He ascribed a role, and it was a vital one, to the performative operation of material culture—to the "manner of living"—in determining identity.

While the focus, as in Duclos's report, is on a small group of French-Indian households in the Upper Mississippi Valley, their experiences had far-reaching implications for the development of theories of difference and an influence in these matters far disproportionate to their numbers. Namely, as seen in extant correspondence, the Illinois Country was deemed relevant to broader questions about colonization, intermarriage, and the social order in French America as a whole, as made clear by Father La Vente and Commissaire-Ordonnateur Duclos. The way these Indian women lived and the three-dimensional image they projected directly influenced how the French in America understood ethnic identity, and how they framed the difference between French and Indian. The key to this influence lay in their material culture expressions, incorporating the furnishings, furniture, architecture, and other living arrangements that provided the performance space for sartorial expression. Duclos had been most vociferous in warning against the "children that come from such marriages [who] are of an extremely dark complexion." In fact, given the continuing demographic imbalance between French men and women, and the strategic and economic importance of kinship to Indians in the Illinois Country, the daughters of French-Indian couples would in turn become desirable as marriage partners for colonists (in numbers that their brothers never came close to). The material culture expressions of these French-Indian daughters mattered, and are incorporated in this study, as are Indian wives in the Illinois Country who were not Illinois.

Part I begins by establishing and interpreting the adoption of French dress by Indian wives and children of Frenchmen in the Illinois Country. In so doing, my discussion of material culture is shaped by consideration of individual acts of agency by particular women. Rather than homogenizing these women's experiences through quantitative analysis, my approach focuses instead on specific women's consumer acts. In dwelling on the nitty-gritty details of material culture consumption by individual women, a layered, collective image emerges to reveal broader patterns about French-Indian cultural exchange in the Illinois Country. My findings reveal that, unlike most intermarried Indian women in French America, these women did become collectively "Frenchified," wearing recognizably European (or more accurately, French Canadian) styles of dressing and eventually living in French colonial settlements, in a process that laid the foundation for their descendants' integration into *colonial* society. The evidence of acculturation is especially challenging in terms of the existing literature on French-Indian intermarriage, scholarship with a rich interpretive framework for emphasizing concepts such as resistance and persistence but that has not always heeded, or known how to interpret, problematic data about material culture. My reading argues that the tension between persistence and acculturation can be reconciled if we accept that consumption is proactive and if we reject the premise of cultural authenticity and purity. As such, I complicate the terms of any discussion of material cultural exchanges in a colonial context, and I suggest that such exchanges influenced French conceptions of difference, slowing the rise of racial ideas.

Contrary to the outcome anticipated by Duclos, and in stark contrast to most intermarried Indian women in North America, these women converts appeared "Frenchified" in their manner of living, lending support to proponents of intermarriage. The material culture of this group of women would therefore prove central to arguments about whether identity was fixed or mutable. This analysis, then, is one that localizes the process of racialization and that stresses the nonverbal expressions of indigenous populations, providing a critical counterpoint to the pronouncements of elites such as Duclos and La Vente.

CHAPTER 1

"Their Manner of Living"

On June 25, 1725, Dame Philippe, the legitimate wife of an agriculturalist and militia lieutenant, died shortly after composing a will and codicil before the local notary, priest, and witnesses. Following her burial within the church that faced her house in Kaskaskia (the largest colonial settlement in the Upper Mississippi Valley), and in conformity with French legal practice, a postmortem inventory was taken of her substantial assets. The valuation of her property, which was held in community with her husband, came to more than 45,000 livres. One of the wealthiest successions in the Illinois Country, the estate was only marginally dependent on the fur trade that had dominated the region's formative period and that had been her French Canadian husband's initial occupation. Instead, its emphasis, as revealed by the inventory, was on large-scale cultivation of corn and wheat, domesticated livestock, and the ownership of one Indian and four African slaves. Like her apparel, which included shifts and jackets, the itemized buildings, outbuildings, and household furnishings were French colonial in style. The extent of the estate is all the more intriguing because Dame Philippe, or Marie Rouensa-8canic8e, was Indian.[1]

With the exception of French explorers Marquette and La Salle, Marie Rouensa-8canic8e is the only widely known figure in the history of the Illinois Country during the French regime. The exceptionally rich and varied sources pertaining to her life—from missionary accounts to parish records and notarial documents including probate records—have provided modern historians with the sort of material that enables them to explore how this Kaskaskia woman was viewed and how she saw her own life: had she acculturated or was she still entrenched in an Indian identity notwithstanding colonial elements of her lifestyle?[2]

Marie Rouensa's cultural shift toward Frenchification began with her conversion, as indicated by Jesuit missionary Father Gravier in his 1694 annual report to the Society of Jesus.[3] That Gravier had mentioned Rouensa in his relation was a reflection of her importance to the Jesuits' missionary project in the Illinois Country. She had been his greatest success story. This woman, who wore French-style garments, and who died in her French colonial-style house built opposite the parish church and furnished with walnut tables, chairs, and armchairs, was the daughter of the chief of the Kaskaskia Illinois Indians. She was a fervent and influential convert whose first sacramental marriage to a Frenchman would usher in an unusual chapter in the missionary and colonizing project in French America, leading other women to follow in her footsteps. Residence in French colonial settlements and immersion in French colonial material culture would become hallmarks of this distinctive population that developed in the Illinois Country as a result of Indian women's conversion to Catholicism and sacramental marriages to Frenchmen. Their daughters would extend this pattern of Catholicism, intermarriage, and integration within the French community. Together, these women provided a collective image of acculturation that would influence how colonists understood them, signaling that identity might well be flexible and mutable.

In 1715, Commissaire-Ordonnateur Jean-Baptiste du Bois Duclos had warned against French-Indian intermarriages by decrying that Frenchmen legally married to Indian women in the Illinois Country had become almost Indians, while their wives had "changed nothing or at least very little in their manner of living." The evidence from Marie Rouensa's probate records contradicts his interpretation, yet for Duclos, this emphasis on the manner of living was the crux of the matter in evaluating the risks inherent in intermarriage. For while he had raised the specter of "the whiteness and purity of the blood in the children," he also betrayed a continuing belief in the role of culture and environment in maintaining, and imparting, Frenchness.[4] Indeed, the term "manner of living" could encompass a broad range of tangible and intangible practices, including but not limited to dress, household objects, and the built environment. If we are to understand how the French interpreted the appearance of Indian wives and daughters of Frenchmen, we need to visualize the context in which they perceived them. For there was a physical and material environment within which cultural practices could be carried out, and they framed the three-dimensional sartorial image that colonists drew on as they evaluated whether or not Indians could actually become French. Furthermore, the interpretation of this sartorial and household Frenchification reveals that these were calibrated according to the rank and economic status of French husbands, providing nonverbal affirmation that Indians could achieve Frenchness—in all its emphasis on social hierarchy.

A focus on material culture not only invites us to recognize the importance of objects in everyday life, but also draws our attention to objects as alternative evidence about those who are underrepresented in conventional historical sources, whether the poor, slaves, or the Indian women examined here.[5] By showing how Indian women in the Illinois Country lived with French possessions, inhabited them, and used them as a part of their daily activities, we can grasp the nonverbal ways in which they channeled objects to convey their identity. Such an analysis requires a painstaking sifting of evidence from the material record. It is detailed work, but the wealth of information gained from it allows the reader to imagine the objects that surrounded these Indian women, setting the stage for a deeper analysis of race, conversion, and frenchification in the chapters that follow. This abundance of material suggests that the questions about identity raised by Rouensa's case are relevant to other Indian wives and daughters of Frenchmen in the Illinois Country. For her immersion in French colonial material culture was not unique. Rather, it was duplicated among her contemporaries and replicated in the material culture expressions of later generations of Indian wives of Frenchmen and the daughters born of such unions.

Living in the French Manner

Marie Rouensa lived on a large lot surrounded by a picket fence in the French colonial village of Kaskaskia, in a house in the distinctive vertical log construction architectural style prevalent in colonial settlements of the Upper Mississippi Valley.[6] Livestock consisted of cattle, horses, chickens, and hogs; a salting tub filled with 300 pounds of ham signaled the intended fate of the pigs, while milking pails and horsedrawn carts put the other animals to use. Nineteen of the thirty-three arpents they owned were sowed with corn and at least four arpents were sowed with wheat. The land itself may have come to the household through Marie Rouensa, but Michel Accault had become an important landlord in his own right in 1693 when he purchased a half-share in a large landholding and fur trade partnership with Henri de Tonty.[7] The inventory shows that the distribution of Rouensa's houses and land conformed to colonial land use patterns in the area, reinforcing the spatial integration of the household within the French village rather than the neighboring Indian village of the same name. The spatial arrangement did not lend itself to the Illinois practice of "michiki88a," in which women segregated themselves in huts during menses and childbirth (as they did during vision quests), a ritual certainly frowned on by Catholic missionaries.[8]

As with its real estate, the family's movable personal property revealed the growing dominance of French material culture in this distant, isolated colonial outpost of the French empire in North America. Rouensa (and no doubt the family's slaves) used brass, copper, and pewter utensils (frying pans, kettles, cauldrons, grills) to prepare food served on pewter plates and platters and coffee poured from copper vessels at a walnut table and chairs, illuminated by copper candelabra, beside a bed of straw and rope adorned with a cotton sheet. Some items spoke of a distinct degree of refinement, such as the two walnut armchairs and the copper coffeepot. Other items of European derivation, such as kettles, were so entrenched as intercultural objects in native usage that they had already become closely identified with Indians.[9] Though officials made no mention of items of Indian manufacture in their inventory of the Rouensa-Philippe household, it was undoubtedly an omission, and we can assume that items such as buffalo robes for bedding or earthenware for cooking and eating were present, just as they were in other households in the colonial settlements of the Illinois Country.

Yet the post-in-the ground vertical log dwelling in which Marie Rouensa died was starkly different from that in which she was born and in which she lived during her early years of marriage with Frenchmen, when the French resided with their wives within Illinois Indian villages. Marie Rouensa lived through the post-1719 transformation of the Kaskaskia Indian village into a colonial French settlement as a result of the policy of segregating French villages from Indian ones (see Figure 3).[10] When she died, French Kaskaskia was in full expansion mode. The description of her dwelling reflected the increase in her own family, as seen in the careful itemization of new housing and agricultural structures on her property:

> Another lot located in the village of Kaskaskia containing one arpent of land ... facing the church. On this lot there is a house of *poteaux-en-terre* 36 x 20 feet in which there is a stone fireplace, with neither floor nor interior walls. And another framed [house] 40 x 22 feet ... a small cabin ... stable of *poteaux-en-terre*. The said lot is half enclosed with pickets of mulberry.
>   Estimated at 5500 livres.[11]

Another house of the same size was being constructed on the same lot and two barns were also itemized, as well as planks, shingles, and ironwork intended for finishing the houses.

This household was marked by the communal living practices familiar to French and Illinois, even if the specific definition of kin and of who should live with whom differed. But if living arrangements shared this feature, the physical appearance of Marie Rouensa's lot differed from that of neighboring Illinois Indians' dwellings. Not only was the configuration of the housing, cooking, livestock, and agricultural structures distinctive, and demarcated from its neighbors by a picket fence enclosure, but the building materials and methods also differed. In these respects, Marie Rouensa's living arrangements in her final years with Frenchmen represented a dramatic transformation from conditions she would have experienced growing up as an Illinois Indian. While it is difficult to precisely date the various stages in the transformation of French-Indian couples' housing arrangements, some evidence suggests a lengthy transitional period. This evidence makes it all the more important to understand the differences between Illinois Indian and French colonial housing practices as experienced initially and over time by households formed by intermarriage. Permanent as opposed to temporary housing and settlements was a crucial point of distinction, one that had been a focal point of colonists' observations of the Indians they first encountered in Louisiana, with implications for the way they interpreted these Indians' culture.[12]

Permanency was a hallmark of French vernacular architecture, and as such was harnessed in plans for conversion and colonization. In contrast to French plans for the establishment of fixed villages, Illinois Indian villages varied seasonally since the Illinois resided half the year in dispersed winter hunting camps before reassembling in conglomerated summer agricultural villages the rest of the year.[13] Pierre Charles de Liette, a cousin of the explorer Henri de Tonti, left a more precise description of the architectural method for winter housing in his 1721 account:

the women who remain [in the camps during the summer hunts] go off in canoes, of which they have as many as three in each cabin, to cut reeds with which they cover their cabins. These are a kind that grows in their marshes. They procure bundles of them, which, after removing a skin that encloses several blades conjointly, they dry in the sun and tie together with twine which they make of white wood, with

ten or twelve bands at intervals of about six inches. They make these
up to ten fathoms in length. They call them *apacoya*, a word which
serves not merely to designate these, but which is a generic term for
all sorts of coverings. They use the same term for bark boards, and
two of these *apacoyas*, one on top of the other, protect one from the
rain as well as the best blanket. These are the cabins which they use in
autumn and winter; even if they leave their canoes, the women carry
these on their backs.[14]

Though pots and receptacles might be left buried in cache pits at each site,
as de Liette had specified, the housing itself was mobile, made and carried
by women.[15] Colonist Antoine Simon Le Page du Pratz had emphasized
this gender division of labor with his depiction of women alone laboring
to carry housing and household goods from site to site during the winter
hunt.[16] French fur traders who settled with Indian women beginning in the
later seventeenth century were initially absorbed into their wives' modes of
housing, but French males introduced and imposed their own traditional
construction methods, as a result of which the native division of labor was
altered. Women's responsibility for housing was displaced as Indian villages
were turned into French colonial settlements purged of Indians who did not
belong to French households. It was in this new kind of settlement that Marie
Rouensa, in 1725, passed away.

The demarcation between French and Indian settlements was a momen-
tous change for Indian women already married to Frenchmen. Yet, though it
was not until 1719 that the French carried out their formal separatist policy,
a shift in living patterns had predated this moment. In 1680, exasperated by
voyageurs (fur trade workers) who kept deserting, La Salle separated the location of the French fort from the Indian village of Grand Kaskaskia, though
he failed to stop interactions between both settlements.[17] It would fall instead
to Illinois women converts to achieve partition between French and Indian
populations. In 1680, when La Salle had reached the Tamaroa village, he had
found that the inhabitants had gone on a hunt; the total absence of anyone in
the village was underscored when he and his companions had to leave gifts of
knives and beads hanging on a branch "to let these *sauvages* know that their
friends had passed by there."[18] But by the end of the seventeenth century, eyewitness accounts began reporting that Indian wives of Frenchmen customarily stayed with their husbands rather than leave with their villages on winter
group hunts. For example, in praising the mission at Peoria in 1699, Father

Jean François Buisson de St. Cosme (who within a few years of his departure from the Illinois Country was reputed to have sired the future Great Sun of the Natchez Indians of Lower Louisiana) noted that

> We had not the consolation of seeing all these good Christians often, for they were all scattered down the bank of the river for the purpose of hunting. We saw only some women sauvages married to Frenchmen, who edified us by their modesty and by their assiduity in going to prayer several times a day in the chapel.[19]

This pattern was directly linked to conversion and to the teachings of missionaries. In his 1694 letter describing the mass conversion of the chief of the Kaskaskia and many of his people, Father Gravier had carefully singled out his new Kaskaskia converts, noting that "All of the people left for their winter quarters on the 26th of September, excepting some old women, who remained in 14 or 15 cabins, and a considerable number of Kaskaskia."[20] Chief Rouensa may not have been among those, however, for in 1702 Father Gabriel Marest traveled "thirty leagues from my village to see Roensa [*sic*] in his winter quarters."[21] Yet ten years later in 1712, Marest noted once again that "our village is the only one in which a few Sauvages are permitted to remain during all these journeys; many of them raise chickens and pigs, in imitation of the Frenchmen who have settled here; . . . Father Mermet . . . remains in the village, in order to instruct them."[22] André Pénicaut, a French carpenter-soldier on detachment there in 1711, corroborated these missionary accounts of converts' increasingly less nomadic life and their reorientation toward French food staples and domesticated animals.[23]

In his account, Pénicaut described Kaskaskia Indians' talent for European agriculture techniques, and he underlined the role of Jesuit missionaries in introducing the plow for the cultivation of wheat, and for establishing gristmills:

> they plow them with a plow, which has not yet been done elsewhere in the Missicipy [*sic*]. They acquired a knowledge of the plow from the Reverend Jesuit Fathers more than sixty years ago. . . . The Reverend Jesuit Fathers had come there by way of Canada to get down to these Illinois and had converted almost all of them to the Catholic religion. . . . Near their village they have three mills to grind their grains: namely, one windmill belonging to the Reverend Jesuit Fathers,

which is used quite often by the residents, and two others, horse mills, owned by the Illinois themselves.[24]

Given the role of missionaries (especially Jesuits) in promoting this kind of agriculture over Illinois methods and technology for cultivating corn, this shift to settling in one place may also have been a key factor in the eventual dominance of market agriculture (specifically, the flour trade, which found an important market in Lower Louisiana) over fur-trade activities in these settlements.[25]

From 1697 to 1714, a ban on unlicensed fur traders had reinforced Frenchmen's immersion within, and reliance upon, native communities in the Great Lakes area. Yet as early as 1710, the physical environment inhabited by Indian women married to Frenchmen already showed the influence of missionary activity, which replaced mobile fur trading activities with a sedentary agricultural lifestyle and the concomitant Frenchification of village life.[26] Indeed, by 1725, Marie Rouensa's probate inventory revealed the minimal presence of trade goods from fur trading activities—about twenty-five ells of cloth, mostly woolens. Valued at a modest 233 livres out of a total value of over 45,000 livres for all the movable property and immovable real estate in her household's possession, these ells did not constitute solid evidence of her husband's "continuing employment as a fur trader."[27] Rather, the inventory revealed the reliance on French agricultural tools and the dominance of large-scale agricultural production, with over nineteen arpents under cultivation with maize, four arpents with wheat, and a further ten arpents indeterminate. Frenchification also appeared in the description of the buildings, furniture, and furnishings with which Marie Rouensa was surrounded.

Rope Beds, Tablecloths, and Armchairs

Historians are fortunate that Marie Rouensa died in 1725, as it was only after the 1719 separation of French and Indian villages that succession records of the community property held by French-Indian couples survive. Collectively, these records reveal a pronounced and established adhesion to, and interest in, French colonial material culture. An extraordinarily rich body of evidence survives to illuminate the unusual material culture expressions of Indian women and their mixed-blood daughters in the Illinois Country, and helps explain why onlookers might have understood them as having "become *Frenchified*," to quote Duclos.[28]

French-Indian couples lived in a smattering of permanent French villages and forts that were carefully isolated from Indian settlements. The French colonial villages were compact, centered on the parish church and surrounded by a system of open-field agriculture, features that further contributed to creating cohesive, nuclear communities.[29] The houses themselves would reveal the presence of French-style furniture and household effects interspersed with indigenous ones. Collectively, all these elements provide a visually distinctive backdrop to the appearance of the Indian wives and daughters of Frenchmen in the Illinois Country.

In the French villages, mixed couples lived in houses made in the colonial style that developed in the Illinois Country. As opposed to the Illinois Indians, with their portable rush cabins whose contents could be conveniently carted from site to site on the backs of women, the French cleared forests and brought in engineers to build permanent forts from wood planks held together with nails and other iron hardware. A slew of French and Canadian masons, carpenters, stone cutters, and others in the building trades built houses influenced by both Canadian and Caribbean architectural styles. For the most part, the houses were constructed in one of two dominant styles: with vertical logs that were either planted in the earth palisade fashion (*poteaux-en-terre*, or post in ground) as in the Bequette-Ribault House (see Plate 2), or placed upright on sills (*poteaux-sur-sole*, post on sill) as in the circa 1740 Cahokia Courthouse (see Plate 3). The areas between the logs were filled with a mixture of mud and straw, or clay and pebbles; both types of houses were whitewashed. Beginning in the 1730s, wealthier inhabitants built stone houses.[30] In 1723 we find the first reference to a wraparound porch (*galerie*) that could run along two, three, or four sides of a house.[31] The gallery highlights the material dimension of this colony's place at the intersection of New France and the Caribbean, for it was a common feature of colonial architecture in France's warmer colonies across the Caribbean and the Indian Ocean, but one unknown in New France. Like the vertical log construction and the usual picket fence, the *galerie* and the double-pitch hipped roof that helped support it would eventually become key elements of Illinois Country houses as seen in surviving mid- to late eighteenth-century buildings in Cahokia, Prairie du Rocher, and Ste. Genevieve, including those shown in Plates 2 and 3.[32]

Until the mid-eighteenth century, documentary evidence of the gallery was relatively rare. For example, in 1739, shortly after the death of his wife,

Ignon Ouaconisen, Louis Marin de la Marque paid one hundred livres for a gallery to be added to the "two long faces" of his house at Kaskaskia.[33] Also known as Françoise Missouri, Ouaconisen was unique among Indian wives of Frenchmen in the Illinois Country in having set foot in France. The details of her visit to France and of her life upon her return to the Illinois Country provide a rare glimpse into French metropolitan *and* local colonial responses to Indian women converts who married Frenchmen. At the behest of the explorer Etienne de Véniard de Bourgmont, a delegation consisting of four Indian chiefs and Ignon Ouaconisen (chosen to represent the Missouri nation) traveled to Paris in 1725. The party also included Nicolas Ignace Beaubois, a Jesuit priest posted to the Illinois Country, and an unnamed female Padoka slave.[34] Over a two-month visit in late 1725, the delegation was greeted by officials of the Company of the Indies, and presented to the court. The caused a storm of public interest as they were shown taken the sights in Paris and at the châteaux of Versailles, Marly, and Fontainebleau, and were presented with gifts of clothing and other objects for themselves and their people. She converted to Catholicism in Notre Dame Cathedral, and took the name Françoise (meaning "French") underscoring the dual symbolism of this public ritual that turned an Indian into a subject of the Roman Catholic king of France. There she also married Dubois, a Frenchman who had accompanied the group from Louisiana and who had been promoted to the rank of officer. Upon their return to Louisiana, she moved with him to the Illinois Country and, upon his death, entered into a new sacramental marriage with Louis Marin de la Marque.[35] Since the gallery they commissioned in 1739 was to be added to an existing building, we can assume that the house she shared with her husband in Kaskaskia was built according to the local colonial style.[36]

Charles Danis and his wife Dorothée Mechip8e8a (or Mechiperouata, Mici8e8a) lived in a more transitional model. According to a 1724 account, their plot contained a house forty-five feet in length, with an outdoor oven, and a "hut covered with bark." The latter is clearly suggestive of the architectural practices of Illinois women. They had also accumulated a large quantity of bark in addition to that covering the hut: on Danis's death in 1724, eight tons of the material was divided between the widow and her children.[37] The couple's other real estate included a range of French colonial farm buildings: a stable, a mill, and a fifty-foot barn on a separate plot.

Apart from this bark-covered hut and the occasional references to slave cabins, all other descriptions of plots and houses in the historical record document the presence exclusively of French colonial structures with fireplaces, windows (unlikely to be glazed) and often, partitioned rooms. Marie Rouensa-8canic8e's residence was a *poteaux-en-terre* house with fireplace measuring thirty-six by twenty feet, the same approximate size as the extant post-in-ground Bequette-Ribault House (see Plate 2).[38] In 1721, Catherine 8abankinkoy (also 8ebana8ic8e, Ouabanakicoué or Ouabanakicouerare) and her husband Louis Texier (or Tessier) were improving on their real estate, consisting of a house measuring thirty-six by nineteen feet, a large stable, a barn, and a mill, constructed from mulberry posts. In that year, they had laid aside the sawn wooden boards required to put flooring, partitions, and windows in the second floor of their house.[39] The 1723 records relating to Jacques Bourdon, a fur trader who emerged as one of Kaskaskia's wealthiest inhabitants and captain of the militia, and who had been married to at least two Indian wives, show that the house of *poteaux-sur-sole* that he shared with his wife Marguerite Ouaquamo Quoana (or Ouaquamoquaano) was forty feet long and included partitions into different rooms; it was also thatched, with a double chimney of stone.[40] Marie Rouensa and her French husband lived in a thirty-six-by-twenty-foot *poteaux-en-terre* house facing the church of Kaskaskia, the same approximate size as the extant post-in-ground Bequette-Ribault House (see Plate 2).[41] The 1726 succession records of Suzanne Keramy's second husband reveal that they lived in a house of posts in the ground measuring forty-six by twenty feet wide.[42] In 1748 in Cahokia, Marie Catherine Illinoise and her husband Jean-Baptiste Baron were in the midst of building a new house with a garden, an (outdoor) oven, and "other lodgings and commodities," and even a stone cellar; in other words, this was a compound virtually indistinguishable from French *paysan* and Canadian *habitant* dwellings.[43]

As these examples suggest, the living quarters of these Illinois women and their French husbands were a vernacular architecture that could accommodate the ownership of hefty wooden furniture, the hanging of large mirrors, the space for a wide range of cooking and serving utensils, and the storage, laundry, and use of household linens and wearing apparel, all inventoried in these houses. Furnishings were imported from France though they might be finished on site (napkins hemmed, for example). While we can assume that some settlers included small-scale furniture items in the cargoes of goods they brought into the Illinois Country for their own use, no furniture items are itemized in the commercial shipments of merchandise for trade in the Illinois Country. Furniture was made by craftsmen from locally harvested wood, using French carpentry methods and tools.[44]

The transitional period during which Indian-French villages were forcibly remade into French colonial villages seems to have been brief, as illustrated in the first extant inventories of French-Indian couples. These records date to 1721, just two years after the policy of separating French and Indian villages came into force, and they reveal that by then the colonial settlements (including the dwellings of French-Indian couples) were already saturated with varying degrees of French material culture. Following his death in 1721, the community property between the late Pierre Roi and his Illinois widow Marianne Mascoutin Ki8ea (identified in 1744 as an Illinois Indian) was shared between her and their two surviving children. The household effects were modest, consisting of tools, five kettles and cauldrons (including one with legs and handle, or *poêlon*), and a bucket, as well as Pierre Roi's wardrobe, which was similar to that of a typical French Canadian habitant. There were virtually no fur trade goods except for half a pound of vermillion. But there were references to French livestock and staple crops: chickens (and records of sales of poultry and eggs to colonists), as well as a few cattle and a field ready to be sown with wheat.[45] The sparseness of her French household belongings did not hinder the widow's prospects at remarriage, and she contracted to marry colonist Pierre Glinel, giving birth to their daughter in October 1723.[46]

In contrast to the lack of trade goods in the Roi household, that of Catherine 8abankinkoy and her late husband Louis Texier was replete with quantities of trade shirts, trade hats, wooden combs, and cloth that could have appealed as much to colonists as to Indians, given the range of the textiles and the uses to which they could be put. As storekeeper for the Company of the Indies, Texier would have been able to take advantage of his position to profit from trade. Beyond these trade items, the household goods encompassed a full complement of kitchenware, poultry, hogs, horses, a smithy with tools, quantities of wheat and flour, and buildings that included a stable and a mill; enslaved Africans and Indians were also inventoried. Once again, few items of furniture were inventoried, though this might reflect the fact that their substantial house was not yet completed. The thirty-six-foot long, two-story house had been erected, but the boards to make the upstairs floorboards, partition walls, and windows were still in storage awaiting installation. It is difficult to conceive of the official storekeeper building a house with such refinements and not planning for contents of a corresponding caliber and Frenchness.[47]

Within two years of these inventories, we find more pronounced evidence of the establishment of French material culture norms, even in modest households.[48] The 1723 inventory of the Bourdon-Ouaquamo Quoana house-hold reveals how swiftly Kaskaskia had been transformed into a French colo-nial village. The widow's share of the property included the forty-foot house (with a cellar), along with furniture including a walnut dresser, a sideboard, a table, two chests, and a bed. Placed in, on, and around these pieces of fur-niture were fireplace implements, a salt cellar, plates and platters of pewter, glass bottles, an iron tablespoon, and prestige items including a silver cup, six silver plates, and two silver spoons. Unlike peasant and modest French households this family did not need to eat from the same pot but could have their own plates, and some had their own spoons.[49]

Archaeological finds of household goods from colonial sites in the Illi-nois Country (both domestic sites and military fortifications) confirm the consumption of such goods there, with the pottery consisting overwhelm-ingly of French-manufactured coarse lead-glazed and tin-glazed earthen-ware, mostly but not exclusively plain and decorated faïence from Rouen (see Plate 4). Such artifacts have also been found in Illinois aboriginal villages.[50] As such, these finds also serve to refine the information derived from docu-mentary sources, which tend to leave out details of the patterning, types, and sourcing of household ceramics, glassware, and metalware, while giving only general data about age, condition, original cost, and quality.[51] And though textiles and furs do not survive to be documented in archaeological reports, they were present in French-Indian households. The Bourdon household included embroidered linen napkins and tablecloths that either someone in the household or a paid village washerwoman would have maintained using skilled and labor-intensive European laundering and ironing techniques.[52] The clothing of the deceased was made of imported cloth, with the furs, large quantities of trade shirts and bolts of cloth likely reserved for trade with In-dians as with local residents. Rounding out the contents of this property were frying pans and various kettles including a covered one.

This household also revealed the presence of various indigenous items. It made use of three buffalo robes (used on the rope bed for bedding), an earth-enware jug filled with oil, and two "colliers" (probably wampum belts). The corn crop was also mentioned.[53] Echoing this retention of indigenous items, we find that of all the items another Indian wife, Suzanne Keramy, might have wanted to purchase at the 1726 auction sale of her late husband's ef-fects, the only one on which she outbid everyone else was a storage container full of local maple syrup.[54] This circumstance is suggestive of her retention of a taste for native foods and flavorings. Other French-Indian households also incorporated indigenous objects, yet here again they were limited to specific categories of goods, such as earthenware or baskets (not always of native local manufacture, since the Illinois traded their earthenware from other distant tribes) and buffalo robes for bedding, while their food stores revealed a taste for native and wild foodstuffs or flavorings of the kinds the French commonly traded from Indians throughout Louisiana (see the depiction of bear oil and preserved meat in the foreground of Plate 1). In the Bourdon household, the wampum, buffalo robes, and maize were unequivocally indigenous, but the earthenware jug filled with oil could as easily have been an imported Spanish jar filled with olive oil as a native pot traded from Indians in the Lower Mississippi Valley (perhaps in imitation of a Spanish olive jar) and filled with bear oil; both types were identified in archaeological excavations.[55]

Conversely, some provisions of European derivation, such as lard and tallow, were found in mixed households, while spices like cinnamon, nutmeg, cloves, pepper, chillies, and coffee and sugar were available.[56] But it is important to note that it was not only in French-Indian households that indigenous items were found. French-only households of the Illinois Country commonly used buffalo robes for bedding and consumed native foods including corn, peas, squash, melons (all presumably grown by Indian women) bear oil, and maple syrup, stored in baskets and earthenware. This finding underscores the difficulty of interpreting the presence of indigenous items as unambiguous markers of cultural retention by Indian wives of Frenchmen, since the same items were found in all-French households.[57]

And, dwarfing the references to items of indigenous manufacture and local food staples within French-Indian households, those colonists charged with inventories and appraisals made note of a plethora of French goods and imported or domesticated foodstuffs, evidence consistent with the archaeological record of colonial sites in the Illinois Country.[58] Appraisers noted, as they had in Jacques Bourdon and Marguerite Ouaquamo Quoana's inventory, that such dwellings were furnished with colonial furniture (at minimum a bed and sideboard) and decorative objects, embroidered linens, kitchen implements, and European bedding. In other words, while native products were present in French-Indian households (and were certainly vastly underrepresented in these and in French-only inventories), these couples also acquired and used a full complement of French household items. Ironically, it was Indian Marguerite Ouaquamo Quoana, widow of Jacques Bourdon, who contributed the bulk of the French material culture items to the household she shared with her new husband Nicolas Pelletier de Franchomme, an officer. A key modification during her marriage to Franchomme was in the bedding, with the buffalo robes now supplemented with but not supplanted by woolen blankets and quilted bedcoverings (perhaps at the insistence of Franchomme, a minor aristocrat born in France).[59]

Another household headed by an officer was that of Ignon Ouaconisen/ Françoise Missouri and her first husband Dubois, whom she had married in France. In 1730, in an attempt to bring some legal order to the estate of her first husband, and thus protect her marriage community of goods with her new husband Marin de la Marque, she provided an inventory of the community property held with Dubois in the Missouri. This revealed a clear preference for French standards of bedding and decoration, some of it quite refined and incorporating twenty-eight used napkins, bedsheets, and even a large mirror worth 50 livres, as well as sixteen heads of cattle. And while at the time of Dubois death, the household measured its wealth from quantities of traded furs and three enslaved Indians, it was also characterized by trade of another kind of product, in the form of 1,600 pounds of wheat flour and forty hams; all these trade goods were being kept in Kaskaskia.[60]

Marie Ma8e8enci8ois (or Ma8ennakoe), the Kaskaskia Illinois wife of two Frenchmen, died in 1740. Her household effects included a table with drawers, chairs, and armchairs, linen sheets for her bed, and a sideboard with its *vaisselier*—the better to display her pewter plates, platters, and copper candlesticks.[61] In 1724, following the death of Dorothée Mechip8e8a's first husband Charles Danis, the household's property was divided between his widow and her children. The household goods had consisted of a dresser and sideboard complete with pewter spoons and iron forks; five old walnut chairs, one walnut armchair; and firedogs, as well as "a table and two walnut benches left to the widow for her chamber." Kitchenware consisted of multiple kettles, but also pie dishes, a frying pan, a roasting spit, and a grill, while basins and two irons for ironing served to maintain the linens and apparel. Other assets included enslaved Africans and Indians, large quantities and varieties of cloth, trade goods, furs, livestock, and foodstuffs, ranging from corn to oats and from oil to tallow.[62] Also striking were the three pairs of hinges possibly intended for doors, windows, or an armoire. By the time of her death in 1747, she and her second husband Louis Turpin lived in a substantial three-story stone house flanked by galleries. It was the largest house at the time in the village of Kaskaskia, and the furniture must have reflected and the contents matched the architecture. This level of Frenchness in the material culture of the household would certainly have acclimated their daughter Marie to life in the New Orleans Ursuline convent where she would become a nun (see chapter four).[63]

Suzanne Keramy Peni8aasa, or Padoukiquoy, a Plains Indian woman who thrice married Frenchmen, died in 1747 in Kaskaskia. Her material surroundings can be traced through the records pertaining to her three marriages to Frenchmen and her own postmortem records. The first of these marriages, to Pierre Milleret, can be dated from 1713 at the latest, the year her eldest daughter, born in 1711, had been baptized as legitimate. By 1726 her second husband had died, and by 1728 she was entering her third marriage, to Daniel Legras. By 1747, at the time of her death, she lived in a household comfortably furnished with three beds and assorted bedding, a sideboard, table, and six chairs, a large and a small tablecloth, eleven napkins, the usual assortment of French-made copper or brass kettles and pans, grill, terrines for one-pot meals, pewter tableware and basins.[64]

It is tempting to see this ownership of French goods as a consequence of a change in immigration patterns by the 1740s, one that witnessed the growth of French and French Canadian populations in the Illinois Country.[65] However, as with the inventory of property held by Marguerite Ouaquamo Quoana in 1723, Indian women's ownership of French goods was not a new development, though it must have accelerated with the increase in quantities and varieties of imported goods aimed at the colonial population. Through immigration and apprenticeships, there was also steady growth in the number of French craftsmen living in the Illinois Country, including carpenters, joiners, stonecutters and blacksmiths.[66] Six tailors are also known to have lived in the Illinois Country during the French regime (four additional references to tailors do not identify them by name), along with three shoemakers and three wigmakers.[67] Women and enslaved Africans constituted two other important groups involved in the making and maintenance of furnishings and apparel though they do not tend to leave formal records of their work.

Suzanne Keramy's own household records reflect this shift toward increasing availability of French goods. Following her second husband's death in 1726, her share of his estate had included land, livestock, African slaves, plus a bed and bedding, a sideboard, two chairs, a walnut table over which could be draped a red linen tablecloth, buckets, kettles, and cauldrons, candlesticks, and an earthenware terrine.[68] In other words, while her 1747 postmortem inventory was replete with French goods, her 1726 household already revealed key components of the material culture of French households.

As gauged from the descriptions found in probate records, French-Indian households did not limit adoption of items of French derivation to purely functional ones. As we have seen, they also decorated their dwellings with French imported decorative objects including artwork. The dwelling in which Marie Catherine Illinoise and her trader husband Jean-Baptiste Baron lived was, like Françoise Missouri's interior, decorated with an expensive wall-hung mirror. The Illinoise-Baron household was in fact characterized in a 1748 inventory by its ownership of luxury or protoluxury furnishings that were still far from established as the norm even in Europe. The couple hung brown linen and calico curtains at the windows, used embroidered table-cloths and napkins, forks and knives, silver and crystal goblets at table, and slept in a bed with a straw mattress, pillow, bolster, calico rug, feather bed, and green wool blanket.[69] And, a feature shared with at least five other mixed households, they owned an armchair (in addition to their seven chairs), allowing household members and guests to sit on chairs rather than the motley tables, beds and other random furniture that provided seating in modest metropolitan French households.[70] While this feature speaks to the wealth and prestige accrued by certain of the more exalted French-Indian households, less affluent mixed couples demonstrated the same incorporation of French material culture, if not the same quantity of goods or the same degree of luxury.

The acculturation to French furniture and furnishings was passed down to daughters of Frenchmen and Indian women. In the contract for her second marriage to a Frenchman, Suzanne Keramy's daughter Hélène Danis negotiated a carefully worded clause to have her new spouse dower her with the substantial sum of three thousand livres, "to be chosen from the finest and best of the property of the said future husband."[71] As suggested by the emphasis on quality in this pro forma contract, a number of daughters of Indian women who married socially prominent Frenchmen betrayed the same emphasis on gentility as that found in the households of their mothers. For example, Marie Rose Texier (daughter of Louis Texier and Catherine 8abankinkoy) unequivocally consumed the more refined and expensive European goods available in the Illinois Country and consistent with her rank. Wife of Nicolas Boyer and widow of marine lieutenant Pierre St. Ange, Texier left on her death in 1747 a substantial succession. Her house was furnished with an armchair, dresser, and chest, while cooking was done in a (French) frying pan as well as in multiple kettles of the type used in French cooking. And her food was seasoned using luxury crystal salt cellars of the kind that were listed among the merchandise being taken to the Illinois Country in 1740.[72]

This adherence to French food preparation and presentation methods in the households of Indian wives and their married daughters suggests that French husbands refused to entirely forsake their native habits and the status such material trappings of Frenchness expressed. But it also reiterates their wives' (and daughters') willingness to embrace specialized European customs, luxuries, and tastes. Just as enslaved Indians and Africans were made to learn French ways of preparing food (which they enhanced and improved with their own techniques and tastes), so did Indian wives and their daughters stock their kitchens with coffee pots, cooking kettles, frying pans, pie dishes, covered dishes, and roasting spits with dripping pans to catch the juices from roasting meats.[73] Even the presence of kettles in mixed households highlights the differences between French and indigenous households. When Illinois Indians used kettles, they had to adapt them to changing living quarters; at the start of each summer hunting season, for example, they had to begin anew the process of setting up their kettles, "going into the woods to cut three poles of which they made a large tripod from which they hung a big kettle."[74] In colonial houses, metal hooks and chains permanently affixed to stone chimneys supported the weight of the kettles.[75]

The French also adapted indigenous implements to their housing practices. As in virtually every other French household in the Illinois Country, Texier's household linens included a buffalo robe, an aspect of Illinois Indians' material culture that had become ubiquitous in French colonial households. But unlike the Illinois, who traveled with their robes, using them flexibly for adornment as well as bedding, in French colonial households appraisers always noted the robe's fixed location on the bed. It was also but one component of bedding. For example, mixed households might use a buffalo robe as bedcovering. But sleeping itself was done on a rope bed padded with a feather bed and mattress, pillows, bolsters, sheets, and blankets (a white woolen one in the Texier household), and sometimes counterpanes and bedcovers—all necessary elements of a complete French bedchamber. Some households, such as those of Texier and of Marie Catherine Illinoise were also decorated with rugs that conformed to European conventions of the time since they were inventoried as bed or table covers rather than used on the floor.[76]

The relationship of the half-Indian Marie Aubuchon and her French or Canadian stepmother provides a direct comparison of French and French-Indian household furnishings. Unusual among daughters of Indian women integrated within French colonial villages, Aubuchon, born in the parish of Kaskaskia, was illegitimate. Though she had three legitimate, church-sanctioned marriages to Frenchmen between 1743 and 1767, her own parents had not married. Her mother's name is not known, but her father, Pierre Aubuchon, remained involved in her life. He was present at her first wedding, where he was acknowledged as her "natural" father and formally gave his consent. Pierre's wife was also present at Marie's wedding, suggesting that her father and stepmother had raised the illegitimate girl, not a unique occurrence.[77] Their presence at the signing of the contract made explicit that Marie was integrated in French colonial society and that she was a suitable candidate for marriage to a Frenchman. The marriage contract was certainly an advantageous one for her, for it stipulated that Marie's future husband, a trader, granted her a generous *douaire prefixe* of 1,000 livres. Her father and stepmother provided a dowry consisting of Antoine, a young enslaved African; they gave virtually the same dowry (a ten-year-old female slave valued at 500 livres) to their legitimate daughter Catherine on her marriage in 1757.[78] It is notable that Catherine could sign her name but Marie could not, suggesting that the illegitimate child was treated differently in the matter of education. Her illiteracy did not hinder her marriage prospects or her rise in social and economic status. By her third marriage in 1767, twice-widowed Marie Aubuchon, now living in Cahokia, was wealthy enough to enter into a contract with the man of her choice, Réné Locat, who declared that "he was bringing nothing" to the marriage community.

As calculated from the inventory of her goods upon her 1767 marriage to René Locat, the widow brought substantial assets, including land and profits from fur trading activities. What is especially notable from this list of her property is that Marie Aubuchon's material possessions were almost a perfect match for those owned by her French stepmother in an inventory taken just four years later in Ste. Genevieve. Among the items, or classes of items, that they both owned were a walnut wardrobe, sideboard, hutch, table with drawers, chest, mirror, chimney firedogs, candlesticks, and the inevitable bed with its mattress, feather bed, bolster pillow, striped blankets, and buffalo robe. Copper and brass kettles, frying pans, and earthenware vessels were present in both kitchens, while serving and eating in both households was facilitated by glassware, plates and platters of pewter and crockery (faïence), and silver and pewter cutlery, with plain and embroidered sheets, towels, napkins, and tablecloths adding texture to the furnishings; Marie's stepmother owned in addition some porcelain items and silver goblets.[79] In other words, this comparison of two near-contemporary households, in Cahokia and Ste. Genevieve, provides some precise data through which we can establish, first, that a wide range of consumer goods drawn from around the world were present in these sites; second, that there was a high degree of consistency across the colonial villages of the Illinois Country; and third, that intermarried French-Indian households maintained standards of living associated with colonial, not indigenous households.

As a component of material culture, furnishings and kitchen implements provide important evidence about the contours of Indian and French-Indian women's lived experiences. But archaeological and documentary evidence about furniture, furnishings, and household implements makes it hard to know the extent to which an Indian wife used a particular object. Beds and bedding were shared and probate records show the matrimonial bed was uniformly associated with the widow, providing incontrovertible proof of a preference for European sleeping comforts, with only the ubiquitous buffalo robes providing a link to indigenous practices. Likewise, while we cannot be certain that they ate hams and other imported foodstuffs, we can be sure, given that food preparation fell within the female division of labor, that the women became familiar with colonists' food preparation methods and food-stuffs. It is less clear from the available records whether an Indian wife ever sat in an armchair or if this was reserved for her husband in his role as head of household. But the ownership of multiple chairs, and of tables and beds to sit on, certainly suggests that there were other options for Indian wives than sitting on the floor when eating meals. Furniture such as tables and chests would have been put in daily use by all members of the household, while the imported textiles hanging from windows and adorning beds and tables, and the presence of wall decoration, cutlery, glassware, and crockery all provided a specific kind of aesthetic in the interiors of colonial houses. Notwithstand-ing the underreporting of indigenous household goods and food staples, it is significant that Indian wives of Frenchmen, and their children, lived in colonial-style houses surrounded by French and imported goods to which they had become acclimated.

Dressed "in the French Manner"

Houses and household goods set the tone and established the spatial envi-ronment for the ways Indian wives presented themselves. The analysis of housing provides an important index of styles of living, but it does so from the communal and collective perspective of all those living within a dwelling (one built by Frenchmen). If household goods may be open to interpretation, since the end user cannot always be presumed, clothing, which was personal to an individual wearer, provides a more precise means of evaluating the degree to which individual women adhered to French material culture. And the extant records of the belongings of Indian wives and daughters of Frenchmen also emphasize that their houses and household effects provided a matching spatial backdrop to their ownership of French-style dress.

As they began to convert the Kaskaskia, missionaries sought to inculcate converts into French ways of dressing that conformed to Catholic teachings. For Marie Rouensa in 1694, as further examined in the next chapter, this meant "her jacket [justaucorps], her stockings, her shoes, and her trifling ornaments," worn over an undergarment (a shift).[80] By the time officials began to produce probate inventories the data are more precise and chart a scale and sophistication in Illinois women's adoption of European forms and materials of dress that invite scrutiny. In other words, it is not that the women did not own Indian attire (moccasins at the very least), but appraisers did not formally record such items. What is especially striking, and significant, is that the same appraisers carefully noted the *inclusion* of all the necessary components of full European dress among the belongings of Indian women and their children, and that they did not differentiate their wardrobe contents from those of French women settled in the Illinois Country. The depth and breadth of this sartorial Frenchification raises questions about the process whereby Indian and half-Indian women learned how to dress in the French style, including the culturally specific body care, layering of foundation undergarments, and deportment associated with wearing such garments.

A French-Indian woman like Marie Aubuchon would have become comfortable with the presence and deployment of French material goods through living in her French stepmother and father's house. Other half-Indian women, raised in French villages by their Indian mothers, experienced this acculturation through interactions with their mothers and the French women living in the villages. Indian women converts, especially those like Marie Rouensa in the late seventeenth and eighteenth centuries, acquired the knowledge needed to dress in the French styles more indirectly.

These women never visited France to witness first-hand what it meant to be French in eighteenth-century France, with the exception of Ignon Ouaconisen, daughter of the Missouri chief. During her 1725 visit to Paris, the members of the Indian delegation from Louisiana were showered with gifts, the most expensive of which were items of clothing. The general director of

the Company of the Indies presented Ignon Ouaconisen with a fine and expensive gown made of "flame-red colored damask silk brocaded with a design
of gold flowers," with "petticoat of the same fabric," to be worn over the hoop
petticoat and one of the "two corcets, six trimmed shifts, six pairs of sleeve
ruffs . . . gold and silver ribbons along with a pair of silk stockings" that he also
gave her. He omitted hair ornaments "because she always went bare-headed."
Likewise, while the four male chiefs accompanying her were also presented
with the full complement of apparel "à la française," for them too the head was
kept distinct: the wig that was a requisite part of a gentleman's formal dress
in 1725 was not included. As explained by the director, these were gifts of apparel with which to "to clothe yourself while here [in Paris]."[81] Instead, and no
doubt for strategic reasons as well as entertainment value, the Indian delegation were often presented to the French public in Indian dress.[82] But religious
decorum would certainly have required Ignon Ouaconisen to wear full French
dress and cover her head during her baptism and marriage ceremonies, and
no doubt on those occasions she did wear the gown with its accessories.

On her return to Louisiana, Ignon Ouaconisen, now named Françoise
Missouri, and her husband settled in the Illinois Country, where Dubois, bolstered by his accession to the rank of officer and appointment as the king's
interpreter in the Illinois, became a trader in the Missouri (dealing in furs
as well as flour and hams).[83] With her marriage, Françoise Missouri's path
diverged from that of the four chiefs who had accompanied her to Paris.
Colonist Jean-François Dumont de Montigny described how the chiefs were
reintegrated within their communities, by being "covered with presents" on
their return to their villages and feted with "dances and festivities in the entire village." His account of Françoise Missouri's return was one in which she
became primarily and customarily immersed in French colonial life. Using
her married name, Dumont described how "Madame Dubois lived in the fort
and went from time to time to visit her family."[84] Dubois was killed in 1728,
and in 1730 Françoise entered into a new marriage with a captain of the militia at Fort de Chartres, Louis Marin (self-titled Sieur de la Marque). Related
to a prominent fur-trading family in the Fox Wisconsin region and involved
in regional trade, Marin and his wife traveled while also keeping a house in
the French village of Kaskaskia.[85] She had passed away by 1739, leaving two
children from her first marriage and three from her second. One daughter
from her first marriage entered into a legal and sacramental intermarriage of
her own in 1740, with a local trader who operated between New Orleans and
the Illinois Country.[86]

Françoise Missouri's first-hand knowledge of France and of the diversity of French material culture marked her out from her peers. In the Illinois Country, the first European woman (and therefore the first woman in full French dress) to be seen was Madame Le Sueur, who accompanied her husband there in the early 1700s. "Very tall, slender, very blonde," and with her "well-shaped face," she and her children (likened to "the little Jesus that Father Gravier shows us every day [in engravings]") caused as much of a stir among the Illinois as Françoise Missouri would among Parisians and the Versailles court.[87] But by the time this Frenchwoman was seen by the Illinois, they had already become acclimated to European standards of dress.

Illinois women developed knowledge of the appearance of European dress and households even before the construction of the first French vernacular house or barn, and the arrival of French furniture, furnishings, textiles, and clothing in the Illinois Country. The engravings of the Gospel that missionaries exposed them to first established their familiarity with the material culture expressions and deportment of Europeans. These images were essential tools for conversion and religious instruction, and Father Gravier described how "To the adults I explained the whole of the New Testament, of which I have copper-plate engravings representing perfectly what is related on each page."[88] Such engravings survive in ecclesiastical collections from New France, among them Gerónimo Nadal's 1593 *Evangelicae historiae imagines*, an illustrated volume (with engravings by Hieronymus Wierix) that St. Ignatius of Loyola commissioned for use in mission work. It was fairly frequently reissued, with revisions that included increasing the size of the plates, more extensive annotated text, and a new arrangement of the plates to concord with the Roman missal's liturgical calendar.[89]

As envisioned by Loyola, such visual tools would themselves stimulate interest in Catholicism and serve as a point of entry in mission work, as made explicit in the later seventeenth-century anonymous painting *France Bringing Faith to the Hurons*, in the Ursuline museum of Quebec.[90] The Spiritual Exercises were a method of prayer based on contemplation of the image.[91] Father Gravier in the Illinois Country would have agreed, commenting that "curiosity to see the pictures, rather than to hear the explanations that I gave, attracted a great many [Kaskaskia]" to his instruction on the New Testament.[92] Yet, as becomes clear from Indians' reception of religious imagery, they did not accept these images as purely didactic, but endowed the objects themselves with power and ritual.[93] The plates were composed using new techniques of perspective that provided realistic-looking depictions of biblical scenes, while the compositions incorporated a large number of interior and farming backdrops based on contemporary European farming practices and material culture. Such images would not only have served to complement missionaries' religious instruction, they would have introduced new converts to the material culture of Europeans. And they would have provided female converts with examples of women who modeled European standards of sartorial performance and domestic life.

We know from Father Gravier that Marie Rouensa was particularly intrigued by, and assiduous about, studying the copperplate engravings, that Gravier let her borrow some of the plates for her private study, that she in turn instructed other Kaskaskia Indians (especially women and girls) about the content of the images, and that she often spoke "of nothing but the pictures or the catechism."[94] This degree of visual scrutiny would have introduced her and other Kaskaskia to the architecture, interior furnishings, and objects of everyday life in Europe: fully furnished bedchambers; chimneys and andirons; chairs, stools, and chests; cookware (including kettles hanging from hooks in fireplaces); embroidered tablecloths, napkins, plates, platters, glasses, and cutlery; lamps and candelabra; and even copper bed warmers (see Figure 4). Indians studying these images would have become acclimated to the European farming implements, techniques of wheat cultivation (see Figure 5), and barns missionaries would introduce into the Illinois Country and which would eventually dominate French-Indian households like Marie Rouensa's.[95]

Missionaries conveyed sensorial information about the appearance, feel, and sound of woolen, linen, silk (and occasionally cotton) textiles through the clothing they wore and the plain and patterned liturgical textiles they brought with them to conduct masses and other rituals.[96] The engravings used as conversion aids built on this information, since they contained representations of contemporary European dress. Most of the plates in the *Evangelicae historiae imagines* depicted generic drapery and exotic, or ancient Jewish, dress (as conveyed through headwear; the rest of their garb depicting fashionable European dress) familiar from the canon of Western European religious art. But just as in that tradition, the engravings used for missionary work also contained numerous depictions of fashionable contemporary dress.[97] An Illinois woman who studied the images, as the Jesuits instructed them to do, could not have missed the body-concealing conventions of European dress, the full-length garments, aprons on servants, and almost always concealment of the hair underneath caps and other head coverings.

FERIA VI. POST DOMIN. IIII. QVADRAGESIMÆ.
Mittuntur nuncij à fororibus de graui morbo Lazari.   76
Ioan. ix.   Anno xxxiij.   lxi

A. Bethania Caſtellum Mariæ &
   Marthæ.
B. Lazarus grauiter ægrotans de-
   cumbit, inſeruiunt ei ſorores.
C. Mittunt nuncios ad IESVM
   Bethabaram.

D. Bethabara, oppidum trans Ior-
   danem, in tribu Ruben.
E. Deueniunt ad IESVM nuncij & tamen hæret Be-
   thabaræ, donec veniat ad
   quatriduanum.

Figure 4. *Feria VI. Post Domin. IIII Quadragesimae.* From Gerónimo Nadal, *Evangelicae historiae imagines, ex ordine evangeliorum quae toto anno in missae sacrificio recitantur, in ordinem temporis vitae Christi digestae* (Antwerp: [Martin Nutius], 1593), plate 76. Reproduced from the original held by the Department of Special Collections of the Hesburgh Libraries of the University of Notre Dame.

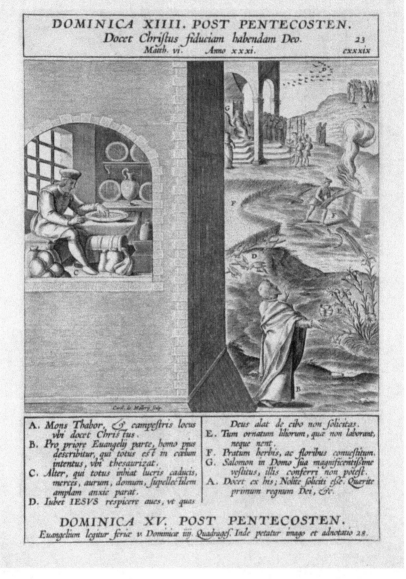

Figure 5. *Dominica XIIII. Post Pentecosten*. From Gerónimo Nadal, *Evangelicae historiae imagines, ex ordine evangeliorum quae toto anno in missae sacrificio recitantur, in ordinem temporis vitae Christi digestae* (Antwerp: [Martin Nutius], 1593), plate 23. Reproduced from the original held by the Department of Special Collections of the Hesburgh Libraries of the University of Notre Dame.

These images were not simply tools of religious conversion; they were also intended as means of cultural dissemination. With their realistic depictions of daily life as rendered in scenes from the Gospels, they laid the initial groundwork for Illinois Indian converts' material Frenchification, well before the establishment of colonial villages and the incursion of actual objects of French material culture into the Illinois Country. This consumption of images developed Indians' visual lexicon of French material culture, provided role models for the performance of gender, and seem to have fostered a taste for the objects and lifestyle depicted.

Furthermore, European goods—actual garments, textiles, and accessories—had already trickled into the region through existing Indian trade networks even before the first incursions of Canadian traders into the Illinois Country.[98] This explains why Father Marquette, on his first arrival in the area in 1674, could feel reassured by Illinois welcoming ceremonies "and much more so when I saw them Clad in Cloth, for I judged thereby that they were our allies." The Illinois were prominent as middlemen in the region and in this instance, according to Marquette, the Illinois had procured their cloth through trade with the Ottawa.[99] By 1674 the French were already quite familiar with the sight of Illinois Indians coming to French trading posts to exchange furs for imported manufactured goods.[100] This demand for nonlocal novelty trade goods added to existing networks of trade among different Indian nations. For example, the porcupine quills that the Illinois used in decorating their moccasins came from intertribal trade with the Potawatomi and Ottawa who "furnish them these, for there are no animals of this sort among [the Illinois]."[101] The arrival of French-imported goods would be a natural extension of this consumer interest, as confirmed in archaeological finds from indigenous sites in the Illinois Country.[102]

In a 1723 letter to his brother, Jesuit missionary Sébastien Rasles provided the fullest eyewitness description of the Illinois (unstated by him, his focus was on males):

The Illinois are covered only around the waist, otherwise they go entirely nude; many panels with all sorts of figures, which they mark upon the body in an ineffaceable manner, take with them the place of garments. It is only when they make visits, or when they are present at Church, that they wrap themselves in a cloak of dressed skin in the summer-time, and in the winter season in a dressed skin with the hair left on, that they may keep warm. They adorn the head with feathers of many colors, of which they make garlands and crowns which they arrange very becomingly; above all things, they are careful to paint the face with different colors, but especially with vermilion. They wear collars and earrings made of little stones, which they cut like precious stones; some are blue, some red, and some white as alabaster; to these must be added a flat piece of porcelain [shell] which finishes the collar. The Illinois are persuaded that these grotesque ornaments add grace to their appearance, and win for them respect.[103]

With his audience in mind, Father Rasles's description dwelled on what he considered exotic, namely the nudity and tattoos that were also featured in visual depictions of Illinois men, for example, in Louis Nicolas's *Codex canadensis* (see Figure 2), or in Alexandre de Batz's 1735 drawing of Indians of various nations (in which the second male from the left is identified as Illinois; see Plate 1).[104] Though he downplayed the incursion of French goods, mercantile records show another side. An extant inventory of trade goods taken into the Illinois Country in 1688 revealed the availability already by this date of imported European-manufactured textiles and clothing in the area, including *capots* (men's hooded coats), stockings, linen and woolen cloth, and thread.[105] By the start of the 1720s, traders were ubiquitous in the area and a French official, Diron d'Artaguiette, reported the dramatic encroachment of French dress among the Illinois Indians, noting that "The men as well as the women wear buffalo robes. . . . But with the arrival of the French in their lands, they have begun to adopt the habit of dressing in the French manner."[106] Just as Father Marquette had recognized as allies Illinois "Clad in Cloth," so did Diron d'Artaguiette's account ascribe a positive value to the adoption of French articles of dress.[107] D'Artaguiette was referring specifically to Illinois Indians living in tribal villages, not Indian wives of Frenchmen who lived in French villages and forts. As we have seen, each had distinct spatial and architectural backdrops to the deployment of French material culture. This in turn would affect how the French perceived the groups, based on a three-dimensional image of their identity.

"Clad in Cloth"

The analysis of dress draws especially on probate records of the belongings of Indian wives of Frenchmen, and their progeny.[108] The dress of mixed-parentage daughters is especially important when considering the long-term goals of Frenchification policies, transforming converted Indians and their progeny into French men and women. The analysis of this source material confirms a level of acculturation that matches the more ample record pertaining to household effects and is similarly surprising in its absoluteness.

All the textiles used in the apparel listed in probate records were imported from Europe or Asia (via Europe). In contrast to the English colonies, none of the materials used in clothing in Louisiana were homespun, and no European spinning or weaving implements were listed in any inventories. This was a result of protectionist economic policies directed at promoting and preserving metropolitan industries, which banned textile production (spinning and weaving of cloth). Official attempts were periodically made to exploit the natural resources of the colony for textile manufacture, but these were to provide raw materials for export rather than finished textiles in the colony.[109] In 1721, the Crown even passed an edict forbidding cultivation in the colony of hemp and flax, which were needed locally for cording. It is telling that a marginal notation (presumably by a local official) reported that, in any case, colonists were uninterested in producing textile goods.[110] In other words, and contrary to recent conjecture, no conclusions about acculturation can be drawn from the lack of weaving and spinning by Indian wives in the Illinois Country, because French and French Canadian women also abstained from these activities in the seventeenth and eighteenth centuries.[111]

Prices charged for manufactured goods in the Illinois Country were high. Until 1731, the company stores were held to be the only legitimate source for imported goods in the colony, and goods there were sold at tariffs set in France that reflected transatlantic shipping costs as well as the markup incurred in transporting goods from Lower Louisiana to the different posts.[112] In contrast to the ban on making cloth, authorities did not subject the production of garments to any restrictions beyond those dictated by the gender division of labor of French guild structures (as a general rule, men made tailored garments, women untailored ones). Instead of looking to homespun textile production as an index of identity, a more accurate picture is provided by the range of textile types in Indian and French-Indian wardrobes. Contextualizing the textiles in terms of the garments worn provides a richer interpretive framework for the analysis of the women's absorption of French and French Canadian material culture. These also help us interpret the purpose of the textiles listed in inventories, for instance, whether European cloth handed over to Indian wives on the death of their French husbands was for personal/family use or for trade with Indians.[113]

Large varieties of imported fabrics in infinite grades of quality and price were used in making garments in French, Indian, and mixed households, as revealed by the records of commercial shipments of goods into the Illinois Country. The majority of the goods in these cargoes consisted of textiles and ready-made apparel, with hardware, household goods, and alcohol distant seconds. In 1728, one trader had a stock of ready-made shirts, men's and women's silk stockings, hats, caps, sets of buttons, handkerchiefs, and bolts of linen, cotton muslin, and woolens.[114] In 1729, ensign and storekeeper Terrisse de Ternan noted that green everlasting (wool) was selling briskly, and there was demand for stockings, women's shoes, and ribbon.[115] In 1737, extant records from the ship *La Reine des Anges* from La Rochelle show that traders purchased goods worth nearly 8,000 livres for shipping to the Illinois Country. While some of this merchandise was of a type to appeal to Indian customers, the bulk was for French colonial consumers: textiles (plain and patterned woolens, silks, linens, and cottons from France, Holland, and India) together with thread, needles, thimbles, and pins, but also stockings, shoes, handkerchiefs, plain and ruffled shirts and hats, white leather gloves, gauze headdresses, silk mantles, fans, crystal perfume bottles, and no fewer than fifteen different types of lace.[116]

Key among the articles of apparel worn by French and Canadian women in the Illinois Country, as by Indian wives of Frenchmen and their daughters, was the *mantelet* jacket. The *mantelet* spread to Louisiana via Canada rather than France. In France and New Orleans the *mantelet* was understood as a short hooded mantle, a mostly decorative garment usually made of silk, muslin, or some other fine lightweight material.[117] In Canada and the Illinois Country the term denoted a loose knee-length jacket or short gown of basic construction (usually unpleated). It was usually worn over a petticoat, sometimes with a wrap-over front, often kept in place by an apron worn over it, and occasionally lined, as was the "old lined mantelet" inventoried among the possessions of the widower of Marie Rouensa.[118] Adoption of this garb by Indian women did not so much denote that they had "Frenchified" (as showcased by the flame-red silk damask gown given to Ignon Ouaconisen/ Françoise Missouri in Paris) as evoke the immediate French Canadian precursors of this style, with corresponding variations in French and Canadian nomenclature.

In Canada, this garment was commonly worn by the working and middling class; it was well adapted to physical work as well as childbearing and child rearing. The *mantelet* was available for purchase in the Illinois Country as a ready-made garment imported from Montreal and Lower Louisiana; for example, in 1736, one trader shipped in nine *mantelets* from Montreal. The cut and construction of this garment was also straightforward enough that women with even basic sewing skills could make one themselves. Its styling was minimally affected by changes in fashion, explaining its longevity as a garment of choice throughout the French regime in the Illinois Country.[119] Variety was provided by the range of textiles from which it could be made, depending on the fiber, weave structure, and finish (all of which affected texture and even sound), the color, and whether the fabric was plain or patterned, as it is in a surviving mid-eighteenth-century jacket and matching petticoat of *siamoise* (see Plates 5 and 6). The *mantelet* owned by Marguerite Ouaquamo Quoana, or Madame Franchomme, was made of *indienne*, a patterned printed cotton calico (see Plate 7). She left it behind when she temporarily abandoned her husband in 1725, along with three petticoats.[120]

Virtually every female inventory in the Illinois Country (Indian or French) included at least one *mantelet*, and usually several from different fabrics, often paired with a matching skirt or petticoat.[121] Probate records from the 1740s provide especially detailed lists of wardrobe contents and confirm the influence of Canadian women's dress and the correlation between the dress of French/Canadian women and Indian wives and daughters of Frenchmen in the Illinois Country. For all, the broad outlines of dress consisted of a shift; a petticoat or skirt; some form of short gown or jacket (usually the *mantelet*), more rarely a gown; a cape, handkerchiefs, and head coverings. A rare surviving doll from circa 1690–1700 shows the sequence in which such items of female dress were layered on the body, underscoring how essential each of these garments was to the performance of sartorial femininity (see Plates 8–13). In the Illinois Country, the preferred type of foundation garment for wearing over the shift was the "corcet," an unboned padded or quilted bodice (also known as jumps), as seen in Plate 18, rather than the boned stays seen in Plate 11 with which the term "corset" is now associated and which was rarer.[122]

The wardrobe contents of women living in the French villages of the Illinois Country perfectly match those depicted in a circa 1780 genre study of inhabitants of Canada (see Plate 14). On the upper level are shown five male and two female Indian figures incorporating varying degrees of French garb: shirts and jackets for the men; cloth petticoats, shifts, and a man's hat for the women. On the lower level are two French Canadian couples framed by two other male colonists. The dress of many of the Canadian men correlates with that of the Indians in that they have incorporated aspects of indigenous dress such as moccasins, finger-braided sashes, leggings, and snowshoes. In contrast to this cross-cultural openness, the Canadian women (on the lower level) wear *mantelets* with petticoats (one of them in matching printed cotton), worn with a neckerchief and an apron. A cap adorned with a red ribbon is visible on the head of the figure to the right; a bright red hooded cape envelops the female figure to the left, a necessary feature of winter dress as Sempronius Stretton emphasized in his depiction of a Canadian man and woman (see Plate 15).[123] This was the model for the dress of Indian wives and daughters of Frenchmen in the Illinois Country. Unlike male colonists who adopted elements of Indian dress, with the exception of moccasins, French women there did not Indianize their appearance. They also did not marry Indian men. This was an indirect reflection of Frenchification policies that almost exclusively envisaged French men marrying Indian women, not the reverse, French females marrying Indian males. Given their simultaneous belief in the superiority of the French over Indians, and of males over women in the context of gendered anxieties about aristocratic *mésalliance*, it was nearly inconceivable that a French woman be subjected to the marital authority of an Indian husband.[124]

Like Marguerite Ouaquamo Quoana and Marie Rouensa before her, Marie Catherine Illinoise wore a *mantelet*; she owned several, along with petticoats and aprons. But her other articles of dress allowed her to exhibit a far greater refinement and luxury consistent with the high quality of her household furnishings. Wife of trader Jean-Baptiste Baron from Cahokia, she died in 1748. She bore her husband three children before they officially married and two subsequently. This factor did not hinder the offspring's marriage prospects, for one of her daughters would marry Jacques Barrois, son of the royal notary at Fort de Chartres, in 1747 at Cahokia.[125] The assets left at Marie Catherine Illinoise's death came to 20,153 livres, an important sum reflected in the variety, quality, and luxury of her wardrobe.[126] Most prominent were her two gowns (of printed calico and of cotton) with matching petticoats and made to be worn with boned stays over a shift and pocket, as seen in the fashion doll's stages of dress (see especially Plates 12 and 13).[127] Appraisers did not list any stays in her inventory, but whalebone was shipped to the Illinois Country. Stay-making was a specialized craft and no stay-makers are known to have operated in Louisiana; it is more likely that the whalebone was for repairs rather than for making a new pair of stays.[128]

Gowns were more expensive and of higher status than jackets or short gowns such as *mantelets*, as confirmed by the quality and value of the textiles from which they were made. In contrast to the *mantelet*, which could be purchased ready-made or manufactured at home using modest quantities of cloth, the more complex cut and construction of gowns dictated the use of trained seamstresses. Since they were full-length garments, worn with a petticoat, gowns also used far greater quantities of fabric, as apparent in the surviving formal gown in Plate 13. From the 1720s on, the outline of full-length gowns was magnified by hoops, as seen on the female figures taking a promenade in New Orleans (see Plate 16).[129] Furthermore, gowns inherently showcased the wealth and rank of the wearer, since the value of garments in the eighteenth century lay in the price (and quality) of the cloth rather than the cost of the tailoring. The appraisals of the two formal gowns confirm this point. They were priced collectively at 250 livres in a lot also including a nightgown; more than twice the value of her bed and bedding. The nightgown itself was made of silk taffeta with a matching petticoat. This "robe de chambre" did meant not a garment worn at home at night and in private, but a fashionable informal garment (which might have been bought readymade), worn indoors in company, and in which the doll is dressed in Plate 12. This garment would have made it possible for Marie Catherine Illinoise to adhere to European etiquette and conventions of formal and informal dress (and undress). Adding to her collection of gowns and dressing gown, and helping complete her wardrobe, were four gowns, eight skirts and petticoats, eight *mantelets*, five caps, six handkerchiefs, an apron, four pairs of silk stockings, and a pair of embroidered shoes.[130]

Suzanne Keramy's apparel was given to her children. It consisted of "two calimanco skirts, two cotton skirts, one old skirt of everlasting [wool], three *mantelets*, four shifts in poor condition, one blanket of blue *limbourg* wool, the whole used."[131] These garments, made from *limbourg*, a common trade woolen, or calimanco, a usually colorful glazed worsted (see Plate 17), seem to betray no trace of her prior identity as a Padoka, or Plains Apache, captive.[132] A 1724 journal of a voyage by the French to the Padoka made note of their dress: "The women cover themselves with robes of dressed skins. Their shifts and skirts have fringe all around, made of the same material."[133] This dress was represented on a female being captured, depicted in a surviving buffalo robe (see Figure 6). Instead of clothing made of hides, with edges cut into the decorative fringes characteristic of Plains dress, Keramy's textiles and apparel were virtually indistinguishable from the sturdy, utilitarian clothes

Figure 6. Anonymous, *Battle scene with riders*, buffalo robe, nineteenth century (detail). Musée du Quai Branly, Paris Acc. 71.1931.5.27. Photo © Musée du Quai Branly/Scala/Art Resource NY.

in Illinois Country inventories of most female colonists of French and of Illinois-Indian descent.

Like their mothers, children born into legitimate marriages between Indian women and Frenchmen customarily dressed according to colonial standards. The half-Indian Marie Jeanne (also known as Marianne) Faffart was the widow of Nicolas Quadrain, and then the wife of Jean-François Becquet. While no inventory of her dress was drawn up after her death, documentation following her widower's death in 1739 referenced a number of used female garments that would have belonged to his late wife. The items left by Marie Jeanne included two *mantelets* (one of calico), four skirts in different fabrics, and an apron, all in poor condition.[134] Once again, the textiles, forms, and styles of these garments marked them as French Canadian.

More exalted and voluminous than Marie Jeanne Faffart's wardrobe was that of Marie Rose Texier. Her apparel was extensive, consisting of three *mantelets*, two of calico and one of calimanco lined with wool flannel, plus two calico petticoats, one of calimanco and one of embroidered cotton, and numerous shifts. She also owned a few ells of linen cloth and quantities of thread that hinted at the cutting and sewing skills that allowed most French and Canadian women to make and maintain their own household's basic linen garments. Alternatively, they could commission the making of their clothes from seamstresses known to operate in the Illinois Country, such as Madame Parant, or they could delegate this work to their African or Indian slaves.[135] Perhaps most distinctive in quality and cost were her silk stockings, four lace-trimmed muslin kerchiefs, headwear consisting of eight coifs and two quilted caps, and silver-mounted diamond earrings.[136] Unlike Françoise Missouri, who "always went bare-headed" during her 1725 visit to Paris, Texier, like Marie Catherine Illinoise, clearly adorned her hair with French-style headwear. No recognizably Indian items were listed in Texier's inventory. Even if these had been excluded from the inventory rather than altogether absent from her possessions, Texier's wardrobe contained all the key elements that would have given this half Indian wife of Frenchmen a "Frenchified" appearance, and one with trappings of gentility and luxury.

The illegitimate Marie Aubuchon, raised in her French father and French/French Canadian stepmother's household, and who entered into three legitimate, church-sanctioned marriages to Frenchmen between 1743 and 1767 had a more utilitarian though well-furnished wardrobe that provided a good match to her furnishings, described above. The inventory taken prior to her third marriage in 1767, after the death of her second husband, was explicit in identifying the widow's own clothes. Their aggregate value was 460 livres and consisted of nine *mantelets*, nine cotton skirts, five calico petticoats, eighteen shifts, twelve linen and fourteen red- and blue-colored cotton handkerchiefs (actually headkerchiefs, not pocket handkerchiefs) , seventeen caps trimmed with lace, and a camlet wool cape.[137] Here again were listed all the components of French Canadian female wardrobes, with their emphasis on *mantelet* and petticoat combinations, head coverings, and handkerchiefs, and incorporating the ubiquitous cape.[138]

Her children's clothing was also inventoried, consisting of forty-seven shirts of all sizes and in varying condition, for an indeterminate number of children, plus two pairs of trousers ("grandes culottes"; see Plate 29), and "for the use of the eldest boy," two waistcoats and a wool *capot* (as worn by the Canadian male inhabitant in Plate 15). The presence of multiple shifts, articles of headwear, and handkerchiefs—all made of washable linen or cotton—meant that Aubuchon could have had her servants/slaves or professional washer-women launder them on a regular basis, since the family would have spare clothes to wear while others were being cleaned. Multiple units of the same garment also meant that she (and her children to a lesser degree) could exhibit daily variety in colors, patterns, trimmings, cut, and quality of the textiles of her dress, speaking to this half-Indian wearer's interest in and taste for full French dress.

This wholehearted concern for the forms, varieties, and standards of French dress among Indian wives and daughters of Frenchmen is notable for its deviation from the selective adoption of French dress by Indians living outside French settlements. For example, Aubuchon's ownership of handkerchiefs marked her out from indigenous consumers who did not respond enthusiastically to French traders' repeated attempts to market handkerchiefs to them; rather than use handkerchiefs as the French (and Aubuchon) did as neckerchiefs, they restricted them to ritualistic and allegorical purposes.[139] They similarly resisted the lure of stockings. This is explicit in the circa 1780 image of Canadian *habitants* (Plate 14), in which not one of the male or female Indian figures in the upper half of the drawing are seen in stockings. Rather, they wear leggings (*mitasses*), made from imported textiles rather than hides.[140] Their utter rejection of stockings stands out from the presence of stockings among the effects of Indian wives and daughters of Frenchmen in the Illinois Country (and the general popularity of men's and women's silk, woolen, linen thread, and cotton stockings in cargoes of goods dispatched to the Illinois Country for the colonial market), providing yet another index of the latter's unusual deployment of French-style dress in all its layers.[141]

The half-Indian Marie Anne (or Marianne) Danis, daughter of Dorothée Mechip8e8a and Charles Danis, had moved to New Orleans with her French Canadian husband, Philippe Chauvin *dit* Joyeuse. He predeceased her, and though he was from a prominent Louisiana family, his death left her living in penury but as a respectable French widow.[142] At the time of her death in 1747, she owned a wardrobe notable for its rich (if worn out) array of European dress and accessories: eight shifts, three gowns (of muslin and printed cotton), two linen jackets (*mantelets*), three petticoats, three neckerchiefs, ten caps, two pairs of embroidered shoes, six pairs of stockings, two headdresses, two handkerchiefs, and a cape, a gold ring, and a mirror. One of her gowns, of calico, was sold at auction after her death, where it fetched thirty-five livres (the low price a reflection of its poor condition). The gown was bought for resale by Veuve Gervais, an established retailer of new apparel and reseller of second-hand clothes in New Orleans, emphasizing that Chauvin's clothing met the requirements of French consumers.[143] Most of her apparel was handed over to her children, especially her eldest daughter, including a *corset* (jumps, as shown on Plate 18) that provided the necessary foundation for the trappings of French female propriety. Madame Chauvin had also dispatched two other *corsets*, made of silk taffeta, to the Illinois Country for resale there, along with a cotton gown, a silk gown, and two petticoats, showing that she recognized a market in her birthplace for such goods.[144] While the *corset* lacked the tightly packed whalebone strips characteristic of stays (*corps* in French), it too provided a degree of rigidity as it flattened the chest and pushed back the shoulder blades.[145] Madame Chauvin's probate inventory made reference to two other crucial culturally specific components of a Frenchwoman's appearance—neatness and cleanliness. Like her Illinois mother, she owned a pair of irons and a laundry pail, and she left a debt to a washerwoman, written on the back of an old playing card, for laundering her household linens.[146]

While she had lived her widowhood in pecuniary need, Marie Anne Danis had maintained French decorum and regulations pertaining to her status as a widow. Mourning dress was worn across a broad socioeconomic range of Louisiana's settler population from the affluent to the destitute. In New Orleans, this specialized garb was supplied by retailers and second hand clothes dealers as well as the Ursuline nuns.[147] Madame Chauvin followed French mourning customs, as documented by the presence at her death of a *miramiole*, the distinctive black peaked headdress worn by widows. She also ensured that her daughter was educated at the Ursuline convent, in the privileged capacity of a paying boarder. There, the girl would have worn her own clothing (not the more standardized and spartan garb supplied to orphans).[148] Among her clothes would have been those items the appraisers and notary had handed over from her deceased mother's wardrobe, just as they had bypassed the formal division of goods by handing over clothing and bedding items to her young male and female siblings. Among the items the officials deemed right to hand over to the girl was a wooden bed with a bolster pillow, a sheet, and a woolen blanket, as well as a chest and a cupboard. The clothing included the *mantelets*, petticoats, neckerchiefs, caps, handkerchiefs, cape, gold ring, and one *corset*, thereby ensuring that this granddaughter of an Illinois Indian woman unequivocally sided with her French forebears in the matter of dress, accessories, and deportment.

"A blanket of blue *limbourg* wool"

It is significant, if perplexing, that there is so little evidence of the continuing
relevance of Indian material culture to the Indian women living in French
society. Indian wives of Frenchmen living in French villages, and their
mixed-parentage daughters, slept in French beds fitted with French bedding,
ate from pewter and crockery, and drank from glass and silver. Where records survive, there was absolute consistency in the descriptions of how they
dressed: exclusively in European garb. If they had the means and inclination,
they wore silk or cotton gowns; if not, *mantelets* with matching petticoats
were the norm. Their hair was covered with caps, their bodies and deportment sometimes shaped and distended by the wearing of *corsets*. In other
words, appraisers and notaries had meticulously documented the presence of
clothing that was European and Canadian in style and provenance.

Contrary to the assumption that these women would remain permanently linked, materially, to their originary clothing practices, virtually no
documentary evidence supports this premise. It is valid to explain this lack of
evidence as the result of the invisibility of native dress in the eyes of French
notaries and appraisers. But all these Indian and French-Indian women
owned European-style dress made from imported textiles, clearly supporting
a shift to colonial ways of dressing. This was clothing that perfectly matched
the wardrobe contents of French and Canadian women in the Illinois Country (and its precursor, the dress of women from the Montreal region). And
it jarred with the visual images of female Indians in Louisiana produced in
that colony (for example, Figure 15 and Plates 1, 19, 32). In images made primarily for European audiences, generic Indian women (their nation was not
usually identified) were shown for the most part bare-breasted, their hair un-
contained by French-style caps, their bodies unconstrained by fitted bodices.

In contrast, written sources were more specific, as André Pénicaut fleshed
out in 1711:

> The Cascassias Illinois women are very skillful: they commonly spin
> buffalo hair, which is as fine as wool off an English sheep. This wool
> is spun as fine as silk and is very white. With this they make materi-
> als which they dye in three colors, such as black, yellow, and deep
> red. Out of this they make gowns that are almost like the gowns of
> the women of Brittany or else like the dressing gowns of our ladies

of France, which trail down to the ground—if to their collar a coif were sewed to cover the head. They wear beneath their dresses a petticoat and a bodice that comes halfway down their thighs. They sew with deerskin thread, which they make in this way: when the deer tendon is quite free of flesh, they dry it in the sun twice in twenty-four hours, and after beating it a little they stretch the tendon-thread as fine and as white as the most beautiful Mechlin thread, and it is still very strong.[149]

In his description, he clearly assigned a greater degree of body covering than Dumont or de Batz's drawings reveal, and he drew repeated parallels with informal or regional French dress, blurring the differences between the two cultures. But his remained a description of indigenous clothing practices of Indians living in the Kaskaskia Indian village, not those of the French-style clothing itemized in the probate inventories of Frenchified Indians residing in colonial villages.

Much of this French apparel was passed on to children, who remained within colonial society, sowing the material seeds of intergenerational continuity.[150] This practice of passing clothes to French-Indian children, typical of French colonial successions, is all the more striking here since Indian death rituals favored keeping garments (especially prestige ones) with their owner, rather than transferring them to another. De Liette had described in 1702 how the Illinois "paint [the deceased's] face and hair red, put on him a white shirt if they have one, and new *mitasses* [leggings] of cloth or of leather, and moccasins, and cover him with the best robe they have." And as late as 1723, Jesuit missionary Sébastien Rasles was still finding that "It is not their custom to bury the dead; they wrap them in skins, and hang them by the feet and head to the tops of trees."[151] In contrast, priests buried Frenchified wives in the Catholic cemetery (or the church in Marie Rouensa's case). Having paid for the French medicine with which she had been treated in her illness, Suzanne Keramy's heirs bought a wooden casket for her burial, capping her life with a final Catholic rite. While her corpse (no doubt enveloped in a shroud or old sheet pinned over her naked body) was buried in its casket, her clothes extended their lifespan on the bodies of her own children.[152]

Notaries documented the same outcome for the body and clothing of Marie Anne Danis, the half-Indian widow of Philippe Chauvin Joyeuse, who died in New Orleans in 1747. The great majority of her linens and clothing were handed over to her young children to wear, including stockings and other miscellaneous garments. Also handed over was a bedsheet to be made into shirts for them, along with "the half of another [sheet] which had been used to shroud" their mother.[153] Here, too, it was European-style garments and imported manufactured textiles that were passed down from one generation to the next with the approbation of family and officials. For example, if most of the goods left by the half-Indian Marie Jeanne Faffart were sold to settle the debts of the community, some items were retained by the heirs, even bypassing official probate with the blessing of the appraisers and notary (sometimes in ways against the letter of the law). Officials were undoubtedly swayed by pragmatic concerns for the material well-being of children in financially precarious households. But in continually condoning the transfer of French-style dress from deceased parent to offspring, these officials also contributed to the wearing of French dress by French-Indian children.[154]

Yet, if the form and materials of the dress worn by Indian wives of Frenchmen in the Illinois Country were derived from Europe, what of laundering practices, ornamentation, and other avenues for personalization and customization of apparel? Lacunae in the evidence of stylistic details of dress impede analysis of the aesthetic appearance of clothes, a problem heightened by reliance on probate records—products of the colonial order, with their own legal mandates and cultural priorities for recording possessions, and their disinterest in documenting Indian retentions. The only items of clothing in extant inventories that were remotely ambiguous as to Indian or European provenance were the embroidered items (a cotton petticoat and shoes). These references spoke to a decorative technique common to French and Indian alike. The pair of embroidered shoes borrowed by Suzanne Baron from her mother Marie Catherine Illinoise could equally have referred to embroidered moccasins as French embroidered shoes.[155] French footwear was regularly imported ready-made into the colony, and as early as 1729, there were requests from the Illinois Country for women's shoes to be shipped for sale there.[156] The French term "souliers" described both moccasins and European shoes. Yet the former were usually qualified as "souliers sauvages" (or "souliers de boeuf" when made of the hides of domesticated cows).[157] The embroidery, not being described in the inventory, could have referred equally to a French or Indian convention and aesthetic. The shoes could even have been European in form, but embellished by their Indian owner, the direct concrete result of cultural and sartorial mélange. In other instances, there are clues in the type of garment the embroidery adorned. For example, the embroidered footwear owned by the half-Indian Marie Anne (or Marianne) Danis in New

Orleans was unambiguously French in form and style: fashionable slip-on mules.[158] There is, however, one other indication of the continuity of native sartorial practices. This is the *limbourg* wool blanket owned by Suzanne Keramy, which, like her clothes, was described as well worn (*limbourg* was a cheap, usually blue or red, coarse woolen cloth developed for the Native American trade, comparable to the duffels used in the English colonies).[159] As previously noted, Keramy's clothing at the time of her death in 1747 was itemized in one single paragraph (not listed singly): four shifts, five skirts, three *mantelets*, and "a blanket of blue *limbourg* wool."[160] The question arises whether she used it as a European would, for a blanket and as bedding, or, as an Indian man or woman might, as a mantle and postcontact substitute for the buffalo robe commonly worn across a wide swath of the continent, including by Plains Indians such as the Padoka.

As seen in household inventories in the Illinois Country, buffalo robes were prevalent in colonial settlements where they were, however, reserved for bedding. This is in contrast to the indigenous usage of robes, used as apparel and adorned with hand-painted designs that evoked the wearer's military prowess (if male) and kinship, while reflecting a rich symbolic, religious, and aesthetic program (see Figure 6 and Plates 22, 23). Documentary references to buffalo robes in inventories of Illinois Country households are uniform in their lack of reference to any painting on the robe. It is likely therefore that the robes used by colonists in bedding were unadorned, and, given their quantities, that they were developed for the French colonial market, just as moccasins were.[161] Illinois painted buffalo robes were, however, available as a trade or proto-tourist item, with many taken to Europe for the market in curiosities.[162] In 1775, William Bartram found "several buffalo hides" of Illinois origin "with the wool on them" at a trading house in Manchac, a (British) military and trading post in Lower Louisiana, and he noted that "The subjects or figures in the composition were much like those inscriptions or paintings on the bodies of the chiefs and warriors. Their borders were exceedingly pleasing: red, black, and blue were the colors, on a buff ground."[163] A number of extant robes attributed to Illinois Indians and dating from the eighteenth century survive in European collections. These reveal a preference for abstract designs with linear and geometric patterns. The designs correlate closely to those in other artifacts including apparel. As Bartram underscored, they also matched the abstract tattoo designs preferred by Illinois men, as represented, for example, in Figure 2 and Plate 1.[164]

In their use of buffalo robes, French colonists in the Illinois Country eliminated this apparel function, limiting their use to an indispensable component of bedding. At home, on a bed, a buffalo robe suffered none of the functional disadvantages of fur worn out in the elements, and especially in watery conditions. French colonists (some of whom came from modest backgrounds where fur was a luxury they were not entitled to wear) raved about the softness of buffalo wool. Conversely, Indian consumers made clear their preference for imported woolen blankets in various colors and stripe patterns. The old and newer style mantles are depicted side by side in Philip Georg Friedrich von Reck's *Indian King and Queen of Uchi, Senhaitschi* (Plate 21), in which the Creek king wears a buffalo robe as a mantle, but the queen has substituted a white blanket with a red border; the dress of both also included items of blue wool. Suzanne Keramy's blanket was blue (though of *limbourg* wool), but in contrast to the queen of Uchi she lived as a Catholic in a French colonial village in the Illinois Country with her French husband.

As with the queen of Uchi, I suggest that Keramy's buffalo robe served a primary function as a mantle, an article of clothing in continuation of indigenous practice, rather than a blanket used exclusively in bedding as in other French colonial households. Although *limbourg* cloth was used interchangeably with blankets (French *couvertes*) to make trade coats, breechclouts, skirts, and other clothing worn by Indians and some poorer colonists, it is unusual to find a blanket of this textile in the records relating to the Illinois Country.[165] Furthermore, almost without exception in Illinois Country inventories, *couvertes* were itemized singly or, more commonly, grouped with other components of bedding.[166] Suzanne Keramy's is the only inventory where a blanket was itemized in a lot consisting exclusively of apparel: petticoats, jackets, and shifts. That the inclusion of this blanket among her *clothes* was not inadvertent is demonstrated by the fact that in two other documents relating to her succession it was again itemized with clothing not bedding.[167] Hence, this Indian woman's blue *limbourg* blanket must be considered an article of apparel, a wrap, rather than bedding.

Whether its use was confined to informal, indoor dress (like bedding, not open to the gaze of outsiders) or worn in public can only be guessed at. Her use of European-manufactured cloth to make a garment previously crafted from a skin (Plate 22) offers a potent image of the creative juxtapositions in the wardrobes of Indian wives of Frenchmen in the Illinois Country. In the sphere of dress, it remains a uniquely documented example, but among Keramy's possessions it was not the only singular object.

Suzanne Keramy also left at her death two boxes, each containing a packet of spun buffalo wool.[168] As early as 1716, propaganda reports on the colony had mentioned the potential for exploiting the fine wool of the buffalo in the manufacture in France of hats and cloths.[169] In 1721 a former officer in the colony (based in Lower Louisiana) reported that "they [the Indians] have wild cattle that have long hair ["cottoné"] like wool, which they spin and make into rugs, braids, belts, and other things for their use."[170] These accounts—endorsed by eyewitness testimony of Le Page du Pratz and Péni-caut—agreed that long buffalo hair was both fine and soft (a fact implicitly confirmed in the popularity of buffalo robes for bedding), and that native women, especially from the Illinois nation, were skilled in spinning, dye-ing, and weaving it for personal adornment.[171] As quoted above, Pénicaut had referred to Kaskaskia women as skilled in spinning buffalo hair, and he drew analogies with French and French provincial dress.[172] The French never succeeded in their hopes of taming and farming buffalo. But the initiative met with modest success, ironically, in the household of one Illinois Indian woman married to a Frenchman in the Illinois Country: two tamed buffalo were listed in 1724 among the assorted livestock owned by Dorothée Mech-ip8e8a and Charles Danis.[173]

Consistent with French plans to exploit raw materials from Louisiana, there was renewed interest in channeling this product for use in France by the 1740s, when local officials in Louisiana attempted once more to give the product a wider press. The commandant at Fort de Chartres, M. de Bertet, had been charged with rounding up a sample of the wool, as recounted in an official dispatch from 1749. Bertet died before this was done, so new orders were given to gather a ball of this wool and send it the next year on the con-voy of boats going downriver to New Orleans.[174] Given the coincidence in the timing of this new push toward a commercial use for buffalo wool, and the records of one Indian woman in the Illinois Country (admittedly not an Illinois) who died in 1747 owning such wool, the possibility that the first led to the commissioning of the latter cannot be discounted. Whether Suzanne Keramy owned this wool for her own use, in a continuation of her native material culture, or whether it was intended for sending to France (in which case she could presumably have traded it from Indian village women rather than spinning it herself) cannot be conclusively answered.

Keramy may have been an exception in French colonial Illinois: an In-dian-born woman who married Frenchmen, lived in a French village, and wore full European dress while also retaining some components of her native sartorial traditions, while her peers forsook most such material reminders.

Her status as a Padoka former captive rather than Illinois Indian may have played a role in this pronounced evidence of cultural retention, further complicating the question of persistence and acculturation. The wool was divided into two lots that fell, according to customary law, to her widower and children. As with the buffalo mantle, it is unknown how her heirs regarded this inheritance, how familiar they were with it, and whether they valued it as a reminder of the deceased, an object associated with her in life, and a mnemonic device in death.[175]

This is not to discount differences in the way Indians and French apprehended French goods. For example, the colonist J. B. Bossu had recounted how Françoise Missouri had shown him the "beautiful repeating watch adorned with diamonds" she had received as a gift from Louis XV during her 1725 visit to Paris.[176] The 1730 inventory of the community property owned in the Missouri by Françoise and her late first husband, Dubois, does not list a watch. Nor was her apparel inventoried.[177] According to Bossu, however, the watch was her most prized possession. It was treasured as a status symbol surely, given its royal provenance and rarity, as a reminder of her extraordinary visit to France, and as a curiosity. Françoise must also have valued it in terms consistent with her native aesthetic, cultural, and religious values, for the metallic qualities of the watch, like mirrors, had spiritual resonances in many Indian belief systems.[178] Bossu himself noted that Indians called it "a spirit, because of its movement, which to them appeared supernatural."[179] As this example reminds us, the same objects could carry different meanings. Thus it is the meaning of the object, not the object itself, that we need to consider in investigating the tension between acculturation and cultural persistence.

Notwithstanding problems with data and ambiguities with interpretation, with the exception of Suzanne Keramy's mantle and buffalo wool, virtually no evidence supports the view that Indian wives of Frenchmen retained their original clothing practices in the period after their residence within French colonial villages had been well established. In this respect, these women present a distinctive response to colonialism specific to their particular experiences of race, ethnicity, class, religion, and the confrontation of cultures at a given time. But far from signaling the elision of indigenous culture, the analysis of Illinois societies in the later seventeenth and early eighteenth centuries suggests that Frenchification represented a means of cultural retention.

CHAPTER 2

"Nothing of the *Sauvage*"

Shifts, *mantelet* jackets, skirts, and coifs, all made of imported cloth: once they began producing inventories in the 1720s, this was the ubiquitous garb nota-ries recorded as worn by the Indian wives and daughters of Frenchmen who lived in French villages in the Illinois Country, in colonial houses equipped with French-style furniture and household goods. These women who pro-jected an image of Frenchness had been encouraged in this direction by reli-gious missionaries and local officials. But it was the women themselves who first promoted legitimate, sanctified unions between Frenchmen and Indian converts. And this material culture response could only have been produced with the consent of the women themselves. Although this book focuses on French views of identity, in this chapter I address the indigenous perspectives that are integral to the study of French-Indian relations in the Illinois Coun-try. Here, too, we remain largely dependent on records by missionaries and colonists, with their inherent biases, but we can read these sources in such a way as to shed some light on indigenous motivations and strategies for con-version, intermarriage, and acculturation. We can also locate an alternative font of information in the analysis of Indian women's nonverbal expressions, namely, their deployment of material culture.[1] In particular, I address the fact that these wives and daughters of Frenchmen appeared to have for the most part forsaken indigenous norms of dress. This evidence of acculturation would appear to anticipate the definitive shift of the region toward European dominance and the cultural eclipse of the Illinois nation over the eighteenth century. I suggest, however, that a gendered analysis of indigenous and colo-nial societies in the late seventeenth and early eighteenth centuries provides material for an alternative reading of the same evidence.

Illinois wives adopted French dress and furnishings, thereby communi-cating their affiliation with the French. Rather than interpreting this evidence as an example of assimilation into the hegemonic colonial and religious order, or as motivated by a desire by wives to make concessions to their husbands, I argue that this practice should be seen as a sophisticated response to the arrival of the French, one that demonstrates the persistence of native social and gender modes of thinking about the role of French material culture. It was also highly specific to this time period and region. While some non-Illinois former captives who married Frenchmen would also convert and Frenchify, this was a pattern particular to Illinois Indians, a nation with a history of openness to new cross-cultural exchanges. It was also primarily focused on the Kaskaskia, and their special response to Catholicism and to intermarriage. The founding story of Marie Rouensa-8canic8e, which weaves together French and indigenous themes of religion, conversion, intermarriage, trade alliances, gender and filial roles, and material culture, will allow us to explore the religious and geopolitical roots of the pattern she helped establish. These factors will lay the groundwork for the analysis of the question of persistence, assimilation, and identity. Read in the context of marital alliance traditions, captive adoption rituals that deployed material culture to achieve metamorphosis into a new identity, and other indigenous practices premised on the fluidity of identity, this analysis further begs the thorny question of whether Frenchified Indians saw themselves as having actually become French upon marriage.

The Illinois: Conversion and Intermarriage

Religion was the building block on which intermarriage and Frenchification were mapped, and missionaries consistently singled out Illinois Indians for their exceptional openness to conversion, praising them from earliest contact as "the fairest field for the Gospel."[2] In Father Marquette's first visit among the Illinois on his way down the Mississippi, he had characterized these Indians as having "an air of humanity that we have not observed in the other nations that we have seen upon our route."[3] It was a reputation colonists throughout the colony would continue to uphold for decades to come.[4] In acknowledgment that not all Illinois Indians were amenable to Christianity, secular and religious observers alike identified the Kaskaskia in particular for their high conversion rate; as Pénicaut wrote in 1707: "The Cascassias illinois nation is Catholic. . . . This nation is highly civilized."[5]

By the time of Marie Rouensa's conversion and the pattern of intermarriage she was to initiate, missionary activity in the region had been taking place for twenty years, since Marquette's 1673 expedition to the Illinois Country with Louis Jolliet. Though this visit led to the establishment of the fledgling Mission of the Immaculate Conception, at that time the Jesuits were not alone in seeking to establish Catholicism in the Illinois Country. Already by 1680, when La Salle made his second expedition to the Illinois Country (the first in 1677), he was accompanied by a Recollect priest, Louis Hennepin. Thereafter, the Jesuit mission to the Illinois Country had to contend with competition from this order for religious control of the region's inhabitants, Indian or French. The Recollect priests favored assimilation policies (including support for intermarriage), hoping that by *first* acculturating Indians, they would succeed in converting them. The Jesuits dispatched to the Illinois Country initially favored an inverse, more syncretic approach, expressed by Father Marquette as to "keep a little of their usage, and take from it all that is bad."[6] This approach entailed learning the Illinois languages. It was an ideal that would evolve and be reversed, but not before the completion of impressive French-Kaskaskia dictionaries and translations of religious texts into Illinois tongues.[7]

Competition with the Recollect provided one backdrop to missionary activity in the Illinois Country in the later seventeenth century. But the Jesuit mission also found itself in the midst of a contest between religious claims centered on the conversion of Indians, and competing claims from officials and traders that emphasized fur trade relations and exploitation of local resources. Marie Rouensa found herself caught in the middle of this contest, as highlighted in the February 1694 description that Jesuit missionary Jacques Gravier provided in his annual relation to the Society of Jesus.[8] That Father Gravier had mentioned Marie Rouensa at all was a reflection of this woman's importance to the Jesuits' missionary project in the Illinois Country. She had been his greatest success story, and he presented her as a high-profile convert to Christianity. He celebrated her in particular for her steadfast religious fervor in the face of tribal and kin pressure to marry a French fur trader, and simultaneously for eventually conceding to the marriage as a means of furthering the goals of Christianity among the Kaskaskia.[9] Parsing the details of her story through Gravier's description of his missionary work reveals the extent of *her* agency in shaping the outlines of conversion, Frenchification, and intermarriage in the Illinois Country.

Following her conversion, this daughter of the chief of the Kaskaskia Illinois had actively participated in the evangelization of other Kaskaskia

Indians (especially women and children), even explaining the Old and New Testament to them using Gravier's copperplate engravings "without trouble and without confusion, as well as I [Gravier] could do—and even more intelligibly, in their manner."[10] She also engaged in self-mortification practices, making "for herself a girdle of thorns. This she wore for two whole days, and she would have crippled herself with it, had she not informed me of this mortification, when I compelled her to use it with more moderation."[11] Self-mortification was a feature of the saints' lives that Gravier (like other missionaries in French America) had exalted and that the priests in the Great Lakes region also practiced. Rouensa's girdle of thorns was no doubt intended to simulate a cingulum (worn around the waist) or a cilice (worn around the leg or arm), like the one made of wire looped and twisted into sharp points recently discovered at Fort St. Joseph, Michigan. These were private forms of penance, intended to facilitate piety, not advertise it.[12]

Marie Rouensa's practice of self-mortification paralleled those undertaken by other female Indian converts across French America. As with the contours of those women's conversion, it remains an open question if their affinity for Catholicism emanated from shared rituals amenable to multiple interpretations. Also among the Catholic rituals with indigenous precedents that lent themselves to the practice of Catholicism by Indians "after their fashion" were fasting and feasting. Unlike female converts elsewhere in French America, Gravier did not describe Marie Rouensa as engaging in fasting.[13] But since de Liette did describe ritual fasting for pubescent Illinois girls, it is not unlikely that she incorporated fasting into her self-mortification practices, especially since she also used her room as an oratory, isolating herself there as an Illinois girl might sequester herself during a vision quest punctuated by fasting.[14]

The opposite of fasting—feasting—provided another point in common. While Marie Rouensa took her first communion on the "feast of the Assumption of Our Lady," her parents each gave gender-segregated feasts to celebrate their own conversion. That Gravier grasped the underlying meaning of "superstitious" feasts for the Illinois was underscored at the feast he gave "to all the Christians, according to [their] custom," an act that would have allowed Gravier "to acquire the esteem of the savages and of all their nations in a short time," if we are to trust Father Jean François Buisson de St. Cosme.[15] Given the political and ceremonial importance of this practice, it is likely that on the day of Marie's marriage this indigenous custom was also followed. Beyond these examples, Father Gravier noted the compatibility between rosary beads and the pieces of wood young female converts counted to help them remember their sins, a mnemonic device similar to the way wampum beads were deployed.[16]

Having publicly and privately professed her faith in Christianity, Father Gravier reported in 1694, Marie Rouensa felt a calling "to consecrate her virginity to God," and "resolved never to marry, in order that she might belong wholly to Jesus Christ."[17] As presented by Gravier, this was a logical response to Jesuit condemnations of indigenous marriage traditions, their focus on instruction about "the bonds of Christian marriage" ("true marriage" as opposed to sins of sexuality), and their emphasis on the Virgin Mary and other celibate female saints.[18] Marie Rouensa was the first Illinois woman convert to choose celibacy; Father Gravier would describe the case of at least one other Illinois (a widow) who would succeed in remaining celibate in marriage with the acquiescence of her second husband.[19] Another would surface in 1712 to reject her parents' and brother's choice of a suitor, declaring to Jesuit missionary Gabriel Marest, according to his relation, "no, my Father, I will never have any other spouse than Jesus Christ."[20] Her ultimate fate is unknown, but Chapter 4 will introduce the daughter of one Kaskaskia Illinois convert who, in 1751, would achieve her goal of becoming a nun.

Gravier's support of Marie Rouensa's desire for celibacy was consistent with his disapproval of intermarriage at this time. This position was not so much because he had doubts about Indian women converts but was premised on his anxieties about the influence of dissolute Frenchmen on Indian women. The girl's father, Chief Rouensa, had different ideas about intermarriage and the deployment of women in alliance formation. After a public two-day struggle between father and daughter, sometime prior to spring 1693, Marie consented to marrying her parents' choice of husband, overriding her resolve that "she did not wish to marry, that she had already given all her heart to God, and did not wish to share it."[21]

Marie Rouensa was seventeen years old.[22] Her bridegroom was Michel Accault. A French fur trader and explorer thirty years her senior, he was "famous in all this Illinois country for all his debaucheries," according to Father Gravier, who left out the fact that around the time of the marriage the literate Accault became one of two major landlords of the Illinois Country.[23] Unlike the widow who succeeded in remaining celibate during her second marriage (living with her husband like "a sister"), Marie would bear Accault two sons before he died, taking "for her special patronesses the Christian Ladies who have sanctified themselves in the state of matrimony . . . whom she invokes many times during the day saying things to them that one would not believe from a young *sauvage*."[24] Following Accault's death, Marie married another Canadian and had an additional six children; all her children outlived her.[25]

Ecclesiastical and legal records documented the contours of Marie Rouensa's conversion and the details of her married life. Material culture was a fundamental part of each of these experiences. The negotiations over her marriage to Accault pitted Marie, and the other young women converts in her village, against her father the chief, who saw the marriage as a way to strengthen the alliance between the Kaskaskia and the French by having a Frenchman as his kin. It would also pit Marie's ally Father Gravier against the prospective groom and the French establishment, both of whom anticipated political and economic benefits from the marriage. This crisis would find material expression in a forceful act of stripping that reveals Illinois women converts' adhesion to elements of French dress in the 1690s, at the very cusp of the new pattern of French-Illinois sacramental intermarriage.

At the height of her refusal to marry the French fur trader, as the tussle escalated, the two Kaskaskia protagonists deployed dress as a tool to assert control over the situation, with Marie's father seeking to pressure his daughter by throwing her out of the home, "after depriving her of her jacket [*justaucorps*], her stockings, her shoes, and her trifling ornaments." This she bore "without a single word of remonstrance or a single tear from her. But, when he wished to take away what covered her, 'Ah! my father, what are you trying to do," she told him. "Leave me; that is enough. I will not give you the rest; you may take my life rather than tear it away from me.'"[26] In response, her father drove her from his house and "not daring to be seen in that state, she hid herself in the grass by the water's edge, where an elderly catechumen who was coming to the chapel found her and threw her his jacket, with which she covered herself before coming to the chapel."[27]

In this account, Chief Rouensa was given the role of authoritarian *sauvage*, his daughter that of pious and civilized convert. What Father Gravier appeared especially intent on conveying to his readers was that Marie—a recent convert—understood a basic tenet of Catholic teaching and could make the distinction between pride in appearance and modesty in covering the body. In a letter from 1723, Father Sébastien Rasles had hinted at the role played by missionaries in facilitating sartorial assimilation. Focusing on the dress worn in holy spaces by mission Indians in the Illinois Country, as cited in the previous chapter, he noted that "The Illinois are covered only around the waist, otherwise they go entirely nude. . . . It is only when they make visits, or when they are present at Church, that they wrap themselves in a cloak of dressed skin in the summer-time, and in the winter season in a dressed skin with the hair left on, that they may keep warm."[28] As seen in this quote, the assimilation into European notions of bodily modesty was calibrated according to space and context, and presence at church invited specific sartorial behavior taught by missionaries that was centered on covering the body.

Marie Rouensa was willing (up to a point) to forsake extraneous or external items of outer dress and adornments such as stockings (or leggings), shoes, and *justaucorps*, a formal fitted French jacket given and traded in the Great Lakes area (including to women, and associated with a number of female Indian burials).[29] But she was unwilling to have her body altogether uncovered by the removal of undergarments—her linen shift (*chemise*) that "covered her." No contemporary visual depiction of Marie Rouensa or any other Illinois woman is known for the French colonial period.[30] The presence on her body of the chest-concealing shift can be contrasted with contemporary images of native women as bare-breasted, as in Alexandre de Batz and Jean-François Dumont de Montigny's drawings of generic Indian women in (Lower) Louisiana (see Plates 1, 19, 20, 32).[31] These eyewitness images, with their emphasis on the "exotic" and depiction of women naked from the waist up, stand in contrast to Gravier's verbal depiction of Marie Rouensa's sartorial modesty. Neither de Batz nor Dumont de Montigny had visited the Illinois Country (although, as long-term inhabitants of Lower Louisiana, they were familiar with Illinois Indians' regular visits to the governor in New Orleans).[32]

Significantly, extant descriptions of the dress of Illinois women suggest that the chasm between French and Illinois styles of dressing was not altogether irreconcilable. The carpenter André Pénicaut had drawn an analogy between the tricolored dress of Kaskaskia women and "the gowns of the women of Brittany or else . . . the dressing gowns of our ladies of France, which trail down to the ground."[33] As in Pénicaut's description of those outer gowns, worn over a bodice and thigh-length petticoat, Father Claude Allouez also emphasized modesty, commenting in 1677 that "The women usually behave well, and are modestly dressed, though the men are not, having no shame of their nakedness."[34] In their general descriptions of Illinois converts, Pénicaut and Allouez seemed at first glance to echo the depictions Jesuit missionary Claude Chauchetière had made of the dress of female converts at the Iroquois mission of Kahnawake. The portrait Father Chauchetière made of

his celebrated convert Catherine Tekakwitha has not survived (the attribution of the painting at Saint Francis-Xavier Mission at Kahnawake is incor-
rect; it is a nineteenth-century copy based on an early eighteenth-century
engraving).[35] But Chauchetière also left a verbal portrait of her, one that
conforms closely to his illustrations of converts at Kahnawake in his manuscript account. In this account, he described her wearing a rough hairshirt.
This term referred to a shift made not from linen but from coarse goats' hair
or horsehair and worn by the devout as a form of penance and a means of
self-mortification. Chauchetière further noted that she and the other female
Iroquois converts who had joined her in severe ascetic rituals that exceeded
those advocated by the missionaries had "promised God never to put on their
fancy attire (for the Indian women have considerable charm and take pride
in adorning themselves with beaded necklaces and with vermilion, which
they apply to their cheeks, and with earrings and bracelets)."[36] In Kaskaskia in
1694, twenty years later, Marie Rouensa's sartorial performance of conversion
played out somewhat differently.

As attested to by Chauchetière, missionaries counseled their charges to
relinquish ornamental trappings. Gravier was as assiduous as Chauchetière
in his evocation of Marie Rouensa as a paragon of Christian virtue and female modesty. But his text describes his young charge as having dressed
herself in *justaucorps* and stockings to wear with her shift and shoes. These
are ambiguous terms in late seventeenth-century Jesuit missives from North
America. The references to stockings and shoes were likely shorthand for leggings and moccasins as described to a French audience unfamiliar with those
indigenous garments. The terms *justaucorps* and *chemise* were more precise
and contrast with the "robe made of several skins sewed together" that Pénicaut had described Illinois converts wearing to church.[37] Marie Rouensa's
justaucorps and *chemise* were specific genres of apparel and signaled a particular European style and construction of fitted man's or woman's jacket worn
over a linen shift, a style that would eventually morph in women's dress into
the looser *mantelet* jacket listed in her second husband's probate inventory.[38]
Marie Rouensa's apparel bore but a formal relation to the cloth leggings,
moccasins, hairshirt, and loose-fitting mantle of the converts at Kahnawake
and the Indian women shown in the circa 1780 scene of Indians and habitants
in Canada (see Figure 7 and Plate 14). Her stockings/leggings and moccasins
were direct continuations of her native dress traditions; her combination of
shift (worn as underwear; see Plate 8) and structured jacket were not, showing that already by 1694 Illinois women converts were incorporating articles

Figure 7. Claude Chauchetière, S.J., *Quelques personnes embrassent la virginité, la continence* (Some embrace virginity and continence). 1686. From "Narration de la mission du Sault depuis sa fondation jusqu'en 1686," series H 48 Jésuites, plate 8. Courtesy of Archives Départementales de la Gironde, France.

of French dress that could express their religious sensitivities in new, material ways.

With her shift and jacket, Marie Rouensa's distinctive apparel visually proclaimed her adoption of key forms of French dress, worn by the daughter of an Illinois chief, at the time of her very public conversion to Catholicism, but preceding her wedding to a Frenchman and two decades before the French policy of separating Indian and French villages in the Illinois Country. The nebulous distinction Marie Rouensa had drawn between forms of clothing that were essential (her shift, "that which covered her" and which she refused to relinquish) or supplemental (the jacket whose removal she did not resist) took on added resonance in the colonial context, where missionaries and other Europeans directly linked acceptance of European dress conventions with reception of Christianity.[39]

Marie Rouensa had in fact drawn a subtle distinction, one that missionaries would have appreciated given the complexity of their own prescriptions. In 1702, the three Jesuits at the Illinois missions requested a shipment of a dozen trade shirts, six blue *capots*, and six ells of wool for making breechcloths. The missionaries intended for Indians to use this clothing, since they had made separate requests for clothing items for their own use.[40] Twenty years later, a proposal to set up a missionary school for Indians in Lower Louisiana earmarked a *capot* and two trade shirts per year as clothing allowance for the students. But for one of their special charges—a promising young convert who served them as a clerk—the missionaries advocated fuller European dress, with stockings among the garments bought for this boy to wear.[41] In both examples, the missionaries were themselves drawing out the contrast between diverse degrees and forms of European dress, reinforcing the same apparent correlation between unconditional conversion and fuller European dress that we find in the sartorial description of Marie Rouensa, and which the celebrated accounts of her devotion make clear. This sartorial association including the rejection of tattoos provided a religious basis for the wholesale adoption of French dress by Indian wives and daughters of Frenchmen living in colonial settlements.

While his focus was on describing his success in converting Marie Rouensa, Father Gravier never lost sight of his audience's interest in the broader picture of the Catholic missionary project in French America. Marie Rouensa's conversion and her acquiescence to the marriage did lead her parents back to the faith, as she had anticipated. Gravier also credited her with returning her French husband to his Catholic roots. In turn, her parents' very public conversion led to that of the other villagers and was presented by Father Gravier as a key moment in his missionary project in the Illinois Country. Her parents' conversion, then, paved the way for the foundation in 1703 of the relocated French-Indian village of Kaskaskia.[42] This was the settlement that would eventually segregate, being reserved after 1719 for the French (including their Indian wives and children) while the Kaskaskia Indians were removed away with a further relocation (see Figure 3). By this date, Kaskaskia Indians had reason to resent French intrusion into their lives, but the tensions were not centered on intermarriage per se.

Marie Rouensa's own conversion and her marriage to a Frenchman thus served as the crucial catalyst in the Jesuits' missionary agenda in the Illinois Country. Her ascetic practices, her attempt at celibacy, her rejection of (Indian) parental control, and her role in the mass conversion of her people were key themes in colonial accounts of female Indian converts in North America.[43] Her two marriages and continued immersion in secular life meant she was not destined for veneration. But she never abandoned the Christian faith, wore French items of dress, lived the last years of her life in a French-furnished, colonial-style house that faced the church of the Immaculate Conception in the colonial village of Kaskaskia, and was buried not in the cemetery but under this church, the only woman (French or Indian) to be so honored. While external political developments played their part in the transformation of Marie Rouensa's household into a French colonial one, its roots can be traced to the formative period that began with her conversion and union with Michel Accault, when we can already locate evidence of her metamorphosis into a woman who would help establish the local definition of a French colonial wife. This transformation had incorporated a sartorial element, revealing the significance of appearance to the construction of a religious identity as a Catholic convert.

With his celebration of Marie Rouensa's marriage to Michel Accault, Father Gravier launched a fresh chapter in the history of sacramental intermarriages in New France and initiated the practice in the Illinois Country. But Marie Rouensa herself had in all likelihood pushed for her marriage to Accault to be a Christian one. The original idea for a marriage between the trader and the daughter of the Kaskaskia chief was hatched between the father and prospective groom sometime before spring 1693. Both men would have expected that it would be a marriage "à la façon du pays," the main model of intermarriage practiced in the Great Lakes region at that time. In other words, they anticipated a marital union celebrated according to Kaskaskia rituals that would not have been recognized as legitimate by the Catholic Church or the French state.

According to Father Gravier, Marie Rouensa was opposed out of her religious convictions to marriage of any kind. He also hinted at the fact that she may have been repelled by a suitor who was a fur trader thirty years older than she was.[44] She only consented to marrying Accault out of concern that her parents would take even more extreme action "against prayer," and in the hope "that by marrying [she would] win [her] family to God."[45] Given her religious motivations, it is to be expected that only a sacramental marriage would be acceptable to her. Given his teachings to the Illinois, so many of which centered on "true" Christian marriage, Father Gravier would have had to give his consent to such a marriage, even if he originally entertained doubts about intermarriage and sought to make this marriage a celibate one that produced no offspring, as discussed in Chapter 3.[46] He probably did not realize at the time that the girl's marriage to Accault would establish sacramental marriage as the norm for French-Indian intermarriage in the Illinois Country. It is surprising that historians have not made more of Marie Rouensa's agency in expecting a *sacramental* marriage, for this was an important consideration in light of Frenchification policies aimed at Indian converts like herself.

While Marie Rouensa was the first and the most prominent of the brides whose intermarriages were celebrated in the Illinois Country, others from Illinois villages and beyond would join her. Some of these women would similarly have ties to influential chiefs. Dorothée Mechip8e8a, wife of Charles Danis and then of Louis Turpin, was the daughter of Grand Rieur (French for "Great Laugher"), the inclusion of his name in the parish register signaling his status.[47] Catherine 8abankinkoy, who married Jean Gillemot *dit* Lalande and then Louis Tessier, was likely to be related to Marguerite Ouabankikoué, who had entered into a Church-sanctioned marriage with a Frenchman at Detroit. Marguerite Ouabankikoué (like Catherine 8abankinkoy) was Miami Illinois and related to chief Wisekaukautshe from the Atchatchakangouen (crane) band.[48] As befitting the relative of a Peoria chief, and as with Marie Rouensa's progeny, Catherine 8abankinkoy's daughter Marie Rose Tessier married especially well, beginning with her first marriage to Pierre Grotton de St. Ange. Like Marie Rouensa, these women initiated, or at least acquiesced to, Catholic marriage rites and they too adopted colonial ways of living and contributed to the pattern that would last well into the eighteenth century.

The sociocultural and economic environment of the Illinois Country in the late seventeenth century suggests some possible factors for Illinois women's collective openness to conversion and to a Christian model of marriage. For the Illinois, the period when the French first arrived in the area was marked by the stresses of prolonged warfare and disease leading to the decimation of the population and an uneven sex ratio (perhaps up to four women for each man) and early marriage.[49] Indeed, Illinois women had been adversely affected by the major upheavals of the previous decades. Concomitant with these geopolitical shifts, French commentators noted the sexual abuse of women in polygamous marriages, and this too seems to have been a factor in driving Illinois women toward Catholicism with its focus on monogamy. Among the forms of sexual abuse documented by Europeans were mutilation, including scalping, and gang rape as retribution against unfaithful wives; as Brett Rushforth has argued, these were punishments primarily reserved for secondary wives who were former captives.[50] But if the genesis and extent of this sexual abuse is in contention, Catholicism does appear to have offered Illinois women an alternative to plural marriage. That at least was the message implicit in Father Gravier's account of the celibate widow and her "horror of everything that may be contrary to purity," and which he claimed she told him was "due to the aversion that she felt for all that she heard and saw done by the married people of her country."[51] Through conversion, Illinois women may have found a new means of enhancing "their own prominence and authority."[52] Yet ironically they might have escaped native varieties of sexual abuse but were in turn exposed to French husbands' abuse of their wives, which was openly condoned by French law.

For example, Dorothée Mechip8e8a, wife of Louis Turpin, would have been privy to the abusive treatment her brother-in-law Jean-Baptiste Turpin exacted on his French wife Marguerite Faffard. In 1741, several witnesses testified that Turpin had physically abused Faffard, cutting off her hair in a violent rage while they were at Detroit some decades earlier, and then attacking her with an ax, events that led her to flee the marital household. Turpin was never prosecuted, and the abuse only came to light because property was at stake when, on his death in 1737, the question of inheritance came into play. His family claimed Marguerite Faffard had implicitly given up her rights to his estate when she had left him; her family claimed she remained his heir as she had only left her husband because of the abuse. In other words, both families had something to gain financially from the outcome. The court in New Orleans took a neutral position and divided the estate between the Turpin and

Faffard family members. Madame Turpin herself was not involved in the litigation: highly unusual among French women, she twice left her husband for Indian men while she was living in Detroit. The first was an Ottawa named Pintaloir; the second was a Huron, 8yta8ikigik, with whom she seems to have gone to the English around 1715–16 while living in Detroit, although a report back to her sister in 1736 was assiduous in noting that she had retained her Catholic faith while there, in spite of rumors to the contrary. Marguerite Faffard's experience offers a rare opportunity to consider how a French woman might have been influenced by indigenous marriage conventions that, unlike Catholic ones, allowed for (limited) change in partners.[53]

As this case brings out, French observers might have made much of the dismal conditions for Illinois women, but they remained blind to related problems in their own societies. Beyond their focus on sexual practices, missionaries and other onlookers found much to be negative about in their assessments of Illinois societies. For example, they were stark in their critiques of the gender division of labor among the Illinois as reflecting poorly on the virility of indigenous men. As described by de Liette, based on observations made in 1704, "While the women are working, as I have already related, from morning till night, the men remain under awnings which the women set up in front of their cabins to keep the heat of the sun from entering."[54] Fleshing out the details, Father Marest reiterated de Liette's dismissal of men's work by emphasizing women's activities: "Hunting and war form the whole occupation of the men; the rest of the work belongs to the women and the girls,—it is they who prepare the ground which must be sowed, who do the cooking, who pound the corn, who set up the cabins, and who carry them on their shoulders in the journeys."[55] These interpretations belonged to a broader critique (and misunderstanding) of native male work practices, predicated on European constructions of gender that perceived native women as "drudges" lacking power and authority.[56] As with this example, Europeans' understanding of female Indian identity was incomplete and colored by preconceived notions of women's work. These observers were also blind to evidence of the continuity of matrifocal households and to fulfillment provided women by their role as mediators in trade and alliance formation. These features provided Illinois women with direct access to power that marriage to Frenchmen extended and enhanced.[57]

Marie Rouensa's story opened a window into the religious and spiritual incentives for Illinois Indian women to marry Frenchmen. Taking account of Indian perspectives on intermarriage (and the role women should play in it) is crucial for this analysis that links religion, sexual customs, alliance forma-tion, and the gender division of labor. For example, in her struggle to refuse Michel Accault, Marie Rouensa could draw strength from Father Gravier's religious instruction and inspiration from the models of Catholic woman-hood that he had introduced her to. Centered most especially on the Virgin Mary, his instruction also encompassed the whole of the New Testament, based on the copperplate engravings Marie Rouensa borrowed "to refresh her memory in private" (see Figures 4 and 5).[58]

Marie Rouensa's initial rejection of the marriage alliances with the trader was also compatible with the rights of unmarried Illinois women to control their sexuality.[59] However, this agency was limited and could be subsumed by the interests of her immediate family, under whose authority (often that of brothers) marital alliances were negotiated for political and economic gain. Father Gravier's account conferred Marie Rouensa with a degree of control in her stand-off with her father. It was she who decided to marry, Gravier asserted, once she had come to the realization that she could influence her fa-ther to convert if she did so. Marie Rouensa was indeed right that she would be instrumental in having her father and mother convert, their previous in-terest in prayer having been interrupted during the struggle over the mar-riage; Gravier also made much of the fact that she had brought her husband back to the faith. These achievements, combined with her frequent role as godmother to newborns and new converts alike, as champion and instruc-tor of the faith among other Illinois women and girls, directly contributed to her status in the eyes of Gravier. Such patronage actions also established her authority in her native community (just as her mother's feast-giving had done), underscoring the importance of looking simultaneously to indigenous and French Catholic precedents and practices.[60] Doing so helps recover In-dian women's frames of reference as they chose Catholicism and intermar-ried with Frenchmen.

In the gendered framework of the fur trade, Indian men defined Indian women in terms of their role as mediators in developing and cementing the kin relations deemed essential to trading relationships. French traders and officials invested in the fur trade also tacitly acknowledged this role, as re-flected in the desirability of forging strategic unions with Indian women.[61] A memorandum by the official Diron d'Artaguiette in 1722–73 had described how the *habitants* of the Illinois Country traded furs "quite cheaply" from the Indians, which they then sold at a very high price to traders who had traveled from Canada to obtain furs in exchange for merchandise. This document made explicit the role of white settlers as mediators in procuring furs from the Indians. But both Illinois and French men understood and proposed Illinois *women* as the crucial intermediaries in these fur trade exchanges and the broader alliances that facilitated them. The tensions surrounding Marie Rouensa's marriage to the fur trader Michel Accault underline this point that women were seen as central to alliance formation because of their sexual and procreative functions. As recounted by Father Le Petit in 1730, the Illinois proclaimed themselves to be "inviolably attached to the French, by the alliances which many of that Nation had contracted with them, in espousing their daughters."[62] It was women who linked Indian and French, and material culture would come to signal that association.

For example, with Marie Rouensa's agreement to the marriage, preexisting customs pertaining to marriages "à la façon du pays" were set in motion. Courtship in patrilineal Illinois communities was mediated by, and at the service of, male family members.[63] These arrangements usually incorporated gifts, which French officials sometimes misinterpreted as a form of prostitution rather than gift exchange of women in marriage. More familiar with the dowry than the bride price system, confused French officials claimed that Illinois parents expected payment for their daughters and that they even gambled them away.[64] Yet French suitors quickly recognized that marriage alliances in the patrilocal Illinois society depended on the ritual exchange of gifts for the right to a wife and seem to have followed this convention.[65] For example, Pénicaut described how French suitors of Indian women followed French and Illinois courtship practices, incorporating native customs of gift giving with a visit to the priest and the publishing of bans.[66] Indian daughters were deployed in forging kin alliances, but these alliances were advertised and expressed through the distribution of material goods.

Illinois women indirectly helped forge alliances that benefited males (and by extension those males' communities). But women could also play a more direct role in mediating between French and indigenous culture when they personally engaged in trade. Their roles as mediators between their trader husbands and Indian suppliers can be surmised in spite of the few references to women's participation in the trading process itself. For one mixed marriage, the records are explicit in revealing the evidence of the female trading that usually remains invisible in French legal and commercial records.[67] The 1723 probate records of Sieur Jacques Bourdon included references to eleven Indians among his customers; one of these was 8ape8yrata, who was indebted to him for a buffalo robe.[68] But further records pertaining to his estate reveal that he was not the sole trader. His first wife, Domitille Chopinquata, was also personally involved in trade, keeping a small warehouse in which she sold and traded imported manufactured goods.[69] His second wife, Marguerite Ouaquamo Quoana, probably followed suit. A couple of brief notations pertaining to the period of her second marriage to the officer Franchomme showed that she had directed some trading activities, with a group consisting of creditors, debtors, and her own slaves making declarations about the goods Madame Franchomme had sold and bought.[70] But even when they were not participating directly in trading activities, women were involved as mediators in material culture exchanges between French and Indians, facilitated by their residence in French villages after 1719. In other words, they may well have retained key aspects of their tribal identity, but they did marry out, and the analysis of their nonverbal material culture expressions showcases one way they chose to identify with the French.[71]

Within Louisiana, the Illinois intermarriage strategies regarding the French were not replicated in any other nation, for example, because these heterogeneous nations were matrilineal and endogamous, or because they simply did not share the Illinois nation's history of establishing trade and diplomatic alliances through marriage.[72] But a parallel with the outcome in the Illinois Country can be drawn with the material culture of one woman, Marie Josephe LeBorgne de Belisle, who lived in Île Royale (Cape Breton). Her father was a French Acadian from a seigneurial family and her mother was the legitimate offspring of a French-Mi'kmak union. Born in 1711, Belisle, like others from mixed communities in this particular area, lived not in aboriginal territory but integrated in the French colonial settlements of Acadia (the province of New France from which the great Acadian immigration to Louisiana took place from 1765 on).[73] These integrated Indians were classified as Acadian, not Indian, in late seventeenth- and early eighteenth-century censuses, speaking to the pragmatic openness of French census takers. From adolescence on, Belisle lived in Louisbourg, where she had been sent to live with her father's sister. This experience among Louisbourg's administrative and mercantile elite culminated in a first marriage in 1733 to the treasurer of the colony and her remarriage on his death by 1750 to a French officer, an act that would have required formal approval of his commander, as was the case for all military officers wishing to get married while in service. Her households through both marriages were engaged in mercantile activities that contributed to their growing wealth.

Like those of her mother and her Mi'kmak grandmother, Belisle's

marriages were consecrated according to French rites and laws (though aboriginal rituals may have also taken place), and her Mi'kmak ancestry does
not appear to have impeded her access to the rights and privileges of colonists. As Annie Marie Lane Jonah has argued, the key to her trajectory lies
in "the conscious process of acculturation . . . which enabled Belisle to enter
Louisbourg society without arousing censure" and to leave at her death in
1754 the richest postmortem inventory of any woman in Louisbourg.[74] That
the material belongings of this granddaughter of a Mi'kmak encompassed
the full range of French dress and furnishings offers a parallel to the wives
and daughters of Frenchmen in the Illinois Country; her specific ownership
of expensive gowns, jewels, crystal, silver, and fine dishes for the table can
be compared to the material possessions of elite French-Indian wives and
daughters like Marie Catherine Illinoise, Marie Rose Texier, or Marie Aubuchon, whose households were similarly furnished with imported luxury
goods.[75]

A looser (and ahistorical) parallel can be drawn with the material culture of elite Métis families in Green Bay a century later. A photograph of the
daughter born of one of these Métis marriages survives (Figure 8). Taken
around 1849–50, it depicts Rachel Lawe Grignon, daughter of Judge John
Lawe of Green Bay and his half-Indian wife Thérèse Rankin, wearing hybrid
ceremonial garb, with a multistranded bead necklace, a large cross pendant,
trade brooches, and prominent cone earrings, all of which had belonged to
her mother. Her trade blanket worked in silk-ribbon appliqué appears to be
that worn (and likely made) by her mother.[76] In many of these details, Grignon's photograph can be compared to George Winter's portraits of Potawatomi and Miami Indians around the same period in Indiana (formerly New
France).[77]

Yet, notwithstanding the image of Indian cultural continuity expressed
(indeed, celebrated) in the photograph of Rachel Lawe Grignon, these hybrid
adornments were worn with a silk gown and a hairstyle in the (American)
fashion of the period, the blanket itself being arranged as a fashionable shawl
rather than as a mantle in the generic Indian style; the outline of her corset
(by the nineteenth century the word had taken on its modern meaning of
boned stays) and its structuring of her upper body can also be discerned.[78]
In contrast to the majority of Métis households at Green Bay (inhabiting
sprawling settlements rather than a nuclear village), Grignon's family lived
relatively integrated in white church, social, and educational structures, usually wearing fashionable Euro-American dress.[79]

Figure 8. *Rachel Lawe Grignon (1808–76), daughter of Judge John Lawe of Green Bay, Wisconsin*, ca. 1849–50. Wisconsin Historical Society Image WHI-2136. Courtesy of the Wisconsin Historical Society.

Indeed, family records reveal that the dress shown in the photograph was not Rachel's regular clothing. Her choice of attire in the photograph was dictated by reverence for her maternal patrimony, not a representation of her daily appearance. As seen in another photograph from the same period (Figure 9), this time taken with her husband, her dress was identical in all respects to that of any other respectable Euro-American woman circa 1850: not only the dark silk gown with its long pointed and ruched bodice fastening at the front, and fashionable pagoda sleeves with short oversleeves trimmed with fringe, but also the black mittens, lace cuffs and collar, cameo brooch at the neck, parted hair smoothed down over the ears and coiled into a knot at the back, dangling earrings and long chain, and clearly visible telltale line of the corset that provided the requisite rigidity for the area below the breast. That Grignon was not unusual in her dress is underscored by surviving photographs of her brother's family similarly wearing full Euro-American garb, just as her sisters did.[80]

In the previous century, Illinois wives of Frenchmen living in French villages, in colonial-type houses furnished in the French style, subject to the laws and religion of France, had similarly worn Frenchified dress paralleling that of their French and Canadian neighbors. They too had confounded superficial assumptions about the inevitability, and form, of cultural retention. In all these cases of ambiguous identity, material culture was the frame on which the construction of ethnicity rested, and this would in turn provide the basis for colonists' interpretations of Indian and French-Indian women's identities in the Illinois Country.

All these women shared a pronounced and distinctive degree of appropriation of French material culture. Theirs was an experience marked by Catholicism and by their immersion within colonial life in all its material aspects. In this respect, their lives contrasted with those of women married "à la façon du pays" and cohabiting with Frenchmen in Indian and Métis communities, isolated from French religion and law. The material culture expressions of Belisle and Grignon show that the experience of the Illinois Country was not exclusive to the wives and daughters of Frenchmen there. But only in the Illinois Country do we find large-scale evidence that some Indians seem to have "Frenchified" in their material culture expressions.

Figure 9. *Pierre Bernard Grignon and Rachel Lawe Grignon*. Neville Public Museum of Brown County, Image 8254.18. Courtesy of the Neville Public Museum of Brown County, Wisconsin.

Assimilation or Persistence?

In her important study of Indian wives of Frenchmen in the western Great Lakes, Susan Sleeper-Smith shows that women of the Illinois tribes who married Frenchmen served as the primary negotiators between French and Indian worlds in the Illinois Country. She singles out these women for their key role in shifting the strategies in place for the attainment of the "symbolic capital" that such kin-based societies relied on to signal family honor, protection, and prestige, and which in turn could be converted into economic resources for the benefit of the kin network (an emphasis on the material that may have echoes in Illinois spirituality).[81] Following Marie Rouensa's agreement to marriage with a Frenchman, her father, Chief Rouensa of the Kaskaskia informed "all the chiefs of the villages, by considerable presents, that he was about to be allied to a Frenchman," thereby also participating in the redistribution of European-imported goods.[82] In this example, behavioral patterns used in the struggle for symbolic capital were modified in response to the new post-contact environment, which for the Illinois represented crucial economic matters such as control of the fur trade and access to imported manufactured goods. This explanatory model also suggests that the high rate of Christian conversion of these women can be attributed in part to a deliberate shift in behavior stemming from the struggle for authority in this system. Such an adaptation to changing situations might be read not as assimilation into the colonial system but as deliberate accommodation that reinforced Illinois practices and increased Illinois women's centrality within native social structures.

Personal appearance, like the appearance of dwellings, was crucial in signaling Indian wives' access to the "symbolic capital" that marriage to Frenchmen signified. In the Illinois Country, the dynamics of the fur trade, whereby furs were exchanged for European manufactured goods (primarily cloth and adornment), brings into sharp relief how the display of such European goods on the bodies of Indian wives of Frenchmen was instrumental in communicating status within French colonial *and* native societies. For these Indian women, absorption of *French* material culture may in fact have "proved a socially innovative mechanism that enhanced female authority and mitigated female submission to male authority."[83] In this reading, adoption of European material culture facilitated continuity of tribal autonomy in fur trade exchanges by advertising and displaying the wearer's status as having access to desirable trade goods.

Conversely, we find some French men consciously and successfully adopting articles of native dress with a view to temporary immersion in tribal villages for purposes of trade. But the visual appearance of Indian wives of Frenchmen may have been more imperative to the fur trade than Frenchmen's, laden as this process was with strict notions of the distinct male and female roles in these kin-based societies. Theirs was a gendered response, the wearing of French dress belonging to a prolonged contest for female authority among Illinois women. As explored through the story of Marie Rouensa, their struggle found one outlet in the Catholic missionary project. In the next chapter we will see how French law provided the women with access to another source of control, facilitated by the fact that their material culture expressions were read as evidence of successful Frenchification. Women who married Frenchmen in the Illinois Country built on their role as primary mediators between French and Indian cultures by using dress to signal their privileged access to trade goods by virtue of their marriages.

Congruent with her assessment of women as enthusiastic consumers who produced surpluses in order to acquire new goods, Tanis C. Thorne has suggested that "Women might eagerly desire unions with outsiders for the tangible advantages they would enjoy: more material items, more leisure, higher status, and more political power as intermediaries."[84] As acknowledged by Thorne, to emphasize women's strategic actions is not to ignore other motives, including a consumer desire for novelty goods. At the same time, we need to acknowledge that their material culture choices were not likely to be straightforward examples of a desire to emulate French women, few of whom were even present in the founding period. Rather, their common ties of religious conversion and Catholic identification; their status as wives and daughters of Frenchmen rather than of Illinois men; meant that material culture was intended to create and maintain peer cohesion *among* these women.[85]

In delineating the role of material culture—specifically dress—in channeling encounters between indigenous and colonizing peoples, this analysis engages with the debate about assimilation and persistence, change and continuity in one community. But in some ways it also puts into question the very terms of the discussion and lays bare some erroneous preconceptions about Native American culture in particular. If we foreground Illinois Indians, for example, we are faced with the fact that their cultural borrowings and taste for exotic goods did not begin with the incursion of the French in North America. In the period preceding contact with the French, these Indians had traded goods and absorbed aesthetic influences, directly and indirectly, from nations as far away as the Southwest.[86] This inter-Indian cultural borrowing might result in loss of tribal manufacturing traditions, a loss possibly as extreme as that caused by contact with the French. For example, as discussed in the previous chapter, the Illinois obtained decorative porcupine quills in trade with Potawatomi and Ottawa Indians, underscoring the same consumer interest in acquiring indigenous novelty and ornamental objects from intertribal trade that they would display in their appetite for French kettles, striped blankets, sewing thread, or ribbons.[87] Imported via France, some of these objects, like the ubiquitous seed beads, were in fact for the most part produced elsewhere in Europe and as far away as Asia.[88] Illinois Indians also no longer produced their own pottery once they began to import Lower Mississippi Valley aboriginal pottery, which they then used alongside another import, colorful French glazed faïence ceramics.[89]

How then do we characterize the decoration the Illinois applied to their garments and other ornamental or functional objects, and how do we determine the contours of the Illinois (whether Kaskaskia, Peoria, or Cahokia) aesthetic that was ostensibly threatened by the adoption of French goods? For example, Chapter 1 introduced the existence of embroidered shoes among the items owned by Marie Catherine Illinoise and asked whether these were Indian-style moccasins or French-style footwear. If the former, then in light of the fact that any porcupine quills used to embroider the shoes were likely sourced from outside the tribe, should we qualify this embroidery as Illinois or Potawatomi/Ottawa? Likewise, should we throw up our hands at the fact that Lower Mississippi Valley pottery had displaced Illinois production (and techniques) of pottery making? And if not, then we should shine a light on the discrepancy in viewing French-Indian exchanges as leading to the erosion of Illinois culture, but Illinois-Oto ones, for instance, as not doing so. It is with these examples and questions in mind that we should heed art historians Janet C. Berlo and Ruth B. Phillips's caution that the idea of a pure Native American aesthetic is a fallacy resulting from Euro-centrism.[90] Focusing too narrowly on the dichotomy between indigenous and imported goods feeds into that pitfall and obscures the rich interactive dynamic between appropriation and assimilation.[91]

Such a view also impedes the commitment to understanding the range, complexity, and heterogeneity of the responses of particular groups of Indians to European and colonial influences, as these occurred at different times and in different places. The alternative is to run the risk of conflating all Indians in opposition to Europeans, thereby losing sight of the flexibility of the living (not frozen) cultures of *individual* North American tribes. But if we free ourselves from the impossible search for a pure and authentic past, the analysis of the material culture decisions of Indian wives and daughters of Frenchmen in the Illinois Country reveal less obvious ways of using objects to *retain* aspects of tribal culture. In other words, it should be stressed that it is not necessary to shy from the evidence of the appropriation of novelty goods in order to highlight the persistence of indigenous uses and meanings attributed to these objects. Sometimes it was enough for the context and the meaning to survive, even if the actual objects used were French ones. For Indian consumers, replacing a buffalo robe with a mantle/blanket made of *limbourg* wool did not necessarily mean they felt they had become French, though for some it may have. In the case of exogamous converts living with French husbands in French colonial villages, perhaps there was a shift in their ways of thinking about the object in question. Perhaps it is precisely to objects we should look for answers to these questions.

In this context it pays to reconsider, through a material culture lens, the practice of deploying women in alliance formation, a practice mapped onto the use of women to secure cross-cultural clan alliances and that predated the arrival of the French, like the practice of exchanging children with a view to alliance formation.[92] For the existence of this indigenous practice suggests that Indian women recognized the need to transgress their own (individual or collective) identities upon marriage to someone from outside their tribe. In those instances, the women would be required (and surely had been conditioned to accept the need to) permanently take on the garb of their new tribe. Marriage to Frenchmen and life in colonial settlements should be seen therefore as a continuation, not an interruption, of a precontact custom of cross-cultural marriage alliances. Sylvia Van Kirk has shown how these elements became formalized in the early nineteenth century in Métis fur trade unions at North West posts, as seen in her description of the ritual undressing and redressing of new Indian brides of Frenchmen:

> The trader usually visited the Indian encampment to claim his wife, and then the couple would be ceremoniously escorted to the fort. It became customary for a new Indian bride to go through a cleansing ritual performed by the other women of the fort, which was designed to render her more pleasing to the white man. She was stripped of her skin garments, scoured of grease and paint and re-dressed in a

more European style. At the North West Company posts, wives were clothed in "Canadian fashion" which consisted of a shirt, short gown, petticoat and leggings. Then the trader conducted his bride to his quarters, and from thenceforth they were considered to be man and wife.[93]

The process described by Van Kirk applied to marriages "à la façon du pays," and speaks therefore to a ritual primarily governed by indigenous beliefs and carried out by Indian women. Indeed, as with the process of colonization generally, the French—whether metropolitan officials or colonists—did not have a monopoly in establishing the meaning of events in the colony; but neither did Indian males. These women's agency through intermarriage—and the negotiations over their role—are key to unraveling the meanings that they attached to European goods, including the dress that they wore and the identity that they projected. The next chapter will foreground the ways that Europeans imbued dress with the potential to "Frenchify" natives. But so did native belief systems allow for ritualized transfers of clothing that could accomplish the transformation to a new identity.

Among the transformations that hinged on dress were intermarriage, captive adoption, and, among the Illinois, gender reassignment of the *berdaches*. Berdaches (as the French called them) were boys raised as girls, in a practice familiar from accounts of seventeenth-century Illinois Indians but not unique to this nation.[94] According to these French eyewitnesses, the process of becoming a berdache was twofold. A boy who showed an affinity for female occupations (in leisure and work) was first veered toward female activities, next he was forbidden access to male privileges and status, and then he was dressed in women's clothing. No information survives about the process of replacing the berdache's male garb with female dress, but given that a metamorphosis lay at the heart of this change of clothing, we can expect that there was a stripping and redressing ritual to be followed. The redirecting of the boy's gender identification was confirmed on reaching adolescence as a result of a religious vision quest that also conferred a role as shaman or manitou onto the berdache. The sources are unclear as to any link to homosexuality or intersexuality; they do specify that berdaches could have sexual relations with both males and females. While occupational and even linguistic factors played their part in their transformation, it was dress and appearance that were essential to constructing and marking the berdache identity. As described by de Liette in 1702:

they are girt with a piece of leather or cloth which envelops them from the belt to the knees, a thing all the women wear. Their hair is allowed to grow, and is fastened from behind the head. They wear also a little skin like a shoulder strap passing under the arm on one side and tied over the shoulder on the other. They are tattooed on their cheeks like the women and also on the breast and the arms, and they imitate their accent, which is different from that of the men. They omit nothing that can make them like the women.[95]

Father Marquette had also noted that once they had "while still young, assume[d] the garb of women," they retained it "throughout their lives," a permanency that was a particular feature of North American berdaches.[96]

The example of the Illinois berdaches speaks to Illinois Indians' belief in the fluidity and potential for gender identity to be modified, a belief shared with early modern Europeans.[97] An example of Illinois beliefs in the malleability of identity that was not gender specific pertains to captive adoption. Captive adoption was both a demographic and a spiritual strategy, in essence a mourning ritual aimed at replenishing depleted populations. In this ritual, some enemies, whether men, women, or children, who had been seized in raids, were selected for adoption as replacements for the deceased, to quicken or "cover the dead." Among Algonquin societies, it was women who held the authority to make these life or death situations, alongside their central role in the torture of captives, such as that of the female victim depicted in the upper left corner of Figure 10.[98] For those spared torture and death, through the process of adoption, the captives' previous identities (with the exception of tattoos or other permanent markings) were literally stripped from their bodies along with their clothes, and a new name was conferred after the washing of the body (including the erasure of any face or body paint), the cutting or restyling of hair, and the putting on of new articles of dress. Permanent markers such as mutilated body parts (stemming from captive adoption rituals) or tattoos remained as signs of a past life but were not impediments to the assumption of a new identity.[99]

Through the process of captivity and adoption, the identity and even the clan affiliation of the captive were reinvented, and any children born to him or her thereafter were considered free; in contrast to French slave codes, this kind of captivity was not hereditary.[100] As captive adoption practices expanded to accommodate French needs for slaves, some of these aspects may have been altered. For example, the stripping of captives could become part

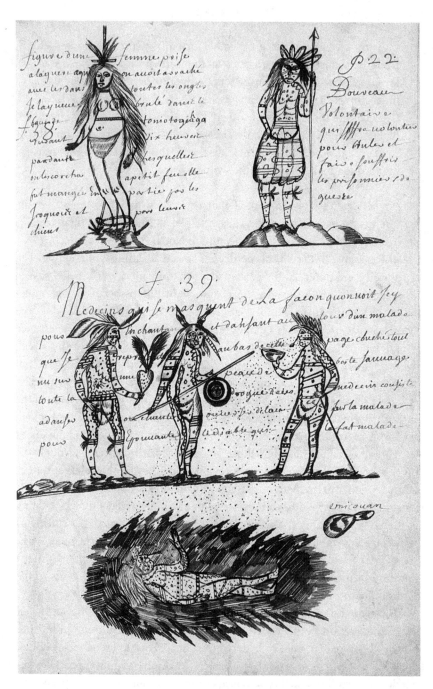

Figure 10. Fr. Louis Nicolas, "Figure d'une femme prise à la guerre à qui on a arraché avec les dans toutes les ongles," *Codex canadensis* (ca. 1675), 22. Gilcrease Museum, Acc. 4726.7.022, 22. Courtesy of the Gilcrease Museum, Tulsa, Oklahoma.

of a process of acquiring desirable consumer goods. This was described, for example, in accounts of the 1729 Natchez Indian uprising in which colonists' clothes were taken to be worn by captors, with the more fashionable articles of dress especially desirable. As Dumont de Montigny and others emphasized, of the two Frenchmen kept as slaves by the Natchez after their attack, "one was a tailor in order to have him alter the clothes of the French to their size."[101]

The Illinois were among those who captured enemies with the explicit goal of covering the dead. Other captives were killed after being stripped of all clothes (until they were "naked like the hand," as Marc-Antoine Caillot had described the torture of a boy by the Natchez in 1729) and then slowly tortured.[102] This practice predated the arrival of Europeans in North America. But as a result of contact with the French, the system stretched, and eventually fractured, through the increased use of captivity in warfare and trade.[103] For example, the Illinois came to deploy captives not only to cover the dead and as servants/slaves, but as a commodity, to barter for other goods or to present as diplomatic gifts, as with the captive the Illinois offered to Marquette on his first visit in 1673.[104] Women were especially valuable as objects of captivity, and we can presume that the wives of Frenchmen identified as Padoka (the French ethnonym for Plains Apache in the first half of the eighteenth century) or *panis* (often a generic term for Indian slave) had been captives.[105] The importance of women as captives is emphasized in the extant buffalo robe showing the capture of an adult female with a distinctive Plains-style fringed dress. The image is a violent one, and the female figure is drawn vertically upended, these visual cues signaling both her powerlessness and the coming inversion of her identity (see Figure 6).

That the capturing tribe could assert its will on captives and confer a new identity on them is to be taken for granted. How captives felt about being reassigned to a different tribe and being expected to assume the identity of a specific person (if not restricted to the role of servant/slave or made a secondary wife) is more problematic to determine. It has been suggested that captives (and captors) saw their adoption as an external performance and that rituals aimed at alienating the captive from the original tribe did fail, with some adopted captives (especially adult males) remaining loyal to their original kin and clansmen.[106] But there are many examples to the contrary, usually but not always involving those adopted as children.[107]

A court case from 1773 in Ste. Genevieve offers an extraordinarily rare, if not unique, glimpse into the thoughts of one former captive who was now a slave of the French, Marianne.[108] Marianne had gotten involved with a Frenchman, Céladon, who had convinced her to run away with him (Céladon would be accused of the murder of another Indian slave, hence the creation of a large body of documents about his actions and those of Marianne). The mother of two children, Marianne left her sons behind, in slavery, when she fled the village. Marianne would remain free (though under the control of Céladon), but her boys would remain enslaved. Yet she had planned a different outcome for them, as her son Jean-Baptiste testified recounting the night Céladon convinced his mother to run away:

> At once, the said sauvagesse said to [Jean-]Baptiste her son to come with her; he said that he refused saying that he didn't want to go without his little brother, which his mother had not wanted saying he would hinder them too much. But that since he [Baptiste] did not want to come he just had to stay quietly and that she was going back to her country, that this winter she would come back with some sauvages [from her country] to fetch him.[109]

What is especially noteworthy in this account is that Marianne was here asserting her kinship to her original nation (likely a Plains nation), even after a lifetime among the French as their captive hundreds of miles away, signaling the tenacity of her tribal self-identification.

But Marianne's story also complicates the assessment of captives' beliefs about their identity. While she clearly wished to communicate to her son her memory of their tribal affiliation, her religious convictions were more ambivalent. Marianne had once before experienced being permanently wrenched from family and kin, when she was first made captive, and she seems to have realized that her current condition (as an escapee dependent on a man who would never allow her to return to "her country") would also keep her permanently separated from her sons. Ste. Genevieve resident Jean-Baptiste Becquet testified that when he came across Céladon and Marianne at their encampment about six months after her escape, she had entreated him for news of her sons. And she seized her opportunity to assert an indirect link to the boys through a religious identification this time: she asked Becquet to help ensure that her sons' owners raised them as Catholics.[110]

Marianne was a captive kept as a slave by the French. Notwithstanding all the limitations on her movement, economic activities, and family and religious life this role imposed on her, she actively identified herself as a Catholic and sought to transmit that identity to her children. In contrast to the enslaved Marianne, the actual degree of agency of former captives who converted to Catholicism, were manumitted, and then married Frenchmen in the Illinois Country presents a distinct set of questions to which material culture offers some fresh perspectives.[111]

While the Illinois Country was characterized by its pattern of church-sanctioned and/or legal intermarriages between French men and Indian women, not all the women were Illinois. Suzanne Keramy Peni8aasa or Padoukiquoy, who twice married Frenchmen, died in 1747 in Kaskaskia. She was identified in some records as a Padoka, in others she was listed as a Panis Indian. She was probably therefore a freed captive who had entered into serial and legitimate marriages with Frenchmen. Her third husband, Daniel Legras, had even owned a Padoka slave whom he had emancipated in 1726, two years before his marriage to Keramy; Legras even supported the slave's marriage to a free Arikara Indian, surely with the approval of his wife.[112]

It is unclear under what circumstances Suzanne Keramy had been freed, but she was not the only free Padoka Indian in the area. A "Marie Therese Patoka [sic], sauvagesse libre" was married to François Dionnet *dit* Lafleur. We can infer that she was baptized and that theirs was also a legitimate marriage since she was registered as the godmother in a 1746 baptismal record.[113] Another identified as Padoka, Marie Anne Padoka Desricaras (likely a reference to her being of the Arikara or Caddo nation), had moved to Cahokia from Ville Marie in Quebec with her first husband, Louis Richard. After his death, she entered into a new marriage at Cahokia, to Joseph Dorion, her marriage contract stipulating that her future husband had granted her the substantial sum of 2,420 livres as her *douaire préfixe* (an allowance reserved for her in the event of his death, on top of her share of their community property), assets composed at least in part of French furnishings.[114] These women's offspring were in turn identified as French, consistent with French patrilineal conventions that traced lineage through fathers (a key exception being the children of enslaved women, as articulated in the 1724 Code Noir).

The French had integrated all four of these Padoka-identified women, thanks to some degree to pressure from missionaries who wanted to avoid "disorder."[115] For Suzanne Keramy this integration was confirmed in the 1726 inventory of the property from her first marriage, which consisted of farmed land, livestock, enslaved Africans, and a house furnished with a bed with bedding, a sideboard, two chairs, and a walnut table with a red linen tablecloth, buckets, kettles, cauldrons, candlesticks, and an earthenware terrine.[116]

On her death in 1747, the furniture and furnishings had grown by an additional three beds with bedding, a sideboard, table, and six chairs, a large and a small tablecloth, eleven napkins, assorted copper or brass kettles and pans, grill, terrines, pewter tableware and basins.[117] As for her wardrobe, there was the blue woolen blanket she likely used Indian-style as a mantle (as discussed in the previous chapter and seen worn in Plate 21). But she also owned all the items a respectable French woman would own (and many multiples of these), "two calimanco skirts, two cotton skirts, one old skirt of everlasting [wool], three *mantelets* [jackets], four shifts."[118]

In evaluating the material culture of former captives who were now married to Frenchmen, it is important to recognize that they came from tribes that also practiced covering the dead, as did the Illinois. Both former captives and Illinois Indian women might even have benefited from the practice when their villages incorporated new slave laborers or when one of their own relatives had been resuscitated through captive adoption. And they anticipated it as a fate that might befall themselves or their own, as the Choctaw did when they engaged annually in a ritual in which they flogged "boys, girls, old and young . . . to teach them to have no fear of the evil their enemies can do to them."[119] This intimate knowledge of captivity as a way of life (and death) forces us to reconsider how former captives understood the implications for their own lives of the *premise* underlying captive adoption, that identity could be reprogrammed through rituals and acts of assimilation. Exchanges of children and ritual exchanges of clothing at councils, stripping and re-dressing of adopted captives, shift to new ways of dressing as a result of cross-cultural marriage alliances in patrilineal societies, regendering of transvestite berdaches through dress all drew on indigenous beliefs in the premise of a fundamentally fluid tribal and gender identity, influencing how Indian wives experienced marriage to Frenchmen.

As seen through all these examples, dress lay at the core of ways to construct and, as needed, to modify identity. It is in this light that we should revisit the account of Chief Rouensa trying to strip his daughter of her clothes. Father Gravier presented the incident as a violent assault on the girl's morality by her yet un-Christian (and uncivilized) father. The daughter had given in to her father when he removed her outer garments and only resisted when he attempted to strip her of "what covered her" (what Gravier signaled to be her shift). In other words, the priest had highlighted her modesty and linked this to the girl's successful transformation into a pious Catholic. And indeed, this association between conversion and French dress was precisely what

Marie Rouensa and her father had been contesting. But the Jesuit, in relaying this incident, was oblivious to the meaning of the act of stripping in the context of indigenous beliefs.

Both daughter and father recognized the significance of Marie's garb of *justaucorps*, shift, and stockings as signaling acceptance of a new social and spiritual identity. It was just that the acquiescence to this change by one family member was contested by the other, even to the degree of the father wishing to reverse that new influence. He would do so by physically stripping his daughter of its sartorial markers, just as a new captive chosen to "resuscitat[e] the dead" would be humiliated, physically assaulted, dishonored, and stripped prior to the conferral of a new identity.[120] This stripping and reattribution of identity was itself seen not only as a sign of the fluidity and malleability of identity but also as reversible, as in the attempts by family members of captives to secure their release.

Antoine Simon Le Page du Pratz provided a self-serving anecdote about such an attempt to recover a former captive, when he described how the father of his female Chitimacha slave, having recognized his daughter, offered to have his nation buy her back. According to the author, his slave (with whom Le Page du Pratz seems to have had relations, and who may have considered herself married to him) refused because "I had treated her with much kindness, she had attached herself to me," and besides, he added, "she had lost the habit of living and going almost naked as in her country." Her father must have insisted, however, for Le Page du Pratz added that the daughter went on to convince her father that he was too old to help her, proposing instead that he settle with his kin near the Natchez post, where the colonist and his slave were intending to move.[121] This case of buy-back failed, although implicit in Le Page du Pratz's text is the premise that he did not object in principle to her return to her father. In contrast to the ample evidence concerning captive adoption rituals, there is little information about rituals involving returned captives. But since they were ostensibly dead to their former kin, it was necessary to conduct a new captive adoption ceremony that would have reinscribed them as members of their originary nation. For those who practiced captive adoption, identity was mutable and reversible.

In attempting to assert his will on his daughter, Chief Rouensa must be understood as simply guarding the authority over female members of his family that his status as a Kaskaskia male granted him. Bolstered by her collusion with a Catholic priest, Marie Rouensa resisted that authority, and Chief Rouensa failed to strip his daughter of her identity as a convert. Father

Gravier presented her eventual acquiescence to the marriage with Accault as an assertion of her spiritual agency, one that led her parents back to the faith after a period in which they had contested the authority of the Catholic Church. But, conversely, Chief Rouensa could also claim that he *had* ultimately succeeded in enforcing his decision that Marie marry Accault. This contention carried implications for how the chief viewed his relationship with the girl after the marriage and its legitimacy. And it helps explain one other eventual consequence of French-Indian marriages and its legitimacy: the Kaskaskia's acceptance of the fact that their daughters would remain with their husbands in the segregated colonial villages reserved for the French after 1719, rather than move to the new Kaskaskia Indian village.

In conformity with Illinois conventions, once she had married out in accordance with her family's wishes, Marie Rouensa was no longer under the jurisdiction of her male Kaskaskia kin, but belonged to her French husband's group. Kaskaskia chief Mamantouensa clearly articulated this understanding during his 1725 visit to Paris. Addressing Louis XV at Versailles, Mamantouensa referenced the arrangement he had been forced to accept at the time of the 1719 policy of separating Indians from French colonial villages in the Illinois Country: "[Commandant Boisbriand] promised me that they wouldn't worry me in my village, that they would not make me change my village again, to make way for the French, my brothers *and my sons-in-law*; I left [the village] but I still fear a change, change is bad for prayer and disturbs my young people and the Black Robe, who gets weary of building, is not eager to follow us; our wives and our children suffer from this; this is why I wish to be the master of the land of my village, & that one does not speak to me soon of [more] change" (my emphasis). Chief Mamantouensa's gendered language is instructive about how the Illinois—including Marie Rouensa therefore—viewed intermarriage with Frenchmen: the women were now dependents of French husbands and members of colonial, not Kaskaskia Indian, communities.[122] In marrying out and living in colonial households with their French spouses, the material culture expressions of Indian wives of Frenchmen and their children would pave the way for the question at the core of the next chapter, of how the French comprehended the identity of these Indian women.

In 1762, seventy or so years after Marie Rouensa married Michel Accault, the parish priest in Kaskaskia celebrated a new marriage, the terms of the marriage contract registered by a notary. This marriage united Pierre Frederic d'Arensbourg to Elisabeth de Celle Duclos. The groom was identified as a "Swedish gentleman," an aristocratic officer in the marine. The father of the bride was an officer and therefore high-born. Her grandmother was Marie Rouensa. Elisabeth's male siblings would similarly enter into noteworthy marriages. Another of Marie Rouensa's granddaughters, Agnès Chassin (daughter of Agnès Philippe and Nicolas Chassin), married aristocratic French officer Jean François Tisserand de Montcharvaux, commandant of the Arkansas post from 1739 on.[123] If respectable and well-born Frenchmen gradually ceased to enter into legal, sacramental marriages with full-blooded Indian women, the same was not true for marriages to the children and grandchildren of legitimate Indian wives of Frenchmen. Far from "remain[ing] part of their indigenous communities," these wives, daughters, and granddaughters had extended Illinois (therefore exogamous) marital alliance practices that required them to appropriate the identity of spouses who happened to be French, not Illinois.[124]

In the same year that Marie Rouensa's granddaughter married d'Arensbourg, France began to divest itself of the Province of Louisiana when the area west of the Mississippi River was ceded to Spain. The following year, 1763, the area east of the river was ceded to Britain. Seventy years later, in 1832, the remnant Indian populations of the state of Illinois left the Upper Mississippi Valley, their descendants now known as the Peoria Indian Tribe of Oklahoma, a federally organized tribe. But the Upper Mississippi Valley is not altogether devoid of descendants from the Illinois nations. Like Cece Boyer Myers, whose ancestry traces to Marie Rouensa, many of those descended from the sanctified unions between Indian women and Frenchmen live on in the former French settlements of the Illinois Country.[125] Their continued presence in the area highlights the role of material culture in collapsing the lines between appropriation and assimilation, adaptation and persistence. And it forces us to develop alternative interpretations of acculturation in order to explain the blurring of difference between French and Indian in the Illinois Country in the eighteenth century. In 1694, Father Gravier had described Marie Rouensa's religious fervor as having "nothing of the *sauvage* in it."[126] His statement would prove prescient in terms of the ways the French perceived the Indian wives, daughters, and granddaughters who wore French garb within French colonial villages. For, however these women thought about their identity, the image they presented to French onlookers would in turn come to influence colonists' very conceptions of ethnicity.

CHAPTER 3

"One People and One God"

In 1627, as the French began in earnest to colonize and evangelize North America, they established a charter for the Company of New France. Among the preoccupations expressed by the document was the question of the Indian inhabitants of the land claimed by France and the plans for converting and Frenchifying them. One clause of that charter touched directly on those Indians who would convert, declaring that they

> will be considered natural Frenchmen, and like them, will be able to come and live in France when they wish to, and there acquire property, with rights of inheritance and bequest, just as if they had been born Frenchmen, without being required to make any declaration or to become naturalized.[1]

Almost one hundred years later, Marie Rouensa-8canic8e, daughter of the chief of the Kaskaskia Illinois, widow of Michel Accault, wife of Michel Philippe, and mother of eight legitimate children, began to fulfill one part of that vision for Indian converts. On the feast day of St. Anthony of Padua, Wednesday, June 13, 1725, she lay on her rope bed, with its straw mattress and cotton sheet, at home in her vertical log post-in-the-ground house facing the parish church in the French colonial village of Kaskaskia. "Sick in her body, but healthy in her mind and understanding, and with free will," she had called in the notary.[2] In his presence, and that of her priest and two other settlers serving as witnesses, she drew up her will, dictating it in her native tongue. Though these events took place in North America and not in France, the men who attended Marie Rouensa on her deathbed were there to formally recognize the right of this Indian convert to "acquire property, with rights of inheritance and bequest, just as if [she] had been born [French]."

Even the fact that she spoke in the Illinois language was not an impediment to the granting of such rights; after all, one could be considered French in France even if one only spoke Provençal or some other regional dialect.[3]

In her will, Marie Rouensa recommended her soul to God, the Virgin Mary, and all the saints, and requested that her husband have prayers said on her behalf both in the French Kaskaskia parish Church of the Immaculate Conception in which she would be buried, and in the original Indian mission church in which "she had been raised." Then, citing the Coutume de Paris—the customary law that governed civilian matters in Louisiana—she affirmed that her children would inherit her property according to this law. The Coutume de Paris was far less flexible than English law in terms of inheritance; it mandated that the surviving spouse (male or female) took half the assets after debts were paid off, while the deceased's children (again, whether male or female) inherited equal shares of the remaining half. But Rouensa used her will to bypass this law (a problematic legal maneuver) and request that her son Michel Accault be disinherited.[4] She justified her rejection of the inheritance rights of this son by citing his choosing to "remain among the *sauvage* nations." She also cited his "disobedience" in the marriage ("à la façon du pays," with an unbaptized Indian woman) that he had entered into "despite his mother and his relatives."[5]

Seven days after drawing up her will, and shortly before her death and burial under the Church of the Immaculate Conception, a still bedridden Marie Rouensa dictated a codicil to her priest, modulating her rejection of this son's inheritance rights on condition that he stop living among the "nations sauvages" and repent. The consensus among historians is that Michel Accault fulfilled the terms of his mother's will in 1728, three years after her death, when he legally entered into his inheritance; as we shall see this was not precisely the case.[6]

The will and codicil were dictated and produced by the Kaskaskia Indian wife of a Frenchman. These legal documents illuminate one Indian convert's understanding of Illinois and French kinship norms, and of her relationship to the Catholic Church, to French law, and to the colonial lifestyle. If we swivel our perspective, we note a group of Frenchmen implicated in supporting Marie Rouensa's claim to an identity as Catholic and as a "natural French[woman]." Together, her husband, her priest, the notary, and the sundry inhabitants who had assembled by her deathbed codified her last wishes according to French norms, as did the appraisers who would later value her assets at the massive sum of more than 25,000 livres. These male colonists

lent collective support to her efforts to keep French property in the hands of
Frenchified Indians and out of the hands of those who "remained among the
sauvage nations" (including her own kin). On one level, these men were acting to protect their fledgling settlement's economic integrity. But in doing so,
they were also acting according to a belief system more redolent of the one
enshrined in the 1627 Charter (which had posited the potential for Indians
to become French) than of the new protobiological notions of identity that
were coming to dominate discourses on race and skin color in the eighteenth
century.

"Natural Frenchmen"

The assets Marie Rouensa denied her eldest son were varied: land and livestock farmed according to French methods (though the farmland might have
been originally cleared by Illinois women); a share of her multiple colonial-
style lodgings and outbuildings; and a random smattering of her French-style
furniture and household goods. In other words, she had not simply deprived
her son of an abstract right to inheritance. In addition to depriving him of
land, she had also denied him actual access to French material goods. Specifically, these were trappings of French material culture that Indian wives
and daughters of Frenchmen in the Illinois Country had appropriated and
displayed. In its emphasis on property rights, the 1627 Charter had similarly
underlined that material goods (movable and immovable) were not only financial assets but attributes of Frenchness.

Chapter 1 established that Indian wives and daughters of Frenchmen in
the Illinois Country deployed French material culture with a remarkable
thoroughness. In this chapter, I leave aside the nitty-gritty details of material
culture expressions. But Marie Rouensa's will is a reminder of the intrusion
of material culture into the construction of identity, and I build upon this
evidence to explain the process whereby Indian women were co-opted by the
colonization project. For the question of how the French among whom she
lived viewed Marie Rouensa and women like her is a fundamental one for
grasping how colonists defined identity as pertaining to French and Indian. It
was Frenchmen who produced the records we now use to trace the outlines
of the lives of Indian wives and daughters of Frenchmen in the Illinois Country. It is they who recorded the location of these women's abodes through reference to other French colonial buildings and environmental modifications,

whether those of a parish church or of neighboring farms and lots. How the wives and daughters of Frenchmen looked and performed mattered to the male and female *habitants* who shared their lived experience of colonization with such women, and who daily had to make sense of the three-dimensional figures they saw before them. And it mattered beyond the Illinois Country, as this primary site for Indian conversion and intermarriage became the lightning rod in debates about the viability of Frenchification policies and its underlying premise that identity was mutable.

In other words, the story of these women from the Illinois Country is not simply a regional illustration of important facets of French-Indian relations in the context of conversion and colonization. Indian women had played a crucial role in French-Indian exchanges in the Illinois Country and beyond. But women such as Marie Rouensa, Suzanne Keramy, and others like them could not have achieved standing within *French* colonial villages without the complicity of the local French missionaries, officials, husbands, and other male and female colonists who interacted with them in daily life. Armed with their visual knowledge of intermarried Indian women converts in the Illinois Country, these members of the colonial population deployed Catholic sacraments, French customary law, and a dose of pragmatism in order, first, to reclassify Indian wives and families of Frenchmen as French and, second, to uphold the women's access to the social, cultural, and legal trappings of Frenchness. Chapter 2 posited that these women may have begun identifying themselves as French upon marriage and acculturation to their husbands' material culture; that this was consistent with the patrilineality of the Illinois; with conventions of exogamous and cross-cultural or cross-clan marital alliances (with the French as one variant group); and with practices such as captive adoption premised on the fluidity of identity. But it is one thing for an Indian woman to see herself as French; quite another for a French colonist to accept her as such, to accept that being "culturally French" equaled being French, as the 1627 Charter of New France had anticipated.[7]

Intermarriage practices and Frenchification policies in colonial Louisiana were not met by a uniform response, but by wide variations in the standpoint and the actions (rather than merely the words and policies) of missionaries and officials. These variations did not follow a progressive chronological course. Nor can these discourses and practices be reduced to a clear-cut opposition between religious and secular views, for the different religious and missionary factions in place in the Illinois Country fought with each other—and among themselves—about intermarriage. And neither can the debate be reduced to disparities between colonial versus metropolitan views, since even among those in the colonies and those in France, views about intermarriage—and the conceptions of difference that grounded these views—varied.

Rather than situate the debate about intermarriage in terms of intellectual and religious binaries, or positing a clear distinction between the views of Frenchmen in the colony and in France, I propose that we look instead to the Frenchified bodies and performances of intermarried couples and their children. For my analysis suggests that the tensions between supporters and opponents of intermarriage and *métissage* in Louisiana was primarily located in their degree of familiarity with the uncommon outcome of such practices in the Illinois Country. It is in fact the material culture expressions of these women that permit us to understand the process through which French colonists determined how to define Indians in the early modern period. Or, to put it more compellingly: the way Indian women performed Frenchness through material culture helps us grasp the implications of priests in the Illinois Country justifying intermarriage there by asserting, in 1732, that "there was no difference between a Christian *sauvage* and a White."[8]

Eighteen years before this statement, Henri Roulleaux de La Vente, priest of the foreign missions and former vicar-general of the bishopric of Quebec, had similarly advocated marriage between Frenchmen and Indian women from Upper Louisiana, on the basis that the latter were "more hardworking, more adroit, better suited to housekeeping and sweeter" and "whiter" than their counterparts in Lower Louisiana.[9] La Vente had made his statement about the color and disposition of Indian women from Upper Louisiana in a broader missive supporting French-Indian intermarriage. It was a cause he had publicly championed since at least 1708, two years after entering the fray by allowing his priests to celebrate four intermarriages.[10] It was in response to La Vente's statement that Commissaire-Ordonnateur Jean-Baptiste du Bois Duclos had issued his shrill condemnation of the practice. Also pointedly singling out the Illinois Country, as quoted earlier, Duclos had declared that

> Although there are several examples of Indian women who have contracted such marriages especially at the Illinois, it is not because they have become Frenchified, if one may use that term, but it is because those who have married them have themselves become almost Indians, residing among them and living in their manner, so that these Indian women have changed nothing or at least very little in their manner of living.[11]

So, here were two influential men—the first the well-established and politi-
cally connected religious figure who had even fought off a previous governor,
the other the newly arrived direct representative of France's administrative
interests in the colony. Theirs was a debate initiated in Louisiana but with
the same audience in mind: that of the minister of marine in France. Father
La Vente had invoked "skin color" and Duclos had alluded to "whiteness"
and "dark complexion" in referring to *French-Indian* marriage.[12] Yet both
interlocutors also harked back to the premise of religion and culture as the
foundations of identity. For instance, La Vente's reference to Illinois wives'
housekeeping skills was not a recognition of their mastering of universal
qualities; rather it implied their acculturation to French, therefore culturally
specific norms. As for Commissaire-Ordonnateur Duclos, in choosing the
word "Frenchified," he was making an explicit allusion to France's century-
long policies toward the Indians of New France.

To Frenchify (*franciser*) had lain at the heart of France's plans for colonizing New France and asserting demographic control over the region by
turning the Indians there into French subjects of the king.[13] Already in 1603,
Samuel de Champlain promised his Indian interlocutors that once a settlement was established at Quebec, "our young men will marry your daughters,
and we shall be one people," to which they reportedly answered, laughing,
"Thou always sayest something cheering to rejoice us. If that should happen,
we would be very happy."[14] But intermarriage was just one route to Frenchification. As Marc Lescarbot pronounced in his 1618 history of New France,
colonization itself would lead the French to "civilize the [indigenous] people and make them Christians by teaching and example."[15] The 1627 charter
granted to the Company of New France formalized this objective of Frenchifying Indians as a means of increasing the number of subjects loyal to the
king of France. As articulated in that document, which decreed that Indians
could become French, religion provided a fundamental, non-negotiable basis
for Frenchification. While conversion was the crucial factor in the earliest
discussions of assimilation, the question of intermarriage between French
and Indians quickly became intertwined with plans for Frenchification. For,
as initially perceived (and promoted) in seventeenth-century New France,
intermarriage was a sacramental union that would facilitate the assimilation
of Indians into Frenchified subjects of the king.

By 1666, Jean-Baptiste Colbert, Louis XIV's influential minister of fi-
nance, reiterated the role Frenchification could play in the colonial project.
"There is nothing," Colbert asserted, "that would contribute more greatly [to

this goal] than to try to civilize the Algonquin, the Huron and other *Sauvages* who have embraced Christianity, and dispose them to come and settle with the French to live with them, and raise their children according to our mores and our customs."[16] The following year, Colbert would echo Champlain and declare that Indians and French would "become one people and one blood."[17] Those charged with the actual job of Frenchifying Indians were more sanguine about the challenges they faced. By 1668, Marie de l'Incarnation (1599–1772), founder of the Ursuline convent in Quebec and an early champion of Frenchification, had become dejected about the potential for Indian girls to be transformed:

> It is in fact a very difficult, if not impossible, task to Frenchify or civilize them. . . . We have had Hurons, Algonquins, Iroquois girls. The latter are the prettiest and most docile of all. I do not know if they will be more capable of being civilized than the others, nor if they will maintain the French politeness in which we raise them. I do not expect this of them, as they are sauvages, and that is enough to temper our hopes.[18]

One year later, her tone had become more impatient and critical as she pleaded with a patroness for more funds to carry out the Crown's instructions:

> His majesty . . . desires that we Frenchify the Sauvages little by little in this way, in order to turn them into a polite people. . . . But though we had raised them since we are in this country, we have nonetheless Frenchified only those whose parents had agreed to this, and a few poor orphans whose mistresses we were; the others were only here in passing and stayed with us a month or a little more, then they left their place to others. But now we have to Frenchify them all and dress them in the French style, which is no small expense.[19]

Allied to this fresh push for Frenchification, Colbert had reoriented formally advocated intermarriage between Frenchmen and Indian women, a move swiftly followed by the commitment of funds to provide dowries for Frenchified Indian female converts to marry male colonists.[20] This promotion of (legal, Church-sanctioned) marriages between Frenchmen and Indian women converts was gendered and specifically intended to make up for the shortfall in the ratio of French women to men in the colony.

But this vision of Frenchification could be even bolder, for missionaries and officials in New France had also advocated that converted and French-ified Indian women marry Indian men, anticipating that this too would increase the number of French subjects. Intendant de Meulles explained, in 1682, "Being brought up in this spirit, I do not doubt that once married to *sauvage* men, [these women] would gradually introduce their husbands to this way of life which could lead them to dress, eat, and live like us and would, with time, get the *sauvage* mind out of them."[21] Echoing statements made by missionaries and officials at the very onset of the colonization of New France, there was an expectation that conversion and Frenchification ("get[ing] the *sauvage* mind out of them") were mutually dependent. And it is telling that this continuing support for the Frenchification of *Indian* converts occurred simultaneously with the elaboration of the 1685 Code Noir. That document would likewise promote the conversion of Africans to Catholicism, and it would allow limited leeway for legal French-African inter-marriage and for free blacks to become subjects of the king. But the premise underlying the 1685 code was the opposite of the mutability thesis inherent in Frenchification policies; its goal was to fix the identity and condition of Africans as permanent chattel.[22] This disparity was reproduced in French-Indian and French-African relations in the Illinois Country and in Louisiana.

Frenchification policies were originally fully supported by the religious mission of the Ursulines in Canada, whose Indian students were among those promised a dowry on marriage to a Frenchman. But the lack of any lasting success with Frenchification would temper the order's early belief in the feasibility of change.[23] Even the Indian bride dowry scheme was dropped, its eventual abandonment presaged by the greater focus, and ex-penditure, on dowries for French "filles du roi"—single women shipped to the colonies for the express purpose of serving as brides to colonists. Whether this shift of funds from Indian to French brides was motivated by "a racial reorientation" away from the Frenchification project remains in contention, but it was followed by a new emphasis in the convents of New France on converting female English captives who had been brought to them.[24]

By the late seventeenth century, as the pace of racialization picked up, support for Frenchification would be by no means either universal or con-sistent. Yet, with the colonization of Louisiana, the topic would gain fresh momentum. In 1700, Pierre le Moyne d'Iberville requested approval for Frenchmen to marry Indian women. The next year he received his answer:

His Majesty has examined the proposal made by the Sieur d'Iberville, namely, to allow the French who will settle in this country to marry Indian girls. His Majesty sees no inconvenience in this, *provided they be Christians*, in which case His Majesty approves of it. (my emphasis)[25]

As reiterated in this document, conversion continued to serve as the key precondition in these marriages, since scriptural law forbade that Roman Catholics marry outside of the faith.[26] Iberville was intimately familiar with the Illinois Country and would have had knowledge of the Church-sanctioned intermarriages that had been celebrated there from 1693 on. Such direct experiential knowledge of intermarriage in the Illinois Country would become a key factor in the continuing support for Frenchification.

That Indian women in the Illinois Country had apparently succeeded in becoming "Frenchified" was especially problematic for the French in the eighteenth century. This period was witnessing the contraction of an earlier model of ethnic flexibility that Frenchification policies had epitomized. New notions of difference were now ascendant, influenced by the formation of (African) slave societies in the French Caribbean islands, premised on fixed identifiers and characterized by the permanency of skin color. There remained lingering references to the potential for Frenchification in the eighteenth century, and the occasional allusion to this beyond the Illinois Country, for example, in the description of Tunica chief Cahura-Joligo as "baptized and almost Frenchified." But though he was observed as dressing in the French manner and owning a complete suit of French clothes, at least one chronicler described him as preferring to carry his breeches rather than wear them.[27]

In the face of the overwhelming failure to integrate Indians in most areas of French North America, the Illinois Country appeared to provide a rare validation of the potential for Indians not only to be converted but also to be Frenchified, making through intermarriage "one people and one God" with the French (as Dumont de Montigny would write as late as 1747).[28] This outcome in turn influenced how contemporaries perceived intermarriage and *métissage*.

Frenchification policies were mapped onto the theory of monogenesis that still dominated European thought in the seventeenth century. This concept was premised on a hierarchical construction of identity not as fixed or biological, but fluid and malleable. Identity was seen as "improvable" (to quote Karen Ordahl Kupperman) and was explained through a confluence of corporeal and spiritual or intellectual characteristics.[29] Skin color was itself seen as mutable, a result of the climate, physical environment, or application of grease to the skin, and also as an external sign of culture and of religion.[30]

The theme of religious conversion as a route to Frenchification had important parallels and precedents in France, for example, with respect to Jews, whose conversion was believed to lead to the whitening of their skin color.[31] In Louisiana, if there were no explicit comments about *changes* in skin color, eyewitnesses did implicitly link conversion with both white skin and acculturation. The Illinois were "the fairest field for the Gospel," but also, according to another Jesuit, had "an air of humanity that we have not observed in the other nations that we have seen upon our route."[32] Others dwelled on the Kaskaskia, "The Cascassias illinois nation is Catholic. . . . This nation is highly civilized" wrote Pénicaut in 1707.[33] Even Chief Rouensa, once he had been won over to Catholicism and just five or so years after his daughter's marriage to Accault, was praised for his "politeness," which was that "not of a *sauvage*, but of a well-bred Frenchman."[34] Thirteen years later, Father Marest, yet another Jesuit based among the Kaskaskia, described how:

> our Illinois are very different from these Sauvages [those who still believed in manitou spirits], and from what they themselves were formerly. Christianity, as I have already said, has softened their fierce habits, and they are now distinguished for certain gentle and polite manners that have led the Frenchmen to take their daughters in marriage. Moreover, we find in them docility and ardor in the practice of Christian virtues.[35]

For all these eyewitnesses, conversion had clearly resulted in Indians becoming civilized ("polite"), and indeed Frenchified.

Once Indian wives began to intermarry and live with their husbands in segregated French colonial villages, we begin to find that the skin color of Illinois converts was emphasized. As we have seen, La Vente had referred to the whiteness of the skin of Indians from Upper Louisiana. Those on site in Upper Louisiana would single out the Illinois for their whiteness. In 1718, commandant of Fort Pontchartrain Jacques Charles de Sabrevois described Illinois women as "especially comely and not at all black."[36] Three years later, de Liette characterized the Illinois as "tolerably fair for Indians" and having "faces as beautiful as white milk, insofar as this is possible for Indians of that country."[37] By the 1720s, even those without direct knowledge of Illinois Indians reported on the reputed whiteness of their skin. Caillot lumped all the Indians of the colony together, describing the flesh of the men as "a dark reddish color," and their women the same. But he too reiterated the Illinois' reputation for exceptionalism, identifying them as being those "who have the whitest skin compared to the other Indians, and the women there are very beautiful." But Caillot had then described a young *French* girl who had caught his eye as having "a complexion as white as the snow," beautiful red cheeks, and unsurpassed blue eyes.[38] As made explicit by Caillot, and echoing other comments cited above, the French may have been describing the Illinois as exceptional *among Indians* for their skin color, but their whiteness was relative, presaging racial thinking elaborated with reference to skin color.[39]

All these aspects of conversion, Frenchification, skin color, and acculturation were brought to bear on the evaluation of the distinctive marriages between Frenchmen and Indian women in the Illinois Country. In turn, the pattern of intermarriage Marie Rouensa initiated (on a scale specific to the Illinois Country, though it would eventually encompass non-Illinois women) provided evidence of concrete, material, and sartorial Frenchification. And this evidence would influence how colonists thought about race. For the question of identity was what was at stake in how the French in eighteenth-century Louisiana conceived of conversion and intermarriage. Were conversion and Church-sanctioned intermarriage still seen as useful and valid tools in enabling the Frenchification of Indians, a goal that had lain at the heart of seventeenth-century plans for colonization? And could Indian women converts who had married Frenchmen, such as Rouensa, become French, as La Vente hinted? Or did their French husbands become Indian as a result of their immersion in native life, as Duclos asserted? Could the French even conceive of the possibility for the metamorphosis of an Indian woman into a French one (and its opposite, that of a Frenchman into an Indian) in a period when views of ethnic difference were hardening into protoracialist ones?

The actions of those most involved with intermarriage provide an invaluable point of entry into these questions of how the French perceived Indian wives and daughters of Frenchmen, beginning with the priests who consecrated their marriages and the men who married them, and ending with the local officials and proxy officials, like those who served Marie Rouensa upon her death, who upheld these women's right to legal status as French. In so doing, we will also examine how these colonists responded to French metropolitan laws and proscriptions against intermarriage.

"A certain article of furniture"

We begin with religious figures because it was Jesuit missionary Father Gravier, in conjunction with Marie Rouensa, who launched the distinctive pattern of *sacramental* intermarriages in the Illinois Country. In doing so, he reversed the Jesuits' opposition to intermarriage in the last decades of the seventeenth century, stemming in large part from disillusionment with conversion and intermarriage in New France.[40] As we have seen in the previous chapter, it was Marie Rouensa, once she had relented to marry Michel Accault, who had initiated the idea for this to be a Catholic marriage. Gravier would have been in a difficult position had he wanted to refuse to celebrate the union, since instruction about "true marriage" was so central to his teachings to the Illinois.[41] But it is also unlikely that the priest had anticipated the extent to which this model of French-Indian intermarriage would become established in the Illinois Country.

Like Marie Rouensa, Father Gravier had initially resisted her marriage to the fur trader Michel Accault. He may also have hoped and he certainly prayed that it might be a Josephite wedding—in which both spouses took a vow of celibacy. For though Gravier claimed to have instructed Marie fully on the obligations of marriage, he had in fact singled out as a model the marriage of St. Henry and St. Cunegund, which at the time was believed to have been celibate. A perusal of his letter reveals that he had also instructed her about a further five married saints "who have sanctified themselves in the state of matrimony."[42] This plethora of models of celibacy in marriage—headed of course by that of the Virgin Mary—certainly raises fundamental questions about Father Gravier's convictions concerning the suitability of sexual relations and procreation between Indians and Frenchmen (even those within the "bonds of Christian marriage"). But once he had witnessed the effect of the consummated marriage on Accault, and on the wider Kaskaskia community, he would begin to champion intermarriage as a means of religious and secular assimilation.

The Rouensa-Accault marriage was the catalyst that led Chief Rouensa and his wife back toward Catholicism, culminating with the mass conversion of many of their people. Father Gravier exulted in this triumph of his missionary endeavors in the Illinois Country. But his 1694 letter shows that one other success may have trumped even this, namely, the return of Michel Accault to his Catholic faith. For, though Accault "was quite ashamed of being less virtuous" than his wife, who had spoken to him "in so tender and persuasive a manner" about her (unsuccessful) hopes that he would consent to a celibate marriage, "the first conquest she made for God was to win her husband." Gravier dwelled at length on Accault's transformation:

> He is now quite changed, and he has admitted to me that he no longer recognizes himself, and can attribute his conversion solely to his wife's prayers and exhortations, and to the example that she gives him. "And how can I resist," he has often told me; "all that she says to me? I am ashamed that a *sauvage* child, who has but recently been instructed, should know more than I who have been born and brought up in christianity, and that she should speak to me of the love of God with a gentleness and tenderness capable of making the most insensible weep; and my experience convinces me that she tells the truth when she says that there is no joy except for those who are good. Hitherto, I have never been satisfied; my conscience has always been troubled with a great many causes for remorse," he continued, "and I have such a horror of my past life that I hope, with the assistance of God's grace, that no one will ever be able to make me abandon the resolution I have undertaken to lead a good life in future."[43]

What a metamorphosis indeed, for a man Gravier had described initially as being "famous in this Illinois country for all his debaucheries." His marriage to an Indian convert had in fact done anything but lead him to "become almost Indian," as Duclos would have had it. It is no coincidence that from this moment on, Jesuit missionaries in the Illinois Country who had hitherto opposed French-Indian unions now became among the most ardent proponents of sacramental intermarriage involving women who had proven to be such devout converts.[44]

Marie Rouensa and the other Indian women who followed her in desiring a sacramental union were instrumental in asserting their agency in determining the contours of intermarriage practices in the Illinois Country. But we must not lose sight of French involvement in this decision. We have seen how one missionary was co-opted by Marie Rouensa into blessing her marriage to Michel Accault, and other priests would follow in the ritual of celebrating and registering marriages and baptisms. We now turn to the other participant whose consent to a Catholic marriage was essential, the male spouse.

Michel Accault initially expected a "mariage à la façon du pays" that would enhance his status as a trader and landowner in the Illinois Country. But there is no reason to believe he took this union lightly, especially since he was single when he approached (or was approached by) Chief Rouensa about marriage to Marie Rouensa. Many men then followed Michel Accault in consenting to Christian marriage with Indian women as Frenchmen in the Illinois Country continued to perceive Indian women and their legitimate mixed heritage daughters as worthwhile marriage partners.

Two French-born men left testimony that sheds light on their economic and social strategies for marrying such women in the 1720s. In 1725, Nicolas Pelletier de Franchomme appeared before the Superior Council of Louisiana to petition for a new marriage contract on the basis that the original from his September 1723 marriage in the Illinois Country had been destroyed by rats. He bolstered his petition by referring to the fact that he had married there "to his material advantage," a rationale that would have resonated with his fellow, usually impoverished aristocratic officers.[45] And indeed Franchomme had benefited economically from his marriage, his wife, Marguerite Ouaquamo Quoana, being the widow of Jacques Bourdon, one of the wealthiest traders in the area and himself the widower of an Indian woman.[46] Financial considerations as well as local connections were clearly factors in these marriages.

One other French spouse of a (half-Indian) woman, Nicolas Chassin, was less venal than Franchomme but no less direct in his assessment of the social and affective benefits of marriage in the colonial environment. In 1722, this French-born representative of the Company of the Indies who served as royal storekeeper (*garde-magazin*), found himself enriched by seventeen acres of fertile Mississippi river frontage.[47] Wishing to cement his establishment in the colony, Chassin wrote a letter to a priest of his acquaintance in Paris in the hopes it might lead to securing a wife. He took pains to explain his requirement for a wife, in the context of the demographic situation in the Illinois Country and issues there with finding a marriage partner suited to his rank and standing:

> You see, Sir, that the only thing that I now lack in order to make a strong establishment in Louisiana is a certain article of furniture that one often repents having got and which I shall do without like the others, until . . . the Company [of the Indies] sends us girls who have at least some appearance of virtue. . . . If by chance there should be some girl [in France] with whom you are acquainted, who would be willing to make this long journey for love of me, I should be very

much obliged to her and I should certainly do my best to give her evidence of my gratitude for it. I think that if my sister had come she would have looked after me as much as I had looked after her, but I am beginning to fear that my hopes may have gone up in smoke.[48]

As seen in his letter, Chassin recognized the importance of marriage as an organizing institution in the new colonial settlements, and he linked having a wife with the potential to realize "a strong establishment in Louisiana." He also explained the difficulties that "officers and those who hold any rank" experienced with obtaining a suitable wife in the Illinois Country. He alluded to having tried previously to matchmake his own sister (back in France) with his friend, forty-five-year-old lieutenant Pierre Melique, assuring Father Bobé that "Mr. Melique is still passionately desirous of marrying my sister." But his parents had resisted, not thinking it "proper" and asserting it would be more "fitting that Mr. Melique should go to France to marry her than that she should go to the Illinois to find him." In response to their concerns, Chassin went on to explain in detail how logistically difficult it would be for a prospective groom to travel back to France for a bride. For Chassin, New World conditions trumped Old World notions of what was proper. His long litany of objections is suggestive of the conversations, strategies, worries, and gossip shared by French bachelors of rank in the Illinois Country about what they obviously considered a major problem:

I shall tell you, Sir, that it is very difficult for an officer to go from the Illinois to get a wife in France because of the great expense that it is necessary to incur not only to go down from the Illinois to the sea and to cross over to France but also for the time that he must spend at New Orleans, in France and elsewhere while waiting for means of transportation to return from France to New Orleans and from New Orleans to go back up to the Illinois, without counting several other good reasons, and after considering them all carefully all of us young men here have decided not to go to France to get wives but to do without them until it pleases the Company to furnish us the means of doing otherwise. Several are becoming impatient but we let them grumble. The Company has already four or five hundred girls, but officers and those who hold any rank cannot make up their minds to marry such girls who in addition to the bad reputation that they bring from France give reason to fear that some also bring remnants of infirmities of which they have been imperfectly healed. It would be rather easy to have girls come from Canada, but a libertine who came here from that country makes us fear that among those who might come from there, there might be some of the same sort.[49]

Melique never did secure Chassin's sister as his wife. The lieutenant died in 1727 at fifty. But though he lived without a legitimate wife, he had an illegitimate daughter with an unknown Indian woman. This daughter was acknowledged as Melique's, and she would inherit his house with its wraparound porch (*galerie*). Endowed with this property, she would contract a legitimate marriage in the Illinois Country; her daughter would in turn secure a member of the prominent Chauvin *dit* Joyeuse family for her legitimate husband.[50]

While he had written back to France for help finding a wife, Chassin must have also talked to his fellow officers and informed local inhabitants of his desire for a wife. Just four months after his letter to the priest, in November 1722, Chassin managed to contract a marriage with just such a "piece of furniture," though one procured locally and who would no doubt have seemed unusual in the eyes of a Parisian priest. For Chassin took as his wife not a woman from France or Canada as mentioned in his letter, but an especially prominent half-Indian woman, Agnès Philippe, Marie Rouensa's daughter.[51] Her mother had initiated French-Indian intermarriage in the Illinois Country, and Agnès Philippe would become the first legitimate child born from such an intermarriage to enter a legitimate marriage of her own with a Frenchman, and one with a relatively high ranking Frenchman.

Agnès's grandfather was Kaskaskia chief Rouensa; her father was Marie Rouensa's second husband, Michel Philippe, whose rise in prosperity as a trader and landowner owed much to his wife's status and trade connections. Michel Accault before him had similarly known how to draw benefit from his marriage. Immediately following his marriage to Marie Rouensa, he purchased a half-share of an important landholding and fur trading partnership with Henri de Tonty (who had inherited his share directly from Robert Cavelier de La Salle).[52] No doubt this legal title to land had also served her second husband well, and may have been among the substantial landholdings distributed to her heirs upon her death.

The marriage contract between Chassin and Agnès Philippe does not survive, but three years after her marriage she inherited a sum of nearly 3,000 livres from her mother's estate alone; she would inherit other assets on the death of her father in 1738.[53] Marie in her will would turn to Chassin and her daughter Agnès to ask them to take in and educate her two youngest children.[54] Agnès's marriage to Chassin in turn laid the groundwork for further amelioration of their household's financial situation and social standing. Chassin would become a pioneer in the agricultural development of the Illinois Country, though his "strong establishment" would be short-lived.[55]

In November 1725, not long after his Indian mother-in-law's death, and following the birth of three children, he was recalled to New Orleans "for bad conduct." The recall was officially related to the way he kept his ledgers. Historians have debated whether his marriage to the half-Indian Agnès Philippe was a factor in his public disgrace, while assuming that he never returned to the Illinois Country as a result.[56] Records produced locally tell another story about his whereabouts and show his continuing integration in the colonial settlements of the Illinois Country, where priests and officials alike continued to uphold his standing in the community. Chassin was present there in February and October 1727 when he witnessed the marriages of his two sisters-in-law, and in August 1728 he bid (and won) a waistcoat and stockings of black silk at the auction sale of the effects of the deceased officer Franchomme.[57] Chassin had died by 1730, when his wife renounced her community property with him (and reclaimed the assets she had brought to the marriage as permitted by the Coutume de Paris); she waited until 1737 to remarry, to the surgeon René Roy.[58]

In the Illinois Country, Accault, Chassin, and Franchomme were not alone in taking an Indian or mixed-Indian wife. A number of other officials contracted legitimate marriages with Indian women or their daughters. Among the especially prominent officers who married daughters of Indian women and Frenchmen were post commandant Pierre Grotton de St. Ange and François-Marie Bissot de Vincennes, founder of the Vincennes post, who in 1730 married Agnès Philippe's first cousin and received a substantial dowry. Even as fresh influxes of European settlers, including women, moved into the area (and ostensibly negated the need for Indian wives), Frenchmen continued to contract marriages with Indian women and, especially, their mixed-heritage daughters. In fact, they seem to have actively sought out marriages to Indian women or their offspring, often marrying Indian women in sequence (as they became widowed), and even turning to Indian women following the death of a French spouse.[59]

These women and their daughters were excluded from the role of concubine which Indian slaves continued to occupy throughout the French period in the Illinois Country as elsewhere in Louisiana. Instead, permanent inhabitants of the Illinois Country and French bachelors stationed there deemed them worthy marriage partners. Clearly, there were financial and social benefits to intermarriage with Indian widows and their daughters, as Franchomme had indicated.[60] The community also benefited from the increased cohesion created when French men and women served alongside Frenchified Indian converts (and their children) as witnesses at marriages, as godparents (as Chassin did for a French-Indian child), or in any other official role mandated by ecclesiastical and state law.[61] Together, these French and Indian inhabitants of the Illinois Country codified their approval of intermarriage by virtue of their presence at these official events, cementing relationships that could prove especially advantageous for outsiders needing to establish themselves in the fledgling settlements.[62] And, if few French bachelors stationed in the Illinois Country recorded their thoughts about marrying Indian women or their daughters, as Franchomme had done, their actions and beliefs in taking their vows of marriage shows that they could put aside any reservations they may have felt.

The material culture objects with which these Frenchmen surrounded themselves—the French-style furniture, bedding, cookware, and architecture, and the dress with which their wives adorned themselves—provide nonverbal confirmation that they understood their households as French colonial, not native. So did the officials who inventoried and appraised these objects and notarized the results, as did those who drew on this evidence and that of the women's dress as they went house to house in the Illinois Country to compile census records. Beginning with the census of 1726, Indian spouses and progeny of French habitants were included among the ranks of colonists, signaling their official amalgamation within the colonial population and advertising the villages' demographic growth. In contrast, enslaved Indians and Africans were enumerated separately. The censuses of 1732 and 1752 would follow the same model.[63]

The censuses were mandated from France and they provide a valuable index of the way agents of the Crown who had direct contact with intermarried couples chose to mark their status. Such mandates, and the writing of new laws pertaining to intermarriage, are useful for understanding how protobiological proscriptions dictated from outside the Illinois Country were dealt with locally. Just as the framers of the 1627 Charter of New France had foregrounded property and inheritance, so did opponents of intermarriage in the Illinois Country attempt to control intermarriage by limiting Indians' rights to the provisions of this law. Precise rules regulated inheritance in Louisiana, based on community property rights between spouses and between parents and progeny, as stipulated by law. The legal framework for legitimate intermarriages in the Illinois Country was the Coutume de Paris, which Marie Rouensa had invoked in her will and which was a community property law. On the death of a spouse, the household assets (land, buildings, crops, furniture, and so on) were itemized, appraised, and added up. These assets were divisible into two equal lots, half going to the surviving spouse and the other half to be shared equally among the male and female children, after expenses and privileged debts. A widow was usually entitled to her bed, clothing, and other personal effects (so these were usually excluded from the inventory and appraisal), as well as any dower (*douaire prefixe*) stipulated in the marriage contract; the living spouse was entitled to a set sum known as the *preciput*; both the *douaire prefixe* and the *preciput* were considered privileged debts.[64]

Although most unions in the Illinois Country were legitimized, they were not always formalized through marriage contracts, as required by the Coutume de Paris (a problem not restricted to French-Indian marriages). In theory, this complicated probate matters, causing problems, for instance, when an Indian widow wanted to secure her rights to the community property, or when she wished to contract a new marriage.[65] In practice, local officials in the Illinois Country endeavored to deal equitably with the problem, just as they did with the marriages of French spouses in the same position. They would do so even as government officials in Lower Louisiana and the metropole pressed them to act otherwise. It is therefore to the struggle between the authorities in the Illinois Country and beyond that we now turn.

"No difference between a Christian *sauvage* and a White"

In December 1728, three years after Marie Rouensa had successfully asserted her right to distribute her wealth according to the Coutume de Paris, her errant son finally re-entered French colonial society long enough to claim his inheritance.[66] In the same month and year, a sequence of events originating in the Illinois Country was set in motion that resulted in eroding the right of Indian women like Rouensa from controlling their estates according to the terms of the Custom of Paris. This happened as the result of a ruling by the Superior Council of Louisiana in 1728. The Council, in New Orleans,

presented its ruling as the result of a request initiated from the Illinois Country by Jesuit missionary Father Antoine-Robert Le Boullenger. Le Boullenger's report does not survive, but the council described him as having asked
for clarification pertaining specifically to Indian wives' inheritance rights. Le
Boullenger had apparently explained that he was accustomed to resolving
conflicts among his parishioners. But he now needed further guidance on the
matter of the *legitimate* marriages between Frenchmen and "Indian women
from the Illinois nation," with respect to two issues. One was that some widows might decide to return to their Indian nation and take their inheritance
with them (that is, remove their community property out of French settlements). The second was that the (Indian) parents of childless Indian women
with knowledge of French inheritance laws might claim their share of the
community property upon the women's death. In both cases, and this is a key
point that the council may not have sufficiently heeded, Le Boullenger was
referring to the dangers caused by non-Frenchified Indians, or those women
who relinquished their links to the French. Not surprisingly, given his long-
standing support of intermarriage, Father Le Boullenger had said nothing
whatsoever to contest the inheritance rights of Frenchified, Catholic Indians,
or of their legitimate children. To the contrary, he had in fact been instrumental in upholding this demarcation between Indianized and Frenchified
Indians.

In her will, Marie Rouensa had disinherited her eldest son for leaving
the French settlement and living "among the *sauvage* nations." It was Le
Boullenger who had composed the codicil to Marie Rouensa's will on her
behalf. This was the document in which she had promised that her son's inheritance would be preserved, provided he repent and reenter colonial society. And in 1728, the very year his request was brought to the attention
of the Superior Council, Le Boullenger wrote to his sister, an Ursuline nun
in New Orleans, for her help in starting a convent in the Illinois Country
"to teach Christianity to these poor Illinois sauvages" (meaning those living
outside French settlements, not the converts married to Frenchmen).[67] Le
Boullenger had clearly not given up on the potential of Indians to become
French. He retained a fervent commitment to Frenchifying Illinois Indians through religious instruction, a process begun with his authorship of a
French-Kaskaskia dictionary and ending with a half-Indian becoming a nun
under his guidance.[68]

The Superior Council of Louisiana would echo Le Boullenger's distinction between legitimate, Frenchified Indians and those who had relinquished

Frenchness, though it did so in a more muted way. In response to Le Boul-lenger's request for clarification, the Superior Council of Louisiana issued a binding decision that was then upheld by the king. It overrode the Coutume de Paris by mandating three separate rules relating to the succession rights of Indian wives of Frenchmen. The council began by asserting that Indians could not inherit from the French, then added the following exceptions and clarifications. First, the assets of Indian wives of Frenchmen who died child-less became the property of the Company of the Indies (meaning the share that would have gone to the woman's parents as next of kin in the absence of children, not her widower's share). Second, widows were prohibited from controlling the assets left them after the death of their husbands; instead a guardian would be appointed (just as if they were minors) and the women would receive annually one-third of the income from the estate, the remain-der to go to any children. In the absence of children, all of the assets would be administered by the attorney for vacant estates. Finally, the ruling for-bade "all Frenchmen or other white subjects of the King from contracting marriages with Indian women until such time as the King let his will be known."[69] Neither the Superior Council of Louisiana nor the minister of ma-rine in France alluded to the Crown's demand in 1716 that intermarriage in Louisiana be prevented as far as possible, underlying that it had been a prag-matic request rather than a binding ruling, and that in the intervening period thoughts about intermarriage in the Illinois Country had receded from their concerns.[70]

Beyond Le Boullenger's input, the 1728 decision also cited an individual dispute in which the French spouse of an Illinois Indian woman had wished to suspend his pregnant wife's right to his estate. Accusing Marie Achipi-courata of infidelity, Guillaume Potier had asserted the child she carried was not his (he did not question the legitimacy of their first two children, one of them Chassin's godchild), and had made a will disinheriting her. It was not the first case of adultery brought against an Indian wife in the Illinois Country, though the outcomes were different. As part of its 1728 ruling, the Superior Council invalidated Potier's will, dismissing his claims as the result of jealousy and on the basis that the child had been born during the mar-riage. Therefore, the Council decreed, the children would receive two thirds of the estate and their guardian would provide Potier's widow with one third of the income from the community property "so long as she remains among the French, whether she remarries or not, but from the moment that she returns among the Sauvages to live there in their manner the said pension would no longer be paid to her."[71] In other words, the Superior Council had used this case to put its new rule into practice. How it was subsequently applied in the colony brings out the contrasts between the actions of officials in Upper and Lower Louisiana.

In Lower Louisiana, the 1728 ruling seems to have been enforced, to a degree. In New Orleans in 1745, Pascagoula inhabitant Charles Hegron *dit* Lamotte made a will in favor of his wife and children that made no reference to the 1728 decision, though he named a friend, Durantay, to carry out the terms of the will. When the will was brought before the Superior Council of Louisiana for ratification, Durantay joined with the attorney general to successfully request that one guardian be appointed for the minor child and one for the widow, "given her quality as an Indian." Yet Lamotte had specified that he bequeathed *half* his succession to his Indian widow Françoise, with the other half to be divided between their children. In other words, he used his will to uphold a wife's right, under the Coutume de Paris, to inherit half the community property, rather than the one-third mandated by the 1728 decision. In its ratification of his will, the Superior Council let that clause stand.[72]

In the Illinois Country, the evidence suggests that the regulations mandated from New Orleans and France were manipulated, so that Indian wives continued to be treated as full-fledged *habitantes*. The three marriages contracted by Marguerite Ouaquamo Quoana before and after the 1728 ruling are illustrative of this pattern. On the death of her first husband, Jacques Bourdon, in 1723, this Indian widow inherited half his estate; since he died childless, his heirs in Canada also inherited a share.[73] By March 1728 (before the ruling), her second husband, the officer Franchomme, made a will that specifically addressed the fact that his heirs might make a claim on his still childless Indian widow's property. Since, he asserted, it was she who had brought much of the wealth of the household to the marriage, her rights should stand.[74] After Franchomme's death, his Indian widow stayed within the colonial settlement, and for the third time, in August 1729, she married a Frenchman, Pierre Blot (and once more would bear no children). That marriage contract made no reference whatsoever to the 1728 decision; on the contrary, it formally upheld the Coutume de Paris (and its provision that half the community property—not a third—was owed to the surviving spouse). It also included both a mutual donation in the case of a childless marriage, and a *preciput* of 1000 francs to the survivor. The spouses had of course negotiated the terms of the contract in the presence of the groom and bride's witnesses and "friends," among whom was the lieutenant commander of the

Ouabache post, Michel Philippe (Marie Rouensa's widower), and even Jean-Baptiste Potier, whose brother Guillaume had been partly responsible for setting in motion the 1728 ruling.[75]

The 1729 marriage contract signed by Blot and Marguerite Ouaquamo Quoana was not unique in its blatant disregard of the 1728 decision. In 1739, Marie Tetio (also written as Tet8kio), widow of Jacques Lalande, contracted a new marriage with Jacques Lefevre. Again, the Coutume de Paris (not the 1728 decision) was cited as the legal framework for the marriage and future inheritance issues. Sieur Buchet, the attorney for vacant estates, was present among the bride's "family and friends" but no reference was made to her being under his guardianship or that of any other guardian. On the contrary, the document was rife with allusions to Marie Tetio's autonomy and absolute control over her property. With Attorney Buchet as a witness, the contract also transferred the guardianship of her children to the joint control of Lefevre and their Indian mother.[76]

From such examples, in no way could one argue that the 1728 decision had altered the fabric of marriage contracts, and intermarriage conventions, as they were applied on site in the Illinois Country.[77] Instead the evidence suggests a pragmatic response to individual cases. For instance, in 1744 an Indian woman was kept out of the proceedings for the division of her late daughter's property. Though she should have been among those chosen to represent her granddaughter's interests, she was excluded because she was an Illinois Indian "not remotely informed about these kinds of affairs."[78] Conversely, the previous year—again in clear contradiction of the 1728 ruling—the Indian brother of a childless Indian woman was successful in upholding his legal right to dispose of property inherited from his late sister *and* her French husband.[79] The point here is that locals such as Le Boullenger, Attorney Buchet, and the other French colonists who joined forces as spouses, witnesses, friends, priests, or notaries to uphold the system of intermarriage in place in the Illinois Country were for the most part intent on protecting the rights of *Frenchified* Indians. Local institutions serving the colonial order supported Indian women converts in their role as French colonial wives, when metropolitan and New Orleans authorities did not. Not only were Frenchified Indians systematically counted as colonists in census records, but laws were also applied locally in such a way as to ensure their rights as full-fledged members of the settler community.

Yet as new officials posted from France to Lower Louisiana were made aware of the extent and contours of intermarriage in the Illinois Country, they continued to protest it. They did so in terms increasingly direct about their racial motives, concerns sometimes echoed by supporters of intermarriage. In two letters written in New Orleans to the minister of marine, dated July 1732, governor Étienne Périer and Commissaire-Ordonnateur Edmé-Gatien Salmon initiated a new onslaught against intermarriage in the Illinois Country. Périer focused on the problem caused by "most of the inhabitants of that quarter [who] have married Indian women. They have themselves become *sauvage*, that is to say, very difficult to discipline, and they speak ill to their parents and against the Commanders and the Missionaries."[80] A few days earlier Salmon had framed the problem as a broader one involving land disputes and the political imperatives of the Illinois nation (not Indian wives per se). But his stance also betrayed his dismissal of earlier hopes for forging alliances (and Indian loyalty to the French) through marriage.

Notwithstanding the belief that in the Illinois Country there was no difference between Indian converts and Whites as the Commissaire-Ordonnateur had quoted a missionary as asserting, Salmon's letter represented the culmination of years of disappointment with conversion and Frenchification policies in French America.[81] It was as a result of this fresh wave of criticism against intermarriage that, in October 1735, a new order was formulated for Louisiana. Still shy of a strict prohibition against intermarriage, the order cautioned priests in the Illinois Country and stipulated that intermarriages would now require formal approval of no less than the governor, the Commissaire-Ordonnateur, or post commandant.[82]

Men in the military were already required to obtain authorization to marry, though marriage with Indian women seemed to attract additional scrutiny. For example, the 1742 registration of Limoges-born soldier Martial Bardoux's union with the Indian Elisabeth warranted a notation in the parish register that Bardoux had had to obtain the commandant's approval in order to get married (just as required by the 1735 edict). But Elisabeth had the distinction of being a freed Indian slave, not the legitimate daughter of a Frenchman. Born in the parish, she had been freed by her previous owner (also her father?), Mr. Blot. In her case, whether or not she was Blot's daughter, her status was that of a freed Indian slave, not a Frenchwoman.[83] Other marriage contracts from after 1735 show no concession to the new requirement for approval. That of Joseph Dorion and Marie, Padoka Indian widow of Louis Pichard, was executed at Cahokia in 1749 and made no mention of requiring permission of the commander. One sergeant was present, not to give his approval but to represent the interests of the bride in his capacity as "among her friends"; in any case, as a sergeant he did not rise to the rank of post commandant.[84]

That 1749 contract was executed by a missionary priest "in the absence of a notary" at the Cahokia post. And indeed, in a 1735 letter to the Crown from governor Jean Baptiste Le Moyne de Bienville and Commissaire-Ordonnateur Salmon, both men had blamed missionaries for celebrating these "mixed marriages" without the commandant's permission, the priests having apparently claimed a higher spiritual power with regard to marriage, and that the word "of a Governor or Commandant was not sufficient for them."[85] But in 1739 the marriage contract joining Jacques Lefevre and Marie Tetio/Tet8kio made no mention of the requisite permissions, and it was done before the royal notary himself.[86] Clearly, it was not simply missionaries who condoned intermarriages in the Illinois Country. Nor should we discount the continuing willingness of Frenchmen in the Illinois Country to marry Indian women (whether Illinois or former captives) into the 1740s, if sporadically by then, as well as their legitimate daughters. This included French-born and high-ranking men who might be expected to hold the same protobiological views on Indians as the governors and administrators who continued to lobby against intermarriage from their distant vantage point in Lower Louisiana.[87]

Blood and progeny were at the core of the new wave of anti-intermarriage discourses. The debates about the merits of sanctioning (and sanctifying) intermarriages touched directly upon the question of the tension between the European influence on the one hand, and the Indian influence on the other, and of how this might affect those individuals in mixed marriages. But at the core of these discussions was the matter of progeny and how the mixing of French and Indian might manifest itself in the identity of children. Ideas about degeneracy and civilization informed and contributed to the nascent racial theories that framed these debates, as they did in English settlements.[88] In French America, the concept of Frenchness had added another layer to these notions, since the achievement of Frenchification by Indians (and their progeny) carried with it the promise of full-fledged and inheritable rights as French men and women.

But by the eighteenth century new ideas about difference and the permanence of "racial" identity had surfaced in both French and native thought systems. Though they were not yet dominant, they did spread to the highest echelons of power in France and influenced matters in the colonies. In 1751, forty years after Father La Vente had invoked the physical trait of "whiteness," *métissage* was endowed with more portentous overtones when Pierre de Rigaud de Vaudreuil, governor of Louisiana, took up the mantle of fighting intermarriage, instructing his new representative in the Illinois Country to prevent the "marriages which the French there have contracted with native women; such alliances are shameful and of dangerous consequence for the familiarity which these engender between natives and French, and the *bad race* which it produces" (my emphasis).[89] In invoking the trope of "mauvaise race," Vaudreuil was deploying the language of lineage (specifically, the anxieties about the dilution of noble blood through marriage with social inferiors). Here, Vaudreuil was extending this class-premised trope, applying it to formulating a total rejection of racial intermarriage.[90] In the same vein, Commissaire-Ordonnateur Duclos, as discussed earlier, had been adamant in 1715 in warning against the "adulteration that such marriages will cause in the whiteness and purity of the blood in the children, for whatever Mr. De La Vente may say, experience shows every day that the children that come from such marriages are of an extremely dark complexion, so that in the course of time, if no Frenchmen come to Louisiana, the colony would become a colony of mulattoes who are naturally idlers, libertines and even more rascals as those of Peru, Mexico and the other Spanish colonies give evidence."[91] As for Father La Vente, a proponent of intermarriage, even he had stressed biological factors when he argued that "the blood of the sauvages" would not prejudice that of the French.[92]

It is difficult to reconcile these pronouncements with the actual treatment of legitimate mixed children in the Illinois Country. Indeed, the disregard in the Illinois Country toward the 1728 legislation extended to the marriages of half-Indian children. This is seen in their marriage contracts, which are indistinguishable from and gave the same protection under the Custom of Paris as those of French couples.[93] For example, in 1739 Marie Dulongpré (daughter of Étienne Philippe *dit* Dulongpré and Marie Ma8e8enci8ois) was elected guardian of her children on the death of her husband, and no guardian was appointed for her. In other words, and contrary to some historians' assertions, local settlers and officials had no problem electing an Indian or part-Indian woman to this important role.[94] Furthermore, half-Indian children continued to be accorded full rights concerning their inheritance and the complete range of legal maneuvers pertaining to French village life. Marie Anne Danis, daughter of Dorothée Mechip8e8a and Charles Danis, had married a member of the prominent Chauvin family in Louisiana. Her French husband died leaving her and her children destitute, and it was, ironically,

to her Indian mother in the Illinois Country that she looked to for an inheritance, which came to 1,409 livres.[95] In the period between the death (or
disappearance) by 1730 of her first husband and her 1737 remarriage, Agnès
Philippe, Dame Chassin, daughter of Michel Philippe and Marie Rouensa,
was the legal head of her household. She also had full control of the property
she had brought into the marriage and that she had reclaimed in 1730 upon
renouncing her community property with Chassin.[96] Local officials upheld
her right to serve in that role, and she succeeded in initiating one of the earliest land surveys in the area, stemming from a dispute over boundaries.[97] In
other words, no court-appointed guardian had been suggested for her either,
and no impediments were placed on her actions as head of household.

Nor was the 1735 edict on intermarriage formulated to apply to marriages contracted by the children born of mixed-parentage marriages. The
major commanding Fort de Chartres did grant his permission to the marriage of officer Pierre Frederic d'Arensbourg to Elisabeth de Celle Duclos
(Marie Rouensa's granddaughter) but this was required for all the military.[98]
For others, their contracts made no reference to the governor, *Commissaire-
Ordonnateur*, or post commandant's permission, and these couples continued to invoke their rights according to the Coutume de Paris. The half-Indian
Marie Aubuchon, for example, not only reserved the right to her half of the
community property, should she be widowed, but also negotiated a *preciput*
and *douaire prefixe*.[99] Marriage contracts were legally binding documents
produced by notaries or by missionaries in the absence of notaries (in the
latter case usually witnessed by local inhabitants or other secular officials).
The point should be made, then, that if missionaries offered one recognized
source of support for Indian women converts, and their children, living in
colonial villages, local administrators in the Illinois Country could be just
as pragmatic in response to the challenges posed by the needs of a mixed
population.

A century after the 1627 Charter of New France, with its promise that
Indian converts would share in the rights owed to "natural Frenchmen," the
continued recognition in the Illinois Country of Indian widows' rights is notable. It occurred notwithstanding a legally binding rejection of some of these
rights by the governing authorities in France in 1716 and 1735, and in New
Orleans in 1728, and in spite of a definitive shift, by this period, in metropolitan views of intermarriage and identity.

But the rift between those who supported and those who rejected intermarriage and *métissage* rested on differing interpretations of the effects of

intermarriage on spouses and children, whether they looked and acted as French or Indian, as Duclos had formulated it. In nearly every discussion of intermarriage relating to Louisiana, the experience of the Illinois Country was invoked and the manner of living of Frenchified Indians was cited. For example, Father La Vente had given a favorable account of the whiteness of Indian women from Upper Louisiana, but he had also stressed their amenability to French ideals of womanhood centered on docility and mastery of housework. As early as 1699, Indian wives of Frenchmen in the Illinois Country were already being singled out for their acculturation into French housewives. In that year, Jesuit Father Binneteau wrote about "women married to some of our Frenchmen, who would be a good example to the best regulated households in France."[100] Twenty or so years later, a French official in the Illinois Country would describe the "many French inhabitants who are married to Indian women, even the most important ones, and they live very well together."[101] Jesuit Le Boullenger would extend this pattern of support in 1728, emphasizing that the women concerned acquired the status and condition of their husbands.[102] And almost forty years after Binneteau's statement, Father Tartarin would assert that the "bastard métis on the contrary have always gone in greater numbers to the sauvages, without education, without hope of any inheritance; in them, the sauvage blood dominates." In contrast, he argued, "legitimate métis are fixed among the French through education and by the inheritance of property from their fathers." Tartarin added that the majority of these legitimate métis married into French families, thereby attenuating the effects of their birth, which their French education had also helped erase. They "behave like true French" (the original French text "véritables français" is gender-neutral), "moved by the desire to make themselves respected by the true creole Frenchmen and Frenchwomen."[103]

Though they did not document their thoughts about intermarriage, the other priests who celebrated marriages between Frenchmen and Indian or part-Indian women in the Illinois Country similarly upheld the position that these women had been or could be Frenchified. For example, Tartarin had written in support of intermarriage forty-five years after Marie Rouensa's marriage to Michel Accault, and two decades after Duclos's successful appeal to the Crown to limit the practice. This time span underscores that Gravier, Binneteau, Le Boullenger, and Tartarin had charted a continuum of behavior and a consistency in the way that Indian wives of Frenchmen in the Illinois Country presented themselves to colonists.

All these statements served to rebut Duclos's argument (based on hearsay rather than firsthand experience) that "these Indian women have changed nothing or at least very little in their manner of living."[104] There was a gulf between eyewitness accounts from the Illinois Country and secondhand reports by those who had never set foot in Upper Louisiana. This apparent success of Frenchification policies in the Illinois Country informed and bolstered the position by officials and missionaries in those settlements who still believed in the potential for the attainment of Frenchification. Local religious and secular officials drew directly on what they interpreted as the growing evidence of the integration of mixed-parentage children into French society to justify their now controversial policy of sanctifying intermarriages. This success offered support to the proponents of assimilation policies and was crucial to their new or continued support for sanctified intermarriage in the face of the increasing rejection, in Lower Louisiana and France, of Frenchification policies premised on the malleability of identity.

My findings in Chapter 1 refute Duclos's statement that Indian wives of Frenchmen had "changed nothing or at least very little in their manner of living." As we have seen, in the Illinois Country, and unlike most intermarried Indian women in French America, these women did wear recognizably European (or more accurately, French Canadian) styles of dressing and lived within French colonial settlements, in a process that laid the foundation for their descendants' integration into colonial society. Whether or not they considered themselves to have "become Frenchified," Illinois wives of Frenchmen, and their daughters, wound up "residing among" the French and "living in their manner" as a result of intermarriage. And this brings us back to the crux of the debate as framed by La Vente and Duclos, and reiterated by others. For they had settled on the question of the metamorphosis of the spouses, and of their progeny, as the crucial factor in deciding the merits (or dangers) of intermarriage and *métissage*. It is with this in mind that we should recognize the centrality of material culture to the development of belief systems. Experiential knowledge of the appearance of Frenchified Indians was key to ensuring continuing support in the Illinois Country for intermarriage. Indian wives' deployment of French material culture and their performance of Frenchness had convinced missionaries, officials, and fellow villagers that they were French (with a concomitant upholding of the legal rights that this title implied). Officials and colonists in France and Lower Louisiana did not have this firsthand knowledge of the "manner of living" of intermarried couples. Only those on site in the Illinois Country were required to interpret, and to rationalize to themselves, the visual and material evidence presented by Frenchified Indians, since only here did colonists assert the success of Frenchification. This difference explains why colonists across Louisiana did not adhere to the same set of beliefs about identity, ethnicity, and race, and why their views of Indians followed a different trajectory and chronology.

Beginning with her public conversion to Catholicism and followed by her growing immersion in the material culture of French colonial life, Marie Rouensa had asserted her claim to the rights of "natural Frenchmen," and Frenchmen in the Illinois Country had unequivocally granted these to her. She herself had desired celibacy out of religious conviction. But she twice married Frenchmen, lived with her second husband in a large colonial house that faced the church, and at her death in 1725 was buried under this church—the only woman (French or Indian) to be so honored.[105] Her exemplification of Frenchification enabled her own mixed heritage daughters to initiate a related pattern of intermarriage between Frenchmen and legitimate half-Indian children. Her granddaughters' sacramental and legal marriages to elite Frenchmen in the 1760s would not have been so readily achieved were it not for the perception that these girls' Indian forebears had successfully "Frenchified" their appearance.[106] Marie Rouensa's legacy of intermarriage and Frenchification would ensure that as late as the third quarter of the eighteenth century it continued to be tenable for a French-born colonist to conceive of the potential for Indian converts, even enslaved ones, to become French. In 1768 in Ste. Genevieve in the Illinois Country, Marie-Claire Catoire, widow of royal notary Leonard Billeron *dit* Lafartigue, made a will. French-born and literate, Catoire was a *fille du roi* who had married Canadian-born Billeron in Biloxi, Lower Louisiana, in 1721.[107] In her will, she confirmed her conditional manumission ten years earlier of her Indian slave Suzanne, granted as Suzanne was about to marry the freed Indian Joseph Canghé. As a condition of the manumission, Widow Billeron had required that the couple "serve me and my son Leonard, and only us, for the rest of our lives." They did so, living with the widow in a fully furnished French colonial house in Ste. Genevieve. But Widow Billeron added another condition: that Suzanne and Joseph were "to practice the Roman Catholic religion and comport themselves as *free persons of the French nation*" (my emphasis).[108]

Forty years earlier, the officer Franchomme had used his will to protect his Indian wife's property rights. His fear of impending death had also led him to verbalize his hopes and anxieties about her continuing contributions to the local community, for example, by emulating his style of treating their (Indian and African) slaves "gently." He then added another plea: that she do her best to look after a French-Indian boy, Jean Saguingouara, who had been in their care, by ensuring that the boy "not give himself over to the Sauvages," exhorting her "to have him instructed in our Religion as best she can, I would have done this myself if I had lived longer."[109] For Franchomme, there were two outcomes that could befall the boy (who was born to a legitimate French-Indian union and is the subject of Chapter 5): he could become either Indian or French. Franchomme indicated that he understood ethnicity as a quality that needed to be attained and then maintained. Saguingouara would be French providing he continued to be given instruction in the Catholic faith and was kept immersed in French colonial, rather than Indian, society. That Franchomme had given his instruction to his full-blood Indian wife meant that he perceived her as also having attained crucial aspects of Frenchification, even to the degree that he trusted her to teach, and initiate others in, Frenchness. No colonist in the Illinois Country ever extended the same consideration to an African, reiterating their belief in the hierarchy of peoples, and their conviction that Indians might reach the summit of that hierarchy through religion and culture (and that they would want to), but that the chasm between Africans and Europeans was too great. For both Franchomme and Widow Billeron, Indians could successfully Frenchify, in a specific environment and time when religion, allied to material culture, might stand in for racial identification. If in the Illinois Country, these colonists codified their belief in the Frenchification of Indians, in other sites across Louisiana, including New Orleans, such an identification would prove harder to uphold.

Plate 1. Alexandre de Batz, *Dessein de Sauvages de Plusieurs Nations, N^{lle} Orleans, 1735.* Courtesy of the Peabody Museum of Archaeology and Ethnology, Harvard University.

Plate 2. Bequette-Ribault house (post-in-ground style), ca. 1790. Ste. Genevieve, Missouri. Author's photo.

Plate 3. Cahokia Courthouse (post-on-sill style), ca. 1740, Cahokia, Illinois. Courtesy of the Illinois Historic Preservation Agency.

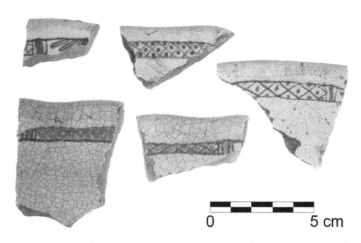

Plate 4. French faïence, Rouen blue-on-white platter shards. Fort de Chartres III, Randolph County, Illinois. Courtesy of the Illinois State Archaeological Survey, University of Illinois.

Plates 5 and 6. Woman's bed gown and petticoat (and detail). Textile ca. 1740–50; reconstructed, 1770s. France or England. Linen warp and cotton weft plain weave (fustian) with wool supplementary weft patterning (*siamoise*) and linen plain weave lining. Mrs. Alice F. Schott Bequest, Acc. # M.67.8.74a–b. Los Angeles County Museum of Art. Digital Image © 2011 Museum Associates/LACMA/Art Resource.

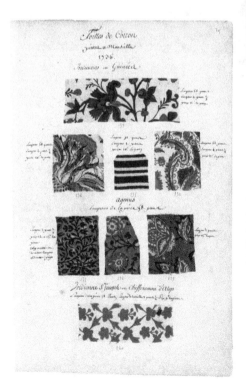

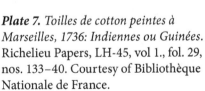

Plate 7. *Toilles de cotton peintes à Marseilles, 1736: Indiennes ou Guinées.* Richelieu Papers, LH-45, vol 1., fol. 29, nos. 133–40. Courtesy of Bibliothèque Nationale de France.

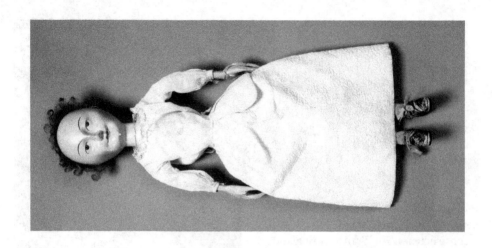

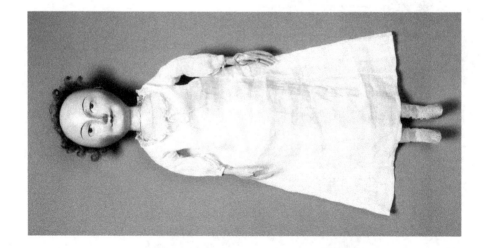

Plates 8-13. Lady Clapham doll (and details). 1690-1700. Victoria and Albert Museum, Acc. # T.846-1974. Photo © Victoria and Albert Museum, London.

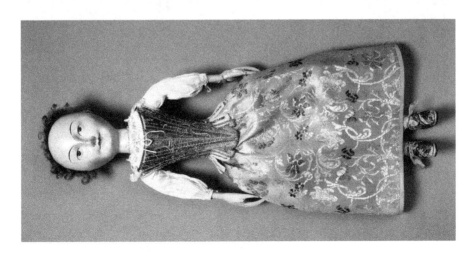

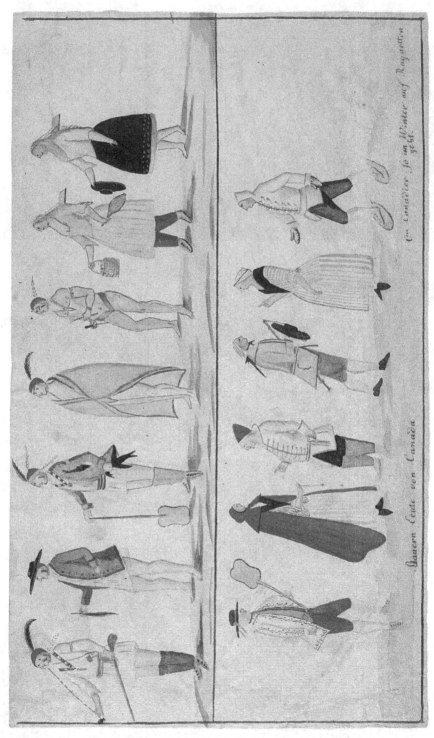

Plate 14. Anonymous, *Genre Study of Habitants and Indians*, ca. 1780. Courtesy of the Royal Ontario Museum.

Plate 15. Sempronius Stretton, *A Canadian Man & Woman in Their Winter Dress, Quebec, Canada November 21, 1805*. From Sempronius Stretton, *Sketchbook*, fol. 19. Watercolor and pen. Courtesy of the National Archives of Canada.

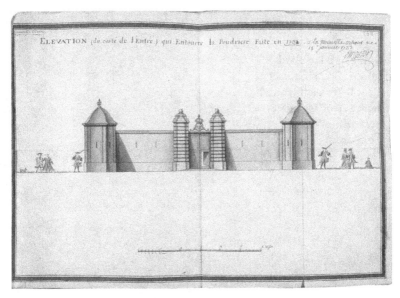

Plate 16. Ignace Francois Broutin, *Elevation (du coste de l'entrée) qui entourre la Poudriere*, New Orleans, 1733, FR.ANOM Aix-en-Provence C13A, vol. 43, fol. 192. Photo © Archives Nationales d'Outre-Mer, France.

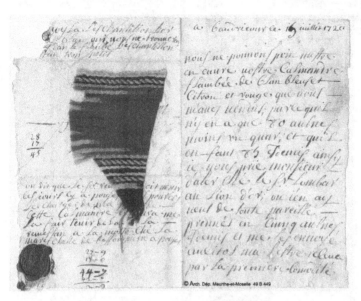

Plate 17. Calimanco (*calemande*) textile sample, 1720. Archives Départementales de Meurthe-et-Moselle, series 49B. Courtesy of the Archives Départementales de Meurthe-et-Moselle, France.

Plate 18. Quilted and padded bodice or jumps (French, *corset*), yellow silk, ca. 1745. Victoria and Albert Museum Acc. T.87-1978. Photo © Victoria and Albert Museum, London.

Plate 19. J. B. François Dumont de Montigny, *Sauvage ... Sauvagesse.* Ms 3459, 160. Bibliothèque de l'Arsenal, Paris. Courtesy of Bibliothèque Nationale de France.

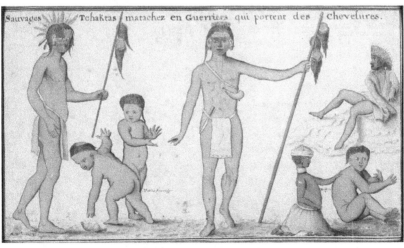

Plate 20. Alexandre de Batz, *Sauvages Tchaktas matachez en Guerriers qui portent des chevelures.* Courtesy of the Peabody Museum of Archaeology and Ethnology, Harvard University.

Plate 21. Philip Georg Friedrich von Reck, *Indian King and Queen of Uchi, Senhaitschi.* 1734. NKS 565. Courtesy of the Royal Library, Copenhagen.

Plate 22. Alexandre de Batz, *Sauvage en habit d'hyver.* Courtesy of the Peabody Museum of Archaeology and Ethnology, Harvard University.

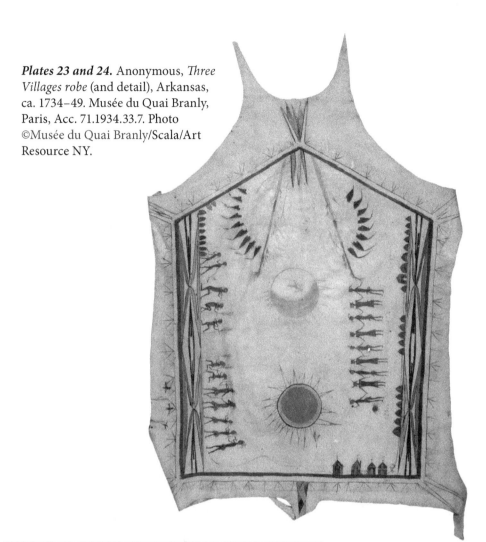

Plates 23 and 24. Anonymous, *Three Villages robe* (and detail), Arkansas, ca. 1734–49. Musée du Quai Branly, Paris, Acc. 71.1934.33.7. Photo ©Musée du Quai Branly/Scala/Art Resource NY.

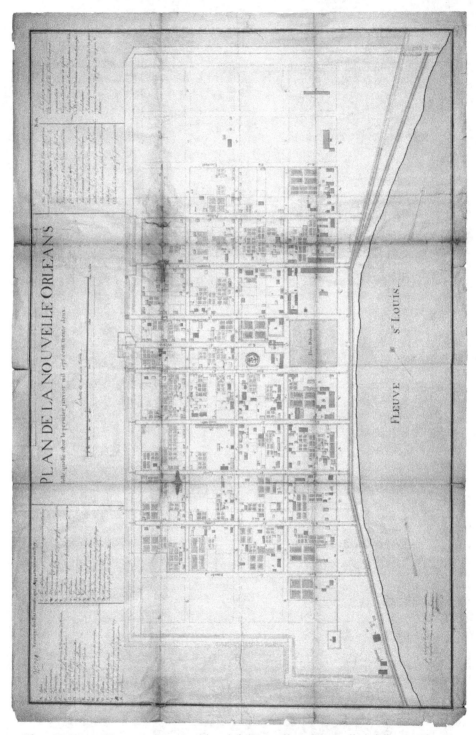

Plate 25. Ignace François Broutin, *Plan de la Nouvelle Orleans telle qu'elle estoit le premier janvier 1732*. New Orleans, 1 January 1732. FR.ANOM Aix-en-Provence 4DFC 90A. Photo © Archives Nationales d'Outre-mer, France.

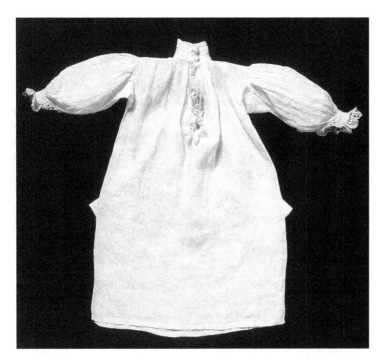

Plate 26. Man's shirt, from Lord Clapham doll, 1690-1700. Linen with bobbin lace. Victoria and Albert Museum, Acc. T.847A-1974. Photo © Victoria and Albert Museum, London.

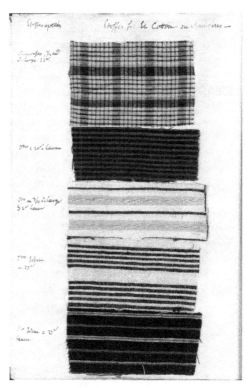

Plate 27. Samples of *siamoises*, 1743. Maurepas Papers, Joseph Downs Collection of Manuscripts and Printed Ephemera, Winterthur Museum Library. Courtesy of the Winterthur Museum, Delaware.

Plates 28 and 29. Michel Le Bouteux, *Veüe du camp de la concession de Monseigneur Law au Nouveau Biloxy, 1720* (and detail). VAULT Ayer MS map 30. Courtesy of the Newberry Library, Chicago.

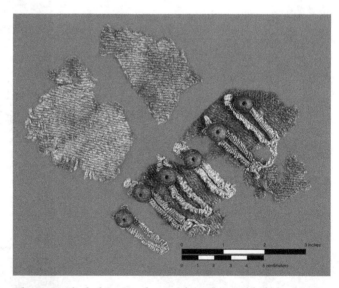

Plate 30. Cloth, buttons, button loops, possibly belonging to La Salle, from shipwreck of *La Belle*, 1686. Courtesy of the Texas Historical Commission.

Plate 31. Masquerade mask from Lady Clapham doll, 1690–1700. Cardboard with silk, vellum, thread, and beads. Victoria and Albert Museum, T.846T-1974. Photo © Victoria and Albert Museum, London.

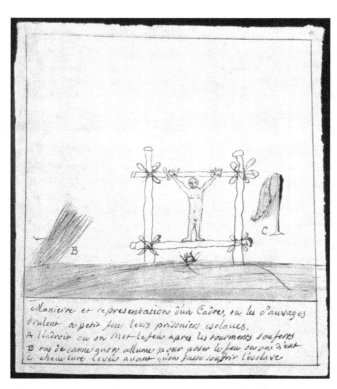

Plate 32. Dumont de Montigny, *Manierre et representation d'un cadre, ou les sauvages brulent a petit feu leurs prisoniers.* VAULT oversize MS 257 drawing no. 5. Courtesy of the Newberry Library, Chicago.

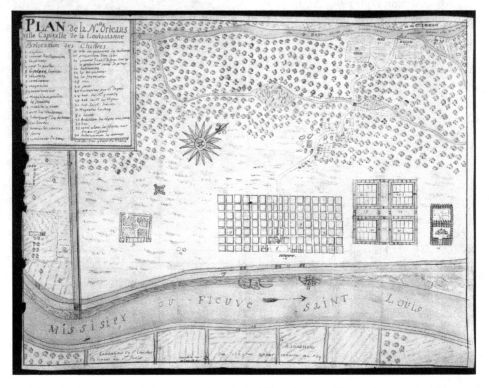

Plate 33. Dumont de Montigny, *Plan de la Nlle Orleans ville capitalle de la Lousianne*. VAULT oversize Ayer MS 257 map no. 7. Courtesy of the Newberry Library, Chicago.

PART II

Frenchified Indians
and Wild Frenchmen
in New Orleans

I N FEBRUARY 1762 in the Illinois Country, one of Marie Rouensa's grand-daughters, Elisabeth de Celle Duclos, signed a contract to marry a Swedish nobleman. Her father, who was also an officer, was present, as was her brother, who served as a gentleman cadet in the troops of the marine.[1] The previous year, in New Orleans, another ritual had taken place, centered on a burial this time, as the Ursuline nuns made note of the passing of one of their own, "our very dear sister Marie Turpin known as Sister St. Marthe."[2] Thirty-two at her death from tuberculosis, and a nun for almost twelve years, Sister Ste. Marthe had been identified by the New Orleans Ursulines as the first "creole" postulant in the colony. While she was not the first woman born in North America (French or Indian) to take vows in New France, she was the first North American-born nun to enter a convent in territory forming part of the present-day United States.[3] But Sister Ste. Marthe's significance goes beyond these firsts. For she was not simply "creole," the term used to designate someone of European (or African) descent born in the colony. She was not related to Marie Rouensa, but like Elisabeth de Celle Duclos and her brother, Marie Turpin hailed from the Illinois Country. Also like them, she was part Indian, and the Ursulines conferred on her a particular status, with its corresponding nun's habit, one that underscored how French-Indians who traveled to Lower Louisiana were perceived in that part of the colony.

The Province of Louisiana was divided by a North-South, Upper-Lower Louisiana axis anchored by the Mississippi River. Marie Turpin physically traversed this line in 1748 as she traveled from the Illinois Country to New Orleans on her quest to be consecrated as a nun. In so doing she moved between two spaces with differing dominant interpretations of ethnicity generally and of her mixed French-Indian Catholic identity in particular. If Marie Turpin's particular goal distinguished her from others who moved from the Illinois Country to Lower Louisiana, the trip itself was not exceptional, for convoys and individual vessels continually plied the Mississippi River (and its tributaries), carting goods and foodstuffs across Louisiana's vast territory. Like Marie Turpin, the passengers who traveled on these vessels also had to negotiate the physical and psychological gulf between Upper and Lower Louisiana, between urban and wild areas, and all the spaces in between. They did so by deploying dress to facilitate the shift from one environment to another, as we will see with discussions of another gentleman cadet, Antoine Marigny de Mandeville, and of the French-Indian voyageur Jean Saguingouara.

In foregrounding dress in these case studies, cultural cross-dressing in particular springs to mind. Cultural cross-dressing has become a fashionable lens through which to understand the hybridization of cultures. But two key problems have characterized much of this scholarship. First, there often lacks a systematic distinction between temporary acts of cultural cross-dressing and the progressive and permanent transformations that develop over time. Second, in the emphasis in this literature on the cultural significance of the process, the actual articles of dress have been relegated to the merely incidental, to serve as visual manifestations of larger ideas. I propose instead that a methodical material culture analysis of details of dress and the context in which it is worn can in fact substantively inform questions about cultural significance and the construction of identity. My reading of cultural cross-dressing in the Louisiana borderlands proposes that even in the hinterlands appearance was not free of considerations of status and rank. Indeed, French-Indian relations relied on dress to denote status and power structures to colonial *and* indigenous audiences (as seen in the records of gift giving and trade, for example). For the French colonial elite, upholding the social and, indeed, the moral order was especially crucial to their claim on North America and the implantation there of a "French" society, even as their experiences were subsumed to the requirements of that environment.

Part I established the significance of material culture, Indian conversion, and Frenchification in exploring French anxieties about intermarriage. The first two chapters in Part II elucidate how those of French-Indian descent negotiated the difference between conceptions of difference in Upper and Lower Louisiana. The third reveals that in Lower Louisiana we can detect evidence of colonists' lingering beliefs in identity as both mutable and also dependent on climate and environment. Throughout, I will emphasize the importance of space in contextualizing dress.

Just as clothing was constituted by actual, tangible materials, so too was space a physical reality before becoming a cultural construct. Two images produced in the 1730s serve to express the ideological chasm between New Orleans and the hinterlands. In the "Three Villages" buffalo robe from circa 1734–49 (see Plates 23 and 24), the spatial ordering is a relational one between three Quapaw villages (inscribed by the artist or in another hand) and the French fort (conclusively identified by its church and the number of its chimneys), and punctuated by visual cues to warfare (a battle) and ritual (the sun and moon, calumets, and unisex scalp dance).[4] The birds around the borders of the central medallion also suggest a clan or band affiliation, reinforcing the degree to which this map was preoccupied with underscoring and documenting relationships among Quapaw villages, and between the Quapaw and the French.[5] In the second image (see Plate 25), Ignace de Broutin's idealized drawing of New Orleans in 1732, the engineer has emphasized linearity and rigid structure. No reference to Indians is made in this drawing. Rather, it underlines the density and permanency of a colonial population whose relationship to each other was based on the static arrangement of their property and not their interactions with each other.

Seen together, these alternative renderings of space are suggestive of how we might also examine Frenchmen's movement between the center and peripheries, or "frontiers" of the colony. As Daniel H. Usner, Jr., has suggested, the frontier should not be read as "a boundary . . . across which more 'advanced' societies penetrated 'primitive' ones."[6] Rather, we should understand the concept as a site of encounter, a geographical borderland that functioned both as a zone of contact between ideas and as a space marked by ambiguity. At the same time, these borderlands were also *actual* geographical spaces that literally and physically mediated cultural interactions for colonists dwarfed by the scale of the territory and riddled by anxieties about the risks posed to Frenchness by their presence in a wild environment and in the midst of Frenchified Indians.

"The First Creole from This Colony That We Have Received": Sister Ste. Marthe and the Limits of Frenchification

In 1751, the Ursuline nuns of New Orleans initiated a new member into their fold. After cutting off her hair, they stripped the girl of her clothing. Then they helped her to don the order's black habit, guimpe and bandeau of white linen, cincture of black leather, and novice's white veil. The components of her dress (habit, guimpe, bandeau, cincture, and veil) served to crystallize the transformation of Marie Turpin, born in the Illinois Country to a French father and an Illinois convert mother, into Sister Ste. Marthe. But the cut and construction of her habit and her veil and even the number of knots on her cincture marked her out as a converse (lay or domestic) nun. Marie Turpin had not been accorded the spiritual rank of a full choir nun, raising questions about the worth of Frenchification in Lower Louisiana.

The religious, legal, and material dimensions of "Frenchification" discussed in the previous chapters coalesced in Marie Turpin's experiences as a nun. We can now imagine afresh the French (not Indian-style) dress in which she had presented herself to the Ursulines. And we can trace the culmination of the attraction that other female Indian converts to Catholicism had felt toward aspects of Catholic spirituality and French material culture. In the 1680s, the Mohawk convert Catherine Tekakwitha had felt a calling to be consecrated a nun. In the Illinois Country in the 1690s, Marie Rouensa, Turpin's Illinois precursor, had wished to remain celibate as a result of her new religious beliefs, and she would not be alone in expressing this desire.[1] Conversion had been a key tenet of Frenchification policies, and prominent converts were heralded as success stories. Marie Turpin's story also fits the model of assimilation proposed by the Crown in seventeenth-century New France, one that would have granted her recognition as a "natural Frenchwoman."[2] And indeed the nuns had described her not as a "sauvagesse" but as their first "creole" postulant, using the term for the French born in the colony.[3] But they did qualify her mother as "sauvage" (not as French as the census records of the Illinois Country had marked her). In other ways too, Turpin's experience in New Orleans signaled the limits, not the culmination, of conversion and Frenchification policies. The offspring born in the Illinois Country from a French-Indian intermarriage, she did not remain there but moved from one to the other periphery of the colony, thereby putting into sharp relief the contrasting views of Frenchification held by colonists in mid-eighteenth-century Upper and Lower Louisiana.

Turpin was accepted into the Ursuline order in the inferior rank of converse nun. Her religious name would be St. Martha, "after the New Testament woman who tended to the kitchen while her sister, Mary, sat in conversation with Jesus," as Emily Clark has phrased this distinction in spiritual status.[4] The primary prerequisites for being accepted as a *choir* nun were access to a dowry and literacy, with social status contributing a further, if more nebulous condition. My research suggests that Turpin had lacked access to neither of these and that her rank as a converse rather than a choir nun reflected the way her French-Indian heritage was understood outside the Illinois Country. The experience of this daughter born to an Illinois Indian wife and her French Canadian husband encapsulated the conflict between competing models of difference and the ways this tension might be managed not in the Illinois Country, with its particular history of conversion, intermarriage, and Frenchification, but in mid-eighteenth-century New Orleans, seat of the colonial government of Louisiana. One model still allowed for the possibility of Frenchification and provided legal, religious, and economic support to children born of French-Indian marriages. The other, increasingly dominant model was premised on the rigidity and fixedness of racial categories and imposed limitations on those considered inferior. Marie Turpin's trajectory embodied this tension, and she offers us the opportunity to better understand how colonists in New Orleans rationalized the question of ethnic difference when faced with her embodiment of Frenchifcation. One way the Ursuline nuns responded to Marie Turpin's calling as a bride of Christ was to control access to the visual and material markers of the woman religious's spiritual status: her black and white habit.

Marie Turpin

Born and brought up in Kaskaskia in the Illinois Country, Marie Turpin made her way downriver to New Orleans in 1747. By this date, her father, Louis Turpin, had established himself as one of the wealthiest inhabitants and merchants in the Illinois Country. There, near the church, he had built the largest house in the village, a stone house laid out on three floors, with a shingled roof and stone chimneys flanked by a second-floor gallery on two facades.[5] Marie's mother had died by 1747, but not before leaving her mark on the family home. She had actively and formally participated in the grad-ual transformation of this house over the years, signing with her husband for labor contracts to have eleven *toises* of stone carted to the site (in 1728) and to have the second floor finished (in 1730).[6] Marie's mother, Dorothée Mechip8e8a, was Illinois, identified in a 1720 entry in the parish registers as "daughter of the Grand Rieur" ("Great Laugher"), signaling a previous his-tory of interactions with the French.[7] The Ursulines' register noted that Marie Turpin's Illinois mother was known for her "exemplary worthiness and piety," in an echo of the Illinois women converts whose particular piety had been the subject of many a missionary's account.[8]

She had married Turpin in 1724 after being widowed by another French-man, Charles Danis, with whom she had had two daughters and one son. These children remained in colonial society, entering into marriages with French men and women, with some of them moving to New Orleans, namely her daughter Marie Anne Danis, who had married into the promi-nent Chauvin family in Louisiana. Having been widowed, Marie Anne Danis died virtually destitute while awaiting her substantial inheritance from her mother. Only one of the grandchildren of Dorothée Mechip8e8a is known to have married a part-Indian: her grandson married a girl whose maternal grandmother was Indian, though she too was identified legally as a French-woman and remained integrated within French colonial society.

In 1724, the Widow Danis married Louis Turpin. He had come to the Il-linois Country from Detroit with two brothers and a sister and was himself the widower of a Frenchwoman. Literate, he had swiftly risen to prominence in the Illinois Country as the royal storekeeper (a Crown appointment) and a militia lieutenant, becoming one of the most important land and slave own-ers in Upper Louisiana. He was also the interpreter when Marie Rouensa made her will, underscoring his mediating role in the community and his fluency in the Kaskaskia language.[9] Following Dorothée's death, he married for the third time, to one of her granddaughters from her first marriage.[10] He died shortly after this third marriage, in 1751, the year Marie Turpin took her final vows.

The 1724 marriage contract between Marie Turpin's parents had been witnessed by the five most prominent officers and officials in the Illinois Country. The couple had at least seven daughters together, but Marie's baptismal record does not survive. Few other records survive of her existence in the Illinois Country, but one was a document in which de la Loere Flaucourt, the provincial judge, had given to Marie Turpin and her two siblings a heifer each as dowry, to be held in common until they had married.[11] The registers kept by the Ursuline nuns in New Orleans flesh out the record, specifying for instance that Marie was the oldest child born to her parents (actually the oldest surviving child). Credibility is afforded the Ursulines' account by virtue of other accuracies in her life account: the fact that Marie's father was royal storekeeper—a prestigious office in the limited bureaucracy of the Illinois Country—and that he was the second (French) husband of Marie's mother, for example.[12] The Ursuline registers (notwithstanding the linguistic and religious conventions of this genre of document) also provide more precise and evocative details of Marie's trajectory toward taking vows and of how she performed her duties as a converse nun.

According to the Ursulines' register for the reception of postulants, Marie had been called to her profession "in a most admirable fashion, being born in the Illinois post at 500 leagues from here and having never seen any [women] Religious." Her mother and father had raised her in the greatest piety, "especially her dear mother, who was of exemplary merit and piety and who was filled with religion." Marie's vocation had flourished following her mother's death in 1747, and been cultivated by a Jesuit missionary in the Illinois Country, eventually leading to her decision to take her vows. Her father had consented only with difficulty to her coming to New Orleans to join the Ursulines because he "loved her so tenderly for the virtues he saw in her."[13]

The register noted that her father had also relied on Marie for running his household; indeed, within a short time after her departure, he had married again. As noted above, his third wife, Hélène Hebert, was the granddaughter of his second wife Dorothée Mechip8e8a, from her first marriage to Charles Danis.[14] The Ursulines recorded that it had apparently taken all her father's religious resolve to reconcile himself to his sacrifice in letting his daughter go. Beyond his reluctance to have his daughter leave him permanently for a new and cloistered life in New Orleans, Louis Turpin was also familiar with the conditions and dangers of the weeks-long convoy that took passengers down the Mississippi to New Orleans. Accordingly, for the trip downriver, which he knew well, he entrusted his daughter to the care of a virtuous and pious female acquaintance. Marie edified this woman with her piety, and even the soldiers who accompanied the convoy made it known to the cloistered Ursulines that they had brought down "a sainted girl who kept her eyes downcast throughout the trip and never said an unnecessary word, being always at prayer."[15]

On arrival in New Orleans in 1748, and until the close of the following year, when she took her final vows, Marie underwent six different stages of spiritual advancement to reach her goal. Each phase was marked by a distinct costume, a sign of the importance of appearance to religious communities. She spent fourteen months as a fee-paying boarder at the convent; this was in order to ascertain her calling and the register did not specify if it was done at the request of the Ursulines or of her father (given his initial reluctance to let her go). Once this test period was successfully completed, Marie formally requested acceptance into the novitiate. Her request was granted, though the register specified at this point that the preparation for her status as a novice was premised on her entry into the convent as a converse, not a choir nun.

Four months later the community of Ursulines reassembled and for the first time discussed her case. The community gave their consent for her to take the habit of a converse nun at the end of a six-month trial period. On December 7, 1749, six months after entering the novitiate, the mother superior once again assembled the chapter and, after taking a voice tally, recorded that "my sister Marie Turpin daughter of Mr. Louis Turpin and Mrs Dorotée Turpin *sauvagesse*, legitimately married, inhabitant of the Illinois, was received with all the voices [of the women religious of the order] to receive the habit, in her quality as converse sister." Twenty months later, in November 1751, the chapter was reassembled. This time only a majority of voices supported her taking her final vows.[16] The lack of unanimity seems relevant in her case but was not uncommon and not, therefore, in itself significant.[17] Two months afterward, in January 1752, Jesuit Father Beaudoin made his own entry (in his role as overseer of the Ursulines in New Orleans). After being brought from the convent to the church, Marie was formally questioned; her answers satisfying him as to the "goodness of her vocation," Father Beaudoin granted his consent. The ritual was concluded when she was returned to the cloister and physically handed over to the mother superior.

Marie Turpin had completed her metamorphosis into converse Sister Ste. Marthe. Sister Ste. Marthe's sartorial transformation signaled the death of her secular identity and her rebirth as a woman religious, as emphasized by the funeral pall draped over her body when she professed her vows for the first time as a nun.[18] Perhaps the half-Illinois Marie Turpin also recognized in these practices a parallel with the indigenous rituals of stripping and redressing captives whose own lives were spared so that they could cover the dead, as discussed in Chapter 2.

The entry pertaining to Marie Turpin in another register, that of the *Lettres circulaires*, repeated many of the same details, but also provided additional particulars about her spiritual path in the Illinois Country. Following her mother's death and her ensuing trajectory toward becoming a nun, her *lettre circulaire* noted, Marie had given herself "in a very special manner to assiduous prayer, to the sacraments, to fasting and to mortification." The register credited the Jesuit priest who had taken charge of her religious instruction in the Illinois Country with initiating her into these spiritual practices, and noted that he had done so with much zeal. Though he was unnamed in the register, Jesuit Father Antoine-Robert Le Boullenger, who was in the Illinois from 1719 to 1744, where he served as curate at Kaskaskia, was the one most likely to have contributed to her religious instruction since birth. Father Le Boullenger was deeply involved with developing French-Illinois relations to such a degree that around 1720, as noted earlier, he had authored a French-[Kaskaskia] Illinois dictionary.[19] He was also deeply implicated in the question of intermarriage, and it was in fact he who had initiated the 1728 appeal to the Crown to rule on the legitimacy of inheritance rights pertaining to childless Indian wives of Frenchmen in the Illinois Country. On the matter of the rights of Indian wives who had children with their husbands, Le Boullenger was unequivocal. He had argued that the women concerned ought to benefit from the same advantages as their legitimate spouses, "whose status and condition they follow, living under the same laws to which they are also subject, this serves as their naturalization."[20] This belief must surely have inflected his dealings with Marie Turpin's mother—she of the "exemplary worthiness and piety"—and with the girl herself as he directed her religious leanings.

Father Le Boullenger's particular role in instructing Marie Turpin about "all the practices of the spiritual life" takes on added resonance when we consider that his own sister was a nun in the New Orleans Ursuline convent. This sibling, Marie-Anne, Sister Ste. Angelique, was in fact a founding member of the New Orleans Ursulines. In 1728, the same year that his missive about intermarriage had wended its way to France, Le Boullenger had written to his sister to request her help with forming an establishment in the Illinois Country. The purpose for such an establishment was missionary, "to teach Christianity to these poor Illinois sauvages" (which of course excluded those Indian converts married to Frenchmen and living in colonial villages).[21] His plan for a convent in the Illinois Country was likely modeled on the Quebec and New Orleans convents, both of which had been originally formed with the intention of missionizing Indian girls. Le Boullenger's proposal for an establishment in the Illinois Country was never put in motion, so Marie Turpin, living in the Illinois Country, would have had no experiential knowledge of nuns. But no doubt Father Le Boullenger had described at length his ties to the Ursulines and his sister's role there. Sister Ste. Angelique was still alive (and serving as the secretary) when Marie Turpin entered the walls of the New Orleans convent, and we should not discount the relevance for Turpin of this link back to her religious instructor in the Illinois Country. Indeed, not only could Father Le Boullenger claim a deep and long-standing attachment to that establishment; his direct involvement in the girl's spiritual formation suggests that he played a greater role in leading Marie Turpin to the convent than was acknowledged in the convent's records.

Another direct link between the New Orleans Ursulines and Illinois converts had been forged in 1730 during the visit of a group of Illinois to New Orleans in July of that year (these were Illinois converts from Indian villages, not the wives and daughters of Frenchmen). Writing from New Orleans, Father Mathurin Le Petit, the Jesuit superior of Louisiana explained:

> The Illinois had no other residence [in New Orleans] but with us, during the three weeks they remained in this city. They charmed us by their piety, and by their edifying life. Every evening they recited the rosary in alternate choirs, and every morning they heard me say Mass; during which, particularly on Sundays and Feast-days, they chanted the different prayers of the Church suitable to the Offices of the day. At the end of the Mass, they never fail to chant with their whole heart the prayer for the King. The Nuns chanted the first Latin couplet in the ordinary tone of the Gregorian chant, and the Illinois continued the other couplets in their language in the same tone.[22]

An earlier encounter between that group and the colonist Dumont de Montigny fleshed out the details of the visit, which was headed by an Illinois chief coming to present the calumet to the governor, accompanied by a small group of men, women, and children. The chief "spoke French passably well," Dumont had noted, and "all who accompanied him were Christian." But only the women (or three of them at least) took communion, speaking to their attainment of a higher level of instruction in the Catholic faith.[23]

That these Illinois visitors had been housed by missionaries while in New Orleans spoke of the narrow ties that bound Illinois converts to the Jesuits. That Ursuline nuns and the Illinois visitors had interacted spiritually through chant suggests that these two communities began to forge ties at this time. When Marie Turpin entered the convent, there were three choir nuns still living from the 1730 visit of Illinois Indians; one was Father Le Boullenger's sister. These were ties that the living and institutional memory of the Ursuline convent would surely have sustained, just as the Illinois converts surely did. If this much could be expected of Illinois Indian converts, with their convincing gendered expression of Catholic rituals and prayers, one wonders how much more receptive the nuns were to the spiritual potential of Marie Turpin, a half-French, half-Illinois girl, who spoke French and who was already familiar with the sacraments. Raised within a French colonial village in an impressive French-built stone house with partitioned rooms, wooden floors, and French colonial furnishings, and familiar with French ways of dressing, here was a girl who would have been at ease among the French colonial trappings of the New Orleans Ursuline convent and known how to act as French within its walls.

As was noted in the *lettre circulaire*, upon her arrival in New Orleans, Marie Turpin was already conversant with the fasting and mortification rituals that the nuns themselves carried out as a key component of their penitential practices. Mortification and other practices aimed at humility had a central role in the Ursuline order as in other Catholic religious orders, including the Jesuits, and the letter credited her Illinois Country priest with initiating her into these practices.[24] Yet, ascetic practices such as fasting and mortification also paralleled Algonquin and Iroquois spiritual practices as discussed in Chapter 2 and as evoked, for example, in the rituals practiced by Marie Rouensa, Catherine Tekakwitha, and their followers.[25] In this respect, Marie Turpin's experience was an extension of that of the numerous native women, like Rouensa (and perhaps like her Kaskaskia mother), who had preceded her in their *unfulfilled* calling to take vows of chastity.

It is not known how Marie Turpin's father had reacted to her penitential practices, and whether this interpreter and spouse of Illinois women had recognized the syncretic character of these rituals. But he had initially opposed his daughter's quest to become a nun, and in the Illinois Country he was not alone in his opposition. Indeed, according to the registers, when Marie had announced that she felt a calling to take her vows, she was met with cynicism about the likelihood that the Ursulines would allow her to join their ranks as an equal: "Those who would prevent her from entering the convent told her, that she would be our servant only. Well, she responded, that is what I would wish for, to serve the brides of Jesus Christ."[26]

The statement is ambiguous: did Marie Therese de St. Jacques, the mother superior who authored Turpin's 1761 postmortem *lettre circulaire*, mean to say, as seems most likely, that the Illinois inhabitants foresaw Marie Turpin being treated no better than a domestic servant and not as a nun? This statement, attributed to unnamed persons in the Illinois Country, is important for another reason. In the absence of direct evidence about their self-perception, this anecdote provides a rare glimpse into the ways that those touched by (legitimate, sanctified) intermarriage and *métissage* felt themselves snubbed in Lower Louisiana.

The mother superior's anecdote about Illinois naysayers was intended to exemplify Marie's humility. But she seemed oblivious to the fact that their worries were prescient, since the Ursulines did restrict Marie Turpin to the rank of a domestic nun. For Marie Turpin was not accepted into the ranks of full-fledged women religious; instead, she took her vows as a converse nun, or "servant of the brides of Christ," to quote Elizabeth Rapley.[27] While the entries pertaining to Marie Turpin were registered in the "Book of Entries of the *Choir* Sisters," she was not allowed to reach this status.[28] Rather, as repeated with each mention of her name in the two registers, Marie Turpin was to take her vows only as a *converse* nun. In order to understand this reiteration of her status as converse for a girl of mixed French-Indian heritage, we need to first consider the spiritual attributes of the Ursuline order.

Sister Ste. Marthe

The Ursulines were a cloistered order marked by an educational apostolate.[29] Founded in Brescia in 1532 by Angela Merici, the Ursuline order spread to France in the 1590s, swiftly reaching around the country in a wave of Counter-Reformation fervor. In France, the Ursuline congregations promoted the education of girls as a means to missionize within France by mobilizing women as transmitters of the faith. When faced in 1612 with the imposition of a strict cloister that might have halted their educational apostolate, the Ursulines successfully petitioned for the right to educate within the cloister. Authorities in Louisiana had not initially planned on sending for Ursuline nuns; their need for women religious had been linked to health issues, and officials had originally sought *hospitalier* nuns (a nursing order) to take over the hospital and take charge of the colony's moral and social problems. None expressed any interest in Louisiana, so in lieu of nursing nuns, the Ursulines were approached and accepted the mission. In 1727, twelve women religious affiliated with the Rouen convent made their way to New Orleans; their origins in the Rouen convent meant that the New Orleans Ursulines were also guided by the Rule of the (Ursuline) Congregation of Paris. In the colony, they administered the hospital of the Company of the Indies, took in boarders as well as orphans, taught day pupils, catechized enslaved Indians and Africans, developed a plantation, and successfully immersed themselves in other business activities. They also were instrumental in founding a lay-women's confraternity that was to have a lasting impact on African American Catholicism in New Orleans.[30]

At the time Marie Turpin took her vows, the Ursuline order formally distinguished three categories of nuns: choir nuns, converse (also known as lay or domestic) nuns, and *soeurs tourières*—mature single or widowed women who served as intermediaries between the cloistered sisters and the outside world. To be a converse in an Ursuline convent in the eighteenth century was to have a distinct status. Both choir and converse nuns took the three ordinary vows of poverty, chastity, and obedience. But only choir sisters took the fourth vow of education, a fundamental distinction among the members of this teaching order. And while choir sisters might be called on to undertake household tasks (and might be exalted for doing so), they were primarily charged with singing the praises of God and educating their charges. In contrast, converse sisters were explicitly associated with domestic work and denied the right to sing in the choir and educate; as early as 1618, for example, the papal bull establishing the Ursuline congregation of Bordeaux enunciated that converse nuns, after having taken their vows, "will only be occupied with housework."[31]

Dress, which was a fundamental marker of the identity of men and women religious, made manifest the distinctions between the different ranks of nuns. Though each Ursuline congregation upheld somewhat different garb for their women religious, illustrations of converse nuns consistently showed a clear emphasis on their visual and material differentiation from choir nuns (Figure 11). In order to strictly enforce the adhesion to these regulations, the Ursuline order used fully attired dolls that represented the dress of each order of nun within a congregation. In this, the dolls seem to parallel the way that fashion houses and merchants shipped fully dressed dolls to the provinces and the colonies as a means of diffusing the latest styles. But where fashion dolls communicated stylistic change, for the Ursulines, the *poupée du costume* represented an attempt at replicating consistency in dress, with the rule requiring that a doll be taken along with the founders of each new convent, to help with the initiation of new novices, but also to serve as a mnemonic object.[32]

One such doll, purported to date from the eighteenth century, survives in the Ursuline convent in Quebec.[33] The 1647 Constitution of this Ursuline convent, composed in Quebec, articulated the exact purpose of the *poupée du costume*: "there will be dressed a doll, that will serve as proof and model to posterity, of the form and construction of the habit of this Congregation, and to this purpose shall be carefully kept in a place which shall have multiple and different keys."[34]

As underlined here, and reiterated in the 1647 Constitution's chapter on dress, the instructions pertaining to clothing were at once prescriptive and highly precise in terms of details of textile weave, cut, and construction, down to the last tuck and pleat. As such, and as seen in the passage about the doll, a model (or "proof") would be required for the faithful and authentic replication of this attire.[35] But the passage is just as revealing about the significance of the doll to the convent's mission and, therefore, about the role of dress in forging (and not simply signaling) the nuns' very identity as women religious.

For this "doll of the costume" was kept locked in one of only two chests in each convent that had multiple locks. The chest holding the doll was locked with two different keys kept separately by the mother superior and the *zélatrice* (the nun charged with promoting religious zeal). The value of the *poupée du costume* to the nuns was only exceeded by the chest that contained all the convent's essential documents pertaining to spirituality and business (letters patent, money, property titles, and Constitution), and for which there were three separate keys kept by three different nuns. The doll—and its meticulous reproduction in miniature of the religious habit—served as a kind of relic, a material culture equivalent of the written constitution of each convent.[36]

Converse sisters were visually demarcated from choir sisters by a number

of precise variations that signaled spiritual and material differences in their
identity (see Figure 11, even though this engraving has minimized some of
the distinctive features of the Ursuline converse's habit). First, some of their
apparel might consist of items discarded by their fellow choir sisters. This
evokes master-servant conventions that also stipulated the redistribution of
used clothing from employers to employees.[37] Converse nuns' shorter veils,
gowns, and coats (*manteaux d'Eglise*), their tighter sleeves with split cuffs
(meaning they could be conveniently rolled back), were functional features
that denoted their suitability to menial work. Variations in the colors of their
garments visually proclaimed their lesser spiritual status as compared to
choir nuns; so did the fact that their cinctures had only three knots instead of
the four that represented the choir sisters' fourth vow.[38] This distinctiveness
in converse nuns' uniform signaled another permanent distinction. As a further condition of being a converse nun (and excluded therefore from teaching), Marie Turpin could not vote in the community chapter and she could
never have acceded to the rank of mother superior.[39] There were spiritual
limits to her potential for advancement and these restrictions were imposed
on her body by being inscribed on her garb.

Marie Turpin was not the only converse nun when she entered the New
Orleans convent, but the others had been born in France.[40] The letters patent granted to the New Orleans Ursulines by the Company of the Indies
had prohibited creoles from taking vows. This was a direct result of a demographic imbalance between men and women, which resulted in the promotion of marriage and procreation for women of European descent born
in the colony.[41] With her acceptance into the order, Marie Turpin overrode
that prohibition to become "The first Creole from this colony that we have
received."[42] Comparison with the experiences of those creole converse and
choir nuns suggests that in spite of the Ursulines' decision to apply the term
"creole" to Marie Turpin, this did not level the playing field for her. The nuns
would not lose sight of her mixed identity, and her maternal Indian ancestry
would trump the advantages conferred to her by her (European-descended)
father's status.[43]

Within a few years of her acceptance, other creole girls began to take
vows. Two did so as converse nuns. Both were of minor birth, likely lacking
the access to a dowry that was a precondition of acceptance as a choir nun. As
for those who entered as choir nuns, they came from socially and economically prominent Louisiana families not much different in wealth and status to
that of Marie as the daughter of Louis Turpin.[44] There is no trace of a dowry

T. IV. p. 166.

Soeur Converse Ursuline,
de la Congrégation de Paris.

59.

Figure 11. *Soeur converse Ursuline de la Congrégation de Paris*. From Pierre Hélyot, *Histoire des ordres monastiques …*, IV (Paris: Nicolas Gosselin, 1715), 166. Courtesy of the Wellcome Library, London.

for Marie Turpin in the records of the New Orleans Ursuline convent, but her family's wealth suggests that this would not have been a problem, since her personal assets can be evaluated at between two and three thousand livres.

By the time she left the Illinois Country, Marie Turpin would have been entitled to her inheritance from her mother's estate, since, according to French customary law, she would have received an amount equal to that of her siblings.[45] After distribution to her widower, the assets left from Dorothée Mechip8e8a's estate for her children came to 7,580 livres, to be shared among Marie and her four surviving siblings and half siblings. The children from her mother's second marriage community, including Marie, were each left 1,517 livres plus twelve and a half arpents of land (the siblings from the first community received a slightly lower but still impressive 1,409 livres each).[46] Given that Marie was still a minor when her mother died, her inheritance was held for her by her father, and the law would have granted him control over these funds until her majority at age twenty-five or on marriage. As she began the journey to become a nun, she would have done so in the knowledge that she held legal title to an important sum to contribute to her dowry. In addition, she would have had the value of the heifer (and its progeny) that de la Loere Flaucourt in 1737 had given her to be used as part of her dowry.[47]

As for her inheritance from her father, the records are lost. Since he died in 1751, his property was omitted from the 1752 census, but he had received nearly 8,000 livres as his share of community property with his late wife, and his three-story house alone fetched 17,000 livres in 1763, when the heirs sold it off.[48] A man with this wealth would certainly have expected to provide a dowry to his daughters, a fact the Ursulines would have known when, in 1749, they decided that Marie Turpin would be a converse. Clearly, she was one converse nun with the financial resources to qualify as a choir nun. And since she had also secured her father's consent to enter the convent, this was not in theory an impediment to the transfer of her expected marriage dowry to the Ursulines.[49] Her status as a converse could not be a result of lack of access to a dowry, a matter that in any case turned out to be problematic for at least four choir nuns who entered the convent in the two decades after Turpin.[50]

Other than the dowry requirement, a key qualification to becoming a choir sister was to be literate. All the creole postulants who followed Marie Turpin into the convent would have had the opportunity to be educated by the Ursulines in New Orleans. Since she began her stay in New Orleans as a paying boarder at the convent, Marie Turpin, upon entry into the convent, should have partaken of the education on offer to boarders.[51] But she was already literate, signing her name, "soeur Marie de Saint Mathe," in a bold hand in the Register that recorded her entry as a converse nun on December 7, 1749. There are no extant documents testifying to Marie Turpin's literacy prior to her arrival in New Orleans; however, a record pertaining to her old sister survives in which she signed her name, in contrast to the innumerable crosses dotting the legal documents that illiterate men and women in the Illinois Country could only sign "with their mark."[52] Her father's signature was sprinkled all over documents from the Illinois Country; he served as an interpreter and was therefore bilingual, suggesting that his household may also have been so. Louis Turpin's position as royal storekeeper was contingent on his numeracy and literacy, for those awarded this post were selected on the basis of their education, wealth, place in the tight society of the Illinois Country, and good relations with the authorities.[53] As such he would have been conscious of the need for his own offspring to receive the scholarly and social education to make the kind of advantageous marriages other half-Indian girls were entering into. Marie Turpin's months as a boarder in the Ursuline convent would have further enhanced the education she had received in the Illinois Country, reiterating that the Ursulines' denial of her right to become a choir sister was not due to her lacking the requisite literacy skills.[54]

Access to a dowry, rather than rank or education, carried more weight in decisions about the rank of nuns in this period in France.[55] In New France, the examples of English former captives turned nuns shows that the Ursulines found solutions to the shortcomings in the women's linguistic and educational skills by restricting their access to educational work. But they did not impede the women's access to the rank of choir nun; on the contrary, volunteers had stepped forward to donate money for these English nuns' dowries.[56]

The selection for Marie Turpin of a rank as converse, or domestic, nun in New Orleans (in spite of her French appearance, presumed literacy, and access to a dowry) is especially intriguing given the evidence that this congregation differed from its French counterparts in valuing not merely the primary educational component of their work but especially "work that took a sister into unusual or unknown directions in response to colonial exigencies."[57] The *lettre circulaire* pertaining to one nun, Renée Yviguel (who had witnessed both the 1730 visit by Illinois Indians and Marie Turpin's entry into the order), singled her out for seeking occupations "most humiliating and disgusting." The letter further noted that this choir nun had, during the first years in New Orleans, done the very type of work for which converse nuns had responsibility, and which would have been unimaginable in metropolitan convents. Pertinently, not only had she assumed the duties expected of converse nuns, but she was praised for doing "what our most lowly slaves did. She ground corn and rice, chopped wood, and did the washing."[58]

The denial of Marie Turpin's access to choir status has to be interpreted in the context of this colonial environment. Like Ursulines in France, the New Orleans Ursulines had servants at their disposal for various tasks, a yardswoman among them.[59] But they differed from their counterparts in France (and in New France) in that they also had enslaved Africans and some enslaved Indians at their disposal. The presence of these figures in the New Orleans convent modulated the role played by converse nuns in France.[60] Slaves were a group of workers who, like converse nuns and servants in France, might participate in skilled and unskilled work such as food preparation, laundry, care and treatment of the sick, and manual labor (including, for many, living on and working the Ursulines' plantation). Among the enslaved Africans was an apothecary, a skilled occupation that in France might be the province of a converse.[61] In other words, these slaves were not for the sisters' personal use, but for the work associated with their plantation, hospital, and school.[62]

Overseeing their slaves was not the extent of the Ursulines' contact with Africans or Indians within the boundaries of their cloister. Enslaved African and Indian day students also came "two hours each day for instruction" at little or no cost, sent by their masters to take catechizing classes and, if needed, language classes. The nuns even took in slaves as boarders (perhaps the illegitimate daughters of their masters), for instruction preceding baptism and first communion.[63] The ranks of these students were completed, and complemented, by the presence of French indigent orphans.

Notwithstanding their open arms policy, the Ursulines upheld strict distinctions between their students, for example in the dress allowed to boarders (unrestricted) and that allocated to indigent orphans. A memorandum dating from 1752 has survived in a reused ledger book, showing the linens and clothing provided to the French orphans:

Memorandum of the linens and clothing of the orphan girls
This 6 April 1752
72 sheets

34 large shifts plus 5
64 *idem* medium plus 8
58 *idem* small plus 3
Are made 189
94 linen skirts
32 *cotonnade* skirts
65 colored handkerchiefs
65 white handkerchiefs
30 coifs
41 small caps
31 [*casaquin*] jackets
8 *foureaux* (fitted jackets) of cotton fabric
50 caps, as many of silk as of calico.[64]

The number of orphans housed by the Ursulines at that date is not known, so we cannot make inferences about the quantity of items provided to each orphan; nor was the quality of the garments identified. However, the textiles and composition of their dress were minimal and utilitarian—a shift, linen or cotton-mix (*cotonnade*) skirt, neckerchief, caps and sundry other types of headwear, and a jacket. There were allowances for variations in color and texture: some of the skirts may have been patterned (likely striped, as were many of the cheaper *cotonnades* sold in the colony); there were colored neckerchiefs as well as white ones, and some of the caps were made of silk or *indienne* (printed cotton calico; see Plate 7). With respect to the condition and quality of their dress, the orphans may not have differed too drastically from some of the poorer paying students.

Marie Turpin's own (mixed-blood) niece, Marianne Chauvin, had attended the Ursuline convent as a paying boarder; her father belonged to one of Louisiana's founding families, a connection that would have been as valuable to Turpin as her own father's connections.[65] Like her mother (the legitimate daughter of an Illinois Indian female convert), Marianne Chauvin dressed in the French manner. Records survive that document some of the clothes she was given on her mother's death in 1747 "for her use at the convent." Among these were two old linen *mantelets* (see Plate 14); three petticoats, two of them white linen; three old neckerchiefs, two handkerchiefs, and ten very worn caps and headdresses; a cape (see Plate 15) and a *corcet* (the padded, quilted bodices that were an alternative to boned stays; see Plate 18); she was also left a small gold ring.[66] The used condition of these handed-down garments would have identified her quite clearly as poor, even if she was a paying boarder. But her multiple units of each garment meant that her wardrobe would appear varied. So, if the lesser quality of the textiles and the cut and construction of the indigent orphans' garments was not necessarily unique, the uniformity of their garb would certainly have visually marked out these pupils from the boarders and paying day students, even poor ones like Marianne Chauvin.

The organizational and spatial structure of the convent accentuated the division among students. For example, paying boarders (Marie Turpin among them) were even differentiated from indigent/orphan boarders down to the schedule for assisting with the principal liturgies during mass.[67] The architectural drawings for the original 1732 and rebuilt 1745 convents reveal the way students and boarders were also spatially segregated based on their status. Boarders, orphans, and externs slept in separate dormitories. They were also segregated in daily activities of learning, eating, socializing. Even in illness they were kept separate, as seen in the presence of distinct rooms for convalescence. The physical segregation revealed by the architecture of the convent buildings reinforced visually the social and ethnic demarcations between students (see Figure 12).[68]

The same concern was found in a plan of the Ursuline convent in Quebec, probably made by Sister Marie Lemaire des Anges in 1687–88 following a disastrous fire in 1686. This plan proposed that the classroom designated for the convent's Indian students be isolated from the others. Its exact placement was even more suggestive of this nun's perception of the Indian converts who had been the driving force behind the establishment in 1639 of the convent.[69] For the classroom was to be situated right next to (and in danger of fire from) the kitchens, the exact site where the great convent fires of 1650 and 1686 had originated.[70] This 1686–87 conceptualization of segregated spaces in the Quebec Ursuline convent was, however, a new development in one respect. While classes and prayer time had always been separate, students had previously resided and eaten together, suggesting the rejection by this period of the earlier, somewhat more egalitarian model of living accommodations.[71] The New Orleans convent would be designed to uphold and extend this spatial hierarchy.

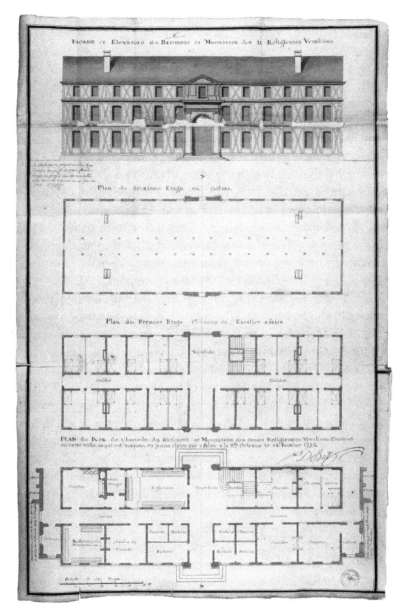

Figure 12. Ignace François Broutin, *Façade et élévation du batiment et monastère des D. Religieuses Ursulines*. New Orleans 14 January 1732. FR.ANOM Aix-en-Provence F3 290/6. Photo © Archives Nationales d'Outre-mer, France.

The Limits of Inclusion

If the New Orleans convent was a heterogeneous space open to all women, its students nonetheless occupied different spaces within it according to their race or rank. As fee-paying boarders in the rebuilt 1745 New Orleans convent, Marie Turpin and her niece Marianne Chauvin would have lived this stratification, one that was modeled after the Ursuline order's rule.[72] It is unclear to what degree these girls with some Indian ancestry might have been kept from mingling too closely with the other, French and creole, boarders. It is certainly hard to conceive, for instance, that slave boarders would have been permitted to mingle socially with French and creole boarders. The New Orleans Ursulines micromanaged their externs according to status, and boarders, too, who were generally drawn from the ranks of the French population, must have experienced a similar hierarchical organization that distinguished between students according to their social and economic rank.[73]

Marie Turpin and Marianne Chauvin were not the only free girls of Indian descent who had attended the convent. In 1729, an Osage was freed by her master (was there an affective or kin relationship between them?), and he left funds in his will to have her instructed at the convent.[74] But she was not necessarily a boarder, nor was she the product of a legitimate union (in French eyes) of the type typical of the Illinois Country. One other Indian, a twelve-year old female Fox (Mesquakie) slave whom a voyageur from the Illinois Country had bequeathed to the Ursulines in 1739, may still have been at the convent at the same time as Turpin and Chauvin.[75] In contrast to these slave and free Indian women, we may wonder how the Frenchified appearance of Marie Turpin and Marianne Chauvin influenced their position in the convent. By the time Turpin had completed her fourteen months as a boarder, the decision had been made to admit her to the novitiate, though only as a converse. This probationary period had presented the Ursuline nuns with a crucial measure for gauging Turpin's qualities and whether they were willing to allow her into the order. But their consideration of Turpin's request for admission was more ideologically charged than would have been the case for a French creole. For their observations and deliberations took place in a cloistered environment steeped in the racial ideologies that percolated through New Orleans's slave society (influenced by the Caribbean). So, if Marie Turpin should have received preferential treatment in the convent by virtue of her economic status as the daughter of one of the Illinois

Country's prominent inhabitants, in New Orleans her ethnicity as a child of French-Indian *métissage* likely trumped this privilege. And the nuns' appraisal of Turpin's identity played out against the backdrop of increasing numbers of French African métis girls who came to the convent for Catholic instruction.

A criminal investigation from 1752 is particularly valuable in shedding light on the nuns' conceptions of the value of their African slaves relative to colonists. The court case revolved around a violent attack by a French soldier on two of the Ursulines' slave women. One of the women, Babette, was too severely wounded and delirious to testify; the other, Louison, though badly injured, did make her deposition to the officers of the court, describing how the attack by the mentally unstable Pochenet had occurred unprovoked while she and a number of other enslaved Africans were doing the laundry by the river, following which her husband was also violently attacked while coming to her aid. The nuns in charge of the hospital were then formally asked if they (in their capacity as the owners of the injured slaves) planned to make their own declaration against the accused soldier, as the court official seemed to expect. Instead, they reported that neither they nor their fellow members of the New Orleans Ursuline community (Marie Turpin among them, at this date) wanted "in any way to get involved in this affair, neither as accusers nor as defendants; that on the contrary, if they could save the life of this man, they would ask for it." In fact, the two Ursulines declared they would rather have their female slave die than do anything to go against "the charity owed to others," others in this instance referring to fellow French men and women.[76]

This focus on difference was not recent. The letters of one Ursuline, Marie-Madeleine Hachard, or Sister St. Stanislas, a founding member of the New Orleans convent, show that she was certainly preoccupied with skin color. In a 1728 letter to her father, she noted humorously that, had Africans wanted to wear beauty patches (small black velvet beauty spots that fashionable women wore to "make their complexion seem whiter," as the *Le Mercure galant* noted), they would need white patches, "which would create quite a funny effect."[77] Yet Hachard's letters drew a clear distinction between the Ursulines' African and Indian charges, revealing diametrically opposite impressions of the suitability of African and Indian women to conversion.

Hachard clearly favored African over Indian women in the missionizing endeavor, a perception probably compatible with that of her fellow women religious at the New Orleans convent as she herself suggests:

What pleases us is the docility of the children, whom one forms as one
wants. The blacks are also easy to instruct once they learn to speak
French. It is not the same for the sauvages, whom one does not baptize
without trembling because of the tendency they have to sin, especially
the women, who, under a modest air, hide the passions of beasts.[78]

The striking appreciation of enslaved African women expressed in this letter was to continue, laying the groundwork for the rich intertwined history
of Africans and Catholicism in Louisiana, one that was mediated by the
Ursulines.[79]

Hachard's markedly less enthusiastic reading of Indian women's propen-
sity for lasting conversion flouts the conventional story of the hierarchical
model on which French conceptions of difference were founded, with Indians seen as below Europeans in their state of civilization, but above Africans.
In Louisiana, such a model was further complicated by the two strands of
influence on the colony's practices with regard to ethnic difference. On the
one hand, the Caribbean exerted its influence as Louisiana developed into an
African slave society; on the other, the history of French-Indian relations in
New France continued to inflect life in the Illinois Country, and by extension
in Lower Louisiana.

Marie Hachard's views about the relative superiority of African girls over
Indian ones in catechizing may also have been a result of her knowledge of
the missionary work at the Ursuline convent in Quebec. As the first Ursuline
establishment in North America, news from there would likely have flowed
back to convents in France. Its founders had envisioned the conversion and
education of Indian girls as the cornerstone of this first project in the New
World.[80] The 1647 Constitution reiterated this mission, hailing the convent's
Indian students as "the delights of [their teachers'] hearts, since one day
they will become the most beautiful floret on their heavenly crown."[81] Notwithstanding the emphasis on Frenchifying "sauvagesses" through religion,
language, dress, and manners, the Quebec Ursulines also absorbed Indian
influences, learning a range of Indian languages, adopting Indian hospitality
practices, and learning (later incorporating) indigenous textiles techniques
in their famed embroidery and gilding workshops.[82] These cultural adoptions
were justified on the basis of the need to appeal to Indians, with a view to
converting and educating them. Thus, the nuns never allowed themselves to
lose sight of their responsibility for inculcating the *sauvages* with the "superior" cultural and spiritual practices of the French, even if the means might

entail their own acculturation to Indian culture. Furthermore, the cloister rendered the Ursuline nuns somewhat more impermeable to indigenous cultural influences than the priests who shared their missionary goals.[83]

The Ursuline nuns taught Indian girls reading, writing, adding, and other skills deemed necessary to Frenchified girls, such as needlework and household skills. This was in addition to the full complement of religious education (catechism, prayers, chanting, confession) and cultural practices (pertaining to eating, dressing, cleaning, and manners). The methods used to instruct seem to have foregrounded gentle approaches rather than punitive or coercive measures. The spiritual and corporeal aspects of the Quebec Ursulines' educational and catechizing mission were further fragmented. Much more emphasis was placed on baptism (with a corresponding change of name) and first communion than other rites, reflecting the length of preparation needed for Indian girls to accomplish these "transformations in their spiritual universe and the attribution of a new identity." As for corporeal practices, Claire Gourdeau has underlined that the Ursulines' pedagogy was heavily weighted toward altering cultural practices pertaining to visual expressions of identity, chiefly through hygiene and dress, rather than food or lodging.[84] This missionary work was premised on the promise of Indian girls as agents of assimilation and conversion, just as education of girls (future mothers, after all) in France was seen as central to the "moral and religious unification and uniformity of the French."[85] It was a gendered mission, wholeheartedly supported by the Crown. In 1667 Colbert masterminded and implemented his plan to provide dowries for these Quebec convent-educated Indian girls to be available for marriage with Frenchmen, representing the culmination of a French policy of population growth through intermarriage with converted, Frenchified Indian girls.[86]

There were some success stories from the Quebec Ursulines' standpoint. In 1668, Marie de l'Incarnation (1599–1672), founder of the Ursuline convent in Quebec, described how "We have frenchified a number of Indian girls, whether Huron or Algonquin, that we have then married to Frenchmen, and they have formed good households." She went on at length about exceptional students such as "one who knows how to read and write to perfection, both in her Huron tongue and in our French, there is no one who can tell her apart nor be convinced that she was born *sauvage*."[87] But by this date she only cited such examples when requesting financial support for the Ursuline mission in New France. In letters to her son, she was more frank about her dejection at the repeated failures "to frenchify or civilize" Indian girls.[88] It was a realization that had already struck her in 1650 when she pondered the fact that none of these girls had declared a vocation as a woman religious and only a few had married Frenchmen.[89]

By 1720, just seven years before the founding of the New Orleans Ursuline convent, the Quebec Ursulines had amended their fourth vow to rescind the goal of educating Indian girls.[90] These failures underline the contrast with the Illinois Country, even if hopes for an Ursuline convent there never materialized. There, missionaries, officials, inhabitants, and parents were complicit in the Frenchification of half-Indian children (especially daughters), supporting these children's integration in French colonial religious, civilian, and marital structures.

But given the Quebec Ursulines' history of failure to permanently Frenchify (and civilize) Indian girls in New France, and in the context of Marie Hachard's cynicism about the conversion of Indian pupils, Turpin's acceptance as a nun *in New Orleans* in the mid-eighteenth century seems all the more remarkable and unexpected. Unlike the "sauvages" referred to in Hachard's letter, Marie Turpin's identity would have been far less straightforward to onlookers. She was the daughter of an Illinois convert sacramentally and legally married to a prominent and wealthy Frenchman. Based on the evidence of sartorial and cultural Frenchification of Indian wives and daughters of Frenchmen in the Illinois Country, we know that Turpin would have presented herself as French, but this did not mean that the Ursulines perceived her as such.

As discussed above, Turpin was not the only girl of mixed French-Illinois heritage that the New Orleans Ursulines had laid their eyes on. As we have seen, by the date of her arrival at the convent in 1749, the Ursulines had had further contact with at least one mixed heritage boarder, Marianne Chauvin. The eleven-year-old was Marie Turpin's half-niece. She was the daughter of Marie Anne Danis, Widow Chauvin, and so was the granddaughter of Dorothée Mechip8e8a from her first marriage to Charles Danis. This meant she was Indian through her maternal grandmother; all her other forebears were of French origin, and she had lived her life in New Orleans.[91] The Ursulines may have been aware of another more problematic family connection when in 1731, Joseph Turpin, Marie's uncle, married Hyppolitte, the Indian daughter of "Catherine, the former servant of Sr. Chauvin de la Frenière." In other words, Joseph Turpin had married a servant (or former slave?) of one of Marie Anne Danis's late husband's relatives; later records would eliminate any reference to Hyppolitte's Indian mother and endow her with Chauvin de la Frenière's last name, for example, when she remarried in 1750.[92]

Despite her relative and temporary penury, Widow Chauvin left on her death in New Orleans in 1747 household effects that adhered to French standards of material culture, notwithstanding their poor condition: beds and bedding (feather beds and pillows, woolen blankets, linen sheets), furniture (cypress tables and chairs), cooking utensils (pewter plates and an array of French copper, iron, and brass cooking equipment), and cleaning and maintenance implements (a bucket and a pair of irons).[93] She also left a voluminous if also worn-out assortment of European fashions. These items included a *miramiole*, the special headdress worn by widows in France to signal their marital status and stage of mourning. This garment paralleled the headdress of women religious (widows and nuns had in common the need to signal sexual abstinence), and it showed the degree to which the widow Chauvin, a half-French and half-Illinois Indian woman, had internalized French conventions.[94] Many of her garments (though not the *miramiole*) were passed on to her daughter for her use at the convent, and the entire family subscribed to French hygiene practices, by hiring laundering services to keep their linens clean. Neither Marianne Chauvin nor Marie Turpin would have turned up at the convent "covered in grease [that their parents had applied to their skin] and wearing only a rag on a body." That had been how Marie de l'Incarnation, writing from Quebec in 1640, had described her newly arrived Indian seminarians whom the nuns had to strip and scrub clean before allowing them to take up residence at the convent.[95] Both girls would have presented themselves to the Ursulines as successful incarnations of Frenchification, fully acclimatized to living in colonial houses surrounded by French furniture and furnishings. These were features that paved the way for the women's pronounced deployment of French material culture and dress, as typified, for example, by the niece's wearing of *mantelets*, *corcets*, petticoats, neckerchiefs, handkerchiefs, caps, headdresses, cape, and gold ring.

In the mission at Kahnawake, the venerated Mohawk convert Catherine Tekakwitha had expressed her calling to become a nun by forming an informal (and unsanctioned) community of women converts bound by catholic fervor (see Figure 7).[96] Marie Turpin grew up with the memory of another role model from her mother's generation and culture, Marie Rouensa, daughter of the Kaskaskia Illinois chief, who had engaged in a public tussle with her parents to be granted leave to commit herself to a life of celibacy and devotion to Christianity. Given the role of Jesuit missionaries in Marie Rouensa's public struggle, it is certain that her story, and variants that were passed from one generation to the next through oral history, served locally as a missionizing tool in the French colonial villages of the Illinois Country. Indeed, as described in the *Lettres Circulaires*, Marie Turpin's own vocation while in Kaskaskia had been nourished and formed by a Jesuit priest. Marie Turpin's consecration as a nun can thus be directly linked to the memory of Marie Rouensa's very public, but unfulfilled, calling fifty-five years earlier "to consecrate her virginity to God" and her resolve "never to marry, in order that she might belong wholly to Jesus Christ."[97] It was doubtless also bolstered by the memory of other Illinois Indian women with similar aspirations, for example, the Illinois widow who would compromise by remaining celibate during her second marriage, or the girl who had declared in 1712 that she would "never have any other spouse than Jesus Christ."[98]

These Illinois Indian women had failed in their calling to remain celibate and consecrate their lives to Christ as nuns did, just as the 1728 proposal for an Ursuline convent in the Illinois Country never materialized. But in 1751, Marie Turpin, daughter of a Frenchified Illinois woman known for her "exemplary worthiness and piety," would succeed in her bid to consecrate her life to a Christian God by taking vows. In so doing, she pushed intermarriage to its limit by entering the highest form of marriage for Catholic women, that with Christ. The new identity of this "sainted girl" was cemented with a new name and took a material form when, following the cutting of her hair, she was stripped and redressed with the order's black habit.[99] It was a ritual that starkly paralleled the stripping and redressing associated with indigenous practices, whether those of marriages "à la façon du pays," of the *berdaches*, or of the metamorphosis of adopted captives discussed in Chapter 2.

On her death, she was praised for having fulfilled her duties as a converse "with much courage, being vigilant, strong, adroit, *and of great cleanliness*" (my emphasis). This last quality was a unique one among descriptions of New Orleans' Ursuline nuns.[100] There are no descriptions of Marie Turpin's sartorial appearance prior to her vows. I suggest that her acceptance into the Ursuline order in New Orleans in 1749 (albeit as a converse nun) was only conceivable because of the peculiar features and material expressions of intermarriage in the Illinois Country. For the conceptions of difference that informed responses to Marie Turpin's identity, and the constraints that were imposed upon her, were not simply fixed by chronology. They were also delineated by geography, by spatial borders and boundaries premised on an Upper-Lower Louisiana axis and inscribed on the body through dress, but also through other cultural practices pertaining to the body, such as cleanliness. In the Illinois Country, material culture had justified and bolstered religious and official arguments in support of *métissage*, arguments that had relied on the potential for Frenchification, premised on conversion, facilitated by intermarriage, and mediated by objects. In acceding to the status of a woman religious, Marie Turpin reached the apex of missionaries' goals for Indian converts in French America. But ironically, her spiritual marriage to Jesus Christ simultaneously marked the death knell of intermarriage. In allowing Marie to leave the Illinois Country to become a celibate nun, Father Binneteau signaled a symbolic rejection of the suitability of such women as lawful marriage partners for Frenchmen and mothers of French children. In New Orleans, Marie Turpin only achieved the rank of converse nun, underscoring the limits of Frenchification in mid-eighteenth-century New Orleans and the emergence in *that* space of racial constraints.

CHAPTER 5

"To Ensure That He Not Give Himself Over to the *Sauvages*": Cleanliness, Grease, and Skin Color

For the duration of the trip that had brought Marie Turpin, future Ursuline sister Ste. Marthe, down from the Illinois Country to New Orleans in 1747 on her quest to be consecrated an Ursuline nun, the girl had been placed in the care of a female acquaintance. The woman was charged with chaperoning the young girl from the French soldiers and voyageurs in the convoy, for this was a predominantly male space. But it was the French soldiers and voyageurs who spoke with authority, upon arrival in New Orleans, not of the Indian or mixed-heritage girl who had accompanied them, but of the "sainted girl who kept her eyes downcast throughout the trip and never said an unnecessary word, being always at prayer."[1] It was the judgment of these intermediaries between Upper and Lower Louisiana, not that of the female chaperone, that counted when the topic concerned their world, that of the river ways.

Frenchmen made up the bulk of those who traveled on the convoys between Upper and Lower Louisiana, as soldiers, voyageurs, and traders, usually accompanied by Indians and Africans.[2] In traveling the Mississippi River and tributaries they, like Marie Turpin, navigated a shifting panorama of practices and beliefs about identity. Travel along the river represented temporary sublimation to the environment. But the fact that travelers were physically contained on the convoy boats meant that they were simultaneously buffered from the wilderness. At the same time, the riverways served as the key conduits between the different colonial settlements. As such, travel between settlements exacerbated colonists' sense of identification with "Frenchness," one that might be temporarily dissolved during the journey, only to reemerge, strengthened, at the conclusion of a trip down or up river, with the resumption of French ways of being. Travelers' bodies played a key role in signaling these metamorphoses and in controlling them. For French beliefs about identity and explanations about differences in skin color relied for their validity on cultural definitions of concepts such as body cleanliness. Intimate body care was a site of cultural difference in early America,[3] but it was also a site of cultural exchange. It is against this backdrop that the interplay of clean clothing and "Frenchness" encapsulated in the material culture expressions of one male voyageur of mixed Indian-French descent becomes significant.

Jean Saguingouara

In 1739, a decade before Marie Turpin's trip downriver, a professional voyageur in the Illinois Country became just one in a long line of men who had presented themselves at the local notary's office to sign a contract for a trip from Kaskaskia down the Mississippi River to New Orleans and back (see Figure 1). The trip downriver would have taken only about twelve to twenty-five days; the return trip up to four months.[4] The contract, a written manifestation of French custom, law, and commerce, engaged the voyageur to work for a merchant-voyageur, Pierre Chabot, who was married to an Indian woman in Canada.[5] In exchange for the work, he was to be paid a wage of 205 livres; in addition "the said Chabot oblige[d] himself to furnish to the said worker tobacco during the voyage and to pay his laundry costs on arrival at the sea." In other words, the voyageur had had a special stipulation included in the contract: that upon reaching the relatively urbanized settlement of New Orleans, his employer would cover the cost to have his clothing laundered. Such a laundry clause was not an uncommon feature of indenture and apprenticeship contracts in this period, as analyzed below. But it was unique among voyageur contracts in Louisiana. The laundry clause stands out for a particular reason, opening a fresh vista on French-Indian relations mediated by material culture. For the voyageur, Jean Saguingouara, was of mixed French-Indian descent.[6]

Jean (or Jean-Baptiste) Saguingouara, was born in the Illinois Country to a French Canadian man and an Indian woman, and raised in another household headed by a French-born officer and his Indian wife. Though some historians have categorized Saguingouara as Indian (likely because of the inclusion in this name of the phoneme "oua" common to Algonquin names), his lineage and early history can be reconstructed and shows that he was in fact of mixed French-Indian heritage.[7] He was born in Kaskaskia in 1713 to an Illinois Indian mother, Marie-Josephe Capi8ek8e. Her husband Joseph was a French Canadian with no Indian blood and whose ancestors can be traced via Montreal to Saintes, in southwest France.[8] At some point in his life the young Saguingouara had been taken under the wing of Nicolas Pelletier de Franchomme, the French officer of noble origin who was himself sacramentally married to an Indian wife in the Illinois Country. The lives of these two men—the one a Frenchman married to an Indian woman, the other born of such a union—were intertwined, though demarcated by differences in rank. The relationship between these two males provides a rare case study of how one French elite figure in 1720s Upper Louisiana, Franchomme, understood ethnic identity, whether that of his legitimate Indian wife or that of a mixed-heritage male under his tutelage. This case study also problematizes our interpretation of *métissage* (of the mixing of French and Indian) when applied to legitimate, baptized French-Indian children who were raised not in Indian fur-trading communities but as Frenchified Catholics in the French settlements in the Illinois Country, where they lived immersed in French colonial culture within French colonial houses (see Plates 2, 3, and 4). Contrary to the assumption that children born to Indian women and Frenchmen necessarily retained an Indian identity and clung to indigenous material culture, the experience of French-Indian children in the Illinois Country presents an alternative response to colonization. Though Saguingouara's 1739 contract was to be canceled for unknown reasons, its existence helps bring to light the process whereby French-Indian children in the Illinois Country were initiated into meanings and practices associated with Frenchness, including how to dress and clean bodies, with implications for views of skin color.

In his will dated 1728, Franchomme invoked the names of both his wife and Saguingouara. In this legal record of his wishes and beliefs, Franchomme made clear his affection and attachment to the boy and endeavored to keep him anchored within the Catholic Church and integrated in the colonial culture. Saguingouara's insistence on a laundry clause must be read in the context of his distinctive experience as a mixed heritage boy raised in another mixed heritage household in the Illinois Country, with its unique pattern of religious conversion and of sacramental intermarriage between French and Indians. Indeed, Saguingouara's laundry clause presupposed ownership of French clothing to be laundered, speaking to his adherence to

French standards of dress rather than indigenous styles. This clause marked one French-Indian Catholic's performance of a crucial cultural component of Frenchness, at least during his stay in New Orleans. But it also signaled his identification with a rank commensurate with that of his unofficial tutor, a member of the minor French provincial nobility. The laundry clause underscores that Saguingouara's cultural practices were colored by a status-based vision of Frenchness that complicates the evaluation of official Frenchification policies in Louisiana. It also signifies his familiarity with European standards of cleanliness more compatible with his French tutor's than with indigenous notions. This was a standard premised on laundered clothing rather than washed bodies. How Saguingouara, a French-Indian male, dressed and cared for his body says something about his subjectivity and how he moved between colonial and indigenous worlds. How the French perceived him, I further suggest, says something about his success in performing Frenchness. But it also illuminates the significance of bodily practices in producing and establishing ethnic identity and whiteness.

These lines of inquiry emanate from the analysis of Saguingouara's particular experiences as a French-Indian male in colonial Louisiana. But the issues raised by his laundry clause transcend the narrow focus on one individual, to illuminate a broad range of questions pertaining to dress, the body, skin color, and the medium of water in a colonial context. This chapter thus proceeds in multiple layers that build on the laundry clause but go beyond it. First, it situates Saguingouara's experiences in terms of his extraordinary relationship to Franchomme and in the context of religious conversion and intermarriage in the Illinois Country. Then, Saguingouara's clause—not a formulaic feature of voyageur contracts—is analyzed in the framework of his occupational status as a voyageur, one who freely made use of French law to protect his interests and fit in as a professional trader. The framing of Saguingouara's position in the French colonial and voyageur communities is thus key to understanding the significance of his request for laundered clothing, one that opens up the question of meanings of cleanliness, and of water, in the eighteenth century.

Information about voyageurs, most of whom were illiterate, is elusive, all the more so for those with Indian blood who seldom left any trace in extant records. Saguingouara fits this pattern, but significant parts of his story can be pieced together from a wide sweep of primary sources incorporating notarial records (including probate records), business documents, baptismal registers, and travelers' accounts, interpreted through the lens of scholarship on race, cleanliness, and material culture. Indeed, while the primary sources are verbal, my analysis of this material is grounded in material culture and dress historical scholarship. In other words, it rests on knowledge and understanding of what it meant and what it looked like, in concrete terms, to have one's clothing laundered but not one's body washed, in the eighteenth century. Bringing this visual and material dimension to bear on the analysis of French-Indian encounters leads to insights about French perceptions of Indians who did *not* launder their clothes. A focus on French beliefs about cleaning allows us, ultimately, to grasp a key way in which colonists explained skin color, so the interpretation of Saguingouara's laundry clause enriches our understanding of conceptions of difference in early America.

Saguingouara's was the only extant voyageur contract notarized in the Illinois Country that included a laundry clause. Among the ranks of voyageurs, this French-Indian Catholic was also distinguished by the elite rank of his unofficial guardian, Nicolas Pelletier de Franchomme. A French-born officer in the French troops of the marine and a member of the French nobility, Franchomme had in 1723 married an Indian Illinois woman legally and sacramentally.[9] In other words, and as with the marriage of Saguingouara's parents, this was not a marriage "à la façon du pays" typical of most mixed and fur-trade marriages but a union backed with the full force of religious and civil authority. The marriage also postdated the 1719 separation of French from Indian villages in the Illinois Country (see Figure 3), meaning Franchomme and his wife lived in a colonial rather than an indigenous settlement, in which Indian wives and children of Frenchmen were immersed in French material culture and classified by officials as French, not Indian.[10]

Born in France, Franchomme hailed from Champagne, where his father served as regional guard-general of the waters and forests of France. Franchomme was not alone in Louisiana, for his cousin Jean Jadard de Beauchamps served as major of Mobile, where he had a distinguished career.[11] It is unclear when Franchomme assumed responsibility for Saguingouara and why. In the Illinois Country, the name Gauthier-Saguingouara (of which Saguingouara was a shortened form) first appears in the parish registers at Kaskaskia. Between 1702 and 1713, four children with this last name were baptized in Kaskaskia. Three were born to Jean Gauthier-Saguingouara and Marie Susanne Capi8ek8e. The last entry was for a boy named Jean, born January 11, 1713, to Joseph Gauthier-Saguingouara and Marie-Josephe Capi8ek8e, and baptized nine days later.[12] The two husbands may have been brothers; the two wives shared the name Capi8ek8e, suggesting they too were related. The priests identified all four children as legitimate, meaning that both sets of parents had been married according to the rites of the Catholic Church. Among the godparents at the baptisms was fur trader and militia captain Jacques Bourdon, who went on to marry, sacramentally, two Illinois women. His second wife, Marguerite Ouaquamo Quoana, would become Franchomme's wife. Also listed as godparents were some of the most prominent intermarried inhabitants of the Illinois Country: Michel Accault and his legitimate wife Marie Rouensa; and Catherine 8abankinkoy, legitimate wife of Jean Gillemot *dit* Lalande. Both godmothers came from prominent Illinois bands.[13]

By the time of Jean's birth in 1713, the occasion of his baptism could only muster a godmother (identified as Marie Saguingouara—the "Gauthier" had already been dropped), but no godfather. These godparent relations, "fictive Catholic kin networks," to use Susan Sleeper-Smith's expression, served to integrate the Saguingouara-Capi8ek8e households in the French-Indian world of the Illinois Country, and they served Jean well once his parents were no longer present. The parental association with Jacques Bourdon, for example, persisted since a Saguingouara (first name not given) was mentioned in Bourdon's 1723 estate among the creditors, for 300 livres, although the specifics are not known.[14] On September 10, 1723, a few months after Bourdon's death, his wealthy widow Marguerite Ouaquamo Quoana married Franchomme. It was her second of three serial marriages to Frenchmen, all consecrated according to French law and Catholic rites, none of which seem to have borne issue.[15]

Jean Saguingouara's name next appeared in Franchomme's will. In March 1728, merely three years after Franchomme's marriage to Bourdon's Indian widow, he left a will.[16] He was to die a few months later when sent to fight the Fox (Mesquakie) in the 1728–33 Fox War, leaving no issue.[17] The Coutume de Paris regulated inheritance laws in Louisiana to the degree that wills are rare, being usually redundant since a wife was automatically entitled to half the estate, with the remaining half shared among the children (if any).[18] Franchomme's will seemed intended to protect his wife's inheritance rights. Indeed, an important subtext to the document was provided by the political maneuverings leading to a ruling by the Superior Council of Louisiana at the end of 1728, which limited the rights of barren Indian widows to inherit their French spouse's property as discussed in Chapter 3.[19]

Claiming that he had married an Indian woman "to his material advantage" and that his original marriage contract had been destroyed by rats, Franchomme, on one of his trips to New Orleans in 1725, had a new contract drawn up and approved by the Superior Council of Louisiana.[20] The will should therefore be read as providing an additional buffer against his wife's disenfranchisement. This included the rejection of any claims on his estate by relatives in France, for the will explicitly stated that "if . . . my heirs should pretend to inherit from the property that comes from my spouse, I declare categorically to them that such is neither my sentiment nor my will, it not being natural that the property she has brought me and which I have used during my life should go to my heirs after my death, and that she have to beg her grain [bread]." Corroboration of Franchomme's claim that his wife had brought property to their marriage community is scattered among a stack of legal filings through which he assiduously pursued and protected her inheritance rights from the community property held with her former husband. This was property Bourdon himself had inherited from his first, Indian, wife, reiterating the role of Indian wives in facilitating their French husbands' trade relations and capital formation. Perhaps therefore Franchomme's legal action to claim his wife's inheritance had been at her urging as much as by his own financial stake in the property.[21] For Franchomme, his Indian wife was the one who brought him wealth, and she was his legitimate heir.

Having worked to secure his wife's property rights, Franchomme turned in his will to other business, including debts and credits. Next, he addressed his wife directly (perhaps in the hope that she would be monitored to ensure she complied with his wishes) concerning their Indian and African slaves, urging her to "treat her slaves as gently as she can as she has seen that I have done and as I have often urged her to, to give them as far as possible their necessities as much for food as for clothing."[22] Finally, referring to his wife's lack of children (he also dismissed the relevance of any other kin relations), he explicitly entreated her to assume responsibility for Saguingouara:

> As my spouse has no parent to whom she has much obligation, I pray that she does as much good as she can to the little Saguingora [sic], and to ensure that he not give himself over to the Sauvages.
>
> I exhort her to have him instructed in our Religion as best she can, I would have done this myself if I had lived longer.[23]

Franchomme perceived the boy in ambiguous and fluid terms: as one who could be either Indian or French. For this French-born officer living in the Illinois Country in the 1720s, the assumption was that identity was malleable and mutable, depending on culture (including religious belief) rather than being inborn, essential, and racial. In this belief, Franchomme subscribed to earlier conceptions of difference premised on the common origin of all men, rather than racial views of Indians. Unlike most officials and religious figures in Lower Louisiana and France who expounded on the subject, Franchomme had come to his beliefs as a result of his personal experience as both a military officer—an aristocratic representative of the Crown—and the husband of an Indian woman (as we have seen, there were others like him).

Franchomme's will was written just a few years after the only known instance whereby a mixed-heritage child born to a sacramentally married couple rejected colonial society. That had been a prominent case, in which the mother, Marie Rouensa, had disinherited her son Michel Accault for entering a non-Christian marriage and choosing to "remain among the savage nations," precisely the course of action Franchomme feared for Saguingouara.[24] This event likely had personal meaning, since his own wife had left him for a period in early 1725. No details are known about this incident, but Franchomme considered it serious enough to commission (and pay for) a full inventory of the contents of his house following his wife's flight.[25] While the timing of these episodes might have been coincidental, Franchomme's admonition to keep Saguingouara from the influence of the *sauvages* nonetheless betrayed deep-seated anxieties about the reversibility of "progression" toward the higher state of civilization represented by Frenchness. Showcasing French ways of dressing, and caring for the body, was one way of assuaging such fears.

Franchomme doubtless had a role in introducing Saguingouara to these French ways. It is likely that the boy had accompanied Franchomme on a trip to New Orleans (perhaps the 1725 trip) and that the voyageur's request for a laundry clause can be traced to the relationship with the officer. His experience accompanying Franchomme would explain how a mixed-heritage voyageur of modest social status became initiated into the custom of having linens laundered on arrival in New Orleans after the weeks-long trip downriver. This was a ritual we can expect of elite Frenchmen like Franchomme, one that would surely have reassured the officer that Saguingouara had not "giv[en] himself over to the Sauvages."

On arrival in New Orleans, bodies that had consumed indigenous products while traveling through the hinterlands were reoriented in colonial settlements toward consumption of metropolitan French dress, architecture, furnishings, food, and drink. For example, the archaeological excavation of the site of Madame John's Legacy in New Orleans, which operated as an inn during the French colonial period, reveals the dominance of traditional French rather than indigenous foodstuffs in the establishment. The same was not true of residential sites in New Orleans over the same period, circa 1720–1760.[26] This contrast between the foods served to residents or visitors to the city highlights the importance of material culture in allowing travelers to re-establish their Frenchness. No record exists about Saguingouara's lodgings on any trip to New Orleans. But it is not likely that a man who cared about clean linens would have wished to camp on the outskirts of the town, where Indian delegations were usually confined. Saguingouara's command of the French language, Catholicism, ties to Franchomme, and laundered linens should have allowed him to expect admission into one of the town's numerous inns and boardinghouses, as a Frenchman, not an Indian.

If Franchomme had initiated Saguingouara into the cultural practices of the French elite, the boy would be deprived of his influence and oversight when he was only fifteen, when the officer died. Following Franchomme's death, Marguerite Ouaquamo Quoana entered her third sacramental marriage with a Frenchman. The sources are silent as to what became of Saguingouara in the immediate period after the officer's death. But within a few years his name began appearing sporadically in formal, notarized contracts that speak to his continuing immersion in French colonial society, albeit in the liminal role of voyageur.[27] Voyageurs alternated between French and Indian worlds and between the imported and indigenous goods central to fur trade exchanges. Saguingouara's occupation as a voyageur ensured that he slipped in and out of contact with various indigenous societies (each with its own way of gauging his identity). Yet his formal, notarized contracts also served to keep him anchored in the colonial society of the Illinois Country.

Voyageurs

Though it was exceptional among voyageur contracts in the Illinois Country, Saguingouara's 1739 laundry clause was but one seemingly insignificant element in an agreement to serve on a trip to "the sea" and back. This was a binding contract backed up with the force of law, and every clause was carefully negotiated, recorded, witnessed, and notarized. The laundry clause was not, therefore, accidental, but served as an index of his active participation in self-presentation and self-definition. The precise terms of his contract thus warrant close scrutiny. Saguingouara's agreement also drew on a rich history of licit and illicit trading activities by French Canadians in the area. Their practices and customs informed the terms in voyageur contracts, terms also derived from the language of French indenture and apprenticeship agreements. While the work was that of a voyageur, Saguingouara's contract actually identified him simply as a "volontaire" (employee). These contractual precedents help explain his place in the economy and society of the Illinois Country and illustrate how his attention to clean clothing contributed to his continuing identification as French.

The fur trade was an integral component of France's official policies toward the indigenous populations of Louisiana, but it was also a commercial venture for large numbers of Frenchmen.[28] As the fur trade became concentrated in the hands of merchants, voyageurs increasingly assumed the role of wage laborers ("volontaires") as they had done in Canada.[29] Whether working for their own account or engaging themselves for work on fur-trading expeditions on convoys traveling between Mobile or New Orleans and the hinterlands (and sometimes between the Illinois Country and New France), voyageurs were critical to the initial formation of a colonial society in Louisiana and instrumental in settling Lower Louisiana as well.[30] Although two terms, *voyageur* and *coureur de bois*, were applied to fur traders, the terms carried distinct meanings that evolved over time and varied by region. *Coureurs de bois* were unlicensed illegal traders, virtual free agents in the New France fur trade. Following the glut in beaver pelts between 1681 and 1716, only twenty *congés* (licenses to trade) were issued annually for the New France fur trade. During this period many voyageurs who were formally excluded from the trade—the *coureurs de bois*—joined expeditions to Louisiana and made the Illinois Country their new base.

That fur traders could act as either legitimate voyageurs or illicit *coureurs de bois* reinforces the fluidity of their work and occupational identity. But in contrast to illicit traders, the status of voyageurs was usually formalized in written, notarized contracts. In Louisiana, voyageurs straddled life in urban centers, military and trading outposts, and the wilderness, not unlike the soldiers posted to the colony.[31] And while their work and lifestyle contrasted with that of sedentary agricultural *engagés* (indentured workers), there was increasing crossover between voyageurs and indentured workers, including in the nomenclature used to identify them.

The work of voyageurs was varied and would have consisted of a combination of paddling and navigating the dugout canoes that could measure up to fifty feet long and carry up to thirty men; hunting and preparing pelts, and preserving meats.[32] They were also responsible for loading and unloading cargoes; the merchandise ranged from varieties of textiles to stockings and shirts, cookware and metal goods, sugar and coffee, alcohol, and trade goods on the way to the Illinois Country; and flour, hams, and furs on the way down.[33] Voyageurs were for the most part illiterate, but they maintained rich oral and musical traditions. Their work was perceived as backbreaking and they were expected "to perform near-miraculous feats of transporting goods and furs over immense distances and challenging canoe routes."[34] In contrast to Canada, with its sparse African slave population, the ranks of voyageurs in Upper and Lower Louisiana were bolstered by heavy use of black slaves as rowers (rather than in more specialized positions on the boats), after the introduction of Africans to the colony.[35] In Louisiana, voyageurs were also likely to be joined by free Africans who bound themselves as full-fledged, professional voyageurs.[36] For, while this was physically taxing labor, it was also skilled work that benefited from some Africans' specialization as navigators on the Senegal River.[37] And if this was a heterogeneous environment, it was also highly demarcated according to skill, experience, class, and ethnicity, as reflected spatially in individual canoemen's position on the boats and in their food practices.[38]

Traveling alongside these men were Indians hired to accompany the convoys on the Mississippi. With the exception of one Michigamia Indian, Penchirois, none of these indigenous men are known to have formally entered into a voyageur agreement.[39] In contrast, the mixed-heritage Saguingouara did practice professionally as a voyageur. For example, he was listed among a group of forty-five "Canadians" (often shorthand for "voyageur") and sixteen Indians hired by Governor Bienville for a horse and cattle drive from the Illinois Country to Fort St. François for use in the Chickasaw campaign of 1736. None of the sixteen Indians hired for this trip entered into a notarized contract and must have been hired informally.[40] Saguingouara, in contrast, availed himself of a notary for this appointment. That he had his agreement notarized, like French hires, suggests that he recognized the value of, and was extended a right to, legal representation according to French law. This legal standing echoed the wording of the 1627 Charter of New France, which granted Indian converts the right to "acquire property, with rights of inheritance and bequest, just as if they had been born Frenchmen, without being required to make any declaration or to become naturalized."[41] Saguingouara's right to legal representation conferred upon him the status of a full-fledged member of the colonial village of Kaskaskia. The son of a Frenchman and an Indian woman, he achieved this status because he acted as a French-man would. His notarized contract made explicit his culturally French iden-tity, telling us something about how he perceived himself and how others in the Illinois Country responded to his co-opting the trappings of French identity. It also illuminates his occupational identity.

Notaries in the Illinois Country who recorded Saguingouara's employ-ment contracts positioned him, unambiguously, in the ranks of French or Canadian, not Indian voyageurs. The way these notaries registered his debts and credits reinforces the reading of his identity as French. Not only was he listed as a creditor in Jacques Bourdon's estate, but other documents reveal his standing in the local financial world. His 1744 partnership agreement with two other voyageurs to hunt on the upper Mississippi formally acknowledged a loan of 164 livres from one of his new partners, intended to allow him to repay two notes he had made to another Frenchman, Jodoin.[42]

Five years prior to this partnership agreement, Saguingouara was merely a voyageur employee. His 1739 contract—the one that anchors this analysis—identified him simply as a "volontaire" (he was identified elsewhere as a "voyageur"). This nomenclature reflected the contractual organization of the labor force and reveals the increasing correlation between the labor practices of voyageurs and those of other employees such as indentured workers. Be-yond shedding light on how Saguingouara presented himself, the way he was identified in legal documents reflected his professional status in the fur trade and influenced how he positioned himself with respect to fellow French, In-dian, and African workers.

As a genre, voyageurs' contracts were standardized legal instruments. As developed in Canada's fur trade, they stipulated the terms of contract includ-ing destination and length of engagement; wages (in kind or notes); food, to-bacco, alcohol, or clothing allowances (if any); and any special rights granted to the voyageur.[43] By virtue of the heavy demand for the skills they had devel-oped living and trading in the wild, voyageurs could enter relatively lucrative work contracts depending on their skill and experience. From 1737 to 1743 in the Illinois Country, wages averaged 200 to 225 livres, usually supplemented with an allowance in kind; from 1743 to 1748, they averaged between 300 and 325 livres. These wages varied according to the skill, experience, and respon-sibilities of the voyageur, and Saguingouara's wage of 205 livres in 1739 placed him in the average range.[44]

The skills they acquired sometimes served to propel voyageurs toward greater power in the marketplace. Their professional involvement in the transport of goods and the roots of their profession as independent traders helped establish their right to personal profit. Some negotiated for the right to hunt for their own account.[45] Other contracts allowed them to trade on their own account, underlining their importance as independent suppliers of goods but also as mediators between the French and Indian goods at the core of fur trade exchanges. In the Illinois Country, such clauses continued to be included even after the decline of the practice in Montreal contracts.[46]

Beyond their specie wages and right to hunt or trade, voyageurs often also negotiated a clause specifying payment in kind. Receiving a wage in kind was not limited to voyageurs' contracts, or restricted to the New World, with apparel (often footwear) constituting an important portion of the wages of domestics in ancien régime France.[47] Yet, notwithstanding some similarities in the format of contracts negotiated in Lower or Upper Louisiana by *engagés*, voyageurs, and apprentices, the details of the terms negotiated with their employers reveals distinctions in the material culture of these distinct groups of nonelite men living and working in the colony.

Voyageur contracts that did contain a clothing provision usually distinguished between the supply of functional clothing for use by the voyageur during the term of the contract and articles of dress given as part payment at the end of the term of service (as was often the custom in European apprenticeships and indentures). The 1738 contract between Charles Eslie and Charles Neau, both of Fort de Chartres, provided a detailed itemization of the duties expected of Eslie.[48] The contract stipulated a wage of 200 livres and a quart of brandy and showed that Eslie had also negotiated the right to trade. In addition to the wage and perks, Neau promised Eslie a *capot* of coarse *mazamet* wool cloth and was to provide him with two trade shirts, a pair of common stockings, and a hat, ubiquitous clothing in the wardrobes of most voyageurs.[49]

Most items of clothing negotiated for in voyageur contracts were occupational, echoing Henri de Tonti's account of fur traders as running around the woods, tattooed, wearing leggings, moccasins, and "a simple breechclout in place of breeches" (see Plates 1 and 21 for representations of leggings and breechclout of European-imported woolen cloth).[50] These were items suitable to the work of the voyageur, none more so than his specialized footwear. In 1746, Pierre Sommelier entered the service of Joseph Desruisseaux, who had been granted the rights to trade in the Missouri River. Though he negotiated for a wage in pelts, he was to receive a tobacco allowance and be supplied with moccasins for the duration of his ten-month term, signaling that this apparel was required for the carrying out of his professional duties.[51] In 1737 the voyageur Louis La Vallée agreed to serve Michel Le Cour on a voyage from Kaskaskia to the Missouri, and from thence to Michilimackinac before returning to Cahokia. They agreed on a wage of 300 livres in beavers or other pelts, with La Vallée being permitted a small amount of merchandise to trade on his own account. In addition, Le Cour was to supply him with a pair of leggings, a breechclout, and two deerskins with which to make shoes (doubtless moccasins) for his own use.[52]

The provision of footwear or materials to make it was a perennial feature of voyageur contracts even where no other clothing was to be issued.[53] A clause pertaining to the provision of the materials needed to make moccasins was distinctive compared to nonvoyageur contracts (such as indenture and apprenticeship contracts). It reflected the recognition that the ability to make moccasins was a valuable skill for early explorers and fur traders, as Henri Joutel explained in his account of La Salle's 1685 expedition to Louisiana.[54] By the middle of the eighteenth century, Dumont de Montigny carefully explained the uses to which bison skins were put: "with [these] our Frenchmen make breeches, waistcoats, leggings, footless stockings [leggings] as well as a kind of shoe which are similar to our slippers."[55] Moccasins and clothes were adapted to river travel and facilitated the work of voyageurs. In other environments, fur traders might choose instead to wear French or French Canadian style dress. For example, in 1740 a voyageur traded a quantity of pelts in exchange for delivery from New Orleans of brandy and the materials for a complete suit of clothing. The document was very specific about the nature of this proxy order, which consisted of a matching silk camlet three-piece suit (with two pairs of breeches), four "beautiful and fine trimmed shirts," silk stockings to match the suit, and the silk buttons, lining material, and padding material needed to provide the shape of a formal, tailored suit. Topping off the commission, he requested a "demy-castor" hat; ironically, given his involvement in the fur trade, this was an imitation beaver hat, far more affordable than one of real beaver fur.[56] This was unquestionably an attempt to dress "à la française." In the same way, Saguingouara's contract, with its laundry clause, alluded to activities and leisure beyond the world of work, exposing the more subtle ways in which material culture could serve to construct an identity as French in a colonial environment.

In this period, having clothes laundered was still a class-based practice. Voyageurs for the most part were issued from Canadian peasant stock, and they subscribed to different sartorial practices from their elite counterparts

in France and North America. Men and women of status who were posted
to outlying areas of Louisiana, including missionaries and military officers
such as Franchomme, imported soap for use in their laundry and ran up bills
with local laundresses.[57] Outside the fur trade, laundry clauses were seen first
in the contracts of upper-middling workers, spreading to a broader range
of indenture and apprenticeship contracts. In the 1724 records of the large
Paris-Duvernay concession in Lower Louisiana, the surgeon alone, Dominique Douat de Janson, negotiated a three-year contract that incorporated
a laundry clause, in addition to an annual wage of 600 livres plus food and
housing.[58] In that period, requiring a laundry clause was distinctly metropolitan in flavor, as well as status-based, and perhaps as in this instance, a
special professional requirement of being a surgeon. In the Illinois Country,
indentured workers and apprentices (when single men) might also negotiate
for their washing to be done as part of their payment, but the records for this
date primarily from the period after 1739.[59]

In this world where laundered clothes signaled Frenchness and status,
one February day in 1739, Saguingouara added his mark (for he could not
sign) to a voyageur contract. He had negotiated his terms with care and
signed up for the trip in exchange for a respectable wage of 205 livres. Where
other voyageurs might insist on being provided with footwear or other payment in kind, such as the right to hunt and trade or a tobacco allowance,
Saguingouara limited himself to the latter. Where no others preoccupied
themselves with negotiating laundry costs, Saguingoura ensured that on arrival his linens would be clean and (if made of higher quality bleached linen)
white.[60] The absence of laundry clauses in other *voyageur* contracts does not
mean that voyageurs did not avail themselves of laundry services on arrival.
Saguingouara's insistence on such a clause was distinctive, however, reflecting his self-perception, when living within colonial spaces, as a Frenchman
bearing the trappings of respectability and high status Franchomme would
have exhibited. These were not, as a rule, the traits identified with voyageurs.
Most pertinently, from a French standpoint, Saguingouara's laundered linens
would mean that he was clean, whether he had washed his body on arrival or
not. Clean clothes meant a clean body. This premise offers an essential lens
for analyzing French-Indian encounters and the role of material culture in
constructing identity.

Water, Linens, and Cleanliness

Definitions of the clean and the unclean are historically and culturally specific.[61] In terms of contemporary European views of cleanliness, Saguingouara's insistence on a laundry clause was not a simple, straightforward yearning for clean *clothes*. It had greater import, for it expressed a desire for a clean *body*. Notions of cleanliness in Europe since the seventeenth century privileged laundering linens over cleaning bodies. Bodies were cleaned by the simple act of removing soiled clothes and replacing them with clean ones. In Europe before the sixteenth century bodies and body parts were stripped of clothing and washed, but the practice went into decline. At the same time, the very notion of bodily contact with water became a source of repulsion and anxiety, with the resurgence of the plague leading to new theories about disease.[62]

As bathing fell out of custom, clean linen displaced washed bodies as a sign of cleanliness. With the exception of the hands, face, and mouth (sometimes the feet and genital areas), water was not applied to the body.[63] For example, Louis XIV of France was widely known and admired for his fastidiousness in keeping himself clean. He was reputed to have changed his shirts multiple times each day, but he did not take baths or wash his body. Contemporaries judged the king of France's bodily cleanliness by the whiteness of his frequently changed shirts, not whether his body had been doused with water or soaped.[64] As asserted in 1688 by Charles Perrault, "We [the French] do not make great baths, but the cleanliness of our linen and its abundance, are worth more than all the baths in the world."[65] As underlined in Perrault's statement, and theorized by Georges Vigarello in his study of concepts of cleanliness in France, the act of changing into clean linen was understood in effect as cleansing the body. It also served to deodorize it, as Alain Corbin has argued, though for elite bodies, powders and fragranced products were also used to mask smells. Soap was not used to wash the body but was restricted for indirect use in laundering clothes. And even parts of the body that were liable to be doused, such as the hands and face, might instead be "washed" through friction/buffing with a dry or perfumed linen cloth, rather than with water, as was the preferred means of cleansing for the French and Indian girls at the Ursuline convent in Quebec in the seventeenth century, for example.[66] In all these situations, cloth performed the act of cleansing; this is perhaps not such an alien concept since, from a material culture point of view, one of the physical properties of linen and cotton fibers is the capacity to absorb grime, dirt, smell, and perspiration.

Once in North America, European-imported notions about the dangers of water might be simultaneously enriched and challenged by exposure to indigenous practices. In New Orleans, indigenous, European, and African beliefs about water and water resources intersected.[67] But since New Orleans was founded by Canadians, they, not the French-born, constituted the founding populations of both Upper and Lower Louisiana. These Canadians would have brought with them notions about water that had been already mediated by exposure to indigenous practices in New France. Indeed, colonists in Canada were perplexed by Indians' relationship to water, and two key tenets of French practices pertaining to water were modified in New France as a result. First, where in France access to fresh water (and the fish and fowl that depended on these) was a privilege of the nobility, in New France "the poor were allowed to move on fresh water." Second, anxieties about water penetrating bodies (driven by fear of the plague) were challenged by observations of Indians safely bathing in, and drinking, fresh water.[68] The brackish rivers and bayous of Lower Louisiana presented colonists with a very different perspective on water from that in much of France or New France. The clear riverways of the Illinois Country would have seemed more familiar.[69] If colonists did alter their perceptions of water, the evidence suggests that social conditioning continued to regulate their washing practices. In France, it was not until the second third of the eighteenth century that bathing by immersion made a cautious reappearance, and only among the highly privileged; even for them bathing was still a rare and irregular occurrence, not necessarily linked to hygiene or morals.[70] In Louisiana, as in France in the period before the colony was split between the Spanish and British empires, changing into clean linens remained the standard by which colonists judged body cleanliness.

The emphasis on laundered linens represented protohygienic concerns in the only way these could be understood: by cleaning bodies through changing linens, and by giving the outward appearance of cleanliness.[71] In Louisiana, this focus on health could be seen, for example, in Governor La Mothe-Cadillac's fight to protect the Crown-appointed midwife from being asked to handle and launder sick soldiers' soiled linens.[72] In the Illinois Country in 1740, the same concern with hygiene rather than aesthetics would dictate hiring Renée Drouin, wife of La Forme, to launder the linens (sheets, shirts, bandages) of the sick at the hospital at Fort de Chartres for one year.[73]

Laundering, in Saguingouara's voyageur contract, referred specifically to the cleaning of small linens ("linges de corps") as opposed to household linens. As a rule, for men these small linens would be limited to shirts, handkerchiefs, stockings, and caps, as well as removable collars, cuffs, and cravats where used. Drawers were not yet universal; instead, as seen on surviving garments (see Plate 26), male shirts had a longer panel at the back that was looped between the legs to form a protective barrier between the skin and the breeches. Outer garments, whatever their fabric, were not subject to laundering, although they might be brushed or dry cleaned in other ways. Saguingouara's laundry clause was very specific in terms of the items of clothing to be washed, and signified that he owned, and wore, small linens or "linges de corps" as components of his attire.

In the late seventeenth and early eighteenth centuries, the renewed ascendancy of linen ushered in this European model of cleanliness premised on laundered linens.[74] Since the medieval period, shirts and other linen items had begun to be worn by men and women as an intermediary between their body and their (woolen) gown, providing an unseen "pliant lining between wool and skin."[75] Rarely owned in multiples, the shirt was seldom changed or laundered until the sixteenth century, when linens became visible, increasingly seen in flashes as ruffs, cuffs, and shirts poked out from the unseen reaches of the body to enrich the appearance of clothing's outer layers.[76] At the same time, ideas about the role of linens in effecting body cleanliness began to emerge, bolstered by a focus on cleanliness rather than external appearance. The seventeenth century saw the continuing rise of emphasis on the role of linen in performing cleanliness, with the whiteness of the linen signaling propriety and seemliness. Paralleling this development, the French word "propre," meaning "clean," was increasingly understood as also meaning "proper."[77]

The emphasis on owning linens was increasingly facilitated by the availability of new washable textiles that did not shrink or otherwise suffer from contact with water. Originally made from linen or hemp, small linens could now be made of cotton or cotton-linen blends; while no longer exclusively restricted to linen fibers, garments made from these new textiles nonetheless retained the nomenclature "linens" and were usually plain (tabby) woven.[78] Cotton textiles had made a spectacular entry into the European marketplace as a wildly popular novelty product first imported from India in the late seventeenth century and adapted for use as inner and outer clothing. Most early cotton imports had been patterned (printed) textiles. But the brighter whites and finer weaves that could be achieved with cotton fibers (as opposed to the fibrous quality of flax), and their suitability to frequent washing, meant that plain white (but also checked and striped) cottons gradually established a strong presence in the marketplace for shirts and other small linens. In spite of opposition from European textile guilds, and prohibition or high import taxes on cotton imports, cottons retained their popularity. An important factor in their success was their novelty, not necessarily their functional advantages over linen. Gradually, cotton cloth was woven in European manufactories using imported thread, adding to the supply of linen and linen mix textiles available to meet the demand for shirts, cuffs, handkerchiefs, and other small linens, as well as some outer garments.[79]

The rise in importance of linens as components of the wardrobe, and as instruments of cleanliness, spread across all social strata over the course of the eighteenth century, with price and quality variations to match. Linens even reached the westernmost extremes of the French empire, as seen in the cultural practices of one French-Indian voyageur in the Illinois Country. There is no information on the composition of Saguingouara's linens, whether linen, cotton, or mixed fibers; nor can we know how they ranked in quality of the fiber, weave of textile, and cut and construction of the garments (whether his shirts were adorned with decorative features such as ruffles at the collar and cuffs, for example). We do not even know whether he had bought them new or second-hand, if they were mass-produced, ready-made linens or custom-made to his size and specifications. All these options were available in the Illinois Country.

As access to linen garments improved, people increasingly owned multiple units of each garment type.[80] For example, Canadian voyageur Jean Ganiot had been hired by his cousin on a trip to the Illinois Country but had died prematurely in 1766. His belongings included a *capot* as well as a waistcoat, breeches, and not one but two shirts in poor condition; a degree of refinement was provided by a hair bag and a pair of silk stockings.[81] The ownership of duplicate linens was the precondition for having clothes laundered and, by implication, for having available clean body-touching clothing into which to change. Owning clean, renewable linen as a sign of distinction was itself relatively novel in the early modern period in France. Daniel Roche's comparison of Parisian wardrobe contents from 1700 and 1789 reveals that "the range of garments was everywhere the same, and the principal linen items general by 1700 . . . what varied was quantity and quality, what mattered was diversity and the capacity to change frequently, thus to proclaim one's cleanliness to the world."[82]

But clean clothes also required soap. While most households still made their own using ashes, tallow, and lye, ready-made soap was increasingly available. More and more of it was made in France for industrial use and available for purchase in the colony where those drawing up probate inventories were assiduous in noting its presence as an article of value.[83] The enthusiasm for this aspect of dress also explains, perhaps, Europeans' blindness to forms of cleanliness, exhibited by Indians for example, that were unconnected to clean linens.

Jean Saguingouara's request for laundry services implied his access to multiple units of washable garments such as shirts. It also implied that he valued clean, grime-free linens, at least when not traveling. In this respect, he subscribed to a notion of cleanliness premised on the display of laundered clothing, and he adhered to a European sartorial model that required that a linen shirt mediate the space between the body and the visible outer layers of garments. His practices stood in contrast to those of nonacculturated Indians, or of French-Indian males who had returned to the "sauvages,"—those who did not subscribe to a notion of cleanliness premised on the display of laundered clothing. At the same time, the requirement for clean laundry in his voyageur contract raises fundamental questions pertaining to Frenchification and the production and transmission of knowledge across cultures.

Gender provided one focal point for this transfer of knowledge, for in European consciousness washing clothes was women's work.[84] Women laundered from the banks of the "little river of Metchicamiare [Michigamia]" in the Illinois Country to the banks of the Mississippi River from Natchez to New Orleans and beyond, sometimes professionally. They boiled linens in tubs of water mixed with homemade or imported soaps, and then met on the riverbank to submerge the linens and scrub and pound them on the riverbanks, before leaving the clothes out to dry.[85] The prevalence of laundry clauses in indenture contracts negotiated by bachelors in Upper Louisiana from the later 1730s and 1740s testifies directly to the gendered character of this skilled work.[86]

French colonists had been swift to play on the association of women—any and all women—with clothes maintenance. In 1747, one female Indian slave and her infant in Kaskaskia fetched a low price when leased because she was considered "infirm and not even capable of working in the fields or laundering," reiterating that this was considered a standard component of the labor of enslaved Indian women.[87] As early as 1713, Governor La Mothe-Cadillac complained that fur traders and soldiers "have female Indian slaves and pretend that they can't do without them for their laundry and for their food, and to keep house." Reading between the lines, Cadillac surmised that this work was cover for illicit sexual relations with enslaved Indian women, and proposed that the men only be allowed to keep male slaves. Cadillac believed that enslaved Indian males could render a number of services to French men, but laundering clothes was not one of them. Instead, he proposed French women be found to take charge of the laundry needs of the entire garrison. Reflecting the demographic imbalance between French men and women in the colony in this period, a later marginal notation conceded defeat; Cadillac admitted that he had not managed to find such a woman, and hiring a man for this job was beyond the scope of his imagination.[88]

Gradually, in Upper as in Lower Louisiana, household washing could be sent out to women who specialized in providing this service for a fee. This was poorly paid, low-status work whose traditional associations with prostitution extended to laundresses in Louisiana.[89] These associations echoed contemporary anxieties about water and bodies. At the same time, African slave women were taught this work, for which they served their masters and mistresses, or for which their owners hired them out by the day. Enslaved women also hired themselves out for their own profit, sometimes commissioned by fellow slaves to launder their clothing.[90] Most references to African slave women laundering appeared not in account books or formal records, but as incidental evidence in criminal investigations into slave infractions. Louis, a Creole slave accused of a number of thefts during his month and a half as a runaway, acknowledged giving three pairs of breeches and two shirts to a female slave "at the bayou" to launder, for which he paid her richly. Clearly, he desired to wear laundered clothes, even when a runaway. Louis was a Creole slave, therefore born in Louisiana (not Africa); hence we would expect to find him acculturated to French ways of dressing. The point is also that Louis could contract out the work.[91] Another reference to enslaved African laundresses appeared in a 1752 criminal investigation against a French soldier accused of attacking a group of female slaves owned by the Ursulines, Babette and Louison. As discussed in Chapter 4, Louison testified that the attack had occurred "while [she and Babette] were doing the laundry at the edge of the river across from the house of the Ursuline ladies, along with some other *negresses* who served at the hospital or belonged to the Ursulines."[92] In all these examples, laundry work was exclusive to women, whether French, African, or Indian.

Saguingouara would have been absorbed into this gendered worldview of laundry work. It fit with the gender division of labor that his mother would have known as an Indian from the Great Lakes area, in which women had oversight of the skilled work of making clothes. European methods of washing clothes were culturally specific, however, requiring skilled knowledge and command of specialized equipment, prescribed steps, and chemical formulas.[93] How Indian wives or slaves, and how African slaves, coped with the laundry needs of their families or masters is seldom alluded to in the sources. One rare exception emerges from the records of the estate of Marie Anne Danis. Born in the Illinois Country, this legitimate half-Indian woman was married to a Frenchman, Philippe Chauvin Joyeuse. Though her husband was from a respectable colonial family and she had married him legally and sacramentally, at the time of her death she was a widow of scant means living in New Orleans with her children. Yet she had ensured that her daughter was educated at the Ursuline convent as a boarder, where her half-sister Marie Turpin was a converse nun (see Chapter 4). Danis's probate records reveal that she dealt with the problem of laundered clothing by paying another woman to do this work. The records reveal that she owed a debt for laundry costs (primarily household linens) in New Orleans, where she lived before her death in 1747. That the debt was scribbled on the back of an old playing card speaks in concrete ways to the low economic status of this kind of transaction.[94] In the Illinois Country, the French widower of Suzanne Keramy, an Indian, also owed money to a laundress one year after his wife's death. It remains unclear if the couple had been in the habit of sending out their washing while Suzanne Keramy was alive, or if the widower needed to hire someone for this work once his wife was deceased and no longer able to provide this domestic work.[95] Either way, this example reiterates the importance of the appearance of cleanliness, of both small and household linens, in French-Indian households. As for Saguingouara, he was raised in Franchomme's high-status French-Indian household, one where slaves, rather than Franchomme's Indian wife, did the laundry.

It is not surprising, given the historical invisibility of women's work, especially "body work," as Kathleen M. Brown has termed it, that we do not know how those who did the laundry learned the specific steps entailed in laundering linens.[96] Indeed, the association of laundering with filth and the unclean was another factor in this invisibility of those who touched dirty linens in order to wash them.[97] That Indian (and African) women were perceived to have the stamina and strength to take on this physically taxing work was implicit in ubiquitous Europeans views of Indian women as "drudges" in comparison with stereotypes of Indian men as "lazy."[98] This European, primarily male view failed to account for the drudgery in female chores as dictated by the European gender division of labor, one that landed European women with similarly monotonous, repetitive, often physically demanding chores such as tending vegetable gardens and chickens, food preparation and preservation, cleaning, and washing clothes.[99] Just as some Indian women became immersed into the work of laundering, so too had Saguingouara been initiated into a French conception of cleanliness as effected through laundered linens. His laundry clause spoke to the influence of French material culture and resulting alteration of indigenous practices pertaining to his body.

Saguingouara's preoccupation with laundered clothing positioned him in a French rather than Indian worldview. Indians tended to emphasize washing the body rather than the display of clean clothing; even where they owned clothes made from the kinds of textiles that could sustain laundering, they were unlikely to wash these. Accounts of indigenous cleanliness practices are consistent across much of North America. Vespucci's account of his 1497 voyage to America made note of the cleaning practices he encountered: "Theyr bodies are verye smothe and clene by reason of theyr often washinge."[100] I would argue that Vespucci's focus on washing the body reflected a lingering interest in late fifteenth-century Europe in washing bodies as a means of effecting cleanliness prior to the sixteenth-century demise of this practice.[101]

In the seventeenth and eighteenth centuries, colonists and explorers did not necessarily view Indians' use of water as signifying cleanliness, especially if the ceremonial washing, for example of captives being ritually adopted, was followed by wearing an unwashed and "greasy" shift.[102] In Louisiana more than two centuries after Vespucci's account, trader Antoine Bonnefoy left an account of his captivity and adoption by the Cherokee in 1741–42. In particular, he recounted the rituals that laid the groundwork for his and his companions' adoption into the group and the conferral upon them of a new name and identity.[103] Having been spared death to replace a dead member of the village, Bonnefoy submitted to the entrance ceremonies and taunts, and following the ritual burning of a parcel of his and his fellow captives' hair, the removal of their collars:

> I followed my adopted brother who, on entering into his cabin, washed me, then, after he had told me that the way was free before me, I ate with him, and there I remained two months, dressed and

treated like himself, without other occupation than to go hunting twice with him.[104]

Beyond this example of the ubiquitous practice of haircutting, stripping, washing and re-dressing of the captive, perhaps the Cherokee also wished to remedy what he saw as an unwashed French body. But this act of bathing would have assumed a familiar dimension for the French, for whom bodily contact with water was now largely relegated to ritual moments associated with weddings, illnesses, and other rites that signaled a change of identity (as in marriage for women) or new life stage.[105] The parallel with baptism is especially startling, given the emphasis on water and clothing consisting of the gift of a (preferably white) shirt and a cross.[106] Both captive adoption and baptism rites played on the mutability of identity, sometimes explicitly. For example, as Marie de l'Incarnation wrote in 1640 from the Ursuline convent she had founded in Quebec to missionize and Frenchify Indian girls:

> There are some sauvage girls who have nothing of the barbarian in them. They lose everything that is sauvage in them as soon as they are washed in the waters of the Saint [holy] baptism, such that those who have seen them before running in the woods like beasts are thrilled and cry with joy to see them gentle like lambs.[107]

In her account, one that predated her later disillusionment with Frenchifying Indian girls, contact with water through baptism resulted in immediate metamorphosis, underlining the interrelationship of conversion and cultural transformation that was at the core of official Frenchification policies.

Contact with water, whether during conversion or captivity ceremonies, also paralleled the ritual mock baptisms celebrated by voyageurs traveling the waterways of New France. This ceremony prescribed specific, controlled steps (including payment of a tip) that incorporated some contact with water, ranging from a sprinkling of water on the head of the novice voyageur, to full immersion in the river as its most extreme expression.[108] This ritual act had its correlation in seafarers' mock baptisms at sea upon first crossing the equator or the tropics, as described by Marc-Antoine Caillot, the employee of the Company of the Indies who was sent to Louisiana in 1729 on board the ship *La Durance* (the ship was illustrated in his manuscript; the ceremony was not). In his account, Caillot emphasized the carefully controlled use of water and the ritualistic aspects of the process. First he described the arrival with great fanfare of the mock "master" of the Tropic of Cancer, on his mock "horse," and accompanied by his mock retinue. In accordance with the mis-rule traditions that regulated mock baptisms, the "master" was accorded all honors by the ship's captain, and in exchange he placed the ship under his protection. A collation and good wine was brought to him, and once the col-lation ended, "[the master] asked to wash his hands, a basin was brought to him which, after rinsing out his mouth and washing his hand, he took the basin and climbed with a little more strength than before on his horse." He then proceeded with the mock baptisms of those who had never before crossed the Tropic of Cancer, using the same basin.[109] Here as in elite circles in Europe, offering water to a guest to clean the hands was in itself a quasi-ritualistic measure of civility and hospitality, one intended to bind together the participants.[110]

Following this first stage of the ritual, Caillot described the actual "bap-tisms" of the men and women on board. Consistent with his predilection for erotic allusions, Caillot's account highlighted the female travelers' subjection to mock baptism:

> When our ladies had heard that [the Master of the Tropic of Cancer] had asked for the persons to be baptized, they tried to hide, but Mr. Aubin represented to them that they would drown from water if they did not submit to everything that the old man ordered them to do, and as for him [Mr. Aubin], he was no longer the master. They gave in after much pain and went to dress themselves in *corcets* and white petticoats. When they came back, the old man sent his two angels to gather those to be baptized and gradually placed us like herrings in a row one after the other. . . . It was one of these ladies who passed first and the others after.

Caillot went on to provide details of the ceremony, in which the first person to be baptized, a woman of status, was asked sundry questions, made to swear her allegiance on a pretend Bible, and then had to tip them. At this point one of the angels "poured water in the shape of a Cross on her forehead and the other angel poured three drops of water between her shift and her skin along her arm."[111] The other women and the men then followed in being "baptized."

As in mock baptisms in the male environment of New France voya-geurs, such rituals served to mark "thresholds to new cultural identities, and new states of occupation and manhood."[112] Beyond organizing and binding travelers, these initiation ceremonies also played a role in the construction and maintenance of masculinity. As with captive adoption rituals, the use of water in these rites was not perceived in hygienic terms, but as spiritual, supernatural expressions whose power had to be manipulated gingerly.[113] Having linens laundered on arrival in New Orleans after a trip in the hinterlands should be read as another ritual, one in which Saguingouara's unofficial tutor may have initiated him. This was a ritual designed to ensure, through clean clothing, that a threshold had been passed and life as a Frenchman resumed.

Skin Color

In the eighteenth century, cleanliness practices took place against the backdrop of these ritualistic uses of water, now no longer equated with cleaning the body. While Vespucci had emphasized the Indians' cleaning of their bodies through washing with water, later travelers and colonists dwelled instead on the grease Indians applied to the face and body. These unguents left a film of grease or color on the skin, as seen in the colorful touches to artists' depictions of Indians in French and British colonies (see Plates 1, 19, 20, 21, 32), while setting the stage for nineteenth- and twentieth-century stereotypes of Indians as dirty. The distinction in native and French concepts of cleanliness is crucial for understanding how Europeans apprehended indigenous bodies and rationalized differences in skin color. In the eighteenth century, and in spite of the emergence of increasingly protobiological notions of a fixed "racial" identity, travelers and settlers continued to explain the development of skin color as resulting from the effects of the environment. As colonist Antoine Simon Le Page du Pratz (in Louisiana in 1718–34) wrote in his *History of Louisiana*, the rays of the sun combined with the application of grease in the production of darkened skin:

> The infants of the natives are white when they are born, but they soon turn brown, as they are rubbed with bear's oil and exposed to the sun. They rub them with oil, both to render their nerves more flexible, and also to prevent the flies from stinging them, as they suffer them to roll about naked upon all fours, before they are able to walk upright.[114]

As suggested by Father Poisson, voyageurs were amenable to a similar transformation, as seen in his description of these men "more sun-burnt and more swarthy than the Sauvages" and, what's more, "clad with but one garment" (undoubtedly an unlaundered one).[115]

While it is rare to find evidence of Indians' views of skin color, there seems to have been a correlating belief in the effect of the sun among some nations. Two brothers, Pierre and Jean-Baptiste Talon, survivors of La Salle's doomed 1684 expedition to the Gulf, had been adopted as children, respectively by the Cenis and Karankawas. In their joint interview upon their eventual return to France in 1698, they described the process whereby their adopters sought not merely to acculturate them, but to cause their external, physical metamorphosis into Cenis and Karankawas. Not only did the two sets of captors initiate the children into new customs and cultural practices such as tattooing, but "they often exposed the said Talons and other young Frenchmen [to the sun] to make them become tanned like themselves."[116] At least, this was how the French boys interpreted their experience with captive adoption and the mutability of skin color, in terms strikingly similar to those associated with Frenchification. Here, it was the sun that acted as catalyst in the mutation of skin color, and this was incremental. In contrast, tattooing was understood by both French and Indians as instantaneous and decorative, though not necessarily as permanent (see Chapter 6). But the effect of the sun was not the only way Europeans explained the skin color of Indians, as seen in Le Pratz's reference to bear oil.

References to the application of grease had appeared in the earliest accounts of travelers to New France as a factor in the color of skin, with one Jesuit missionary noting in 1610–13, for example, that "[Indians] have the same complexion as the French, although they disfigure it with fat and rancid oil, with which they grease themselves; nor do they neglect paints of various colors."[117] Such early accounts described Indian skin as *basané*, or tawny from the effects of the sun and pigmentation. Nancy Shoemaker has noted the increasing tendency from the eighteenth century on, first among the French and then among the English, to describe Indians' skin color not simply as tawny or brown, but specifically as "red," a term that originated with Indians but that we can in fact trace back to the seventeenth century.[118] The Company of the Indies employee Caillot used this terminology in his 1729 account, when he described Indians (he didn't differentiate among them) as "a dark reddish color."[119] Caillot left unspoken the source of the coloration, but others were more precise in their explanations. Beyond the effects of the climate on the production of skin color, travelers to Louisiana repeatedly stressed the role played by the regular rubbing of grease onto the body as a factor in the darkening of skin. This grease was applied to the face and body as means of warding off mosquitoes and the cold as well as for aesthetic reasons, and it was often pigmented.[120] In other words, the practice, for Indians, was simultaneously functional and aesthetic.

Accounts from beyond Louisiana were similarly unanimous in emphasizing the effects of the application of tinted grease as an adjunct to the sun's rays in the explanation of Indians' skin color. An account from 1689 incorporated a section devoted to "THEIR COMPLEXION AND COLOUR. They are of a tawny colour, and they make themselves more so, by anointing their bodies with bear's grease which they do, to preserve themselves from the heat of the sun, which they endure much better than the Inglish."[121] Nearly a century later, James Adair's *History of the Indians*, published in 1775 but based on his experiences as a trader among the Cherokee and Chickasaw in the mid-eighteenth century, provided another detailed explanation of the process:

> the parching winds, and hot sun-beams, beating upon their naked bodies, in their various gradations of life, necessarily tarnish their skins with the tawny red colour. Add to this, their constant anointing themselves with bear's oil, or grease, mixt with a certain red root, which, by a peculiar property, is able alone, in a few years time, to produce the Indian colour in those who are white born, and who have even advanced to maturity.[122]

This emphasis on the effects of the climate and of grease represented a worldview resting on theories of monogenesis, and was premised on conceptions of identity as fluid and mutable rather than permanent and fixed.

This was why the Ursuline nuns in Quebec initiated their Indian boarders (targeted for Catholicism and Frenchification) in the practice of "washing" their bodies by friction and "chang[ing] their linen and clothes often" in order to remove the grease their parents had applied to their skin.[123] That practice dated to the mid-seventeenth century. But the premise underlying this cleaning of the skin, that skin color was mutable, was still being expressed in mid-eighteenth-century publications, even as conceptions of difference were becoming increasingly racialized. Pierre-François-Xavier de Charlevoix was explicit in explaining to his readers that identity was not essential or fixed: "The colour of the Indians does not, as many have convinced themselves, constitute a third species [of men] between the Blacks and the Whites. They are very tawny, and of a dirty and dark red, which is more sensible in Florida, of which Louisiana is a part: but this is not natural to them. The frequent rubs that they use, gives them this red [complexion]."[124] This passage from the description of Charlevoix's travels in New France in Canada dated from 1721, though it was first published in 1744, extending this view of skin color—and therefore of ethnic difference—as environmental and cultural: "manipulable rather than essential."[125] Evidence from a Wisconsin court case suggests that the popular belief in the mutability of ethnic identity survived into the mid-nineteenth century in spite of the ascendancy of biological formulations of race. In this case, whites persistently scrubbed the skin of a boy believed to have "become" Indian after a supposed abduction by an Indian woman, to wash away his new race and return his skin to its original, lighter coloring.[126] This fluid model for explaining how the skin of Indians, or others, had become "tawny"—whether in the colonial period or the nineteenth century—cannot be fully understood, however, without reference to cultural beliefs about how bodies were (or were not) cleaned.

In the mid-nineteenth-century context of the Wisconsin case, soap and water were directly applied to the boy's body to clean his skin and attempt to return it to its original color. In the seventeenth and eighteenth centuries, colonists (the Ursuline nuns, for example) expected laundered linens to achieve the same effect. Focusing on the act of cleaning the skin thus allows us to grasp how the French in eighteenth-century North America saw indigenous bodies, and how they constructed, explained, and represented visual signs of identity including skin color. Indians did not wear laundered linen garments, so their skin had darkened incrementally. Without linens, bodies tanned, and the pigmented grease rubbed into Indian bodies on a daily basis was not, according to French logic, removed.

Washing as an attribute of identity rested on a couple of contrasts. On the one hand, the "nudity" of Indian bodies stood opposed to the invisibility of Europeans' bodies concealed by their "second skin"—linen shifts. On the other hand, the dirtiness of Indians' clothes was contrasted with the cleanliness of Europeans' linens. With his adherence to French laundering customs in New Orleans, Saguingouara clearly marked his body as a French one in that space. A court case from New Orleans puts the juxtaposition of French and indigenous customs in stark relief. In 1748 a band of African and Indian slave runaways had been recaptured following many months in hiding in a Choctaw village in the Louisiana backcountry. Their interrogation confirms a native disregard for clean clothing among the Choctaw, at least. One of the runaways, Joseph, a Chickasaw, was asked if he had seen, among the

Choctaw, any who wore shirts like his. This was an allusion to the fact that Joseph's shirt was of British manufacture. Local officials, ever conscious of imperial competition in North America, could distinguish (based primarily on the weave and fiber in the textiles, rather than the cut of the garment, which was uniform) between French and English manufactured goods as they sought to monitor the incursion of English goods and traders in territory they considered French. Joseph responded that most Choctaw wore deerskin shirts and some had small blankets in very poor shape. One, a man of standing, had a large dog's hair blanket that was black and red striped. Only one young man (a "banaret") had a shirt somewhat like his.

This selective availability of shirts among indigenous populations is confirmed in written sources of trade and gift giving and in visual records of European garments as the province of chiefs and other notables alone, as illustrated in de Batz's depiction of a captive Natchez chief in the top right corner of Plate 20. Unprompted by his interrogator, Joseph pointed out that it was only in being blacker (in other words, dirtier) and in worse condition that this young man's shirt differed from his. As for the enslaved Chickasaw Joseph, the fact that he noted that the Choctaw wore his shirt soiled might have meant his own linens were washed for him. More likely his attention to this feature above any other suggests he was attuned to the value the French attributed to clean shirts.[127]

The Chickasaw slave Joseph's description of the young Choctaw's shirt as dirtier and more worn than his confirms accounts from across North America of Indians wearing their clothes until they literally wore out, without ever washing them.[128] As Gordon M. Sayre has pointed out, the very value of beaver pelts to fur traders (and to the European hatters who manufactured these into hats) resided in the fact that the best ones were not just parchment skins ("castor sec" or dry beaver), but "castor gras" (translated literally as "greasy" beaver and meaning coat beaver).[129] These were pelts

> as have been worn by the Indians, who, having well tawed them on the inside, and rubbed them with the marrow of certain animals, with which I am not acquainted, in order to render them more pliant, sew several of them together, making a sort of garment, which they call a robe, and in which they wrap themselves with the fur inwards. They never put it off in winter, day or night; the long hair soon falls off, the down remaining and becoming oily, in which condition it is much fitter to be worked up by the hatters; who cannot make any use of the

dry [beaver], without a mixture of this fat along with it. They pretend it ought to have been worn from fifteen to eighteen months to be in its perfection.[130]

Because the value of beaver derived from hat manufacturers' demand for pelts that could more easily be felted, and that produced a "firmer, more lustrous, and more durable" hat, greasy coat beaver ("castor gras") that had been worn fetched up to twice as much as untreated and unworn pelts (see Plates 21 and 22).[131] Indeed, an earlier Dutch account specified that "unless the beaver has been worn and is dirty and greasy it will not felt property—therefore those old peltries are most valuable."[132] As emphasized in this description, grease and dirt were interrelated.

The association of worn beaver skins with grease/fat takes on added meaning when juxtaposed with European views of cleanliness. Indian wearers of beaver robes did not wash those robes, but neither did Europeans launder their *outer* garments. They did, however, launder the layer of clothing closest to their skin. The French found it striking, therefore, when they noticed that some Indians, like the Choctaw *banaret*, owned a shirt but did not launder it. They were especially perplexed at the sight of Indians wearing shirts under their clothing, in the French manner (as opposed to wearing it as an outer garment, like a robe). But since these shirts were not laundered, they were unable to provide the necessary function of cleaning the body. For the French, shirts were the garments worn closest to the body and constituted a kind of second skin, an extension of the body, that simultaneously represented the state of dress and nakedness.[133] This corporeal association, this elision of the space between body and clothing, determined the cultural value of laundered linens, one that had added resonance in the context of French-Indian cultural exchanges.

Small linens were intended to mediate between the body and outer garments, but also to serve, through a change of clothing, to cleanse the body of impurities. Indians did not have such a layer (or if they did, they didn't launder it), with the result that their outer garments would have been seen as absorbing the body's dirt, perspiration, and pigmented grease. Since these garments remained on the body, the skin was never purged of these impurities. The linguistic identification of worn beaver skins as "greasy" or "dirty" was consistent with this belief about the role of clothing in absorbing grease, grease that only the presence of freshly laundered linens could serve to remove. The absence of linens to mediate the space between the body and the outer garment was thus a significant factor in Europeans' perception of Indians' lack of cleanliness. In contrast, laundered linen clothing was key to achieving cleanliness and, therefore, key to the evaluation of Frenchification.

As with Indian wives of Frenchmen in the Illinois Country, Saguingouara's hygienic Frenchification may have been one result of his identification as Catholic. Although they may have had concerns about Indians becoming too invested in refinement and body care, missionaries and nuns did stress the importance of their converts' fundamental adherence to *French* ways of cleaning.[134] And water was not the only factor in this binary relationship between clean and unclean (that is, according to European definitions of washing). Soap, whether commercial or homemade, was the other catalyst needed to achieve cleanliness where clothes were concerned. The addition of soap to water for laundering clothes produced a chemical reaction with degreasing and deodorizing functions. But the presence of soap also served to culturally modify the water drawn from local sources, and it was no accident that colonists with the greatest stake in projecting (or having pretensions to) rank or spiritual authority were assiduous in their attempts to procure soap in their postings and encampments in Louisiana's hinterlands.[135] In so doing, they affirmed French ways of being premised on class-based and hierarchical conceptions of difference *among* Frenchmen.

Paying attention to soap, water, shirts, and laundry reveals distinctions in concepts of French and Indian concepts of cleanliness. This focus derives from analysis of Saguingouara's contract, but takes us beyond it, to highlight Europeans' understandings of indigenous bodies and how colonists rationalized differences in skin color according to their logic and knowledge base. In the eighteenth century, and in spite of the emergence of increasingly protobiological notions of a fixed "racial" identity, travelers and settlers continued to linger on the effects on skin color of the environment and of the application of grease. The absence of clothes washing to remove and negate the effects of the application of tinted unguents provided a key logistical step in Europeans' explanations of the visual appearance of Indians' skin color. Saguingouara's voyageur contract shows us how he sought to position himself within the French colonial order into which he had been integrated. The few words encoding his laundry clause also serve as a springboard to illuminate French conceptions of ethnicity as (literally) embodied in cultural practices such as washing. Saguingouara's desire for laundered linens thereby underlines the role that dress played in the construction of beliefs about identity in the early modern period.

CHAPTER 6

"We Are All *Sauvages*":
Frenchmen into Indians?

In 1739, the same year the French-Indian voyageur Saguingouara negotiated for his linens to be laundered, a nineteen-year-old youth of European descent set off on a trip from New Orleans to the military Fort de l'Assomption four hundred miles away in the hinterlands of Louisiana. As part of the preparations for his journey, he acquired two garments of Indian origin: a pair of *mitasses* (leggings) and a breechclout. Contrary to our assumptions about the identity of this nineteen-year-old, he was not a fur trader. Had he been a voyageur, we might have expected him to adopt indigenous dress to smooth negotiations with Indian suppliers. This young man was a cadet in the French troops of the marine. He served in this capacity by virtue of his rank as a member of the petty French provincial nobility, born at Mobile, whose family was embedded in the colonial power structure.

Antoine Philippe de Marigny, Écuyer, Sieur de Mandeville was here being equipped with two of the most identifiably and generic "Indian" elements of male attire first adopted by voyageurs in Canada and found also in the dress of fur traders and sundry other colonists of the "lower sort" in Louisiana. Often worn with a cheap ready-made trade shirt, moccasins, and an outer coat of varying degrees of elaboration, this was the ubiquitous garb of cross-cultural exchange across French and British colonial North America. It was a style created by osmosis and illustrated in countless visual and written depictions of European males journeying through territories claimed by the French and English, and apparently matched by the dress of countless Indians in these territories.[1] If some of these depictions of European men speak to a preoccupation with collecting and "playing Indian," other sources point to the way Indian dress was deployed in diplomatic and trade relations.[2]

In the Illinois Country, probate records reveal that male colonists there were both more thorough and more consistent in their appropriation of articles of indigenous origin. Of the sixty-one extant probate records for Frenchmen in the Illinois Country in which clothing is listed, thirteen contained a reference to *mitasses* (leggings), and eleven listed one or more breechclouts.[3] The voyageur Saguingouara's guardian, the aristocratic officer Franchomme, was among these, for he owned a breechclout, leggings, and moccasins. He also possessed a striking object that allied indigenous aesthetics to European function: a black powder horn decorated with porcupine quills, that perhaps had been made by his wife, an Indian widow of means, from quills traded from the Potawatomi.[4] The inclusion of such items among personal belongings of Frenchmen in Louisiana raises the question of how they viewed their own identity when living in the Indian manner. How *did* colonists like Marigny and Franchomme justify their adoption of Indian dress, and how did they manage the transgressions implicit in cultural cross-dressing and the risk of becoming Indian from their presence in a wild environment?

In 1681, one of the soldiers from La Salle's troops who had destroyed and deserted Fort Crevecoeur in the Illinois Country had lingered long enough to scribble a message: "NOUS SOMMES TOUS SAUVAGES, CE 15 A.... 1680" ("WE ARE ALL SAVAGES, THIS 15TH.... 1680"). Sieur Tonti, one of the leaders of the French expedition, had caused the words to be written in April, and a fragment of the inscription had been snatched off by Iroquois attackers. The message was directed at La Salle, who had sought out the civilizing written reassurance of "some writing or some sign of his men having been there."[5] But the declaration also betrayed the anxieties felt by a man who could feel his Frenchness slip away. As such, this inscription, or graffito, is suggestive of the fundamental instability Frenchmen felt as they colonized North America. For there was a corollary to lingering French beliefs in the mutability of identity as epitomized by Frenchification policies. If Indians could become French, then Frenchmen could become wild, or *sauvage*.

Wild Frenchmen

Clothing provided the means to regulate and control these anxieties, and focused on managing the risks posed to "Frenchness" by Frenchmen's presence in Louisiana. If wardrobe contents document the material means of becoming Indian through dress, so too should we look to individuals' apparel to explain Frenchmen's collective strategies for preventing or reversing Indianization. In Louisiana, cultural cross-dressing evokes Daniel Usner's now classic formulation of that colony as a fluid "frontier exchange economy" that blurred the lines between members of distinct social and ethnic groups. Indeed, young cadet Marigny's acceptance of crossover, indigenous dress for travel to the hinterlands (which he repeated over the course of his ten years in the colonial military forces) hints at the tacit recognition for even the social and military elite to wear clothing in common with Indians, troops, fur traders, and even African slaves. When subjected to a material culture analysis, however, the aesthetic qualities of the dress worn, and the geographical spaces and contexts in which they were worn, betray instead a preoccupation with promoting a rigid social structure in other arenas for sartorial expression. The regular dress worn by Franchomme and Marigny consisted primarily of French clothing that reflected their rank. In other words, the wearing of Indian garb was justified on the basis that it was utilitarian. But the performance of Frenchness further required additional support from the maintenance of social order and class distinction among colonial populations. It was also reversible, helping temper colonists' anxieties about being irrevocably turned into Indians.

*　*　*

Marigny, our young cadet, had been born in Mobile around 1721. Following the death of his father (who had in the meantime had illegitimate children with an enslaved Indian), the boy was placed under the guardianship of his mother's new spouse.[6] His stepfather Ignace Broutin was a royal engineer and surveyor whose architectural credits included the New Orleans military barracks (1732), Fort St. Jean-Baptiste at Natchitoches (1733), and the 1745 reconstruction of the Ursuline convent in New Orleans, among others.[7] Marigny remained under Broutin's tutelage (though he spent some years in France) until he reached his majority at twenty-five. At this age, he expected to enter into his inheritance from his late father. Instead, in 1746, he successfully filed suit against his stepfather to force him to render the accounts of the succession.[8] Broutin complied by submitting an eighteen-page memorandum that detailed every single expenditure on behalf of his stepson over the ten-year period from 1736 to 1745. The bulk of the records of expenditure related to the supply (and occasional repair) of clothing for Marigny's use, from elaborate three-piece suits down to the ribbon for his hair. Meticulously documented by date of expenditure and place of purchase, these records provide evidence of the contrasts between military and nonmilitary types of consumption, between the European and Canadian-derived styles that coexisted in Louisiana, and between the dress worn in relatively urbanized settlements such as New Orleans and in military outposts (as well as in transit between these).

It is in the pages of this memorandum that Broutin had documented spending ten livres on garments of indigenous derivation for Marigny's use for his service in military outposts or on the journey to these. An eyewitness description of the dress worn on campaign by soldiers in New France provided a succinct description of these breechclouts and leggings. The breechclout was "a piece of wool that one passes between the thighs in the fashion of the Indians, with the two ends tying onto a belt; one wears this without breeches to walk with more ease through the woods."[9] One Illinois Country inventory dating from 1755 itemized both the breechclout and its tie or belt among the possessions of a settler, a rare reference to details of cut and construction.[10] Leggings were commonly though not always worn over the breechclout (see the male in Plate 21), partly assuaging the simulation of nudity that was manifest in the wearing of breechclout alone. As described by another eyewitness in New France, these *mitasses* were

> a type of stockings that the Canadians construct from two half-ell lengths of wool, or one ell of [wool] flannel cut into two for each leg and sewn along the length of the leg according to the width of the thigh so that the leg can slip in, such that there remains an excess of fabric beyond the seam, measuring four to five inches in width that one allows to flutter along the length of the leg, or . . . in the shoe; and it is tied at the top with a garter above the thigh.[11]

The visual appearance of the breechclout can be judged from contemporary depictions of Indians by French artists in the colony. Alexandre de Batz's drawings, for instance, show both skin breechclouts (with their jagged edges) and some cut from blankets, with their distinctive white stripe (see Plate 1). In both cases the artists generally emphasized the nakedness of the Indian wearers.[12] The documented purchase of two elements of Indian garb for the use of a young noble gentleman cadet in the military speaks of a marked transformation in the appearance of those colonists who were posted to outlying military forts. Indians had made significant contributions to the development of dress on the colonial frontier, namely with respect to footwear (moccasins) and the use of breechclouts and leggings. In turn, this cross-cultural garb had just as significantly absorbed European influences.

Working for the Spanish Crown in the late 1790s, Nicolas de Finiels, a French engineer, was struck by the distinctiveness of dress in the former French settlements of the Illinois Country. In his account, he attributed these features (derived from New France) to the effects of prolonged interaction with Indians through trade relations mediated by fur traders:

> The proximity of the Indians, the ease of communicating with them, the need to hunt with them and live in their villages in order to trade— these had no small influence on the character of the colonists. They were compelled to adopt many Indian customs and clothing styles: the breechclout took the place of breeches; leggings replaced stockings; doeskin moccasins succeeded European shoes; a loose-fitting tunic covered the rest of the body; a blue kerchief wrapped about the head completed the costume. When cold weather renders this dress inadequate, a cloak of bergopzoom or rough blue fabric, fitted with a hood, protects the body. Some persons don fur hats that cover their necks and ears and a pair of fur mittens attached by a long string that passes over the shoulders like a stole; the mittens hang down on either side in case your hands need protection, but when not required they are out of the way without any danger of being forgotten or lost. With this simple outfit you can move easily through the woods, tracking deer, wildcats, and wild turkeys, and your body learns to endure the fatigue.[13]

While some elements of their dress had kept up with changes in fashion, or been influenced by access to a range of cloths, the main components of voyageurs' cross-cultural garb were seen in this description from the late eighteenth century into the Spanish colonial period: breechclout, leggings, moccasins, hooded outer garment familiar from Canadian voyageurs, and kerchief (see third figure from lower left, Plate 14).

This verbal account was reflected in surviving artifacts and visual images from the Illinois Country in the late eighteenth and early nineteenth centuries. Leggings and breechclouts hitherto constructed from hides were increasingly made from European manufactured textiles that, unlike skins, could withstand and wick off moisture, and also smelled different.[14] Some articles of clothing worn by French and Indian alike, such as the hooded *capot* (a garment erroneously included by Finiels among the "Indian customs and clothing styles" adopted by the colonists), followed the construction method of European garments. The collective sartorial elements of leggings, breechclout, moccasins, and *capot* had evolved to the point that from a distance at least, identifying Frenchman from Indian in the hinterlands was a challenge for Indians and French alike as they sought to identify friend from foe. Failure to make the correct identification could potentially have fatal consequences; in 1733, Osage Indians formally apologized to the French for killing a Frenchman, arguing that they had mistaken him for an (enemy) Indian on the basis of his appearance.[15] In 1680 the explorer Tonti had also been taken for an Illinois by Iroquois attackers, but he was spared when they spotted "from the fact that his ears weren't pierced that he was a Frenchman."[16] In 1729, French escapees from the Natchez massacre almost called out to a man dressed "à la française" only to realize as he came nearer that it was an Indian dressed in clothes stripped from the governor (or commandant).[17] In 1743, adopted captive Antoine Bonnefoy, having escaped from the Cherokee, took pains to convince a group of Alabama Indians he was not an enemy Indian. Only after one of his interlocutors had crossed the river and seen him *up close* was he recognized as a "Frenchman."[18] In the same decade, Jesuit traveler Charlevoix described the reverse, a Native American chief in New France dressed *like* a Canadian voyageur.[19] Notions of tradition, origin, novelty, were collapsed in these profuse accounts about ambiguous identities, but for all this evidence of cross-cultural exchange, distinctive colonist and Indian identities were not entirely muffled. As indicated in all these accounts, each group had stressed that they could ultimately distinguish between Indian and voyageur. Their insistence on this point is suggestive of a need to assuage fears about the slipperiness of French and Indian anxieties.

As travelers' descriptions of leggings and breechclouts suggest, the key factor was the suitability of this garb to moving "through the woods" and rivers. Functionality provided an essential justification for adoption of Indian dress in the hinterlands, building on European precedents for utilitarian garb for traveling. Marigny had acquired utilitarian apparel of French derivation immediately on arrival back from France to New Orleans in February 1737, when he was outfitted with two waistcoats and two pairs of breeches of *siamoise*. He bought another two sets of waistcoats and breeches, of gingham this time, the following year, and a pair of striped cotton dimity breeches in 1739. Marigny might have been expected to procure his clothing in France (where cloth and clothing were cheaper and more varied) prior to his departure for Louisiana. Certainly, his cadet's uniform would have been acquired prior to his departure. And yet, during his transit from France to New Orleans, Marigny had had to borrow a pair of shoes from a fellow cadet (reimbursed at a cost of twelve livres), suggesting that he lacked funds in France or had elected not to use his shipping allowance on coarse inexpensive textiles.[20]

The waistcoats and breeches can be identified as utilitarian by virtue of their textiles. *Siamoise*, dimity, and gingham were three relatively inexpensive but sturdy cotton or cotton/linen-mix cloths, appropriate choices of cloth for daily wear in the colony. Dimity was characterized by a small-scale repeat pattern in the same color as the ground, while gingham was usually checked. *Siamoise* was a French textile made in imitation of popular Indian goods. Identified at the highest echelons of the Ministry of the Marine as ideal for use in the colonies, this textile was indeed suitable for the humid Louisiana climate. In design, samples of *siamoise* manufactured in Rouen in 1743 show that these were brightly patterned fabrics (striped, checked, or floral, depending on the sex of the wearer; see Plates 5 and 27).[21] But though these textiles exhibited a degree of elaboration in their color and pattern, the lightweight *siamoise* and gingham breeches and waistcoats acquired for Marigny in New Orleans would have contrasted markedly with the expensive wool drab of his matching suits, or the rich velvet with which his formal breeches were made.

The inclusion in Marigny's wardrobe of *siamoise*, gingham, and dimity hint at the tacit recognition for even the social and military elite to wear common clothing in some contexts, even if the superior tailoring and new fabric might proclaim the wearer's status. Like Marigny, Alphonse de la Buissonniere, commandant in the Illinois Country, owned waistcoats and breeches of dimity and *cotonnade*, in addition to his rich array of military and civilian clothing.[22] Henri Joutel's relation of his 1685 trip with La Salle confirmed the reliance on textiles suitable for travel wear from the earliest period of European exploration: "for this is what we use the most in this country, where it is never cold. One is most often dressed in shirts, unless one has some lightweight suit."[23] Likewise, the foremost preoccupation for the officer Dumont de Montigny, on being instructed to go up the Arkansas River in 1722, was the selection of appropriate utilitarian clothes for this exploratory trip in search of mineral wealth: "Here I was again obliged to travel.... I had to obey, and after saying my farewells..., taken the necessary linens and clothes, to go to an unknown country where I had never been . . . I went and embarked myself on the pirogue of the Sr. du Freine."[24]

Dumont at this point gave no details of what he considered suitable apparel for the canoe trip to the hinterlands. Later that year, traveling in a pirogue accompanied by one soldier, on his way from Natchez to New Orleans, he was accidentally thrown overboard in the vicinity of Pointe Coupée:

> But fortunately I was at the time dressed only in my plain shirt on the body and a pair of trousers [grandes culottes]; it was July 26th or thereabouts when it was very hot. This mishap merely served as a bath, although it was an involuntary one, since when I re-embarked I was no longer wet.[25]

That Dumont was not wearing shoes as he rode on the pirogue was not surprising, given the need to constantly wade in water or mud, as also described in Joutel's eyewitness account: "We didn't have shoes, these would not have been very convenient in these sorts of voyages, where one often had to get into the water, on top of which, when one found oneself in muddy areas, they [the shoes] would be in danger of staying in the bottom [of the river]."[26]

Both Dumont and Joutel were referring to the role of the weather and circumstance in dictating their dress: shirt and linen trousers alone for use in the hinterlands. Marigny had acquired two pairs of midcalf loose linen "grandes culottes" in anticipation of his posting at the Natchez post. These trousers were staples of both sailors' French metropolitan working dress, illustrated, for example, in the dress of indentured workers on John Law's concession in Lower Louisiana and prominent in the wardrobes of African slaves in the colony (see Plates 28 and 29).[27] The young cadet had similarly procured supplies of cheap shirts while on site in military outposts.

Joutel had emphasized that "One is most often dressed in shirts." His comment suggests that French travelers wore their shirts as Indians did, as a garment (rather than the undergarment of European convention), worn loose and not tucked into nether garments, a cross-cultural style illustrated in the dress of the two Indian males in the top left corner of Plate 14. The cut and construction of shirts certainly lent itself to this style, with its overall length (reaching to midthigh) and extended back panel as seen in surviving examples (see Plate 26). The garment provided basic coverage of the body, though European eyes would still have perceived the nudity of the wearer. No wonder Marie Turpin, future Sister Ste. Marthe, had "kept her eyes downcast throughout the trip" from the Illinois Country to New Orleans. While this "sainted girl" might well have done so because she was "always at prayer," here was also a coded expression meant to convey this half-Indian girl's modesty and imperviousness to the sight of semiclad adult men.

The shirt was successfully adapted for travel dress, where it was worn Indian style. When worn in the European style, this garment was a means of signaling social distinction, based on its cut and fabric. While on site in military outposts, Marigny had favored plain or trade shirts. Trade shirts were ready-made garments, mass-manufactured in Europe from cheap textiles for export to the colonies.[28] Intended for use in the fur trade (see the figure of the captured Natchez chief in the upper right-hand corner of Plate 20 wearing a linen shirt), in Louisiana these were also worn by African slaves and poorer white settlers. In the account of Marigny's expenses, the retail price of these trade shirts was just over four livres each; he also purchased plain shirts (which could be ready-made or custom-made, sometimes of unbleached linen), at six livres a piece. These modest values contrast markedly with the twenty-five to thirty livres paid for each fine ruffled shirt (*chemise garnie*) purchased for him to wear when in New Orleans. Where trade shirts differed from plain shirts in the quality of the linen and of the sewing, *chemises garnies*, in addition to being made of finer bleached linen, were trimmed with ruffles at the collar and cuffs, with the very best ones being distinguished by sleeves very finely pleated with an iron (Plate 26).

Cloth and clothing, ostensibly consistent as *categories* of goods common to large swaths of consumers, were in fact subject to marked and recognizable gradations in quality and style that determined the access to choice. Apparel was also inherently gendered, including basic undergarments like shifts whose different cut and construction for males and females served to uphold gender distinctions (compare Plates 8 and 26). Marigny's consumer options encompassed access to new ready-made shirts of coarse fabric as well as custom-made garments of highest-grade textiles with high-quality trimmings. Those of lesser means also had a choice of fabric, but often driven by what was available on the second-hand market and at the lower end of cheap new fabrics. Though a range of options was available to the soldiers, impoverished settlers, Africans, and Indians who also counted among the ranks of consumers of shirts in the colony, the different qualities of the linen cloth, the variations in cut and construction and in decorative trimmings, meant that social and economic distinctions were signaled in the design of a staple garment such as the shirt.

Although the acquisition of stolen or fenced goods certainly increased the pool of textile grades available to the members of these disadvantaged groups, in no way could these be considered regular or consistent components of the provisioning system. Notwithstanding contemporary discourses about the erosion of class attributes through the deployment by the lower and even middling sorts of clothing deemed above their station, textiles and garments were clearly repositories of status and were earmarked for such a role in mediating social relations. Any deviation from this model represented a significant modulation of the process of deploying clothing to signify social and economic attributes. There were European conventions for the temporary acceptance by elites of practical, nonrefined clothing for travel as exemplified in Marigny's selection of coarse textiles and ready-made trade shirts. But Marigny's travel garb must also be evaluated in light of an environment fraught with physical danger for colonists. The wearing of class-coded apparel helped them resume their Frenchness when back in colonial settlements and even helped during their trips to the hinterlands.

As documented in Marigny's expenditure account, he continued to secure unrefined clothing (trade shirts, trousers, heavy-soled footwear) and indigenous styles (breechclout, leggings) even as he rose through the ranks first of *cadet à l'aiguillette* (gentleman cadet), then second ensign, and nomination to the rank of full ensign (a rank achieved in 1746, followed by final promotion to the rank of lieutenant in 1752).[29] Yet, beyond the question of how articles of travel dress, including those of Indian derivation, might be adapted, used, and viewed by a range of wearers and onlookers, cultural and class cross-dressing incorporates the possibility of *rejecting* as well as accepting particular articles of apparel. In light of Marigny's adoption of breechclouts and leggings worn with trade shirts, the absence in his wardrobe (and officer Dumont's) of the hooded *capot* stands out.

Related to the matchcoat in the English colonies, this garment was prevalent in the wardrobes of regular troops and *voyageurs*, ubiquitous in gifts to Indians in French America.[30]

Indeed, the *capot* had become the quintessential synthesis of European and indigenous sartorial cultures in cross-cultural dressing in New France and Louisiana. It typically represented the regional or occupational dress of Canadians, as seen by the third and sixth figure from the bottom left of Plate 14 and on the male in Plate 15. It was featured among the articles of clothing traded or given to Indians, and was a staple of slave dress (both African and Indian).[31] Its popularity and ubiquity as a component of the dress of soldiers is evoked by the wearing of hooded *capots* rather than regimental coats at the Arkansas Post (see Plate 24).[32] The depiction of relaxed, nonchalant soldiers surrounded by Indian warriors, wearing the *capot* and smoking pipes on duty, one soldier hunting, Indian-style, with a bow and arrow, was a potent image of the French ambivalence toward its military forces in Louisiana.

The *capot* was not part of the regular issue of soldiers' uniforms in Louisiana, but this garment was sometimes included among the shipments of uniforms to the colony and was also sourced locally.[33] Its adoption by troops was justified on the basis of functionality and as well adapted to the climate and physical environment, in contrast to the uniforms worn in France.[34] The presence of the hooded *capot* on the backs of soldiers at the Arkansas and other outposts would seem to validate the same apparently straightforward concern for functionality that was expressed in Marigny's adoption of breechclout and leggings for wear in the hinterlands.[35]

Associated from the onset with marginal groups, including enslaved Africans, the *capot* was in fact noticeably absent from officers' wardrobes in Lower Louisiana.[36] Unlike common soldiers, Dumont (as an officer) and Marigny (as a cadet and later an officer) were responsible for supplying their own military uniforms.[37] This provided a measure of control and individuality, yet officers' selection of apparel for military service followed a pattern. For example, the omission of the *capot* in Marigny's wardrobe was echoed in those of other members of the more affluent and high-ranking military personnel in Lower and Upper Louisiana, none of whom owned the garment.

The records pertaining to the succession of the late Chevalier de St. Agnet, a lieutenant of noble rank, helps contextualize Marigny's deployment of clothing. St. Agnet died at his military encampment in 1740, and separate inventories were made of his effects there and in New Orleans, where he lived with his wife and young child.[38] Scarlet-colored clothing, gold buttons, velvet suits, and fashionable colors ("couleur ventre de biche"—the color of a doe's stomach) were the keynotes of his dress in New Orleans. But when he was on active duty outside New Orleans, his wardrobe made substantial concessions to climate, topography, and social environment. For outerwear at his military encampment, the Chevalier de St. Agnet brought a few articles of more formal uniform attire such as a silk sword hanger. These reflected the prevalence among senior officers of lavish uniforms, including scarlet coats trimmed with gold galloon and accouterments such as stocks, gorgets, and elaborate sword hilts. This special garb was reserved for ceremonial occasions and formal interactions with Native Americans, as when the explorer

Bourgmont wore an elaborate blue and scarlet suit for an official encounter with the Apache, an outfit he ended up presenting to an Apache chief. This pattern of wearing ceremonial dress for diplomacy had been replicated since La Salle's first encounters with Indians. The showiness of color and ornamentation is found in the coat fragment attributed to La Salle and found in the shipwreck of his ship *La Belle* (see Plate 30).[39]

But St. Agnet's wardrobe at the encampment also included two redingotes (outer "riding" coats, or greatcoats), as well as utilitarian leather breeches and breeches made of *mazamet*, the inexpensive, low quality wool flannel so popular with voyageurs and as an object of exchange in the fur trade. Like St. Agnet, the postmortem inventory of de la Buissonniere, commandant at Fort de Chartres, included a redingote, as did that of New Orleans Councillor Bruslé, taken at his death in 1738.[40] For his part, the commandant of the Natchitoches post owned fifteen *surtouts* (a French variant on the redingote), mostly of silk trimmed with braid.[41] Officer Nicolas Pelletier de Franchomme, Saguingouara's guardian, who was married "to his material advantage" to an Indian widow in the Illinois Country, had owned a pair of leggings and used a powder horn of black kidskin decorated with porcupine quills. But he also owned *pitrebourg* wool breeches, a waistcoat, black silk stockings, and an old dress hat edged with silver (worn with a wig) that could be called on to signal his status as a member of the nobility in the French military.[42] As for Marigny, instead of the *capot*, there are a number of references to other styles of overcoat: the *grande veste* altered from his military uniform, or multiple silk-lined volants, another variant on the redingote.[43] These overgarment types, from the redingote and surtout to the *volant*, represented the sturdy all-weather garment worn by men of means in France. They had virtually identical functional qualities as the humble *capot*, but a different, certainly more sophisticated (and unambiguously French metropolitan) cut and construction (see Figures 13 and 14 in contrast to Plate 15).

We have seen how even in their encampments French officers brought soap to ensure their linens could be laundered, thereby upholding elite standards of dress. In the same way, even as the need for wearing a protective, practical over-garment of this type in Louisiana was acknowledged, and the *capot* included in the dress issued to slaves and soldiers, high-ranking colonists repudiated the modest *capot* in favor of related garments that were more appropriate to their rank and that proclaimed the more tailored cut, construction, and fabric of metropolitan French styles and fashions. Form clearly trumped function in the wardrobes of those male colonists who episodically

Figure 13 and 14. Greatcoat (front and back view), ca. 1780, wool. Chester County Historical Society Acc. 1991-7. Courtesy of Chester County Historical Society, West Chester, Pennsylvania.

inhabited the hinterlands, marking the differences between members of distinct professional groups, ethnicities, and ranks, even though on the surface a shared dress code might suggest cohesion and collapsed social and ethnic boundaries.

There was another factor. Most studies of cultural cross-dressing have downplayed or left unexplained the difference between permanent and temporary acts of cultural cross-dressing.[44] Tattooing of course fell into the former category. Used by warriors as a mnemonic device to record and advertise their exploits, the practice was adopted by some Frenchmen. But here too rank exerted an influence on the willingness of Frenchmen to be tattooed. It is rare to find records of elites with tattoos (especially those not dissimulated by articles of dress), as underscored by the renown of the select few who were so marked. Even the permanency of tattooing was contested by the French. Dumont de Montigny and Bossu, for example, claimed to have been tattooed with the cross of St. Louis and a deer respectively. But both also boasted of having discovered the secret to removing the indelible markings. Their assertions put into question their claims of having been tattooed in the first place. Above all, this purported knowledge of how to reverse tattooing underscores that it was vital for French cultural cross-dressers to find a way to resume their French identity.[45]

With the exception of the occasional tattoo (reversible or not), for Marigny and his fellow officers, cultural cross-dressing was *episodic*. Marigny's adoption of breechclout and leggings did not represent one stage in a progressive evolution toward creolization (with attendant risks of descent into savagery as informed by lingering popular understandings of the role of climate and environment on constructing identity and even imparting color to physiognomy).[46] Father Poisson's description of "our travelers" on a voyage from New Orleans to Natchez clearly expressed his disquiet and revulsion: "To see these men, clad with but one garment, more sun-burnt and more swarthy than the Savages,—stretched upon the sand or squatting like monkeys, devouring what they hold in their hand!—one does not know whether they are a company of Gypsies, or of people holding a witches' revel."[47] This worldview would prove tenacious even as new protobiological models of difference surfaced. The concept of the wild man (or woman, or child) predated France's colonization of North America.[48] But according to the way this model was applied in French America, Indians could conceivably "improve" their state through conversion and Frenchification to become "French," as we have seen, just as "civilized" Frenchmen might "degenerate" into wild men by becoming Indian. Dress channeled each of these potential instances of metamorphosis.

Stripped Bodies

Colonists were clearly troubled by the threat implicit in living in isolated French settlements surrounded by more populous groups of Indians. It is notable, for example, that so many colonists' published and unpublished accounts of their experiences of Louisiana incorporated written and, especially visual depictions of torture. This can be seen in the depictions Marc-Antoine Caillot and Jean-François-Benjamin Dumont de Montigny drew for their manuscripts, and colonists such as Antoine Simon Le Page du Pratz ensured were included in their published memoirs. Dress (or rather, the total lack of) was a ubiquitous attribute of these images of captives in the process of being tortured (see Plate 32, Figures 10 and 15). As seen in Company of the Indies employee Caillot's especially vivid account of the aftermath of the 1729 Natchez massacre, clothing was a key factor in colonists' anxieties about the risks that Indians posed to the French and the fears that they too might become *sauvage*.[49]

The Natchez uprising of November 1729 was a well-executed surprise attack that left approximately 200 dead (mostly male) of a population at this settlement of 400 colonists and 280 enslaved Africans. A further 80 women and 150 enslaved Africans were taken captive.[50] Colonists responded with shock to the uprising, culminating in a plethora of written accounts of the attack, the prelude to the attack, and its consequences; fears about possible future Indian attacks or joint insurrections by Indians and Africans colored these reports. Whether describing massacre, captivity, plunder, torture, or as we will see, masquerade misrule, these accounts alternated the passivity of being stripped with the agency of getting redressed (or dressed up).

Caillot's account began with the arrival of French survivors, some of them "totally naked, and others with breechclouts [*cannecons*, or underwear]." His narrative would continue to hone in on aspects of dress and undress,[51] As seen in Chapter 5, from a dress historical standpoint it is essential to note that "nakedness" was an ambiguous term; the more common definition of being "naked," as underlined by Furetière in his dictionary, meant being stripped to one's shift, or underwear. A rarer use of the word was to signal total nakedness, in which case the term had to be qualified. Thus, some of those arriving on the pirogue were "*totally* naked." The women added that when they were freed (following paying Choctaw intermediaries a ransom consisting mostly of dress and textiles, along with some guns and tools), they were "as naked *as when they were born.*" Likewise, a boy who was tortured was "stripped naked *like the hand.*" Dumont de Montigny's account of the torture and death of two other colonists was more detailed, as he recounted that they were first stripped of their clothes, and made "naked as the hand," before their bodies were ceremonially rubbed with the black ointment that sealed their ultimate fate.[52]

Here were examples of the literal and metaphorical loss of identity (not simply the embarrassment) caused by the absence even of the shift, that unseen garment that was an extension of the skin. Conversely, Caillot and Dumont had both described a surfeit of French dress on the bodies of Natchez plunderers and their allies. So, French men, women and children were denuded (or Indian-style, as the colonists understood it), and Indians were dressed "à la française." Into this topsy-turvy world, indeed, in the very middle of his description of the Natchez massacre, Caillot introduced an episode centered on masquerade and Mardi Gras festivities.

Earlier in his manuscript, Caillot had inserted a reference to misrule, in the context of the passage through the Tropic of Cancer, a ritual intended to counter anxieties about crossing new thresholds in the open sea. With his account of masquerade in New Orleans so soon after the Natchez massacre, Caillot offered the earliest known account of Mardi Gras in New Orleans, one that took place during a wedding party in Bayou St. Jean, just north of the city, on Fat Monday. No costumes were available for hire or purchase in New Orleans, and Caillot claimed credit for instigating this Mardi Gras masquerade and for designing the disguises and concocting the masks (see Plate 31). Caillot drew out the description of his own white shepherdess costume, worn over a woman's shift, stays, and hoops, and highlighted by the addition of decorative black silk beauty patches ("mouches") to his closely shaven face and even to his breasts, to simulate women's nipples. He also described the soldiers he had engaged to play music, and the eight "real" enslaved Africans deployed to hold torches as the procession made its way through the wilderness on the path from New Orleans to Bayou St. Jean (see Plate 33). The escort of actual French soldiers and real African slaves protecting French elites as they made their way helped uphold the narrative of a stable and hierarchical colonial order even in the midst of this dangerous environment, a point reiterated by the sudden appearance of four huge bears along the way. It was all the more important for Caillot to reassure his reader on his point, given colonists' fears of a mass revolt against the French by Indians and Africans.[53]

What is especially notable about Caillot's presentation of the masquerade is that the majority of the costumes, like his, were centered on sexual cross-dressing, and followed by strictly heterosexual encounters once unmasked at the party. None of the French had masked in ways that invoked cultural cross-dressing or made any allusion whatsoever to Louisiana's colonial environment. Temporary transgressions of gender and class under the conditions of masquerade were conceivable.[54] In the aftermath of the Natchez uprising, cultural cross-dressing was simply too close to reality, as Caillot signaled with his resumption of the account of the aftermath of the uprising and his cautionary tale of Frenchmen who might become too much like Indians.

Having completed his foray into a colonial-pastoral masquerade, Caillot redirected his reader back to the Natchez massacre with one more story of stripping, this time involving a Natchez woman, as signaled by an in-text drawing of a totally naked woman attached to two squared poles as she awaits her torture (Figure 15). The Natchez woman had been captured by Tunica allies who had presented her to the French for them to take revenge on her and her nation. The governor had officially refused to accept the woman but left her to the Tunica, anticipating they would ritually torture and kill her. Colonists went to witness the torture; Caillot himself, if we are to believe him, and others directly participated in it.

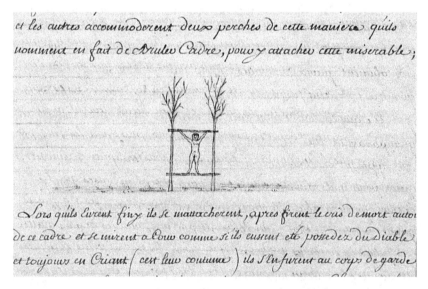

Figure 15. *Relation du voyage de la Louisiane ou Nouv.lle France fait par le Sr. Caillot en l'année 1730.* Ms. 2005.11, 169. Courtesy of the Historic New Orleans Collection.

This French involvement in torturing took place following the ritual burning of her body. As they were about to kill her, "the Frenchwomen who had suffered in her hands at the Natchez each took a pointed cane and larded her." But more was to come than this image of revenge on Indian terms. "I assure you that one must have a firm heart to be able to watch such spectacles," wrote Caillot, but "what I found odious and execrable was a soldier who, while she was dying, cut a piece of her . . . and ate it; as punishment he was put in irons and made to run through the gauntlet." This act almost mirrored a purported eyewitness account of the torture on the frame inflicted on Frenchmen in the immediate aftermath of the Natchez uprising, which began with scalping (Plate 32) and was capped by cutting off their genitals, which were then placed in the captives' mouths.[55] Whether apocryphal or not, Caillot's account of French men and women torturing, and doing so in "the Indian manner" (rather than the French torture techniques mandated for use in judicial court cases) was a frightening warning to colonists that Frenchness was not a permanent and stable condition.

It is with these horrific transgressions in mind that we need to consider the role of dress in reasserting the French identity of male and female colonists. New Orleans inhabitants reacted to the sight and sound of captives and victims whom Indians had stripped down to their skin, by clinging to French dress in all its emphasis on signaling social distinctions. On reentry into New Orleans, for example, the Company of the Indies immediately provided the escapees with new clothing, though Dumont (who would marry one of them) noted they were charged for the privilege.[56] Meanwhile, Caillot and other company employees were placed in militias to protect the town from any other attacks; he and his companions devised and paid for an elaborate dress uniform for this purpose. Consisting of a *volant* outercoat of red camlet, a hat with silver braid, white cotton waistcoat and breeches, and white silk stockings, its primary purpose seemed to be to visually and materially distinguish this group from mere inhabitants. It also stands out from the *capot* worn by soldiers in the buffalo robe depiction of the Arkansas post (see Plate 24).[57]

Travelers like Marigny had similarly tempered the risks that the hinterlands posed to their Frenchness by changing back into French dress upon their return to urbanized colonial settlements. Saguingouara (and his aristocratic guardian before him, no doubt) had similarly reiterated his Frenchness upon arrival into New Orleans by making a point of reestablishing French cultural standards of body cleanliness. Marigny's memorandum makes clear that his trade shirts and cheap, lightweight apparel, his Indian leggings and breechclouts were exclusively reserved for military service in Mobile (itself relatively urbanized), La Balize, Natchez, and Fort de l'Assomption, where he was intermittently posted, or on the journey to these, and that they were often bought or altered in the posts. In New Orleans, more refined and expensive clothes were commissioned or bought for his use in this urbanized environment.

Urbanization was of course relative in colonial Louisiana. But though its population stood at 905 European colonists in 1731, New Orleans had been conceived as a city, and in key respects colonists strove to fulfill that vision of an ordered colonial city.[58] One way they did so was through consumption. In response to a colonial environment marked by demographic dominance of enslaved Africans, elites and middling groups sought to reinforce and extend social cohesion through consumer and leisure activities such as shopping, and by echoing the material culture of their exact peers and kin in France. For example, Augustin Chantalou was a bureaucrat of middling origin; his family's consumption was mapped onto that of their exact peers at La Rochelle, as seen in the style of his wigs and of the apparel and jewelry he ordered from relatives for his wife's use. As for the New Orleans-born wife of a provincial nobleman, the Chevalier de Pradel, she not only shopped with the governor's wife but also ordered an expensive brocaded silk taffeta gown from the governor's Parisian merchant. The chevalier himself based his plantation house, Monplaisir, on the latest French landscaping and furnishing fashions; he also termed it a *chateau*, calling attention to its association with the elite French architecture that this nobleman's kin in France would instantly recognize.[59]

Such settlers also asserted their privileged status through etiquette practices known to the few. Marigny's stepfather and guardian, Ignace Broutin, was well attuned to these aspects. His 1733 architectural drawing of the enclosure of the New Orleans powder magazine depicts two soldiers flanked by two couples promenading (see Plate 16). Even in the Illinois Country, the promenade was an important social ritual.[60] But walking elegantly was a skill elites had to learn to master, and Marigny was served by writing masters, dancing masters, and fencing masters while in New Orleans, for to carry arms, dance, and walk were acquired talents.[61] Aside from such skills, the structure of garments and undergarments, such as boned corsets and hooped petticoats for women or padded coats for men, also affected bearing.[62] These features are visible in Broutin's drawing. On the left side, a soldier from the marine troops stands guard with his gray-white coat lined and cuffed in blue, blue waistcoat, breeches, and stockings, black tricorn hat, and yellow/gold sword hanger. Ambling beside him is a couple (accompanied by a dog) on a promenade, the man in a wig and tricorn hat and a formal three-piece suit with the large "boot" cuff sleeves and fashionably wide coat skirts of the 1720s–30s, the woman in a gown (an open robe "à la française" of the type seen in Plate 13) with a fashionable hat. On the right is another soldier, wearing a red coat lined with blue cuffs, blue waistcoat, breeches and stockings, black tricorn hat and white/silver sword hanger (probably that of the Karrer Swiss regiment).[63] Near him is a group consisting of a man, woman, and child, this time turning their backs to us (the child, trailing behind, appears to be facing the viewer), and revealing the sword and sword hanger that distinguished the man, in his three-piece suit, as elite; the woman and child wear long gowns. The brushwork is minimalist, consistent with that of an engineer's drafting skills. However, the silhouettes follow the general outline of fashionable dress and this drawing may be considered an accurate depiction of New Orleans in the early 1730s, one in which colonists advertised their rank visually, through their posture and deportment, but also through hooped petticoats and embellishments such as wigs. Similarly, when in New Orleans, Marigny rejected Indian and coarse clothing, making sure that his status was visible to onlookers: he wore fine ruffled shirts, silk hair ribbons, silk stockings, formal breeches of rich silk plush, and an expensive three-piece suit of heavy wool drab trimmed with silver filigree buttons that may or may not have contained perfume wafting around him as he walked.[64]

Colonists deployed clothing to uphold the fiction of a French moral and social order in the colony, allowing them to exert control over the hinterlands—a potentially dangerous and alien environment not yet subsumed to colonial rule. The way cultural cross-dressing was regulated along class lines ensured this fiction and resolved one of the implicit conflicts in cross-dressing. Furthermore, like masquerade, cultural cross-dressing by Frenchmen such as Marigny constituted only a *temporary* and reversible mutation or metamorphosis. Wearing Indian dress *in specific spaces* (that is, not in New Orleans) allowed visitors to the hinterlands to temporarily "belong" to that borderland space. Like masquerade, it offered the protection of a disguise, defusing anxieties about venturing into this geographical and ideological space. The social and ethnic fluidity epitomized by cultural cross-dressing was thus contained, restricted to precisely delineated spaces and spheres of interaction that imposed limits on a vast colony that the French only sparsely settled. This temporary yielding to a cross-cultural identity was explained by functionality (such as climate and requirements of travel). But most of all, it was rationalized on the basis of its reversibility, as signaled concretely, materially, through Marigny's change of dress when in New Orleans.[65] Travel in the hinterlands may indeed have exposed the French to "a thousand dangers for both their Bodies and their souls."[66] But I suggest that clothing helped to manage and defuse these risks. Far from enabling the gradual transformation of Frenchmen into Indians, I suggest that colonists saw cultural cross-dressing as a way to avert a permanent change in their identity. French and Indian may have temporarily merged identities as they literally switched clothes and traded spaces on the colonial Louisiana frontier and absorbed something from their exchange of material culture. But as with the performance of masquerade, which colonists understood as hinging on the reversibility of dress and identity, changing back into their French clothes reassured Frenchmen who had temporarily dressed cross-culturally that they had *not* become Indian.

Epilogue: "True French"

In 1725, Kaskaskia convert Marie Rouensa-8canic8e lay dying. As the suspense surrounding her will and codicil was playing out in the colonial village of Kaskaskia, another drama was brewing in the Illinois Country, at Fort de Chartres. Royal storekeeper Nicolas Chassin, her future son-in-law, had called a meeting of the Provincial Council to investigate the activities of Pierre Pericaut, suspected of theft from the storehouse. After being subjected to a court-sanctioned whipping to elicit a confession, on August 13, 1725, Pericaut was deposed and proceeded to describe his activities leading up to, during, and after the robbery. His testimony about the robbery described his theft of sundry trade items such as vermillion and hunting knives, as well as some gunpowder. But the primary emphasis was on textiles and apparel: two lengths of woolen stuff, camlet cloth, a necklace, and a bundle of shifts taken in a hurry "without counting them." From a legal standpoint, this was aggravated theft since he had broken into the storehouse, using a ladder to climb into the building and hiding his plunder in bushes while he went up and down to get more goods. Pericaut also named an accomplice, Pierrot. Pericaut's account of his interactions with Pierrot prior to the robbery described how he had gone "one Sunday to the habitation of M. de Boisbriand [the commandant] in order to make repairs to a *negresse*'s skirt, at the request of her husband." On leaving their house, Pericaut had encountered Pierrot, who asked him to repair his breeches, but he did not have time since he was on his way to the fort to steal, whereupon, the accused asserted, Pierrot joined him in the theft. The court then deposed Pierrot, who denied being Pericaut's accomplice, asserting that his breeches were leather and had no rips. The next day, Pericaut retracted his accusation against Pierrot.[1] Dress suffused this account that combined transgressions against the social (and economic) order; the informal economy; the acculturation to—and desire for—French ways of dressing. And it did so, in this instance, in the material culture expressions of enslaved Africans.[2] For, like Boisbriand's slaves whose clothing he had repaired, Pierre Pericaut and Pierrot were African chattel.

Indian wives of Frenchmen and their progeny had also adopted French dress, an interest matched by their immersion in French colonial furnishings, furniture, and architecture. The Crown, beginning in 1627, had held out the promise that Frenchification, together with conversion, would lead to Indians becoming, and acquiring the rights of, "natural men." Freed African slaves were extended the same right to become "natural subjects," though it was revocable. The slave codes required that masters baptize their African slaves and give them Sundays off, in parallel with the emphasis on conversion in Frenchification policies, but intermarriage was not seen as viable in Louisiana. The 1685 Antilles Code Noir, which was extended to Louisiana, had made limited provision for intermarriage between French and Africans. But there were only rare instances of such marriages in Louisiana in the early period and importation of large numbers of enslaved Africans into Louisiana was from the onset influenced by—and modeled on—the experience of Caribbean and other French colonies with a history of using African slave labor. French encounters with Africans there never allowed for the flexibility and hopes embodied in French-Indian relations. For this population group, racialization had already begun to crystallize, and no colonist, official, or missionary lobbied for French-African intermarriage, or even discussed it. By 1724 a new Code Noir was promulgated for Louisiana, the first major reworking of slave law since the 1685 code. It was mapped almost word for word onto the 1723 Code Noir for the Mascarene islands (primarily Île Bourbon and Île de France, modern-day La Réunion and Mauritius) in the Indian Ocean. In other words, the 1724 Code Noir was not simply an Atlantic product, but a global one.[3] In their 1715–16 debate, Commissaire-Ordonnateur Duclos (who had lived in South America) and Father La Vente (who had lived in Île Bourbon from 1698 to 1702) had made no direct reference to French-African relations.[4] On the surface, their preoccupations lay solely with the matter of French-Indian intermarriage. In 1715, Louisiana had not yet developed a significant African population. But Duclos and La Vente's choice of words was already mapped onto emerging racial beliefs about identity. The 1723 and 1724 Codes Noirs had renamed Europeans and Africans through skin color, as "whites" and "blacks." These terms were absent from the 1685 code with its allusion to *homme libre* (free man) or *esclave* (slave). Duclos and La Vente would similarly refer to skin color in their opposing views of French-Indian intermarriage. But though racial beliefs were already in the ascendancy, and though even proponents, like La Vente, had inflected their support of French-Indian intermarriage with comments about blood and skin color, Frenchification remained valid in the Illinois Country.

At the close of the French regime in the Illinois Country, mixed-heritage women were still being integrated within colonial society. In the 1760s, the granddaughters of Marie Rouensa-8canic8e (and great-granddaughters of the chief of the Kaskaskia) contracted marriages with members of the elite, including a European aristocrat living in Louisiana.[5] One of her grandsons became a gentleman cadet, like Antoine Philippe de Marigny, Sieur de Mandeville, and served alongside French officers of rank. These were the progeny from her second marriage to Michel Philippe, and they personify the value of conversion, intermarriage, and Frenchification in the Illinois Country.

The outcome for her children from her first marriage would be more ambiguous. Marie Rouensa had enthusiastically immersed herself in the Christian religion and colonial lifestyle to such a degree that she consented to Jesuit missionaries' entreaties to send her eldest son, Pierre Accault, to be educated in Canada, possibly with the goal of being trained as a priest in the Seminary College.[6] Pierre Accault disappeared from the record after September 1725.[7] Marie Rouensa's commitment to Catholicism and Frenchification was such that she then renounced another son, Michel Accault, for transgressing what she saw as his appropriate identity as French. In this attempt at controlling her son, her actions were a mirror image of her father's actions to enforce his will over her marital decisions. But where Chief Rouensa dealt with that episode as a matter of control over kin (and over a clan member), Marie Rouensa dealt with her son's rejection of her values by using French legal instruments, first by making a will in 1725, to which she later added a codicil allowing him to inherit if he repented and ceased living "among the sauvages."[8] Michel Accault's residence among the Kaskaskia prior to his mother's will is confirmed by his presence among the three chiefs of the Kaskaskia who had come to Fort de Chartres in 1723 with thirty of their men to ask for the pardon of a French soldier accused of murder.[9] While living among the Kaskaskia Indians, Michel had obviously entered into a marriage à la façon du pays with an unbaptized Indian woman, for Marie Rouensa cited his "disobedience" in the marriage he had entered into "despite his mother and relatives."[10]

In 1728, Michel Accault met the terms of his mother's codicil just long enough to legally enter into his inheritance.[11] By 1738, a missionary priest in the Illinois Country would single him out as the only legitimate "Métis" who had left the French village for a life among the Indians and noted that post commanders had never wanted to alienate or isolate him.[12] He would resume living among the French for a short time soon after the priest's comment, during an illness that eventually killed him.[13]

Marie Rouensa's progeny were not the only members of the Rouensa family whose existence intersected with those of the French. In January 1750, Father Gagnon registered the baptism of Louis, a son born to a *sauvagesse* named Elisabeth Michel Rouensa, "daughter of a chief of the Kaskaskia" and therefore a relative of Marie Rouensa. But Elisabeth lived in the Indian village of the Kaskaskia, not the French colonial village of the same name.[14] The father of the boy was French, named René de Couagne.[15] Both mother and child were baptized, testifying to the lingering influence of Catholicism on later generations of Indian and part-Indian women, even those who were excluded since 1719 from the fold of the French settlements. But the child was categorized as illegitimate; Elisabeth Michel Rouensa's union with de Couagne was not a legal, religious marriage of the kind Marie Rouensa had entered into and that led her and her cohort to be recharacterized as French. Living in an Indian village, not immersed in the French material culture of the colonial villages, Elisabeth remained, in the eyes of the missionary priest who recorded the baptism, a "sauvagesse."

Here was one Indian family with two outcomes predicated on whether its members had lived "in [the Indian] manner" or as materially and legally integrated in a French colonial settlement. Comparison of the two branches reveals that, to the French who assigned and recorded ethnonyms *in the Illinois Country*, birth was not the primary means of distinguishing French from Indian. As seen through Louis de Couagne's baptismal record, it was not Catholicism or the French blood that coursed through their veins that provided onlookers the means to distinguish between wild and Frenchified Indians. It was "their manner of living." Marie Rouensa's progeny from her marriage to Michel Philippe lived within French settlements, and like "the majority of [legitimate Métis]" there, lived "like true French."[16] Material culture marked the divisions between the two families. Proponents of intermarriage could— quite literally—look to the Frenchified appearance of these "true" French men and women to support their views that identity was flexible and mutable. As a result of what they believed they saw, such colonists would act to protect the legal rights of Frenchified Indians, and in so doing, they slowed the spread of racialization.

ABBREVIATIONS

===

AM	Archives de France. Marine. Microfilm copy in Library of Congress.
AMUQ	Archives of the Monastery of the Ursulines, Québec, Canada.
ANOM	Archives Nationales d'Outre-mer, Aix-en-Provence, France. Microfilm copy in Library of Congress.
ASQ	Archives of the Seminary of Québec, Quebec.
AUQ	Archives of the Ursulines of Québec, Quebec.
Ayer	Ayer Collection, Newberry Library, Chicago.
BFTRMM	Business and Fur Trade Records of Montreal Merchants, 1712–1806. Antiquarian and Numismatic Society of Montreal. Microfilm copy in French Michilimackinac Research Project Collection, Western Michigan University Regional Archives
BNF	Bibliothèque Nationale de France, Paris.
CHS	Kaskaskia and Fort de Chartres Collections, Chicago Historical Society, Chicago.
CISHL	Theodore Calvin Pease and Raymond C. Werner, eds., *The French Foundations, 1680–1693*, Collections of the Illinois State Historical Library 23, French Series vol. 1 (Springfield: Trustees of the Illinois State Historical Library, 1934).
DLB	Glenn R. Conrad, ed., *A Dictionary of Louisiana Biography*, 2 vols. (New Orleans: Louisiana Historical Association, 1988).
FFL	Glenn R. Conrad, trans. and comp., *The First Families of Louisiana*, 2 vols. (Baton Rouge: Claitor's, 1970).
HNOC	Historic New Orleans Collection, New Orleans.
JR	Reuben Gold Thwaites, ed., *The Jesuit Relations and Allied Documents*, 73 vols. (Cleveland: Burrows Bros., 1896–1901).
KM	Kaskaskia Manuscripts, Randolph County Courthouse, Chester, Illinois.
Lorient	Archives de l'Arrondissement Maritime de Lorient, France.

MHS   Missouri Historical Society Collections, St. Louis.

MPA   Dunbar Rowland, A. G. Sanders, and Patricia Kay Galloway, eds. and trans., *Mississippi Provincial Archives, French Dominion*, 5 vols. (Jackson: Press of the Mississippi Department of Archives and History, 1927–85).

NL   Newberry Library, Chicago.

NONA   New Orleans Notarial Archives, Parish of Orleans, now in the Notarial Archives Research Center, New Orleans.

NP   Natchitoches Archives, Natchitoches Parish, Louisiana. Microfilm copy in Family History Library of the Church of Jesus Christ of Latter Day Saints.

PFFA   Marthe Faribault-Beauregard, ed., *La Population des forts français d'Amérique (XVIIIe siècle): Repertoire des baptêmes, marriages et sépultures célèbres dans les forts et les établissements français en Amérique du Nord au XVIIIe siècle*, 2 vols. (Montréal: Bergeron, 1982–84).

Rochefort   Archives du Port de Rochefort, France.

RPHD   Research Program in Historical Demography of the University of Montreal, http://www.genealogie.umontreal.ca/en/leprdh.htm.

RSCL   Records of the Superior Council of Louisiana (1717–69), Louisiana State Museum, New Orleans.

SGA   Ste. Genevieve Archives, Missouri, microfilm copy in the State Historical Society of Missouri, St. Louis.

UCANO   Ursuline Convent Archives, Parish of Orleans, microfilm, Historic New Orleans Collection, New Orleans.

VP   Vaudreuil Papers, Loudoun Collection, Huntington Library, San Marino, California.

NOTES

===

Introduction

1. While the term *métissage* (like "race" and "gender") is anachronistic, it is used here (in preference to the English "miscegenation" with its explicitly biological connotations) to convey the full range of sexual and marital unions and procreation.

2. Throughout, *sauvage* will be used in preference to the English "savage" to retain the original French definition of the word as meaning wild or untamed. Notwithstanding critiques of "identity" as too protean (Brubaker and Cooper, "Beyond "Identity"" and Hodson, "Weird Science"), it is this very quality that provides the flexibility needed for my analysis.

3. Aubert, " 'The Blood of France' "; Belmessous, "Assimilation and Racialism."

4. Havard and Vidal, *Histoire de l'Amérique française.*

5. Vidal, "Africains et Européens au pays des Illinois" and "Private and State Violence Against African Slaves in Lower Louisiana"; Ekberg, "Black Slavery in Illinois, 1720–1765" and "Black Slaves in the Illinois Country, 1721–1755"; also Heerman, "That "acursed Illinois venture."

6. Aubert, "The Blood of France"; Belmessous, "Assimilation and Racialism"; Emily Clark, *Masterless Mistresses*; Dawdy, *Building the Devil's Empire*; DuVal, *The Native Ground*; Jaenen, *Friend and Foe*; Hall, *Africans in Colonial Louisiana*; Ingersoll, *Mammon and Manon in Early New Orleans*; Spear, *Race, Sex, and Social Order in Early New Orleans*; Usner, *Indians, Settlers, and Slaves in a Frontier Exchange Economy.*

7. See, for example, Shoemaker, *A Strange Likeness*; Chaplin, *Subject Matter*; Kathleen M. Brown, "Native Americans and Early Modern Concepts of Race."

8. Spear, "Colonial Intimacies" and " 'They Need Wives.' "

9. DuPlessis, "Cloth and the Emergence of the Atlantic Economy" and "Defining a French Atlantic Empire: some material culture evidence," in Augeron and DuPlessis, *Fleuves et colonies*, 291–300; Dean L. Anderson, "Documentary and Archaeological Perspectives on European Trade Goods" and "The Flow of European Trade Goods into the Western Great Lakes Region, 1715–1760"; Dubé, "Les Biens publics," which stresses the importance of textile imports and see in particular Table 6.1 p. 321; Breen, *Marketplace of Revolution*, 56

10. See, for example, Glassie, "Meaningful Things and Appropriate Myths."

11. Key works include Buckridge, *The Language of Dress*; Castro, "Stripped"; DuPlessis, "Circulation des textiles et des valeurs dans la Nouvelle-France" and "Circulation et appropriation des mouchoirs chez les colons et aborigènes"; Foster, *New Raiments of Self*; Little, " 'Shoot That Rogue' "; Loren, *The Archaeology of Clothing and Bodily Adornment in Colonial America*; Mackie, "Cultural Cross-Dressing"; Ann Smart Martin, *Buying into the World of Goods*, esp. chap. 6;

Maynard, *Fashioned from Penury*; Prude, "To Look upon the 'Lower Sort'"; Shannon, "Dressing for Success on the Mohawk Frontier"; Tobin, *Picturing Imperial Power*; Ulrich, "Cloth, Clothing, and Early American Social History"; Waldstreicher, "Reading the Runaways"; White and White, *Stylin'*; Sophie White, "'Wearing Three or Four Handkerchiefs.'"

12. See, for example, Castro, "Stripped"; and Haefeli and Sweeney, *Captors and Captives*, 145–63.

13. Caroline Weber, *Queen of Fashion*, 25–32. This was the custom throughout Europe; see, for example, Welch, "Art on the Edge," 247–49.

14. Belmessous, "Assimilation and Racialism"; "Être français en Nouvelle-France"; and "D'un préjugé culturel à un préjugé racial"; Havard, "'Les Forcer à devenir cytoyens'"; Jaenen, "The Frenchification and Evangelization of the Amerindians in the Seventeenth-Century New France," *Friend and Foe*, and "Miscegenation in Eighteenth Century New France"; Melzer, "The Underside of France's Civilizing Mission," "The Magic of French Culture," and "L'Histoire oubliée de la colonisation française." On the expression "franciser" (to Frenchify), see Belmessous, "Assimilation and Racialism," 323 n. 7.

15. Belmessous, "Être français." On Frenchness and French national identity in this period, see Bell, "Recent Works on Early Modern French National Identity"; Sahlins, "Fictions of a Catholic France"; and the papers presented at the colloquium "Être et se penser Français: Nation, sentiment national et identités dans le monde atlantique français du XVIIᵉ au XIXᵉ siècle," Centre d'Études Nord-Américaines, École des Hautes Études en Sciences Sociales, Paris, October 16–18, 2008.

16. Kupperman, "Presentment of Civility," 193; see also Kupperman, "Fear of Hot Climates in the Anglo-American Colonial Experience" and *Indians and English*, 41–76.

17. Aubert, "'The Blood of France.'"

18. Sala-Molins, *Le Code Noir ou Le calvaire de Canaan*, 108–9.

19. Rushforth, "'A Little Flesh We Offer You'" and "Savage Bonds."

20. My thanks to Guillaume Aubert for offering this nuance.

21. Aubert, "'The Blood of France,'" 451.

22. On the repopulation of the Illinois tribes from the Ohio valley via the southern shores of Lake Michigan to the Upper Mississippi Valley, see Shackelford, "Navigating the Opportunities of New Worlds." Shackelford argues that rather than being driven into the area by the threat of aggression from the Iroquois Confederacy (the orthodox explanation), Illinois Indians were in fact drawn by the possibilities for large-scale bison hunting consistent with their historic subsistence strategies. The precise genesis and meanings of the terms "Illinois" and "Illiniwek" have remained open to debate; for two opposing views see Sleeper-Smith, *Indian Women and French Men*, 173 n. 15; and Bilodeau, "Colonial Christianity and the Illinois Indians," esp. 372 n. 12.

23. Margaret Kimball Brown, *Cultural Transformations Among the Illinois*; Bauxar, "History of the Illinois Area"; Callender, "Illinois"; also Bilodeau, "Colonial Christianity."

24. Settlement patterns in the Illinois Country are discussed by Ekberg, *French Roots in the Illinois Country*; Lessard, Mathieu, and Gouger, "Peuplement colonisateur au pays des Illinois"; see also Briggs, "Le Pays des Illinois"; Belting, *Kaskaskia Under the French Regime*; Giraud, *A History of French Louisiana*, 1:340–47; Richard White, *The Middle Ground*. For a comparative study that does not treat the Illinois Country in isolation from its Anglo neighbors, see Hinderaker, *Elusive Empires*.

25. On variations in her name and on the phoneme "8," see Ekberg, "Marie Rouensa-8canic8e and the Foundations of French Illinois" (earlier version published as Ekberg with Pregaldin, "Marie Rouensa-8cate8a and the Foundations of French Illinois"). For the purposes of this book, the letter "8" will be used, but Brett Rushforth has recently and persuasively argued that the symbol is in fact

ß, the Greek ligature commonly used to render the Latin "ou" (personal communication, January 2012); see also McCafferty, *Native American Place Names*, 21, 24–26 and "Correction," 32.

26. Sleeper-Smith, *Indian Women and French Men*; on the importance to native women of Catholicism unrelated to intermarriage, see also Greer, *Mohawk Saint*; Shoemaker, "Kateri Tekakwitha's Tortuous Path to Sainthood."

27. See, for example, Spear, "Colonial Intimacies" and "They Need Wives"; Sleeper-Smith, *Indian Women and French Men*; Aubert limits his discussion of the different marital models to a footnote ("'The Blood of France,'" 456 n. 37). For an important exception, see DuVal, "Indian Intermarriage and Metissage in Colonial Louisiana."

28. Key works on marriage "à la façon du pays" in French America include Jacqueline Peterson, "Many Roads to Red River" and "Prelude to Red River"; Sleeper-Smith, *Indian Women and French Men*; Thorne, *The Many Hands of My Relations* and "For the Good of Her People"; Murphy, *A Gathering of Rivers*; Van Kirk, *Many Tender Ties*. As noted by Sleeper-Smith, this scholarship is collectively indebted to studies of the fur trade and of the formation of distinctive Métis identity in late eighteenth- to early nineteenth-century Métis culture (168–69 n. 12).

29. Aubert, "'The Blood of France'"; Belmessous, "Assimilation and Racialism"; Hall, *Africans in Colonial Louisiana*; Ingersoll, *Mammon and Manon*; Usner, *Frontier Exchange Economy*; Spear, *Race, Sex, and Social Order*.

30. Key sources on Africans in French colonial Louisiana include Aubert, "'Français, Nègres et Sauvages'"; Caron, "Bambara Slaves and African Ethnicity"; Clark and Gould, "The Feminine Face of Afro-Catholicism in New Orleans"; Hall, *Africans in Colonial Louisiana*; Ingersoll, *Mammon and Manon* and "Free Blacks in a Slave Society"; McGowan, "Creation of a Slave Society "; Spear, *Race, Sex, and Social Order*; Usner, "From African Captivity to American Slavery," *Louisiana History* 20 (1979): 25–48; see also Hanger, *Bounded Lives, Bounded Places*. On the Illinois Country census figures, Vidal, "Africains et Européens au pays des Illinois," 52; Vidal, "Private and State Violence Against African Slaves in Lower Louisiana"; Ekberg, "Black Slavery in Illinois, 1720-1765"; and "Black Slaves in the Illinois Country, 1721-1755." See also Aubert, "Kinship, Blood."

31. On enslaved Africans' role in the making and upkeep of apparel, see Sophie White, "Cultures of Consumption in French Colonial Louisiana."

32. For an example of a popular belief in the mutability of ethnic/racial identity in the mid-nineteenth century, see Sleeper-Smith, "Washing Away Race."

33. Spear, "They Need Wives"; White, *Middle Ground*; Sleeper-Smith, *Indian Women and French Men*.

34. DuVal, "Indian Intermarriage and Metissage."

35. Regional studies of the Illinois Country have incorporated this material. See, for example, Belting, *Kaskaskia*; Ekberg, *French Roots* and *Colonial Ste. Genevieve*; Vidal, "Les Implantations françaises au pays des Illinois au XVIIIème siècle"; Leavelle, *The Catholic Calumet* and "Religion, Encounter, and Community in French and Indian North America"; Morrissey, "Bottomlands and Borderlands."

36. Daniel K. Richter has noted the same preponderance of captive adoptees (as well as women) among those most likely to convert and join Christian missions at La Prairie and Lorette; see Richter, *The Ordeal of the Longhouse*, 124–25. See also Ekberg, *Stealing Indian Women*.

37. *Codex canadensis*, now attributed to Louis Nicolas, ca. 1674–80, Gilcrease Museum, Tulsa, Oklahoma; facsimile published as Charles Bécart de Granville, *Les Raretés des Indes*. Louis Nicolas had accompanied Father Claude Allouez on a trip to the Odawa (Ottawa) in 1667 during which

had he encountered Illinois Indians. In contrast to his images of animals, which were based on published sources, his depiction of the Illinois chief was original and appears factually correct in terms of the depiction of the tattoos. See Warkentin, "Aristotle in New France," esp.80–81, 97–98.

38. Marc-Antoine Caillot, "Relation du voyage de la Louisianne ou Nouvelle France fait par le Sr. Caillot en l'année 1730," Historic New Orleans Collection Ms 2005.0011, 167; Brain, *Tunica Archaeology*, 326–27.

39. Mahé and McCaffrey, *Encyclopædia of New Orleans Artists, 1718–1918*; Sophie White, "Trading Identities," Appendix A; Bushnell, "Drawings by A. De Batz in Louisiana, 1732–1735." De Batz included the figures of two Africans in his depictions.

40. This hide is reproduced in Horse Capture et al., *Robes of Splendor*, plate 22, 136–37, details 28, 140. A reappraisal of the origin, date, and iconographic content of the robe is authoritatively argued by Morris S. Arnold in "Eighteenth-Century Arkansas Illustrated." See also Feest et al., *Premières nations, collections royales*.

41. The earliest known complete surviving garment is a mid-eighteenth-century French man-ufactured trade coat found on the corpse of a Native American man at the Fletcher site in Michi-gan; see Margaret Kimball Brown, "An Eighteenth Century Trade Coat." In terms of chronology, the next securely attributed surviving clothing from the territory originally covered by the colony of Louisiana is a group of garments belonging to one of the founding families of St. Louis, the Chouteaus, now housed in the MHS. Dating from 1786 onward, these belong to the Spanish regime of Louisiana. The absence of any earlier surviving garments is not in itself overly surprising given the relative scarcity of garments from the eighteenth century, for example, in Canada; see also Loren, "Colonial Dress at the Spanish Presidio of Los Adaes," "Threads," and "Beyond the Visual." Some fragments associated with articles of clothing were found in the wreck of La Belle; see Brus-eth and Turner, *From a Watery Grave*. See also Waselkov, *The Archaeology of French Colonial North America*.

42. On the value of archival sources for material culture research and the importance of mate-rial culture to historical research, see Auslander, "Beyond Words."

43. Vidal, "Le Pays des Illinois."

44. For an exception to this pattern, see the June 15, 1736, invoice of merchandise taken by Mr. Phillipeau to the Illinois Country (the items clearly intended for colonists); BFTRMM reel 2, pp. 754–58. For the post-1763 period see the ongoing research by Robert Englebert.

45. Ekberg, "The Flour Trade in French Colonial Louisiana."

46. On African slavery in the Illinois Country, see Ekberg, "Black Slavery in Illinois" and "Black Slaves in the Illinois Country"; Vidal, "Africains et Européens" and "Les Implantations," 534–57.

47. Usner, *Frontier Exchange Economy*; Hall, *Africans in Colonial Louisiana*; Ingersoll, *Mam-mon and Manon*. On the marginalization of colonial (Lower) Louisiana within narratives of Amer-ican history, see Emily Clark, "Moving from Periphery to Centre"; Usner, "Between Creoles and Yankees"; Zitomersky "In the Middle and on the Margin"; Havard and Vidal, "Making New France New Again."

48. See, for example, Carl J. Ekberg, Tracy Neal Leavelle, Robert M. Morrissey, and Cécile Vidal.

49. For the population of Lower Louisiana, see Usner, *Frontier Exchange Economy*, 108, 279; Ekberg, *French Roots*, 154–55 and table 2.

50. My approach to eighteenth-century dress history is especially indebted to scholars including

Baumgarten, *What Clothes Reveal*; Beaudoin-Ross, "'À la Canadienne' Once More," 69–70; Buck, *Dress in Eighteenth-Century England*; Calvert, "The Function of Fashion in Eighteenth-Century America"; Haulman, "Fashion and the Culture Wars of Revolutionary Philadelphia"; Lemire, *Dress, Culture, Commerce*; Paresys, "The Dressed Body"; Pellegrin, *Les Vêtements de la liberté*; Ribeiro, *The Art of Dress*; *Dress in Eighteenth-Century Europe, 1751–1789* and *Dress and Morality*; Roche, *The Culture of Clothing*; Styles, *The Dress of the People*; Vickery, "Women and the World of Goods."

51. See the critique of such views in Berlo and Philips, *Native North American Art*, 16–17, 32.

52. Ibid., 75–77, also 91.

53. On the global sourcing of goods available in Louisiana, with a particular focus on the implications for understanding consumption by enslaved Africans, see Sophie White, "Geographies of Slave Consumption."

Part I Intro. Frenchification in the Illinois Country

1. Minutes of the Council, September 1, 1716, ANOM, C13A, 4:255–57. This summary referred to La Vente's report but the report itself has not been traced. La Vente did strongly endorse intermarriage in a 1708 letter, and this letter is used to flesh out his views. See Abbé Henri Roulleaux de La Vente to Abbé Jacques de Brisacier, July 4, 1708, ASQ, sme 2.1/r/083, esp. 19–20.

2. Jean-Baptiste du Bois Duclos, sieur de Montigny, to Minister of Marine Pontchartrain, December 25, 1715, ANOM, C13A 3:819–24, translation from *MPA* 2:207.

3. Jean-Baptiste du Bois Duclos, sieur de Montigny, to Minister of Marine Pontchartrain, December 25, 1715, ANOM, C13A 3:819–24, translation from *MPA* 2:207–8.

4. La Vente to Brisacier, July 4, 1708, ASQ, sme 2.1/r/083, p. 20.

5. Aubert, "'The Blood of France,'" esp. 467–70.

6. Memo of the King to Srs. de l'Espinay Governor and Hubert Commissaire-Ordonnateur to Louisiana, October 28, 1716, ANOM, B 38, fol. 334, translation from Aubert, "'The Blood of France,'" 470.

7. *FFL* 2:32–34.

8. Macarty to Vaudreuil [1752], VP O/S LO 426.

9. Sleeper-Smith, *Indian Women and French Men*, 42–44.

10. See Lessard, Mathieu, and Gouger, "Peuplement colonisateur au pays des Illinois," 56–65. The authors have identified three distinct phases of settlement. The first, from 1699 to 1718, was characterized almost exclusively by the arrival of Canadian men who overwhelmingly married Indian women. The second phase, 1719–1732, was a period of extensive settlement, mostly by men from France, though also by settlers from Canadian towns. The final phase, 1733–1752, was again dominated by the arrival of mostly male, mostly urban Canadians, with the added distinction that they were usually related to earlier settlers.

11. Important scholarship on intermarriage in early America includes Aubert, "'The Blood of France'"; DuVal, "Indian Intermarriage and Metissage"; Spear, *Race, Sex, and Social Order*, "Colonial Intimacies," "They Need Wives"; Sleeper-Smith, *Indian Women and French Men*; Jaenen, "Miscegenation in Eighteenth Century New France"; Fischer, *Suspect Relations*; Godbeer, "Eroticizing the Middle Ground"; Brooks, *Captives and Cousins*; Plane, *Colonial Intimacies*; Vidal, "Les Implantations françaises"; Jacqueline Peterson, "Many Roads to Red River"; Havard, *Empires et métissages*, 625–80. Recent scholarship on the French colonial experience of intermarriage and *métissage*

has tempered earlier presumptions of a marked contrast between French, Spanish, and English perspectives on these practices, while acknowledging different outcomes. See especially Jaenen, "Miscegenation"; Spear, "Colonial Intimacies."

12. DuVal, "Indian Intermarriage and Metissage."

13. For example Jacqueline Peterson, "Many Roads"; Sleeper-Smith, *Indian Women and French Men*; Thorne, "For the Good of Her People"; Van Kirk, *Many Tender Ties*. Compare this to Richard White's careful delineation of the differences between the married and unmarried Illinois Indian partners of French traders, the factors that facilitated these unions and how these unions affected social, economic. and political life in the region; see *Middle Ground*, 64–75.

14. See, for example, Spear, "Colonial Intimacies" and " 'They Need Wives' "; Sleeper-Smith, *Indian Women and French Men*; Aubert limits his discussion of the different marital models to a footnote (" 'The Blood of France,' " 456 n. 37).

15. Key works on "marriage à la façon du pays" in French America include Peterson, "Many Roads to Red River" and "Prelude to Red River"; Sleeper-Smith, *Indian Women and French Men*; Thorne, *The Many Hands of My Relations* and "For the Good of Her People"; Murphy, *A Gathering of River*; Van Kirk, *Many Tender Ties*.

16. As highlighted by Godbeer, there was an interplay between the acceptance of intercultural sex and resistance against intercultural marriage; see Godbeer, "Eroticizing the Middle Ground"; also Fischer, *Suspect Relations*, 55–97.

17. Spear, *Race, Sex, and Social Order*, 17–51; also Hall, *Africans in Colonial Louisiana*, 16. Contrary to Hall's assertion, lawful relationships between French men and Indian women were not common in Lower Louisiana, and indeed, one of the married men she lists was an inhabitant of the Illinois Country (this was Jean Huet; see Belting, *Kaskaskia Under the French Regime*, 96). See also Higginbotham, *Old Mobile*, 445–45, for an example of a Canadian (a former voyageur subsequently employed as storekeeper at Massacre Island) living with his Chitimacha Indian slave, fathering her children (and having them baptized), and subsequently marrying her. More commonly, Frenchmen in Lower Louisiana provided some support for their Indian mistresses and their children without explicitly acknowledging the relationship. This was probably the case with the Indian slave Rebout left behind, with her young son, in the care of his friend Descairac. She was neglected as her former owner returned to France, her new master having to sue Rebout for the costs of her upkeep. See RSCL 1737111102. See also the references to the three children born to Diron, lieutenant of the king (in Louisiana and then Saint Domingue), and Marianne, who had been "in his service." He had made provisions, including a dowry, for his children. See RSCL 1749082601, 1749083001; Cruzat, "Records of the Superior Council of Louisiana, LXII," 166–67, documents relating to Jean Baptiste and Françoise Panioussa (April 6, July 1 1747).

18. In 1743, two years after the birth of twins to his Indian concubine, the commandant at the Alabama (Fort Toulouse) post, La Houssaye, was told by Governor Vaudreuil to put an immediate stop to his "scandalous conduct" in cohabiting with an Indian woman. In his directive, Vaudreuil further implied that this relationship was the direct cause of La Houssaye's difficulties with his men. See Commissaire-Ordonnateur Salmon to Minister of Marine, March 6, 1741, ANOM, C13A, 26:119; Commissaire-Ordonnateur Salmon to the Minister of Marine, December 7, 1743, VP LO 9, vol. 3, p. 28.

19. Jean-François-Benjamin Dumont *dit* Montigny, "Mémoire de Lxx Dxx officier ingénieur, contenant les evenements qui se sont passés à la Louisiane depuis 1715 jusqu'à present," NL Ayer Ms 257, pp. 372–73. For an edited transcript of the manuscript, see Dumont de Montigny, *Regards*

sur le monde atlantique, 1715–1747; see also Delanglez, "A Louisiana Post-Historian: Dumont *dit* Montigny." Dumont changed his last name from Dumont *dit* Montigny (*dit* meaning known as), to the noble-sounding "de" Montigny.

20. La Mothe-Cadillac to Minister of Marine, October 26, 1713, ANOM, C13A 3:13, 17.

21. Suzanne B. Sommerville, personal communication, 2002, cited in Havard, *Empires et métissages*, 680 n. 126.

22. Spear, "Colonial Intimacies"; Peterson, "Prelude to Red River," 55.

23. These examples are discussed in Vidal, "Les Implantations françaises," 486; see also p. 500. The sanctified marriage took place in 1759 in Kaskaskia, between an Indian brought up by Jesuits in Detroit and a Swiss-born colonist (the contract is abstracted in *PFFA* 2:92). See also the case of Marguerite Faffard, discussed in Chapter 2. For examples of such marriages in New France, see Jaenen, "Miscegenation," 89, 91. Such unions (seldom sanctified) certainly occurred more frequently where European male captives were adopted into tribes.

24. Sleeper-Smith, *Indian Women and French Men*, 42–44.

25. Zitomersky, "The Form and Function of French-Native American Relations in Early Eighteenth-Century French Colonial Louisiana"; also Zitomersky, *French Americans-Native Americans in Eighteenth-Century French Colonial Louisiana*.

26. "Relation de l'arrivée en France de quatre Sauvages de Missicipi," 362 [2844]. On the 1725 Indian delegation to Paris, see Norall, *Bourgmont*, 17, 81–88; Giraud, *History of Louisiana*, 5:488–94; Ellis and Steen, "An Indian Delegation in France, 1725."

27. "Journal of Diron d'Artaguiette," in Mereness, *Travels in the American Colonies*, 67.

28. See Ekberg, *French Roots in the Illinois Country*; and Susan Sleeper-Smith's current research project on Illinois women's agrarian village world.

29. *MPA* 2:208 n. 1.

Chapter 1. "Their Manner of Living"

1. *PFFA* 2:205; for the will and codicil, see KM 25:6:13:1, 25:6:20:1 (the numbers represent year:month:day:sequence). They owned a minimum of thirty-three arpents (some lots were not measured in the inventory). The appraisal did not include twenty arpents of still unharvested maize. No dress was included in her probate inventory, but lack of references to apparel is not unusual among the succession records of deceased women in France and its colonies. At the time of her widower's death twenty years later in 1746, his probate inventory did list an old lined woman's jacket (*mantelet*) that had probably belonged to his late wife, one that reveals her continuing adhesion to French colonial styles of dress; see KM 46:1:17:3. See also the discussion in the next chapter of her dress as described in the *Jesuit Relations*. On her name, see Ekberg with Pregaldin, "Marie Rouensa-8canic8e and the Foundations of French Illinois"; Masthay, *Kaskaskia Illinois-to-French Dictionary*, 33–34.

2. Ekberg with Pregaldin, "Marie Rouensa-8canic8e," which also includes a translation of her probate inventory; Belting, *Kaskaskia Under the French Regime*; Vidal, "Les Implantations françaises" 1995, esp. 485–501; Richard White, *The Middle Ground*, 66, 70–75; Hinderaker, *Elusive Empires*, 62–63; Leavelle, "Religion, Encounter, and Community in French and Indian North America" and "Geographies of Encounter"; Morrissey, "Bottomlands and Borderlands"; Sleeper-Smith, "Women, Kin, and Catholicism" *Ethnohistory*, and *Indian Women and French Men*, chap.

2; Jacqueline Peterson, "Women Dreaming." She even merits her own series of edited texts; see Leavelle, *Why Were Illinois Women Attracted to Catholicism, 1665–1750?*; Sophie White, "Marie Rouensa-8canic8e."

3. *JR*, 64:159–237.

4. Duclos to Pontchartrain, December 25, 1715, ANOM, C13A 3, Fol. 819–24, translation from *MPA* 2:207.

5. For example, Ulrich, "Of Pens and Needles"; Styles, *Threads of Feeling*.

6. KM 25:8:16:1.

7. See "La Forest Sells Half-Interest to Accault," April 19, 1693, *CISHL*, 264, discussed in Morrissey, "Bottomlands and Borderlands," 85–86.

8. For this term, see Masthay, *Kaskaskia Illinois-to-French Dictionary*, 36–37. See also Leavelle, *The Catholic Calumet*, 167–8.

9. Turgeon, "The Tale of the Kettle."

10. Zitomersky, "The Form and Function of French-Native American Relations in Early Eighteenth-Century French Colonial Louisiana"; also Zitomersky, *French Americans-Native Americans in Eighteenth-Century French Colonial Louisiana*.

11. KM 25:8:16:1; translation from Ekberg with Pregaldin, "Marie Rouensa-8cate8a," 158.

12. See, for example, Tonti, *Dernières découvertes dans l'Amerique septentrionale de M. de La Salle*, 332.

13. On the archaeological record pertaining to the Winter and Summer villages, and problems caused by biases in the documentary record, see Esarey, "Seasonal Occupation Patterns in Illinois History"; see also Morgan, *Land of Big Rivers*.

14. His memoir (misattributed to de Gannes) has been published as "Memoir of de Gannes Concerning the Illinois Country," in *CISHL*, 302–96, hereafter cited as "Memoir of de Gannes [de Liette]"; see 340–41. On the misattribution, see Ekberg with Pregaldin, "Marie Rouensa-8cate8a," 148 n. 7. See also *JR*, 66:229.

15. On the contents of cache pits, see Walthall, "Aboriginal Pottery and the Eighteenth-Century Illini," 168. In summer, housing consisted of bark-covered longhouses large enough to house multiple families. They too made use of local materials and female labor and were suited to the climate and to defensive warfare; see "Memoir of de Gannes [de Liette]," 308.

16. "Naturels du Nord qui vont en chasse d'hyver avec leur famille," in Le Page du Pratz, *Histoire de la Louisiane*, vol. 3, plate following 164.

17. Morrissey, "Bottomlands and Borderlands," 81.

18. "Relation de la découverte que Mr de la Salle a faite de la Riviere de Mississipi en 1682," in "Memoranda on French colonies in America, including Canada, Louisiana, and the Caribbean [1702–50]," NL, Ayer Ms 293, 233. Two years later, in July 1682, he once again managed to miss them.

19. "The Voyage of St. Cosme, 1698–1699," in (and translation adapted from) Kellogg, *Early Narratives of the Northwest*, 351. On Father St. Cosme's relationship with Bras Piqué, the female Great Sun, with whom he fathered the future heir, see Sayre, "Plotting the Natchez Massacre," esp. 398–401. Natchez kinship rules stipulated that the Great Sun be born of a female Great Sun princess and a nonroyal. As demonstrated by Sayre, multiple eyewitnesses referred obliquely to this relationship while also implicating both Bras Piqué and her children by St. Cosme (including the Great Sun) in plotting the 1729 Natchez massacre.

20. *JR*, 64:189.

21. *JR*, 66:38.

22. *JR*, 66:253, 255.

23. "Relation de Pénicaut," in Margry, *Mémoires et documents*, 5:489; translation from Péni-caut, *Fleur de Lys and Calumet: Being the Pénicaut Narrative of French Adventure in Louisiana*), hereafter *Pénicaut Narrative*, 137. On the kinds of damage free-roaming hogs might cause to Indian cornfields, and the incompatibility of these two food staples, see Richter, *Before the Revolution*, 279.

24. *Pénicaut Narrative*, 137–38. On the gristmills, see also also Vidal, "Les Implantations," 85.

25. Ekberg, *French Roots*, 172–75. Ekberg links this development to the Jesuit preference for ag-riculture over commerce (which might engender the debauchery of Indians) in the Illinois Coun-try, introducing gristmills, draft animals, and later, African slaves. See also Ekberg, "The Flour Trade." The flour might be carried down in sacks made from deer hides; see RSCL 1738070603.

26. Ekberg, "The Flour Trade."

27. Sleeper-Smith, *Indian Women and French Men*, 42–43, 32.

28. This evidence draws on first-hand records in travelers' descriptions, in missionary ac-counts and official reports emanating from the area, read alongside the sparser architectural and archaeological data. But documents by notaries (or by missionaries who filled in for notaries in their absence) in the Illinois Country provide the richest source of evidence about French-Indian households. Products of European hegemony, they reveal as much about those who created them as about those whose material culture they document and should be interpreted with this in mind. Yet a qualitative reading of these records reveals that information on native practices is encoded in these documents. Among the records produced by notaries in the Illinois Country, extant probate documents are a neglected treasure trove of source material for analysis of household effects and dress of Indian and mixed-parentage women living in the French villages. The analysis of these probate records is, however, complicated by problems with the source type. First, while the par-ish registers of baptisms and marriages that testify to the importance of intermarriage in the two earliest decades of colonization in the Illinois Country survive, few probate records survive (or were produced) during this formative period; these records are, however, prolific, despite some important chronological gaps from the 1720s to 1760s. When notarial records do survive, there are difficulties identifying succession records pertaining to mixed heritage offspring, since a con-sequence of legal and/or sacramental marriages with Frenchmen was the conferral of the father's surname to his children; this practice was in conformity with French patrilineal practices that did, however, ensure that a wife retained her own name in legal records. My research in this chapter has stretched to genealogical work to chart family trees as a necessary step to identifying relevant inventories, although the data inevitably remain incomplete, given the lacunae in later parish regis-ters and other depositories of genealogical information. Second, notarial sources including probate inventories are a notoriously problematic source of evidence, as addressed, for example, in Benes, *Early American Probate Inventories*; Main, "Notes and Documents." See also Sophie White, "Dress in French Colonial Louisiana."

29. Ekberg, *French Roots*.

30. KM 28:6:10:1; Vidal, "Les Implantations," 594.

31. KM 23:6:22:1 and 40:3:24:1.

32. On architectural styles, see Belting, *Kaskaskia*, 30–37; Vidal, "Les Implantations," 593–99; Charles E. Peterson, "Early Ste. Genevieve and Its Architecture," *Colonial St. Louis*, and "Notes on Old Cahokia," esp. 326–30; Thurman, *Building a House in 18th Century Ste. Genevieve*. A synthesis of the different theories about the genesis of Louisiana's creole houses is provided by Edwards,

"The Origins of Creole Architecture"; and Oszuscik, "The French Creole Cottage and Its Caribbean Connection."

33. KM 39:4:13:1. Thurman, *Building a House*, 25, suggests that galleries did not become dominant until about 1750.

34. Lorient, ser. 2P22, liasse 2, no. 4, April 19–December 29, 1726. Bourgmont had acquired the enslaved Padoka woman during his expedition to the Apache. In contrast to Ignon Ouaconisen, she left only scarce traces of her presence there, although she was to remain, marry, and die in France. In 1728, a baptism was recorded in the town of Cerisy, where Bourgmont had retired, for "Marie Angélique, Padouca slave of E. Véniard de Bourgmont." Four years later another record was made, to register her marriage to a Frenchman and the legitimization of her newborn son; see Norall, *Bourgmont*, 88. On the complicated legal status of slaves in France, see Peabody, *There Are No Slaves in France*.

35. Norall, *Bourgmont*, 17 and 81–88; see also Giraud, *History of Louisiana*, 5:488–94. A lengthy account of the Indians' visit was published as "Relation de l'arrivée en France de quatre Sauvages de Missicipi"; the translation is mine but see also Ellis and Steen, "An Indian Delegation in France, 1725." Another account was published in London and reprinted in "First Visit of Nebraska Indians to Paris in 1725." Bourgmont himself was reputed to have married the daughter of a Missouri chief according to Indian custom, fathering a son with her in 1714; see Norall, *Bourgmont*, 17.

36. Although a full inventory, description, and appraisal of her community property with Marin de la Marque was made on her death, the original records do not survive; see KM 39:2:3:3, 39:2:4:1, 39:5:24:2. The community with Dubois did not go through probate but was folded into the new community with Marin de la Marque (RSCL 1730072801), causing inheritance issues between her widower and her offspring from the marriage to Dubois (RSCL 1746022401).

37. KM 24:7:26:1.

38. KM 25:8:16:1.

39. KM 21:9:13:1.

40. KM 23:7:1:1.

41. KM 25:8:16:1.

42. KM 26:5:2:1.

43. KM 48:7:6:1. Other documents describing French colonial dwellings are quoted in Belting, *Kaskaskia*, 31–37; Vidal, "Les Implantations," 593–99.

44. On furniture styles in colonial Louisiana, see Holden et al., *Furnishing Louisiana*.

45. KM 21:6:29:1.

46. KM 21:6:27:1; *PFFA* 2:133.

47. KM 21:9:13:1; also 25:—:—:2.

48. KM 23:9:16:1, 23:9:26:1.

49. KM 23:7:1:1, 23:7:7:1, 23:10:26:1.

50. Walthall, "Faïence in French Colonial Illinois"; Noble, "Eighteenth-Century Ceramics from Fort de Chartres III"; Jelks, Ekberg, and Martin, Excavations at the Laurens Site, 110–11. See entry of 8 June 1736, BFTRMM Reel 2, 767, for a reference to pewter utensils that the trader François Grignon planned to bring from Montreal to trade in the Illinois. The absence of pewter in archaeological sites, in spite of its dominance of the documentary record, is explained by its recycling and reuse as other vessels; see Walthall, "Faïence," 100–101; Ann Smart Martin, "The Role of Pewter as Missing Artifact."

51. As for example with the utterly nondescript faïence shipped in to New Orleans from La

Rochelle on the ship *La Reine des Anges* and subsequently freighted to the Illinois Country in 1737 for resale there; see RSCL 1737081405 and 1737081501.

52. See also Kathleen M. Brown's discussion of this "body work" in *Foul Bodies*, esp. Part III.

53. KM: 23:10:26:2.

54. KM 26:5:10:1. A stoneware *duedalle* was among her effects at her death in 1747; see KM 47:10:31:03.

55. Walthall, "Aboriginal Pottery"; Noble, "Eighteenth-Century Ceramics," 43. On finds in Lower Mississippi Valley French sites of Creek colonoware made in imitation of Spanish olive jars, see Waselkov, "French Colonial Trade in the Upper Creek Country," 41. One mixed household had "two Spanish jugs"; see KM 24:7:26:1.

56. For an example of spices, coffee, and sugar shipped to the Illinois Country from New Orleans, see RSCL 1747052901.

57. KM 48:1:14:1, 23:7:1:1, 28:8:6:1.

58. A detailed analysis of foodstuffs (primarily faunal remains) found at Fort de Chartres is presented in Jelks, Ekberg, and Martin, *Excavations at the Laurens Site*, chaps. 5, 6, esp. 112–17, which note the differences between Illinois Country and other French colonial villages of the Great Lakes. On Lower Louisiana, see Dawdy, "'A Wild Taste'"; and Meredith D. Hardy, "Living on the Edge: Foodways and Early Expressions of Creole Culture on the French Colonial Gulf Coast Frontier," in Kelly and Hardy, eds., *French Colonial Archaeology*, 152–88.

59. KM 25:3:15:1; RSCL 1725021501, 1725021604, 1725022601.

60. RSCL 1730072801. Her heirs would later contest this legal maneuver; see RSCL 1746022401.

61. KM 39:1:22:4, 40:1:22:2.

62. KM 24:7:26:1.

63. KM 63:1:16:1; Ekberg, *François Vallé and His World*, 40–41. The house was sold in 1763 for 17,000 livres.

64. KM 47:10:31:3.

65. Lessard, Mathieu, and Gouger, "Peuplement colonisateur," 56–65.

66. Since Louisiana fell under the administrative control of New France, in theory the guild regulations in New France should have been in effect; however there were no guilds in French colonial Louisiana. Nonetheless, craftsmen in the colony did claim guild affiliation to denote their status, and formal apprenticeship contracts were entered into. On the guild system in New France, and its implications for apprenticeships there, see Hardy and Ruddel, *Les Apprentis artisans à Québec*. On apprenticeships in Paris, see Kaplan, "L'Apprentissage au XVIIIe siècle: Le cas de Paris," and "The Luxury Guilds in Paris in the Eighteenth Century."

67. See Sophie White, "Trading Identities," Appendix B.

68. KM 26:5:2:1, 26:5:10:1, 28:6:7:1.

69. KM 48:7:6:1, 48:7:6:2, and 48:7:8:1. See also the pair of sheets left by Marie Rouensa's sister-in-law Marie Ma8e8enci8ois, wife of Charles Huet *dit* Dulude and widow of Etienne Philippe *dit* Dulongpré; KM 40:1:22:2. For comparative purposes, see Lorna Weatherill's analysis of the ownership of curtains in Britain, 1675–1725, which reveals the scarcity of these in rural areas and in most social groups (though their incidence is more frequent in households belonging to members of the trades and the gentry): "Consumer Behaviour, Textiles and Dress," esp. tables 2 (AD) and 3, 302–4.

70. KM 48:10:9:1. The household of Margueritte Ouaquamo Quoana and the late Jacques Bourdon included one armchair and five chairs of walnut (KM 23:7:1:1), as did that of Marie Rouensa and Michel Philippe (KM 25:8:16:1) and that of Dorothée Mechip8e8a and Charles Danis

(KM 24:7:26:1). The household of the late Marie Rose Texier, half-Indian wife of Nicolas Boyer, also contained an armchair (KM 47:12:13:1). Illegitimate half-Indian Marie La Boissiere and her legitimate husband Joseph Baron owned an armchair and eight chairs; see SGA, Estates, no. 12, 1759 succession records of Joseph Baron.

71. KM 28:11:27:1, 28:11:27:2 for the inventory of her community property with her first husband.

72. KM 47:12:13:1, 47:12:15:1. On the ubiquity of these imported kettles in Illinois Indians' households, see "Memoir of de Gannes [de Liette]," 308–9. For the cargo listing, see 1740070401. The boat was attacked by Indians on the way upriver.

73. For example, KM 25:8:16:1, 28:11:27:2, 47:10:31:3; RSCL 1747061001. On the presence of French cooking and serving implements in colonial Louisiana, see Meredith Hardy, "Living on the Edge," esp. 160–62, 168–72, 176–80.

74. "Memoir of de Gannes [de Liette]," 310.

75. Albala, *Food in Early Modern Europe*, 93.

76. KM 47:12:15:1, 48:7:6:1, 48:7:6:2, 48:7:8:1, 67:10:20:1; some of these rugs were made of calico.

77. See Ekberg's discussion of François Vallé's illegitimate daughter Marguerite, raised in her father and stepmother's household, with her marriage dowry allowing her to bypass the limits on her rights to an inheritance from her father because she was illegitimate. Ekberg, *Colonial Ste. Genevieve*, 115, 188; see also SGA, Marriage Contracts, no. 32; Vidal, "Les Implantations," 584.

78. KM 44:7:5:1 and 57:11:10:1.

79. KM 67:10:21:1 Pierre Aubuchon estate papers, April 22, 1771, SGA, Estates, no. 8, F. 112–13.

80. *JR*, 64:196 (my translation).

81. "Relation de l'arrivée en France," 2833–34, my translation. The translation of the dress and textile terms in Ellis and Steen, "Indian Delegation," 394, contains errors. The color of the gown was "couleur de feu,'" brilliant red"; see Académie Française, *Dictionnaire de l'académie française*, 1:516.

82. "Relation de l'arrivée en France," 2837–38.

83. Folmer, "Étienne Veniard de Bourgmond in the Missouri Country," 296; RSCL1730072801.

84. Dumont de Montigny, *Mémoires Historiques sur la Louisiane*, 2:77–78; translation from Folmer, "Étienne Veniard de Bourgmont," 297.

85. See Brasseaux, *France's Forgotten Legion*, Part 2, 81; and RSCL 1730072801, 1746022401, 1746030501, 1746030502; also Belting, *Kaskaskia*, 93. Many of Marin's relatives in the Fox Wisconsin region had entered into marriages *à la façon du pays* there as part of their trading networks; see Murphy, *A Gathering of Rivers*, 32 and chap. 1 generally. On their house, see KM 39:4:13:1

86. KM 39:1:26:1, 39:1:31:1, 40:11:20:2.

87. "Memoir of de Gannes [de Liette]," 338.

88. *JR*, 64:219, 227.

89. Nadal, *Evangelicae historiae imagines*, *The Illustrated Spiritual Exercises*; Buser, "Jerome Nadal and Early Jesuit Art in Rome"; see also Gagnon, *La Conversion par l'image*. On the engravings in the Ursuline convent in Quebec, see Christine Turgeon, *Art, foi et culture*, 33–35; on other types of artwork used by Jesuits in New France, including full-length paintings, see Deslandres, *Croire et faire croire*, 342–46.

90. Collection du Monastère des Ursulines de Québec, Musée des Ursulines de Québec, accession no. 1997.1017.

91. Nadal, *The Illustrated Spiritual Exercises*, iv–v.

92. *JR*, 64:227.

93. Gagnon, *La Conversion par l'image*, 32.

94. *JR*, 64:229.

95. For the bedchambers, see Nadal, *Evangelicae historiae imagines*, plates 3, 31, 76 (including the bed warmer); for the chimneys and andirons, see plates 1, 2, 3; for the chairs, stools, and chests, see plates 1, 16; for the cookware, see plate 18; for the embroidered tablecloths, napkins, plates, platters, glasses, and cutlery, see plates 15, 18, 31, 48, 49, 60, 73, 102, 103; for the lamps and candelabra, see plates 104, 105, 106, 114, 115; for farming and barns, see plates 23, 38, 39, 72.

96. On textiles brought by missionaries, see Dawson, "An Analysis of Liturgical Textiles"; Christine Turgeon, *Le Fil de l'art*. On liturgical textiles in France in the seventeenth and eighteenth centuries, see Aribaud, *Soieries en sacristie*.

97. Notably plates 2, 15, 67, 73, 74, in Nadal, *Evangelicae historiae imagines*.

98. By the early eighteenth century, Indians from all but the most remote tribes of the North American continent had increasing access to and displayed a growing taste for the European-style goods and novelties available to them. See Calloway, *New Worlds for All*, 44.

99. *JR*, 59:117; Shackelford, "Navigating the Opportunities of New Worlds."

100. For example, see *JR*, 54:174.

101. "Memoir of de Gannes [de Liette]," 339.

102. Archaeological evidence is problematic in that there is a deceptive paucity of finds of organic materials such as textiles. These disintegrate fast, leaving virtually no physical trace. The almost total absence of textile finds in Louisiana and the Mississippi Valley, as elsewhere in North America, has contributed to an overemphasis on pottery and metal goods (including guns) as primary and predominant objects of trade from Europeans to Indians. But the written records show conclusively that cloth and related items of adornment constituted the bulk of trading commodities. For a rare analysis of an important clothing find, see Margaret Kimball Brown, "An Eighteenth Century Trade Coat." On Lower Louisiana, see Loren, "Colonial Dress at the Spanish Presidio of Los Adaes," "Threads," "Beyond the Visual"; also, more generally, Loren, *Archaeology of Clothing and Bodily Adornment*. On New France, see DuPlessis, "Circulation des textiles et des valeurs," "Circulation et appropriation des mouchoirs." See also Dean L. Anderson, "Documentary and Archaeological Perspectives," "The Flow of European Trade Goods."

103. Rasles to his brother, October 12, 1723, in *JR*, 67:165; see also Palm, *Jesuit Missions of the Illinois Country*, 24.

104. *Codex canadensis*, now attributed to Louis Nicolas, ca. 1675–80, Gilcrease Museum, Tulsa, Oklahoma; see also Bécart de Granville, *Les Raretés des Indes*.

105. Good, *Guébert Site*, 8. See also KM 14:4:6:1, a claim from Montreal merchant J. Soumand against Michel Philippe, second husband of Marie Rouensa, for payment of a sixteen-year-old debt (from circa 1698) owed for trading goods.

106. ANOM, 3JJ: 276 [1722–23], Diron's journal. While d'Artaguiette conflated male and female sartorial practices, official gifts from the French Crown to Indian tribes reveal that gifts of clothing intended for Indian women were limited to shifts and decorative *passementerie*. This gender disparity seems to be confirmed in archaeological burial excavations, where women's burials seem to have been less associated with artifacts than men's or children's; see Margaret Kimball Brown, "The Waterman Site."

107. *JR*, 59:117.

108. According to customary law, the right to select a set sum's worth of "furniture or linens or apparel" from the community was granted to the surviving widow and usually taken in the form

of personal clothing, jewelry, and often bedding. Such items were not therefore subject to placing of seals and were often excluded from inventories, appraisals, and sales. Furthermore, most inventories of female wardrobes in the Illinois Country exist for a small window of time, concentrated in the 1740s, and possibly linked to the arrival of a well-trained and more highly educated notary from Canada, Jean-Baptiste Bertlot dit Barrois, who served in the Illinois Country in 1737–1756. The loss of original notarial acts for Kaskaskia for the 1750s has also reduced the sample of extant inventories available for analysis; see Vidal, "Les Implantations" (1995), 620–25. These issues with the available source material pertaining to personal effects hold for all women in the Illinois Country, regardless of origin, marital status, or ethnic identification.

109. For example, two female silk workers were among those engaged in 1722 to work on the Dubuisson concession; see Lorient, series 2P1, liasse 2, no. 13, June 5, 1722.

110. "Ordonnance id du 9. janvier 1721," ANOM, A 23:31.

111. See Sleeper-Smith's assumption, based on the absence of these tools, that native women resisted acculturation; *Indian Women and French Men*, 32. There were the occasional attempts by trading companies to promote commercial textile production but this was not the norm and did not represent instances of women producing textiles for their household use. See Ruddel, "Domestic Textile Production in Colonial Quebec" and "Consumer Trends, Clothing, Textiles, and Equipment in the Montreal Area."

112. CAOM, A 22: 1, September 1712. The price tariff changed with the distance of the different posts from the landing point; see, for example, CAOM, B 43: 83, September 2, 1721, Paris. See also CAOM, B 42bis: 276, April 25, 1719, Paris.

113. For examples of trade cloth bequests to Indian widows, see the inventory of the effects of Catherine 8abankinkoy, widow of Louis Texier, which included floral fabrics and painted handkerchiefs (KM 21:9:13:1); the share received by the widow of Jacques Bourdon (KM 23:10:26:2); the inventory of the effects of Charles Danis (KM 24:7:25:1); and the inventory of the goods of Antoine Beausseron *dit* Leonard (KM 26:5:2:1).

114. RSCL 1728052903.

115. RSCL 1729101301. He was an ensign who served temporarily as Storekeeper; see Ekberg, "Terrisse de Ternan" and Vidal, "Les Implantations," 131. See also the correspondence between Benoist de St. Clair, commandant of the Illinois Country and his partner in New Orleans, the retailer Widow Gervais, discussed in Sophie White, "'A Baser Commerce.'"

116. RSCL 1737081405 and 1737081501; also 1738071901.

117. See de Garsault, *L'Art du tailleur*, 54; also Diderot and d'Alembert, *L'Encyclopédie*, 10:55–56.

118. KM 46:1:17:3. Jean-Baptiste d'Aleyrac, in Canada in 1755, noted that "the Canadiens speak a French similar to ours. With the exception of some words which are peculiar to them . . . . They say . . . mantelet when they mean a casaquin without pleats," *Aventures militaires*, 31. The engineer Louis Franquet, writing in 1752, claimed that Canadian women "instead of a gown, wore a mantelet of the utmost propriety, which only reaches as far as the waist"; cited in Gousse and Gousse, *Lexique illustré du costume*, 38. Pehr Kalm described how the hair of Canadian women was always curled, "even when they are at home in a dirty jacket and a short coarse skirt that does not reach to the middle of their legs" (*Travels in North America*, 2:525). Each of these accounts identified the *mantelet* as a type of short, unpleated jacket worn over a petticoat as an alternative to a full-length gown.

119. Beaudoin-Ross uses "camisole" to describe the *mantelet*; see "'À la canadienne' Once More," 69–70; Burnham, *Cut My Cote*, 20–21. On this style outside French America, see Kidwell, "Short Gowns." For the June 15, 1736 invoice of merchandise taken by Mr. Phillipeau to the Illinois

Country, see BFTRMM reel 2, 754–58; mantelets are listed on esp. 754, 755, 758. Dean L. Anderson has identified thirty references to *mantelets* in outfitters' records, all made locally in Montreal and each using from 1 to 3 ells of cloth (more commonly 2 or 2.5 ells); see Anderson, "Documentary and Archaeological Perspectives," App. A, 179–80. In New Orleans in 1750, officials hired a woman, Dame Roujot, to make a large quantity of *mantelets* and capots; see ANOM C13A 35: 248: 5 dec. 1750. In construction, the garments were probably closely related, cut from one continuous length of cloth (or a blanket for the *capot*) for both front and back, with pieced sleeves; see Burnham, "Cut My Cote," 20–11.

120. KM 25:3:15:1. Ready-made mantelets imported into the Illinois Country from Montreal seem to have been less varied in fabric. For example, of the thirty mantelets identified by Dean L. Anderson, twenty-nine were made of calimanco and twenty-seven of these were lined (of carizé or flannel); see Anderson, "Documentary and Archaeological Perspectives," App. A, 179–80.

121. For example, KM 40:8:3:1, 44:1:3:1, 48:8:5:2. See also engineer Nicolas de Finiels's 1790s description, in *An Account of Upper Louisiana*, 112–13.

122. On the definition of the *corset* in the early eighteenth century, see Thépaut-Cabasset, *L'esprit des modes au grand siècle*, 170 n. 137.

123. It echoes the voluminous outline of the hooded cape worn with moccasins by a woman on an anonymous late eighteenth-century image of a Canadian couple. Archives de Montréal.

124. Havard, "'Les Forcer à devenir citoyens,'" 1002 and Aubert, "Kinship, Blood.".

125. *PFFA* 1:195.

126. KM 48:7:8:1.

127. KM 48:7:6:1.

128. RSCL 1737081405.

129. Ribeiro, *Dress in Eighteenth-Century Europe 1715–1789*, 56–58; also Crowston, *Fabricating Women*, 148–50.

130. KM 48:7:6:1, 48:7:6:2, 48:7:8:1.

131. KM 47:10:31:3.

132. On this French ethnonym, see Ekberg, *Stealing Indian Women*, 48–99.

133. "Journal of the Voyage of Monsieur de Bourgmont, Knight of the Military Order of Saint Louis, Commandant of the Missouri River [which] is above that of the Arkansas, and of the Missouri [Country], to the Padoucas," AM, 2JJ 55; 26: 1–44 [1724], document fully translated in Norall, *Bourgmont*, 159–60.

134. KM 39:9:1:1, 39:9:13:1.

135. The work of female seamstresses was seldom recorded; the activities of Madame Parent in the Illinois Country are only known because she had been commissioned to make clothes for children whose mother had died; see RSCL 1764081701. For an example of a male enslaved African with sewing skills, see KM 25:8:13:1; also Sophie White, "Cultures of Consumption."

136. KM 47:12:13:1, 47:12:15:1.

137. On protobranded textiles in France, which usually emerged from local specializations (and were named for these localities), see Lespagnol, "Des toiles bretonnes aux toiles 'Bretagne.'"

138. KM 67:10:20:1.

139. DuPlessis, "La Circulation et appropriation des mouchoirs," 168–70.

140. In contrast, see Mary Rowlandson's 1682 captivity narrative, in which she described numerous instances of being asked or made to knit stockings for her Wampanoag captors; Rowlandson, *Captivity and Restoration*, 24, 30, 61.

141. References to shipment of stockings to the Illinois Country are found in RSCL 1728052903, 1737081405, 1737081501, 1738071901, 1738072901, 1740040804. In 1729, Terrisse de Ternan wrote to his partner in New Orleans requesting a stock of assorted stockings to sell as there was a dearth of them in the Illinois Country; see RSCL 1729101301.

142. RSCL 1747061001.

143. RSCL 1747061001. On Widow Gervais's place in the mercantile world of New Orleans, see Sophie White, "'A Baser Commerce.'"

144. Ibid.

145. On jumps and stays, see Steele, *The Corset*; Kidwell, "Making Choices."

146. RSCL 1747061001.

147. Sophie White, "Widow's Weeds." On the Ursulines' manufacture and sale of mourning dress, see RSCL 1736100302; their commercial interests are discussed in Emily Clark, *Masterless Mistresses*, chaps. 5, 6.

148. "Mémoire du linge et hardes des orphelines ce 6 avril 1752," Ursuline Convent Archives, New Orleans, General Accounts, October 1797–October 1812, 13.

149. *Pénicaut Narrative*, original French 139 n. 5.

150. For example KM 26:5:4:4, 47:10:31:3; RSCL 1747061001.

151. "Memoir of de Gannes [de Liette]," 357–58; *JR*, 67:167.

152. KM 47:10:31:3. On French burial customs as practiced in colonial Louisiana, see for example Marie Elaine Danforth, "The Moran Site (22HR511): An Early-Eighteenth-Century French Colonial Cemetary in Nouveau Biloxi, Mississippi," in Kelly and Hardy, eds., *French Colonial Archaeology*, 64–80.

153. RSCL 1747061001.

154. KM 39:9:1:1, 39:9:13:1.

155. For moccasins, see KM 48:7:6:1.

156. In New Orleans, merchant Paul Rasteau stocked embroidered morocco leather shoes at 10 livres a pair; see RSCL 1737100201, fol. 10r. For the 1729 letter from Terrisse de Ternan to his partner in New Orleans, see RSCL 1729101301. Sixteen pairs of men's and nine pairs of women's shoes were included in a 1737 cargo for the Illinois Country; see RSCL 1737081405. Other shipments of shoes to the Illinois Country are documented in RSCL 1740031203, 1740051202, 1740070401 (38 pairs of men's shoes), and 1741071406 (20 pairs of children's shoes).

157. For further examples of embroidered shoes clearly of European-style manufacture, even when made of beaver, for instance, see RSCL 1735091201, 1740060604, 1753100104.

158. RSCL 1747061001.

159. See also Alexandre Dubé's work in progress on limbourg.

160. KM 47:10:31:3.

161. On the market for moccasins in the later eighteenth century, see Ekberg, *A French Aristocrat in the American West*, 143, 149; Cangany, "'Altogether Preferable to Shoes.'"

162. Feest et al., *Premières nations, collections royales*. See also Horse Capture et al., *Robes of Splendor*, which contains full color images of the robes, but is problematic in interpretation and tribal attribution. See also, more generally, Phillips, *Trading Identities*.

163. Bartram, *Travels and Other Writings*, 534.

164. Brasser, "Notes on a Recently Discovered Indian Shirt from New France"; Feest et al., *Premières nations*; Horse Capture et al., *Robes of Splendor*; Bécart de Granville, *Les Raretés des Indes*.

165. *Limbourg* was identified predominantly as red or blue, although references to brown and

white might also be found. The symbolic significance of certain colors allied with increasing availability of cloth in these colors led to their proliferation in Indian wardrobes. Kathryn Braund has suggested in her study of Creek consumerism that the increasing popularity of red and blue "had less to do with cosmic concerns than the dictates of native fashion and a love of vibrant colors"; see *Deerskins & Duffels*, 123. For an account of the emergence of blue in the eighteenth century, not only among France's working poor but also in Africa and Canada, see Pellegrin, "Le Goût du bleu." Blue and red dyes carried cost implications at the manufacturing level too; see ANOM, C13A 31:251, May 5, 1747.

166. In the Illinois Country, buffalo robes, used as bedding, were present in fifteen of the sixty-one extant probate inventories; see White, "Trading Identities," 81.

167. KM 47:11:9:1, 48:10:9:1.

168. KM 47:10:31:3.

169. Antoine Crozat, memorandum (prior to February 8, 1716), ANOM, C13A 4:29. Crozat went on to discuss the possibilities for developing silk cultivation in the colony, which would benefit from Indian women's skills in spinning.

170. Drouot de Val de Terre, memorandum on Louisiana (prior to December 9, 1721), ANOM, C13A 6:352.

171. See "Memoir of de Gannes [de Liette]," 339, which specifies that Illinois women made sacks and garters of spun buffalo hair. For a description of the qualities of buffalo wool, see Le Page du Pratz, *Histoire de la Louisiane*, 2:62–63; 66–68 on dyeing buffalo wool.

172. *Pénicaut Narrative*," original French 139 n. 5.

173. KM 24:7:26:1.

174. Commissaire-Ordonnateur Michel to Minister of Marine, August 6, 1749, ANOM, C13A 34:108.

175. For a rich interpretation of the meaning of things as mnemonic devices, see Auslander, "Beyond Words."

176. Bossu, *Nouveaux voyages aux Indes occidentales*, 1:162, The watch was also referenced in the "Relation de l'arrivée en France," *Mercure de France*, 2852.

177. RSCL 1730072801.

178. Bossu, *Nouveaux voyages aux Indes occidentales*, 1:162. On the similarities between some European manufactured goods (such as glass, mirrors, copper) and "spiritually charged native items," including use of the former in ceremonial contexts, see Miller and Hamell, "A New Perspective on Indian-White Contact."

179. Bossu, *Nouveaux voyages dans l'Amérique septentrionale*, 27; translation from Folmer, "Étienne Veniard de Bourgmond in the Missouri Country," 297.

Chapter 2. "Nothing of the *Sauvage*"

1. See Ulrich, "Of Pens and Needles."

2. "Relation of François Le Mercier with Claude Jean Allouez, Thomas Morel, and Marie de Bonaventure (1666–67)," *JR*, 51:51.

3. Translation rom Greer, *The Jesuit Relations*, 200.

4. See, for example, Dumont *dit* Montigny, "Mémoire," NL, Ayer MS 257, fol. 400.

5. *Pénicaut Narrative*, 116–17; also 137, 139 (from the year 1711).

6. *JR*, 54:181; and Morrissey, "Bottomlands and Borderlands," chap. 2 and "'I Speak It Well.'"

7. Antoine-Robert Le Boullenger, French-[Kaskaskia] Illinois Dictionary, ca. 1720, Box 1894, John Carter Brown Library, Brown University; Masthay, *Kaskaskia Illinois-to-French Dictionary*; Anonymous, *Illinois and Miami Vocabulary and Lord's Prayer*; Costa, "An Overview of the Illinois Language;" Morrissey, "'I Speak It Well.'"

8. *JR*, 64:159–237. The annual reports of French Jesuit missionaries in the field represent a particularly important source for understanding the unusual contours of intermarriage in the Illinois Country. They were published in Paris and widely disseminated between 1632 and 1673, after which date, Jesuits such as Gravier continued to submit their relations, but they were no longer published. As Allan Greer reminds us, this was also literary genre, where texts served as "sites where notions of gender difference and racial hierarchy were enunciated, qualified, challenged, and inverted"; see Greer, "Colonial Saints," 324.

9. "Letter by Father Jacques Gravier in the Form of a Journal of the Mission of l'Immaculée Conception de Notre Dame in the Ilinois Country," February 15, 1694, *JR*, 64:158–237.

10. *JR*, 64:219, 225–29.

11. *JR*, 64:213.

12. Ibid.; Brandão and Nassaney, "Suffering for Jesus."

13. Ekberg with Pregaldin, "Marie Rouensa-8cate8a," 154; Sleeper-Smith, *Indian Women and French Men*, 34. On fasting by Catherine Tekakwitha and other female converts at Kahnawake, see Greer, *Mohawk Saint*, 119–20; Shoemaker, "Kateri Tekakwitha's Tortuous Path to Sainthood"; Davis, "Iroquois Women, European Women."

14. "Memoir of de Gannes [de Liette]," 353. On her oratory, see *JR*, 64:223; Leavelle, "Geographies of Encounter," 929–30. On her vision quest, see Jacqueline Peterson, "Women Dreaming," 39.

15. "The Voyage of St. Cosme, 1698–1699," in (and translation from) Kellogg, *Early Narratives of the Northwest*, 353. His example pertained to an especially prominent female chief.

16. *JR*, 64: 209, 179, 185, 163, 175–77.

17. *JR*, 64:203, 193.

18. *JR*, 64:165, 191, 195, 209.

19. *JR*, 64:165–67.

20. *JR*, 66:247–49.

21. *JR*, 64:195. No record of the marriage survives. Contrary to Morrissey's assertion that the marriage took place in 1694, clues present in Father Gravier's February 15, 1694, letter suggest she was already married to Accault by spring 1693, when he mentions baptizing a widow who had *followed* Rouensa in desiring celibacy; see *JR*, 64:167; and Morrissey, "Bottomlands and Borderlands," 85–86.

22. *JR*, 64:229; on the conflicting accounts of her age, see Ekberg with Pregaldin, "Marie Rouensa-8canic8e," 149.

23. *JR*, 64:213. On Accault's presence on a number of expeditions to the Illinois Country, with La Salle and Tonti as well as Louis Hennepin (during which time he deserted, stole, and generally looked after his trading interests before seeking legitimacy and social standing by 1693), see Ekberg, "Marie Rouensa-8canic8e," 209–10; and especially Morrissey, "Borderlands and Bottomlands," 82–86 (but see note 21, above, about dates). On his acquisition of the seigneury, see "La Forest Sells Half-Interest to Accault, April 19, 1693," in CISHL, 264–66.

24. *JR*, 64:211.

25. Belting, *Kaskaskia Under the French Regime*, 14.

26. *JR*, 64: 196 (my translation).

27. *JR* 64:196 (my translation). A catechumen had received religious instruction, but was not yet baptized.

28. *JR*, 67:165–67.

29. Kent, *Ft. Pontchartrain at Detroit*, 2:557. *Justaucorps* "a femme" (for women) are documented in 1673 and 1684; on coats associated with female Indian burials, see 560–61.

30. A number of depictions of Illinois males are known. See, for example, the *Codex canadensis*, attributed to Louis Nicolas, ca. 1675–80, Gilcrease Museum, Tulsa, Oklahoma; facsimile Bécart de Granville, *Les Raretés des Indes*; see also Plate 1, Alexandre de Batz's *Dessein de Sauvages de Plusieurs Nations*.

31. BNF Arsenal Ms 3459; Dumont, "Mémoire," NL Ayer Ms 257.

32. The encounter took place in 1729; see Dumont, "Mémoire," NL Ayer MS 257, 209.

33. *Pénicaut Narrative*, original French at 139 n. 5.

34. "Narrative of a Voyage Made to the Illinois, by Father Claude Allouez," in Shea, *Discovery and Exploration of the Mississippi Valley*, 75.

35. My art historical evaluation of the portrait of Tekakwitha attributed to Chauchetière and now housed in the Saint Francis-Xavier Mission at Kahnawake has revealed that this is in fact a nineteenth-century image. It is not therefore done in Chauchetière's hand, in contrast to the illustrated manuscript that is securely attributed to Chauchetière and dates from the seventeenth century; for the manuscript, see "Narration de la mission du Sault depuis sa fondation jusqu'en 1686," ser. H 48 Jésuites, Archives Départementales de la Gironde. See also the facsimile, Chauchetière, *Narration de la Mission du Sault depuis sa fondation jusqu'en 1686*, ed. Avisseau. Though the painting is not a primary source, it is based on a 1715 engraving that shows a more accurate depiction of dress; the engraving and a 1722 version are reproduced in Gagnon, *La Conversion par l'image*, 25–26.

36. Letter of Father Claude Chauchetière, October 14, 1682, *JR*, 62:176; translation taken from Greer, *The Jesuit Relations*, 152; see 153–54 for Chauchetière's description of the dress of Iroquois mission Indians (including wearing fine white shirts on Sundays and feast days). Emphasizing the overall modesty of this dress, he noted that "They closely fasten the shirt and let it hang down over a petticoat, consisting of a blue or red blanket, a fathom or more square, which they fold in two and fasten simply around the waist. The shirt, which falls over this sort of petticoat, reaches only to the knees" (154).

37. Cited in Schlarman, *From Quebec to New Orleans*, 155–56. Schlarman cites the "Relation de Pénicaut" in Margry, *Mémoires et documents*, 5:448–93, but this passage has not been located. Nor does it appear in *Pénicaut Narrative*.

38. KM 46:1:17:3.

39. For example ANOM, C13A, 8:407, May 26, 1725. See Robert S. DuPlessis's account of the links between the acceptance of European clothing with the reception of Christianity, as formulated by religious figures in "Circulation des textiles et des valeurs," 85. See also Stols, "L'Âge d'or du déshabillé," 282.

40. Good, "Guébert Site," 18–20.

41. ANOM, C13A, 8:409, September 15, 1725 and 407 May 26, 1725.

42. Ekberg with Pregaldin, "Marie Rouensa-8cate8a," 148.

43. The colonial hagiographic themes found in accounts of Marie's conversion echo those found in the accounts of Catherine Tekakwitha's conversion. The latter's death—or martyrdom— (as opposed to Marie's marriage) provided Catherine's champions with the additional ammunition

needed to promote her path to veneration; on the limitations imposed upon Indian candidates for veneration and sainthood, see Greer, "Colonial Saints," 344, 347.

44. *JR*, 64:193, 213.

45. *JR*, 64:205.

46. *JR*, 64:209.

47. *PFFA* 2:124.

48. Marrero, "A Tale of Three Marguerites"; and "Marguerite Ouabankikoue," http://www .leveillee.net/ancestry/ouabankekoue.htm. Thanks to Karen Marrero for this citation.

49. Sleeper-Smith, *Indian Women and French Men*, chap. 2. Raymond E. Hauser argues that the shifts in warfare practices among Illinois Indians in the contact period (from raiding to "communal warfare") were initially advantageous for the Illinois, but contributed ultimately to their decline. Hauser attributes the transformation of warfare practices to the arrival of European trade goods, which offered technological advantages to the Illinois and altered their economic landscape; Hauser's analysis is particularly attuned to transformations in gender and social roles in warfare stemming from these changes. See Hauser, "Warfare and the Illinois Indian" and "The Fox Raid of 1752." The estimate of wives in polygamous marriages was provided by de Liette; see "Memoire of de Gannes [de Liette]," 329.

50. My thanks to Brett Rushforth for sharing chapter 1 of his forthcoming *Bonds of Alliance: Indigenous and Atlantic Slaveries in New France* (Chapel Hill: University of North Carolina Press, 2012).

51. *JR*, 64:167. For a brief contextualization of the practice of retaliatory gang rape among Algonquin-speaking tribes that suggests that this was both widespread and long-term, see Lawrence A. Conrad, "An Early Eighteenth-Century Reference to 'Putting a Woman on the Prairies.'" An alternative view, that sexual abuse was exacerbated by geopolitical conditions and influenced by contact with the French, is provided by Hauser, "The Other Half."

52. Sleeper-Smith, *Indian Women and French Men*, 21.

53. This case was litigated in the Illinois Country and in New Orleans because it concerned a succession dispute. See KM 41:4:28:2, 41:4:28:3, 41:4:28:4; RSCL 1737092401, 1737092501, 1738080401, 1741011701, 1741040401, 1741042801, 1741071501, 1741101705, 1741101709, and esp. 1741011704, discussed in Sophie White, "A Certain Article of Furniture." For another abuse case from the Illinois Country, see KM 40:8:1:1, 40:8:2:1, 40:8:3:1, 40:9:24:1. On Turpin and 8yta8ikigik, see Sommerville, *All Sources Are Not Created Equal*, Part 10.

54. "Memoir of de Gannes [de Liette]," 351; also 339–47.

55. *JR*, 66:229.

56. Pertinent critiques of the interpretation of Illinois women as merely passive "drudges" are offered by Hauser, "The Other Half"; Thorne, "For the Good of Her People." See also Smits, "The 'Squaw Drudge.'"

57. General features of the female experience, including the gender division of labor, plural marriage, marriage gift exchange and the prevalence of clan considerations, are briefly recounted in Hauser, "The Berdache and the Illinois Indian Tribe", and "Other Half." For Hauser, "the enforcement of clan rights reflected both the economic importance of marriage and the power of women while protecting their sphere" ("The Other Half," 8).

58. *JR*, 64:225.

59. "Memoir of de Gannes [de Liette]," 333.

60. *JR*, 64:213, 224–25, 207.

61. Sleeper-Smith, *Indian Women and French Men*; Richard White, *Middle Ground*, 60–75; Jacqueline Peterson, "Many Roads to Red River"; Thorne, "For the Good of Her People."

62. *JR*, 68:203.

63. Hauser, "The Other Half." A thought-provoking account of native concepts of trade (and how these were played out in commercial interactions with Europeans) is offered by Colpitts, "'Animated like Us by Commercial Interests.'" On the deployment of women's bodies as a medium of exchange in diplomatic rituals and economic relations beyond French America, see Godbeer, "Eroticizing the Middle Ground," 98–99; Brooks, *Captives and Cousins*, chap. 1; see also Barr, "From Captives to Slaves."

64. On French misinterpretations of gifts as payment for women, see Denonville to Minister, August 25, 1687, CISHL, 89. On women being gambled away, see Raudot, "Memoir," 391, cited in Morrissey, "Bottomlands and Borderlands," 233.

65. *JR*, 64:211; "Memoir of de Gannes [de Liette]," 331–34; "Journal of Diron d'Artaguiette," 72–73. On Illinois women's dependence on their male relatives for marital decisions, see also "Letter of Father Julien Binneteau, [January] 1699," *JR*, 65:66.

66. *Pénicaut Narrative*, 139–40.

67. On the invisibility of women's trading activities, see, for example, Lemire, *Dress, Culture, Commerce*, 95–120; also Cleary, *Elizabeth Murray*, 71–72; Sophie White, "'A Baser Commerce.'"

68. KM 23:11:8:4.

69. KM 23:9:10:5.

70. KM 25:3:15:1.

71. On the retention of names, language, and tribal identity, see Sleeper-Smith, "Women, Kin, and Catholicism," esp. 426, and "'an Unpleasant Transaction on this Frontier,'" esp. 417.

72. See Kathleen DuVal's comparison of Illinois, Apalachee, and Quapaw strategies for fostering or avoiding intermarriage with the French in Upper and Lower Louisiana in "Indian Intermarriage and Metissage."

73. Brasseaux, *The Founding of New Acadia*.

74. Jonah, "Unequal Transitions." I am grateful to the author for providing me with transcripts of ANOM G3, 2047–1, 115, October 30, 1750 and 2042, June 21, 1754.

75. KM 48:7:6:1, 48:7:6:2 and 48:7:8:1; 47:12:13:1, 47:12:15:1; 67:10:21:1 respectively.

76. Neville Public Museum of Brown County, Wisconsin, photo negative nos. 3.1983.50, 220–22, 601–6.

77. See, for example, George Winter's watercolor portrait *D-Mouche-Kee-Kee-Awh* (observed 1837, executed ca. 1863–71), Tippecanoe County Historical Association, Lafayette, Indiana. The dress in this portrait, and related ones by George Winter, is central to Susan Sleeper-Smith's discussion of Potawatomi and Miami persistence strategies of "hiding in plain view" on the mid-nineteenth-century Indiana frontier; see *Indian Women and French Men*, chap.7.

78. Severa, *Dressed for the Photographer*, 76–77. Severa identifies Rachel's mother as Ojibwe (Chippewa). However, more detailed and contextualized information on Rachel's parents, and their position as a leading family within the Great Lakes Métis community, is provided by Peterson, "Prelude to Red River"; and Murphy, *Gathering of Rivers*, 52–59. Peterson identifies her mother as half Indian, granddaughter of an Ottawa originally from the environs of Mackinac, "Prelude," 43. See especially Murphy's discussion of continuing native influences on the material culture of these elite families, as well as her argument that there was a gendered distinction in the dress of elite Métis men and women in this community, *Gathering of Rivers*, 53–55.

79. Severa, *Dressed for the Photographer*, 76–77. For a summary of Métis settlement patterns at Green Bay (where trading activities and subsistence agriculture continued to be performed according to a gender division of labor), see Ekberg, *French Roots in the Illinois Country*, 17–21. On the emergence of lead mining, also influenced by changes in gender division of labor through French, British, and American control, see Murphy, *Gathering of Rivers*.

80. Neville Public Museum of Brown County, photo negative nos. L1348 (Mrs. George Lawe and her daughter Amanda T. Lawe, 1847), L1350 (George Lawe and his son John D. Lawe, Jr., ca. 1846). On her sisters' dress at St. Mary's Catholic Seminary in Somerset, Ohio, see letter from Maria M. Lawe to John Lawe, April 26, 1838, in Severa, *Dressed for the Photographer*, 76–77.

81. Sleeper-Smith, *Indian Women and French Men*. On spirituality, see Bilodeau's assertion of a "'material' mentality" among the Illinois, arguing that "the Illinois based their relationships with both humans and manitous in part on material exchanges" that was evoked in their practice of Christianity; see "Colonial Christianity," 354.

82. *JR*, 64, 211.

83. I am here adapting Sleeper-Smith's interpretation of Illinois women's Catholicism to a consideration of their dress (*Indian Women and French Men*, 29).

84. Thorne, "For the Good of Her People," 109.

85. I am here indebted to Amanda Vickery's discussion of peer distinction in her analysis of dress; see Vickery, *The Gentleman's Daughter*, 161–94; see also Bourdieu, *Distinction*.

86. Morrissey, "Bottomlands and Borderlands," 63–64.

87. "Memoir of de Gannes [de Liette]," 339.

88. Though see Laurier Turgeon, "French Beads in France and Northeastern North America."

89. Walthall, "Aboriginal Pottery"; Noble, "Eighteenth-Century Ceramics," 43.

90. Berlo and Phillips, *Native North American Art*, 16–17, 32.

91. Laurier Turgeon makes the same point in "The Tale of the Kettle."

92. Bohaker, "Contesting the Middle Ground"; DuVal, "Indian Intermarriage and Metissage."

93. Van Kirk, *Many Tender Ties*, 37; see also Podruchny, *Making the Voyageur World*, 270–71.

94. Hauser, "The Berdache and the Illinois Indian Tribe"; Trexler, *Sex and Conquest*, chap. 4. See also Dumont dit Montigny's description of berdaches among the Natchez; NL Ayer Ms 257, p. 382. Hauser identifies the original term as Ikoneta; Carl Masthay provides two other names from Gravier's Kaskaskia-French dictionary, mentchinikita and ic8e8aïa; see Masthay, *Kaskaskia Illinois-to-French Dictionary*, 172 and 122 respectively.

95. "Memoir of de Gannes [de Liette]," 329.

95. Ibid.

96. *JR*, 59:129; Hauser, "The Berdache and the Illinois Indian Tribe"; Trexler, *Sex and Conquest*, chap. 4.

97. On early modern European views of gender fluidity, see Laqueur, *Making Sex*; also Castro, "Stripped," esp. 119–22. The berdache do also invite parallels with examples such as Thomasina Hall in 1629 Virginia; see Kathleen Brown " 'Changed . . . into the Fashion of Man.' "

98. Little, *Abraham in Arms*, 101–2.

99. Viau, *Enfants du néant et mangeurs d'âmes*, 164; Starna and Watkins, "Northern Iroquoian Slavery."

100. On captivity and captivity rituals in New France, see Rushforth, " 'A Little Flesh We Offer You' "; Starna and Watkins, "Northern Iroquoian Slavery"; also Richter, *Ordeal of the Longhouse*, 66–74; Viau, *Enfants du néant et mangeurs d'âmes*, 137–60; also Claude Charles Le Roy,

Bacqueveille de la Potherie, *Histoire de l 'Amérique septentrionale*, trans. as "History of the Savage Peoples" in Blair, *Indian Tribes*, 2:36–43; also Sayre, *Les Sauvages américains*, chap. 6. For the South, see esp. Barr, "From Captives to Slaves"; Brooks, *Captives and Cousins* and "'This Evil Extends Especially . . . to the Feminine Sex'"; and Snyder, *Slavery in Indian Country*. Lafitau states that breechclouts were not stripped off; see Joseph-François Lafitau, *Customs of the American Indians Compared with the Customs of Primitive Times*, vol. 2, ed. and trans. William N. Fenton and Elizabeth L. Moore (Toronto: Champlain Society, 1977), 151, cited in Starna and Watkins, "Northern Iroquoian Slavery," 46, on stripping see 45; Bonnefoy, "Journal of Antoine Bonnefoy," 246.

101. Dumont, "Mémoire," NL Ayer Ms 257, 225; NL Ayer Ms 530, 54; ANOM C13A 12:57–58v. Two tailors were listed among the survivors. See also the events following the 1704 raid on Deerfield, in Haefeli and Sweeney, *Captors and Captives*, 130–31; also Castro, "Stripped"; on English female captives deploying their needlework skills while in captivity, see Little, *Abraham in Arms*, 123–24.

102. "Relation du voyage de la Louisiane ou Nouv.lle France fait par le Sr. Caillot en l'année 1730," HNOC Ms. 2005.11, 148. See Erin Greenwald's forthcoming edition of this manuscript; also Sophie White, "Massacre, *Mardi Gras* and Torture."

103. Rushforth, "'A Little Flesh'"; Barr, "From Captives to Slaves."

104. *JR*, 67:172–73; Rushforth, "Savage Bonds," chap. 1; Ekberg, *Stealing Indian Women*; Morrissey, "Bottomlands and Borderlands," 61–62.

105. Barr, "From Captives to Slaves;" Brooks, "'This Evil'"; Snyder, "Conquered Enemies," esp. 271–74. On definitions of Padoka and panis, see Ekberg, *Stealing Indian Women*, 48–49; Rushforth, "'A Little Flesh,'" esp. 788.

106. Richter, *Ordeal of the Longhouse*, 72; Starna and Watkins, "Northern Iroquoian Slavery," 42–43.

107. Demos, *The Unredeemed Captive*; Starna and Watkins add that children were seldom marked, on the assumption they would be apt to assimilate completely (and irreversibly?); see "Northern Iroquoian Slavery," 54 n. 6.

108. All references to this court case are from Ste. Genevieve Civil Records, Slaves, no. 196. See also Ekberg, *Stealing Indian Women*, Part II, with thanks to Carl J. Ekberg for sharing his research with me.

109. Ekberg, *Stealing Indian Women*, 162–63.

110. Ibid., 172, 181.

111. On manumission as always preceding legal marriages to Frenchmen, see Ekberg, *Stealing Indian Women*, 80.

112. KM 26:7:26:1; Ekberg, *Stealing Indian Women*, 43–45.

113. *PFFA* 2:237; Ekberg, *Stealing Indian Women*, 47.

114. KM 49:8:10:1.

115. ANOM, C13A, vol. 23, fols. 241–42.

116. KM 26:5:2:1, 26:5:2:1, 26:5:10:1, 28:6:7:1.

117. KM 47:10:31:3.

118. Ibid.

119. *Pénicaut Narrative*, 65.

120. The quotation is from Father Sébastien Rasles; see *JR*, 67:172.

121. Le Page du Pratz, *Histoire de la Louisiane*, 1:112–15.

122. "Relation de l'arrivée en France de quatre Sauvages de Missicipi," 362 [2844]. On the 1725 Indian delegation to Paris, see Norall, *Bourgmont*, 17, 81–88; Giraud, *History of Louisiana*, 5:488–94; Ellis and Steen, "An Indian Delegation in France, 1725."

123. *PFFA* 2:224–25; Ekberg and Pregaldin, "Marie Rouensa-8canic8e," 216.

124. Sleeper-Smith, "Women, Kin, and Catholicism," 426.

125. Personal communication, Fort de Chartres, October 2003.

126. *JR*, 64:191.

Chapter 3. "One People and One God"

1. See "Acte pour l'établissement de la Compagnie des Cent Associés pour le Commerce du Canada, contenant les articles accordés à la dite Compagnie par M. Le Cardinal de Richelieu, le 29 Avril 1627," transcribed in *Edits, ordonnances royaux, déclarations et arrêts du Conseil d'État du Roi concernant le Canada*, 1:10; translation from Aubert, "'The Blood of France,'" 451–52.

2. KM 25:6:13:1.

3. My thanks to Dominique Deslandres for this insight.

4. Olivier-Martin, *Histoire de la coutume de la prévôté et vicomté de Paris*, is the standard reference on the customary law of Paris. For its application in Louisiana, see Baade, "Marriage Contracts in French and Spanish Louisiana"; Baker, Simpson, and Allain, "*Le Mari Est Seigneur*"; Boyle, "Did She Generally Decide?"; Johnson, "*La Coutume de Paris*." See also, on New France, Parent and Postolec, "Quand Thémis rencontre Clio"; Zoltvany, "Esquisse de la Coutume de Paris"; Greer, *Peasant, Lord, and Merchant*, 48–55.

5. KM 25:6:13:1.

6. KM 25:6:20:1, 28:11:13:1; Ekberg, "Marie Rouensa-8canic8e," 217.

7. The term is borrowed from DuVal, "Indian Intermarriage and Metissage."

8. The missionaries' words were reported in Salmon to Minister, July 17, 1732, ANOM, C13A, 15:166v

9. ANOM, C13A, 4:255–57.

10. La Vente to Brisacier, July 4, 1708, ASQ, sme 2.1/r/083; he may also have authored the anonymous report in Summary of Memorandum on Louisiana [1710], ANOM, C13A, 2:563. On the marriages, see Bienville to the Minister of Marine, October 10, 1706, ANOM, C13B 1:5v.

11. Duclos to Pontchartrain, December 25, 1715, ANOM, C13A, 3:819–24, translation from *MPA* 2:207.

12. La Vente to Brisacier, July 4, 1708, ASQ, sme 2.1/r/083, p. 20.

13. Jaenen, "Frenchification and Evangelization of the Amerindians," *Friend and Foe*, and "Miscegenation"; Belmessous, "Assimilation and Racialism," "Être français en Nouvelle-France," and "D'un préjugé culturel"; Melzer, "Underside of France's Civilizing Mission," "Magic of French Culture," and "L'Histoire oubliée"; Vidal, "Francité et situation coloniale." On the expression "franciser" see Belmessous, "Assimilation and Racialism," 323 n. 7.

14. *JR*, 5:210.

15. Lescarbot, *History of New France*, 1:10.

16. Jean-Baptiste Colbert to Jean Talon, January 5, 1666, in Roy, *Rapport de l'archiviste de la Province de Québec*, 45.

17. Colbert to Talon, April 5, 1667, in Roy, *Rapport*, 72.

18. Letter to her son, September 1, 1668, in Oury, *Correspondance*, 809.

19. Letter to Mère C. de S. Joseph, September 1, 1669, in Oury, *Correspondance*, 821.

20. Jaenen, *Friend and Foe*, 163–64; *JR*, 14:19–21, 9:233.

21. De Meulles to Minister, November 12, 1682, ANOM, C11A 6:87–88; translation adapted from Belmessous, "Assimilation and Racialism," 334.

22. On the 1685 Code Noir, see Sala-Molins, *Le Code Noir ou Le calvaire de Canaan.*

23. Deslandres, "L'Éducation des Amérindiennes," and "Un Projet éducatif"; Gourdeau, *Les Délices de nos coeurs.*

24. Greer, *The People of New France*, 17; Aubert, "Blood of France," 452–54; Belmessous, "Assimilation and Racialism," 332 n. 46. On these English captives, see Little, *Abraham in Arms*, chap. 4, and "L'Étrangère."

25. AM B1:152:161v-162, translation from Aubert, "Français, Nègres et Sauvages," 148.

26. Jaenen, "Miscegenation," 96. Spear asserts that the emphasis for missionaries was on "the power of European social institutions such as marriage to convert and "civilize" Indians" ("They Need Wives," 42). On the contrary, as shown in the 1657 edict, conversion was the precondition that would lead to Frenchification.

27. "Relation du voyage de la Louisiane ou Nouv.lle France fait par le Sr. Caillot en l'année 1730," HNOC Ms. 2005.11, p. 167; and Bossu, *New Travels in North America*, 99.

28. Dumont, "Mémoire," NL Ayer Ms,S 257, p. 400.

29. Kupperman, "Presentment of Civility," 193.

30. Ibid.; see also Kupperman, "Fear of Hot Climates," and *Indians and English* 41–76; Shoemaker, *A Strange Likeness*, 125–40.

31. Aubert, "The Blood of France," 449–50 n. 23.

32. "Relation of François Le Mercier with Claude Jean Allouez, Thomas Morel, and Marie de Bonaventure (1666–67)," in *JR*, 51:51; and "Of the first Voyage made by Father Marquette toward new Mexico, and How the idea thereof was conceived," 673–77, in *JR*, 59:125.

33. *Pénicaut Narrative*," 116; also 137, 139. As seen here, such observations were usually presented as statements of fact.

34. "The Voyage of St. Cosme, 1698–1699," in Louise Phelps Kellogg, ed., *Early Narratives of the Northwest, 1634–1699* (New York: Scribners's Sons, 1917), 351.

35. *JR* 66: 241.

36. "Sabrevois memoir on Illinois, 1718," in Edmund B. O'Callaghan, *Documents Relative to the Colonial History of the State of New York* (Albany, 1853–87), 9:890–91, cited in Morrissey, "Bottomlands and Borderlands," 309.

37. "Memoir of de Gannes [de Liette]," 337, 328.

38. "Relation du voyage," HNOC Ms 2005.11, 117, 157.

39. Roediger, *The Wages of Whiteness.*

40. See Robert Morrissey's probing analysis of the motives for this transformation in "Bottomlands and Borderlands," chap. 3; also Aubert, "Français, Nègres et Sauvages," chap. 4.

41. *JR*, 64:209.

42. *JR*, 64:213. It is now recognized that St. Henry and St. Cunegund's marriage did not begin as a celibate one, but that this myth became current after their deaths; see Alban Butler, *Butler's Lives of the Saints*, 65–66.

43. *JR*, 64:213-15. In a later section of his letter, Father Gravier added further incidental information about Accault's newfound zeal for the conversion of the Illinois, the "good service" he rendered to the mission, and that he would speak to his new family about "the ceremonies of our churches, and of the offerings made to God of tapers, blessed bread, etc." (235).

44. In 1707, Gravier would write to his superiors in Rome to request clarification on "the

contracting of marriage by a christian with an infidel"; see *JR*, 66:121–23. It has been argued that this was an index of Gravier's continuing uncertainty about the practice of intermarriage (Morrissey, "Bottomlands and Borderlands," 312). In fact, his request concerned "infidels" (those who had not converted), not the Indian converts whose marriages to Frenchmen Gravier and others in the Illinois Country had been celebrating.

45. RSCL 1725021501, 1725021604. His petition was approved and a new contract drawn up based on his declaration and that of his witnesses (RSCL 1725022601).

46. KM 28:3:6:1.

47. Belting, *Kaskaskia*, 19 n.51. On the potential for garde-magazins to enrich themselves as a result of their position, including the temptation to sell the Crown's merchandise for their own profit, see Dubé, "Les Biens publics," 394–406.

48. Chassin to Father Bobé, July 1, 1722, ANOM, C13A, 4:299v, translation from *MPA* 2:279.

49. Chassin to Bobé, July 1, 1722, ANOM, C13A, 4:297–297v, trans. *MPA* 2:274–75.

50. KM 23:6:22:1; on his daughter's possession of his property following his death in 1727, see 40:3:24:1. Melique's age is given in K-370, Brown and Dean, *Village of Chartres*, 831.

51. KM 22:11:2:1.

52. See "La Forest Sells Half-Interest to Accault," April 19, 1693, *CISHL*, 264, discussed in Morrissey, "Bottomlands and Borderlands," 85–86. Morrissey states that this act predated his marriage, which he dates to 1694. Clues from Father Gravier's February 1694 letter show that they were already married by spring 1693, when he mentions baptizing a widow who became the second (*after* Rouensa) to wish celibacy; see *JR*, 64:167.

53. The marriage contract does not survive, but three years after her marriage she inherited 2,861 livres from her mother's estate alone. See KM 25:8:16:1, 28:11:13:1, 38:10:20:1, 38:10:20:22.

54. KM 25:6:13:1.

55. Vidal, "Les Implantations," 139.

56. ANOM B 43:558, C13A 17:114v, cited in Belting, *Kaskaskia*, 19; *MPA* 2:623; see also Aubert, "Français, Nègres et Sauvages," 173; Spear, *Race, Sex, and Social Order*, 244–45.

57. *PFFA* 2:91m 94; KM 28:8:6:1.

58. KM 30:10:23:1, 37:7:6:1.

59. For examples of the (often favorable) marriages contracted by the children of interracial unions, see Ekberg, "Marie Rouens-8canic8e," 216. Also among those who married half-Indian women was the son of the royal notary in the Illinois Country, Jacques Barrois, who married Suzanne Baron in 1747; widowed, she married another Frenchman, Joseph Clermont; see *PFFA* 1:195, 197. Some widowers actively sought Indian or mixed-parentage women as spouses. Jean-Baptiste Baron, the widower of Marie Catherine Illinoise (parents of Suzanne Baron), contracted a second marriage with Domitille Rolet, the daughter of a settler and Domitille Apanis8 of the Peoria nation (KM 48:8:18:1). Louis Turpin had married Dorothée Mechip8e8a, widow of another Frenchman, Charles Danis; in his case, he had gone from widower of a French/Canadian woman to marriage with an Indian (KM 24:7:25:1 and *PFFA* 2:232). Daniel Legras married Suzanne Keramy, widow of Leonard (Belting, *Kaskaskia*, 81). Nicolas Boyer, widower of the half-Indian Marie Rose Texier, married the half-Indian Dorothée La Boissiere (KM 47:12:13:1, 49:4:21:1). Belting contributes additional data in *Kaskaskia*, 80–83; see also KM 23:4:12:1, 30:6:27:1, 38:12:30:2, 31:4:3:1, 59:2:17:1.

60. For one exception, see the marriage contracted by Jean Olivier with Marthe, a destitute Indian widow whom Olivier had married "to give her bread." See KM 23:9:16:1.

61. *PFFA* 2:147. The parents at this 1721 baptism were Guillaume Poitier-Dubuisson and his wife Marie Apecke8rata (also spelled Potier and Achipicourata); Chassin was joined as godparent by the Indian Marguerite 8asacam8c8e. On Indian Godmothers' role in creating cohesion within the *French* colonial settlements, see Morrissey, "Facebook Kaskaskia."

62. For example, Agnès Philippe (daughter of Marie Rouensa-8cate8a, the latter's father being chief of the Kaskaskia), was godmother to the son of Philippe de la Renaudiere; see *PFFA* 2:125. His godfather was a prominent military officer of noble extraction, Sieur Charles Legardeur de l'Isle. For an example of gift giving, see the gift of a heifer each that de la Loere Flaucourt, the provincial judge, made to the half-Indian Turpin siblings to be used as a dowry (KM 37:10:14:1 and 37:10:15:1).

63. General Census of the inhabitants of the colony of Louisiana, January 1, 1726; and Census of the Inhabitants of Louisiana and Census of the inhabitants of Illinois, dated January 1, 1732, both in ANOM, ser. G1, 464; VP O/S LO 426: [1752]. The first two are published in Maduell, *Census Tables for the French Colony of Louisiana*; also for the 1726 census, *FFL* 2:32–34. This contradicts Jaenen's statement that in New France under the French regime, all native peoples, full-blooded or not, were considered members of the Amerindian population by the French ("Miscegenation," 81).

64. Again, Olivier-Martin, *Histoire de la coutume*, is the standard reference on the customary law of Paris. Johnson, "*La Coutume de Paris*," attempts to explain its application in Louisiana, but does not discuss specifics of the law. More relevant in this respect are Baker, Simpson, and Allain, "*Le Mari Est Seigneur*"; Boyle, "Did She Generally Decide?" See also Parent and Postolec, "Quand Thémis rencontre Clio."

65. For example, RSCL 1746022401. Making a will or donation was one way of remedying the problem (KM 28:3:6:1; RSCL 1745050803 and 1745050804). Conversely, husbands inherited from their wives in much the same way, broadly following the regulations of the Coutume de Paris even if no contract existed.

66. KM 28:11:13:1.

67. As reported in a letter from Marie Madeleine Hachard to her father, April 24, 1728, in Emily Clark, *Voices from an Early American Convent*, 85.

68. Now housed at the John Carter Brown Library, Brown University, see Box 1894, and discussed in Costa, "Overview of the Illinois Language."

69. "Edict of the Superior Council of Louisiana, October 18, 1728, concerning the marriages of Frenchmen with Indian women" ANOM, A, 23:102–3. For other versions, including those from the Superior Council of Louisiana, see "Questions à decider au sujet des alliances matrimoniales des Français avec des Sauvagesses," 1729; ANOM, F3, 242:144–47; ANOM, F3, 11:178–79, 180, 182–83. My thanks to Guillaume Aubert for sharing his transcripts of all these variants.

70. "Memo of the King to Srs. de l'Espinay Governor and Hubert Commissaire Commissaire-Ordonnateur to Louisiana, 28 Oct. 1716," ANOM, B 38:334, translation from Aubert, "'The Blood of France,'" 470.

71. KM 23:6:2:1. The Council convicted the errant wife of adultery and condemned her to two years imprisonment if her husband "is able to have her taken into custody," unless he decided to take her back. Translation from Brown and Dean, *Village of Chartres*, 813–14.

72. RSCL 1745050803,d 1745050804; see also Spear, "'They Need Wives,'" 50, *Race, Sex, and Social Order*, 17. The children had been born before the marriage, suggesting that Lamotte's motive for the marriage (an unusual instance of legitimate intermarriage in Lower Louisiana) was related to inheritance matters.

73. KM 23:10:26:2, 23:11:8:1.

74. KM 28:3:6:1.

75. KM 29:8:24:1.

76. KM 39:1:19:1; 39:1:19:2; also *PFFA* 2: 134.

77. See also KM 35:5:23:1.

78. KM 44:10:31:1.

79. See Vidal, "Implantations," 288 nn. 29–30.

80. Périer to Minister, July 25, 1732, ANOM, C13A, 14:68.

81. Salmon to Minister, July 17, 1732, ANOM, C13A, 15:166–69.

82. October 4, 1735, ANOM, B 63:88v.

83. *PFFA* 1:78.

84. KM 49:8:10:1.

85. May 3, 1735, ANOM, C13A, 20:83–93; see fol. 90.

86. KM 35:5:23:1, 39:1:19:1.

87. Lessard, Mathieu, and Gouger, "Peuplement colonisateur," 57–65.

88. Jaenen, "Miscegenation" and (with caution) Karen Anderson, *Chain Her by One Foot*, 31–54. Two studies of English settlements that bring out the distinctiveness of regional colonial responses to intermarriage and *métissage* are Smits, " 'We Are Not to Grow Wild' "; and Fischer, *Suspect Relations*, ch. 2.

89. Vaudreuil to Macarty, August 8, 1751, VP LO 325.

90. See Aubert, "The Blood of France"; Vaudreuil's father, Philippe de Rigaud de Vaudreuil, governor of New France (1703–25), had deployed similar language in the first decades of the eighteenth century; see Aubert, 457–58. For a broader perspective on the evolution of concepts of lineage, nation, and race in European intellectual thought, see Hudson, "From 'Nation' to 'Race.' "

91. Jean-Baptiste du Bois Duclos, sieur de Montigny, to Minister of Marine Pontchartrain, December 25, 1715, ANOM, C13A, 3:819–24, translation taken from *MPA* 2:207–8.

92. La Vente to Brisacier, July 4, 1708, ASQ, sme 2.1/r/083, p. 20.

93. For example KM 35:11:21:1, 37:7:6:1, 40:9:4:2; 67:10:21:1.

94. KM 39:1:22:4.

95. RSCL 1747061001; CHS 211/6/1747.

96. KM 30:10:23:1, 37:7:6:1

97. KM 33:5:18:1.

98. *PFFA* 2:224.

99. KM 40:9:4:2.

100. *JR*, 65:69.

101. Lallement to Directors of the Company of the Indies, April 5, 1721, in CHS Kaskaskia Papers, Box 207, Folder 23, translation from Morrissey, "Bottomlands and Borderlands," 237.

102. ANOM, A 23:102–4.

103. Memorandum of Father Tartarin, ANOM C13A 23:241, 243. The document is undated; the Archives Nationales has dated it to 1738 although the context suggests a date of 1737.

104. *MPA* 2:207.

105. Ekberg, "Marie Rouensa-8canic8e," 214.

106. This is compatible with the comment by a French military officer in 1755 that marriages of mixed-parentage men with Canadian women had occurred at Lorette reservation in New France precisely because these men were among "the most Frenchised and the best Catholics"; see d'Aleyrac, *Aventures militaires*, 27.

107. Ekberg, *François Vallé and His World*, 29.

108. SGA Estates, no. 30, discussed in Ekberg, *Stealing Indian Women*, 68–74.

109. KM 28:3:6:1.

Part II Intro. Frenchified Indians and Wild Frenchmen in New Orleans

1. *PFFA* 2:224. The groom's father also served the French marine in Louisiana, as commandant at the Poste des Allemands (German Coast).

2. "Registre pour écrire les réceptions des Religieuses de France et postulantes [March 4, 1726–September 20, 1893] et les lettres circulaires [July 6, 1728–January 31, 1894]," UCANO, Reel 2.

3. Kenny, "The First American Nun in this Country"; St. Charles, "The First American Born Nun."

4. See Morris S. Arnold's reappraisal of the origin, date, and iconographic content of the robe in "Eighteenth-Century Arkansas Illustrated"; and Feest et al., *Premières nations, collections royales*. Though the interpretations are more problematic, see also Horse Capture et al., *Robes of Splendor*, plate 22, 136–37, details 28, 140.

5. On animal imagery and clan identity, see Bohaker, "Contesting the Middle Ground."

6. Usner, *Indians, Settlers, and Slaves in a Frontier Exchange Economy*, 6.

Chapter 4. "The First Creole from This Colony"

1. See Father Gabriel Marest to Father Germon, Kaskaskias, November 9, 1712, *JR*, 66:219–95.

2. *Edits, ordonnances royaux, déclarations et arrêts*, 1:10.

3. Compare this to the Quebec Ursulines, who applied the surname "sauvage" or "anglaise" to new Indian and English (former captive) boarders; see Little, "L'Étrangère." The documents relating to Marie Turpin in the UCANO consist of three separate entries. Two are eighteenth-century originals in a bound manuscript volume, the "Registre pour écrire les réceptions des Religieuses de France et postulantes [March 4, 1726–September 20, 1893] et les lettres circulaires [July 6, 1728–January 31, 1894]," UCANO, Reel 2. The third is a nineteenth-century (possibly abridged) copy of the eighteenth-century original, found in the "Lettres Circulaires depuis 1727 jusqu'en 1835," UCANO, Reel 18. I am deeply indebted to Emily Clark for her guidance in navigating these materials.

4. Emily Clark, *Masterless Mistresses*, 70.

5. KM 63:1:16:1; and see Ekberg, *François Vallé and His World*, 40–41, *Stealing Indian Women*, 80. The house was sold in 1763 for 17,000 livres (not 1,700 as stated in Belting, *Kaskaskia*, 37). On the rarity, expense, and prestige of stone houses in the Illinois Country, see Vidal, "Les Implantations," 594.

6. KM 28:6:10:1, 30:8:28:1.

7. *PFFA* 2:124.

8. "Registre pour écrire les réceptions des Religieuses de France et postulantes."

9. Vidal, "Les Implantations," 569; KM 25:6:20:1.

10. KM 51:3:20:3, (51:11:18:1) [Perrin du Lac, *Voyage dans les deux Louisianes*, 39]. Bracketed citations refer to documents in the register of gifts of real property now in the Perrin Collection at the Illinois State Archives. See also Brown and Dean, *Village of Chartres*, D-248, 175–77.

11. KM 37:10:14:1, 37:10:15:1.

12. Vidal suggests that nomination to the office of *garde-magasin* at Kaskaskia, an office that paid 450 livres a year, would have been based on his level of education, wealth, position in society in the Illinois Country, and relations with the authorities; in turn, his status as *garde-magasin* would have further distinguished him from the other inhabitants. See Vidal, "Les Implantations," 146.

13. "Registre pour écrire les réceptions des Religieuses de France et postulantes."

14. See KM 51:3:20:3 and (51:11:18:1) [Perrin, 39], registration and inscription by clerk Barrois of marriage contract between Hélène Hebert and Louis Turpin, dated March 20, 1751; also Brown and Dean, *Village of Chartres*, D-248, 175–76.

15. "Registre pour écrire les réceptions des Religieuses de France et postulantes."

16. The vote was by secret ballot, using beans (black for rejection, white for acceptance); on the procedures for taking the vote, see *Règlemens des religieuses ursulines*, 164–73.

17. Emily Clark, personal communication, April 2007.

18. On the funeral pall ritual and vows as signal of secular death, see Emily Clark, *Voices from an Early American Convent*, 93–94; see also the description of the stages of Marie Hachard's entry into the Ursuline order, 31–32 and n. 11.

19. Now housed at the John Carter Brown Library, Brown University, see Box 1894, and discussed in Costa, "An Overview of the Illinois Language."

20. "Questions à decider au sujet des alliances matrimoniales des Français avec des Sauvagesses," ANOM, F3, 242:144–47, quote at 145.

21. Hachard to her father, April 24, 1728, in Emily Clark, *Voices from an Early American Convent*, 85.

22. *JR*, 68:209–10; see also Leavelle, *The Catholic Calumet*, esp. chap. 1, and "'Bad Things' and 'Good Hearts,'" 363.

23. Dumont, "Mémoire," NL Ayer MS 257, 209–10. Dumont encountered them on their way downriver in 1729.

24. On the role of mortification and other such practices in the history of the Ursuline order, see Pommereu, *Les Chroniques de l'ordre des Ursulines*, 3:133–34.

25. See especially Greer, *Mohawk Saint*, chap. 5.

26. "Lettres circulaires depuis 1727 jusqu'en 1835."

27. Rapley, *A Social History of the Cloister*, chap. 11.

28. This is no different from the other converse nuns. In any case, each mention of her name was followed by the qualification "converse."

29. On the Ursuline order in France, see Annaert, *Les Collèges au féminin*; on teaching congregations in France, see Rapley, *The Dévotes* and *A Social History of the Cloister*. The key source on Ursulines in New Orleans is Emily Clark, *Masterless Mistresses*; see also Ebbs, "Subjected and Productive Bodies," which focuses primarily on their pedagogy; Heaney, *A Century of Pioneering*.

30. Clark, *Masterless Mistresses*, 41–58, "'By All the Conduct of Their Lives': A Laywomen's Confraternity in New Orleans, 1730–1744," *WMQ* 3rd ser. 54 (1997): 769–94; also Emily Clark and Virginia Meacham Gould, "The Feminine Face of Afro-Catholicism in New Orleans, 1727–1852," *WMQ* 3rd ser. 59 (2002): 409–48.

31. *Bulle de Bordeaux*, 24–26, cited in Annaert, "Les Collèges au féminin," 93–95.

32. Annaert, "Les Collèges," 94 n. 19. On fashion dolls, see Roche, *The Culture of Clothing*, 474–76; also Croizat, "'Living Dolls.'"

33. A second doll in the same collection is from a later date.

34. Lallement, *Constitutions et règlements des premiéres Ursulines de Quebec*, 121. See the Introduction for the background to this Constitution.

35. Ibid., 118–21.

36. Personal communication with Christine Cheyrou, director of the Musée des Ursulines de Quebec, May 2008.

37. *Règlemens des religieuses ursulines*, 3:275. On giving used clothing to servants in Europe, see Buck, *Dress in Eighteenth-Century England*, 108, 112–19; Roche, *Culture of Clothing*, 101–2; Crawford, "Clothing Distributions and Social Relations."

38. See *Règlemens des religieuses ursulines*, 2:277–81; also "Constitutions des ursulines de Paris" (Beaugency, A.U.F.N., Ursulines d'Abbeville, B 2G 01, manuscript, ca. 1623), fols. 117v–119r, cited in Annaert, "Les Collèges au féminin," 94 n. 20; on the Quebec Ursulines' distinctions between the habit of choir and converse sisters, see Lallement, *Constitutions et règlements*, 120.

39. Annaert, "Les Collèges au féminin," 93.

40. Emily Clark, *Masterless Mistresses*, appendix 1, 264–67.

41. Ibid., 52–53, 64, 211.

42. "Registre pour écrire les réceptions des Religieuses de France et postulantes."

43. Emily Clark, *Masterless Mistresses*, app. 1, 264–67. In this interpretation I am drawing on evidence that Louis Turpin was not a mere "trader" to rethink Clark's assessment that, while Turpin's ancestry "might have been enough to consign her to converse status," her socioeconomic background "probably equally determined her status at the convent" (72).

44. These women are described in Emily Clark, "A New World Community," 82–83.

45. Olivier-Martin, *Histoire de la coutume*; Jerah Johnson, "*La Coutume de Paris*"; Baker, Simpson, and Allain, "*Le Mari est Seigneur*"; Boyle, "Did She Generally Decide?" See also, on New France, Parent and Postolec, "Quand Thémis rencontre Clio"; Zoltvany, "Esquisse de la coutume de Paris."

46. RSCL 1747061001; CHS 211/6/1747.

47. KM 37:10:14:1, 37:10:15:1.

48. VP O/S LO 426 [1752]; KM 63:1:16:1. See Ekberg, *François Vallé and His World*, 40–41; Vidal, "Les Implantations," 566.

49. See Emily Clark, *Masterless Mistresses*, 211. Elizabeth Rapley has also shown that a sudden change in access to funds could alter the outcome for a nun accepted as a choir or lay nun; see Rapley, *A Social History of the Cloister*, 191–92. On dowry requirements in New France, see d'Allaire, *Les Dots des religieuses au Canada français*.

50. A comparison with the dowries paid by other choir nuns who entered the convent during this period is problematic since for various reasons they did not provide dowries either. See Emily Clark, *Masterless Mistresses*, 211; on the convent's unusual history of dowries under the French and Spanish regimes, see 210–19. As a point of comparison, in 1722 choir nuns in the Quebec Ursuline convent were expected to bring a dowry of at least 2,000 livres, although it is unclear to what degree this was adhered to; see ASQ, sme 2.1/014/4.005 (1722).

51. On their pedagogical aims, see Ebbs, "Subjected and Productive Bodies," 207–38; Emily Clark, *Masterless Mistresses*, 94–96. As Clark notes, though education was the primary distinguishing feature of the Ursuline order in France, "the work that drew the most enthusiastic praise [in the *lettres circulaires*] was that which reached beyond the parameters of the Ursuline project in France" (97).

52. KM 67:12:7:1. Her half sisters from the first marriage, however, do not appear to have been literate, suggesting that Louis Turpin, unlike Dorothée's first husband, Charles Danis, valued the attainment of a degree of education in his children; see KM 29:11:16:1, in which Hélène Danis, who was married to Ignace Hebert, made her mark rather than sign her name.

53. Vidal, "Les Implantations," 146.

54. See KM 49:7:25:1 and 60:11:20:1 for references to the presence of teachers and to parents teaching their children to read and write in the Illinois Country; on general levels of literacy, see Vidal, "Les Implantations," 587–89.

55. Rapley, A Social History of the Cloister, 191.

56. See the cases of Sr. St. Benoit/Mary Ann Davis and Sr. Marie-Joseph/Dorothy Jordan in New France, analyzed in Little, "L'Étrangère." Esther Wheelwright, a captive of Indians and taken to the convent when still young, rose through the Ursuline ranks to emerge as mother superior.

57. Emily Clark, Masterless Mistresses, 97.

58. Lettres circulaires, 228, UCANO, discussed in and translation taken from Emily Clark, Masterless Mistresses, 100.

59. One of these yardswomen, Veuve Dubic, the circumstances under which she came to the convent, and the business she conducted on behalf of the Ursulines are detailed in Sophie White, "'A Baser Commerce,'" 536. While she is not described as a soeur tourière, Widow Dubic's duties and identity in the convent conform quite closely with the functions of données outlined in the Règlemens des religieuses ursulines, 2:308–21.

60. Emily Clark, Masterless Mistresses, 72–73.

61. Ibid. On converse apothecaries, see Rapley, A Social History of the Cloister, 191.

62. See, for example, the agreement between Le Normant and the superior of the Ursulines, December 31, 1744, New Orleans, ANOM, C13A 28:342.

63. Hachard to her father, April 24, 1728, in Clark, Voices from an Early American Convent, 82 and n. 36 concerning a mulatresse whose master owed the Ursulines for unpaid boarding fees.

64. "Memoire du linge et hardes des orphelines Ce 6 avril 1752," 13, General Accounts, October 1797–October 1817, Ursuline Archives, New Orleans (the original was consulted at the Ursuline convent, January 1996, with thanks to Sister Joan Marie Aycock, O.S.U; the microfilmed copy has not been located, but see also Nolan, A Southern Catholic Heritage, 1:120.

65. While it deals with noble clientage, see Noel, "Caste and Clientage," for a discussion of the significance of connections in Quebec convents.

66. RSCL 1747061001.

67. "Délibérations du Conseil, 1727–1902," 24, UCANO, Reel 1.

68. Emily Clark, Masterless Mistresses, 150–56. Clark argues that "even as they sustained this conservative social template [of the hierarchical European social order], the nuns created a site that also subverted it when they invited all women to enter the larger physical space that was their compound and the spiritual space that was the church" (156). See also "An Architectural History of the Royal Hospital and the Ursuline Convent of New Orleans" in Wilson, The Architecture of Colonial Louisiana, 161–220.

69. AUQ, 1A4, March 28, 1639, piece 1, cited in Gourdeau, Les Délices de nos coeurs, 53.

70. Plan de l'aile St. Augustin, 1687–8, AMUQ, accession no. 1/N8, 1.3.1. The attribution to Marie Lemaire des Anges is by Christine [Turgeon] Cheyrou, director of the Musée des Ursulines de Quebec, personal communication, May 2008. On this nun, see Christine Turgeon, Le Fil de l'art, 109–39. On the two fires, see Roy, A travers l'histoire des Ursulines de Québec, 33, 75.

71. Oury, *Correspondance*, 801, letter of August 9, 1668; Deslandres, "L'Éducation des Amérindiennes," 102.

72. Emily Clark, *Masterless Mistresses*, 150, 94–96.

73. Ibid., 151.

74. Ibid., 81.

75. For the bequest from Jean Detharade *dit* La Rigueur, see 1740012203, 1740012201; he had died at Natchez en route from the Illinois Country. My thanks to Emily Clark for the additional information that she was twelve years old and that La Rigueur "gave her to us freely and of his own will in his will without having ever had any relation with our Community which only knew his name on the occasion of this gift"; see UCANO *Deliberations du conseil*, 42. No further information is known about the girl.

76. RSCL 1752061301. See also the testimony of a third witness in this case, Manon, a female slave belonging to another owner, in RSCL 1752061302.

77. Thépaut-Cabasset, *L'Esprit des modes au Grand Siècle*, 213; Hachard to her father, April 24, 1728, in Emily Clark, *Voices from an Early American Convent*, 83.

78. Hachard to her father, January 1, 1728, in Emily Clark, *Voices from an Early American Convent*, 78.

79. Emily Clark, *Masterless Mistresses*, chap. 5.

80. Archives des Ursulines de Quebec, 1A4, March 28, 1639, piece 1, cited in Gourdeau, *Les Délices de nos coeurs*, 53. On the Indian students, see Gourdeau, *Les Délices*; also Deslandres, "L'Éducation des Amérindiennes," and "Un projet éducatif au XVIIe siècle." On the missionary role of Marie de l'Incarnation and other women in New France, see Deslandres, *Croire et faire croire*, 356–89.

81. Lallement, *Constitutions*, 102.

82. On language and hospitality practices, see Gourdeau, *Les Délices de nos coeurs*, 31, 53–54. On the incorporation of techniques for porcupine quill and birchbark embroidery, see Turgeon, *Le Fil de l'art*, 54–60.

83. Gourdeau, *Les Délices de nos coeurs*, 31, 60.

84. Ibid., 72–73, 30–31.

85. Deslandres, "L'Éducation," 91–92; 105–6. For a comparison of the missionary vocations (and actions) of the Quebec Ursulines and Quebec Hospitalières nuns, see Deslandres, "In the Shadow of the Cloister."

86. Jaenen, *Friend and Foe*, 163–64; *JR*, 14:19–21, 9:233.

87. Letters to her son, September 1, 1668, and to Mère C. de S. Joseph, September 1, 1669, in Oury, *Correspondance*, 809, 821.

88. Ibid.

89. Letter to her son, August 30, 1650, in Oury, *Correspondance*, 396.

90. Gourdeau, *Les Délices de nos coeurs*, 96.

91. On the Chauvin family, see Elizabeth Shown Mills, *Chauvin dit Charleville*; Gary B. Mills, "The Chauvin Brothers."

92. New Orleans Parish Registers, Archdiocesan Archives, New Orleans, July 11, 1731, discussed in Vidal, "French Louisiana and Saint-Domingue." See also *PFFA* 2:88, 100.

93. RSCL 1747061001.

94. Ibid. On the parallels in the early development of widows' and nuns' garb, see Taylor, *Mourning Dress*, 66–69.

95. Annales, 5, and Oury, *Correspondance*, 97, letter of September 3, 1640, cited in Gourdeau, *Les Délices de nos coeurs*, 63 and 64.

96. Greer, *Mohawk Saint*, 135–43.

97. *JR*, 64:203, 193.

98. *JR*, 64:165–67, 66:247–49.

99. On the genesis and derivation of the Ursuline habit, see Pommereu, *Les Chroniques*, 132. On parallels with name changes according to life passages among indigenous populations in New France, see Gourdeau, *Les Délices*, 76–79. At the Hôpital-général of Quebec, converse nuns even wore clogs instead of leather shoes; see d'Allaire, *L'Hôpital-général de Québec*, 161–62.

100. "Registre pour écrire les réceptions des Religieuses de France et postulantes."

Chapter 5. "To Ensure That He Not Give Himself over to the *Sauvages*"

1. "Registre pour écrire les réceptions des Religieuses de France et postulantes [March 4, 1726–September 20, 1893] et les lettres circulaires [July 6, 1728–January 31, 1894]," UCANO, Reel 2.

2. On the different kinds of boats, crew configurations, and frequency of convoys, see Surrey, *The Commerce of Louisiana*, chaps. 4, 5.

3. Kathleen M. Brown, *Foul Bodies*. See also the Critical Forum on Brown's "Foul Bodies," *WMQ*, 3rd ser. 68 (2011): essays by Lewis, "Cleanliness and Culture"; Little, "Bodies, Geographies, and the Environment"; Norberg, "Bodies in European and American Historiography"; Kathleen M. Brown, "The Historical Body"; Lewis, "Cleanliness and Culture"; Little, "Where the Boys Were"; Norberg, "Cleanliness and Rights."

4. Surrey, *The Commerce of Louisiana*, 75–76.

5. On Chabot, see Jaenen, "Miscegenation in Eighteenth Century New France," 93.

6. KM 39:2:27:1. On Saguingouara, see KM 23:7:1:1; 23:7:5:2 28:3:6:1; also Margaret Kimball Brown, "Allons Cowboys!" 279. There are a number of spelling variants of the name (which originated in France), including Sakingoara, Saguingorra. For clarity, "Saguingouara" as in the 1739 *voyageur* contract will be used throughout.

7. Margaret Kimball Brown, *The Voyageur in the Illinois Country*, 8, and "Allons Cowboys!" 279; also *PFFA* 2:131–32.

8. References to the Saguingouara and Gauthier-Saguingouara lineage are found in the RPHD; see entry for Pierre Gauthier Saguingorra, born around 1629 in Notre-Dame d'Echillais, near Saintes, the first Gauthier Saguingorra to emigrate to New France, where he married Charlotte Roussel in 1668. See also Tanguay, *Dictionnaire généalogique des familles canadiennes*, 1:257, 4:206

9. KM 28:3:6:1; RSCL 1725021501, 1725021604, 1725022601.

10. See Zitomersky, "The Form and Function of French-Native American Relations"; Ekberg, *French Roots in the Illinois Country*, 70–72.

11. Franchomme first appeared in the records pertaining to the Illinois Country in 1723; see KM 23:7:1:1.

12. See *PFFA* 2:131–32. Both couples had named one child Jean. The Jean born to Jean Gauthier-Saguingouara and Marie Susanne Capi8ek8e was born in 1707. He can be excluded since he would have been twenty-one in March 1728, when he was identified in Franchomme's will as "the small Saguingouara," and since his father was still alive.

13. Marrero, "A Tale of Three Marguerites"; and "Marguerite Ouabankikoue," in http://www
.leveillee.net/ancestry/ouabankekoue.htm. My thanks to Karen Marrero for this citation.

14. KM 23:6:25:1, 23:7:1:1, 23:7:5:2.

15. For the marriage to Franchomme, see RSCL 1725021501, 1725021604, 1725022601; her third
marriage was to Pierre Blot; see KM 29:8:24:1.

16. KM 28:3:6:1.

17. Périer and La Chaise to the Minister of Marine, September 1, 1728, ANOM, C13A, 11:113;
also Belting, *Kaskaskia Under the French Regime*, 49. On the Fox Wars, see Edmunds and Peyser,
The Fox Wars.

18. Olivier-Martin, *Histoire de la coutume* is the standard reference on the customary law of
Paris, in effect in Louisiana.

19. "Arrêt du Conseil Supérieur de la Louisiane du 18 decembre 1728, concernant le mariage
des français avec les sauvagesses," ANOM, A 23:102–3.

20. RSCL 1725021501, 1725021604, 1725022601. The original marriage had taken place on September 10, 1723.

21. KM 23:7:12:1; 23:10:22:2; 23:9:19:1; 23:9:11:1.

22. In 1724, they had one Indian and three African slaves (they also had a hired employee and
twenty acres of cleared land); see census of the inhabitants of Louisiana, January 1, 1726, ANOM,
G1:464, published in *FFL* 2:34.

23. KM 28:3:6:1.

24. See KM 25:6:13:1 for the will, KM 25:6:20:1 for the codicil in which she relented, provided
he repent and return.

25. KM 25:3:15:1.

26. See Dawdy, " 'A Wild Taste.' "

27. Margaret Kimball Brown, *The Voyageur*, 8, "Allons Cowboys!" 279.

28. See Dubé, "Les Biens publics," chap. 8.

29. See Allaire, "Fur Trade Engagés, 1701–1745."

30. Skinner, "The Sinews of Empire," 367.

31. By 1680 in Canada, the term *coureur de bois* had lost much of its currency and was increasingly replaced with the broader designation *voyageur*; see Dechêne, *Habitants and Merchants*, 94.
But Carolyn Podruchny uses their labor status to continue to distinguish between *voyageurs* (understood to encompass *engagés*, servants, and workers) and *coureurs de bois* (independent traders)
in "Baptizing Novices," 166.

32. Surrey, *Commerce of Louisiana*, 75–76; Margaret Kimball Brown, *The Voyageur*, 5, 8–10.

33. For example, see RSCL 1728052903, 1729101301, 1730072803, 1731030402, 1735071602,
1737081405, 1737081501, 1737081503, 1737081604, 1738040901, 1738070603, 1738071901, 1738102001,
1740012203, 1740022902, 1740051202, 1740060801, 1743083001, 1746032802, 1765013105, 1766072105.

34. Podruchny, *Making the Voyageur World*, 86–134, quote 87.

35. For example the three slave leases contracted in August 1737 for the voyage to the Illinois,
each slave earning his master 1,500 pounds of Illinois flour for his work on the trip; see RSCL
1737081503 (lease of two slaves by Louis Tixerand to René Boucher de Monbrun); RSCL 1737081602
(lease of slave by Henry de Louboey to François Rivard). Other similar contracts can be found in
RSCL 1738040901, 1739070602. See also Hall, *Africans in Colonial Louisiana*, 174–75; Usner, *Indians, Settlers, and Slaves in a Frontier Exchange Economy*, 227–30.

36. There are a number of extant contracts between free blacks engaging themselves for the

trip between New Orleans and the Illinois Country and slave owners also contracted out their slaves to other masters for the trip. See for example the contracts entered into by "Scipion Negre Libre" from New Orleans. In 1736 he contracted to travel up and down river as a rower for 200 livres (RSCL 1736082101). Three years later, he engaged himself again, to another *voyageur*, for the same wage in currency but with enhanced terms to trade (alcohol) on his own account, the right of portage for his clothing, and the right to hire himself out while in the Illinois Country; see RSCL 1739031003. The case of Jacques Duverger, a free black identified as a *voyageur* and master surgeon, is discussed in Margaret Kimball Brown, *The Voyageur*, 7. One of the wealthiest residents of the Illinois Country was appointed administrator of his estate, a sign of his importance in the community.

37. See Ibrahima Seck's discussion of the relevance of navigation skills honed on the Senegal River to related activities on the Mississippi River in "The Relationships Between St. Louis of Senegal, Its Hinterlands, and Colonial Louisiana."

38. On labor and other hierarchies, as reflected in positions within the canoe, see Podruchny, *Making the Voyageur World*, 65–71, 121–23.

39. KM 43:11:15:1, discussed in Margaret Kimball Brown, *The Voyageur*, 8.

40. See Margaret Kimball Brown, "Allons Cowboys!" 279, although she has incorrectly identified Saguingouara as Indian rather than mixed heritage. One of these "Canadians" was in fact a master tailor by profession, and his wage was high, 400 livres; see KM 39:3:10:2.

41. See "Acte pour l'établissement de la Compagnie des Cent Associés pour le Commerce du Canada," in *Edits, ordonnances royaux, déclarations et arrêts*, 1:10.

42. KM 44:6:10:1; see also 51:7:19:4, agreement to hire Sagouinguara by De Gruy.

43. On Canadian *voyageurs*' contracts (some relating to the Illinois Country), see Allaire, "Les Engagements pour la traite des fourrures"; Lande, *The Development of the Voyageur Contract*; Skinner, "The Sinews of Empire," 345–71, 117–22. On contracts originating in the Illinois Country, see Margaret Kimball Brown, *The Voyageur*. E. Z. Massicote suggests payments in kind (including clothing) were uncommon prior to the eighteenth century; see "Le Costume des voyageurs et des coureurs de bois," 237–38.

44. Margaret Kimball Brown, *The Voyageur*, 2, 18–19. The bulk of extant *voyageurs*' contracts from the Illinois Country date from 1737–48; most were for trips down the Mississippi, although some contracts were initiated in Canada for the Illinois Country trade. A rare extant *voyageur* contract originating in New Orleans is found in RSCL 1725042901: agreement of Guillaume Aillain (Allain) to accompany Jean Baptiste Le Fevre "for the voyage to the Illinois and for hunting, in a capacity as his indentured servant," for a wage of 200 livres plus tallow, meat, bear's grease, and pecans.

45. Margaret Kimball Brown, *The Voyageur*, 7. Sometimes they negotiated for the right to a proportion of the pelts they had hunted on a trip; see for example KM 43:11:17:1.

46. Skinner, "The Sinews of Empire," 353–54, argues that "in general, engagements for the west in the years after about 1726 were on a strict salary basis. The trading allowances were gone and the men worked for an agreed-upon sum and subsistence." For other contracts with trade provisions in the Illinois Country after this date, see CHS Kaskaskia Collection, Folder 210, 4, April 29, 1738 (KM 38:4:29:2); KM 46:3:19:1; RSCL 1739031003 (contracted by Scipion, a free African slave).

47. Pellegrin, *Les Vêtements de la liberté*, 90.

48. CHS, Kaskaskia Collection, folder 210, no. 3 March 21, 1738.

49. See KM 31:—:—:1 for another contract with near identical provisions. Bearing in mind

these remunerations in kind in addition to his wage, Eslie had negotiated a reasonable payment, given that a soldier at this date would receive 11.10 livres/month after deduction for his retenue; on soldier's wages, see Saadani, "Colonialisme et stratégie," 210. A seal from the town of Mazamet, France, has been found at Fort Michilimackinac; see Adams, *Lead Seals from Fort Michilimackinac*, 23.

50. Tonti, *Dernières découvertes*, 14.

51. KM 46:7:9:1. On Desruisseaux's five-year trading rights on the Missouri River, see VP, LO 64, April 25, 1746.

52. KM 37:9:23:2.

53. Other contracts that specified provision of footwear (or deerskins for making footwear) are found in KM 37:3:9:1, 37:9:23:1, 39:8:11:1, 44:4:4:1; 46:3:19:1.

54. "Relation de Henri Joutel: Voyage de M. de La Salle dans l'Amerique (1685)" in Margry, *Mémoires et documents*, 3:222–23.

55. Quotation from Dumont de Montigny, *Mémoires historiques sur la Louisiane*, 2:149.

56. KM 40:5:10:1.

57. KM 30:5:17:1, 40:2:4:3; 40:11:22:1, 47:1:29:1, 47:2:15:1, 48:1:18:1, 48:1:20:1, 63:6:19:1; for shipments of soap from New Orleans up to the Illinois Country, see RSCL 1738071901, 1740042302 and 1740060801, 1740070401. Benoist de St. Clair, commandant of the Illinois post, arranged for twenty pounds of bulk soap, as well as a shaving plate and two "savonettes" (small cakes of soap, likely fragranced) to be included in a shipment of goods to be sent to him in the Illinois Country by his agent in New Orleans, Widow Gervais; see RSCL 1746052802, 1746080401 and 1748112802; their commercial activities are discussed in Sophie White, "'A Baser Commerce.'" On missionaries, see ANOM C13A, vol. 10, fol. 72 (n.d.).

58. RSCL 1726122801.

59. For example, KM 39:4:4:1, 39:4:16:1, 40:2:20:3, 40:4:7:1, 40:12:10:3, 45:4:19:1, 46:3:27:1, 46:9:14:1; see also 40:12:10:3, when a laundry clause was included as part payment in a land lease agreement.

60. KM 39:2:27:1.

61. Douglas, *Purity and Danger*.

62. Vigarello, *Concepts of Cleanliness*, 7–17; Corbin, *Le Miasme et la jonquille*; also Smith, *Clean*; and Kathleen M. Brown, *Foul Bodies*, 15–41, bibliographic essay, 431–35.

63. Vigarello, *Concepts of Cleanliness*, 45–47; also Biow, *The Culture of Cleanliness in Renaissance Italy*, 26–27.

64. His doctors might prescribe a bath for medicinal purposes (usually lasting a couple of hours, sometimes taken twice a day), but they were clear to distinguish this from "bain de la chambre," of which he did not partake. See Perez, *Journal de santé de Louis XIV écrit par Vallot, Daquin et Fagon*, 156–57 and n. 1. Louis XIV's medicinal baths were steam ones. On the medicinal role of cold bathing in this period, see Jenner, "Bathing and Baptism."

65. Charles Perrault, *La Querelle des anciens et des modernes en ce qui regarde les arts et les sciences* (Paris, 1688), 1:80, quoted in Vigarello, *Concepts of Cleanliness*, 60–61. On baths, see Marschner, "Baths and Bathing at the Early Georgian Court."

66. Gourdeau, *Les Délices de nos coeurs*, 63–67. On dry washing, see Vigarello, *Concepts of Cleanliness*, 17–20.

67. Colten, "Meaning of Water in the American South"; see also Strang, *The Meaning of Water*.

68. Delâge and Dubois, "L'Eau, les Amérindiens et les Franco-Canadiens."

69. For an account of how the French transformed the environment in New Orleans and environs, which emphasizes the need to manipulate water in that area, see Morris, "Impenetrable but Easy."

70. Vigarello, *Concepts of Cleanliness*, 93–94. Richard L. Bushman and Claudia L. Bushman, "The Early History of Cleanliness in America," argue that cleanliness as an attribute of morality only developed in the nineteenth century, when soap also began to assume a greater role in washing the body; see also Keith Thomas, "Cleanliness and Godliness in Early Modern England." See the postcolonial scholarship on washing bodies with soap as a means to enforce class and race-based hegemonic cultural practices in the nineteenth and twentieth centuries in McClintock, *Imperial Leather*; and Burke, *Lifebuoy Men, Lux Women*; also Luise White's review essay, "Sex, Soap, and Colonial Studies."

71. This continued to be the case into the nineteenth century, even as body washing gained in importance, as seen in attitudes toward the populace; see Corbin, *Le Miasme*, 184–86. On the emergence of concerns for hygiene in the early nineteenth century, see Vigarello, *Concepts of Cleanliness*, 168–70.

72. La Mothe-Cadillac to Minister of Marine, October 26, 1713, ANOM C13A 3:19. He proposed instead that one of the Ursuline nuns be charged with this.

73. KM 40:11:27:1.

74. Roche, *The Culture of Clothing*, chap. 7.

75. The phrase is Vigarello's; see *Concepts of Cleanliness*, 49.

76. Vigarello, *Concepts of Cleanliness*, 41–77.

77. Ibid., 78–82.

78. On the transition from linen to cotton, see Lemire, "Transforming Consumer Custom."

79. Though it is primarily focused on Britain, Beverly Lemire's *Fashion's Favourite* is the best treatment of the rise of cotton in Europe.

80. On the emergence of a parallel emphasis on hygiene and on the cleanliness of linens in France, see Roche, *Culture of Clothing*, chap. 7.

81. RSCL 1766073107.

82. Roche, *Culture of Clothing*, 169.

83. See Boulanger, *Mémoires du savon de Marseille*; Vernin, "Savons et savonneries à Nyons au XVIIe siècle." Vernin points out that the bulk of commercial soap was used in the textile industry, not for personal use on the body or for laundry.

84. See Kathleen M. Brown, *Foul Bodies*; also Richard, "Washing Household Linens and Linen Clothing in 1627 Plymouth"; Blow, *The Culture of Cleanliness*, 95–143.

85. Other than bills for laundry costs, incidental references to women (including slaves) doing laundry work are found in numerous documents. In Lower Louisiana at Natchez, see RSCL 1725041202, and 1727092001; for New Orleans and its environs, see RSCL 1752061301, 1752061302, 1764090401, 1768111402. In the Illinois Country, see KM 40:11:27:1; also 37:9:1, in which a number of women washing at the river witnessed the drowning of a slave. One of the women, Dame La Chenay, worked professionally as a washerwoman: see KM 48:1:10:1. On washing practices, see Belting, *Kaskaskia*, 47; Richard, "Washing Household Linens." On the spatial arrangements for washing, see Ungerer "Les Valeurs urbaines du propre."

86. See, for example, KM 39:4:4:1, 40:2:20:3, 45:4:19:1, 46:3:27:1; see also KM 39:4:16:1 (an apprenticeship contract) and KM 40:12:10:3 (a land lease), and KM 46:9:14:1 (a partnership agreement) for other examples of bachelors negotiating for their laundry to be provided in part payment.

87. KM 47:4:29:1.

88. La Mothe-Cadillac to Minister of Marine, October 26, 1713,

89. See KM 39:3:7:1, which discusses the suit that Dame La Chenay, the laundress, had filed to demand a public apology for having been accused of keeping a brothel. On her activities as a laundress, see note 85 above.

90. See, for example, the invoice in the Azemar succession for 3 livres 15 s, the cost of two days' laundry work by African women slaves ("deux journées de negresse qui ont blanchy le linge") in RSCL 1768111402. See also the list of slaves on the De Noyan plantation, which included two specialist washerwomen, Calamboüe and Catherine, both in their twenties and appraised respectively at 1,800 and 1,500 livres, more than the female domestic slave and the same as the two seamstresses on the plantation; see RSCL 176310220.

91. RSCL 1765090902; on the dress of enslaved Africans in colonial Louisiana, see Sophie White, "'Wearing Three or Four Handkerchiefs.'"

92. RSCL 1752061301. See also the testimony of a third witness in this case, Manon, a female slave belonging to another owner, in RSCL 1752061302.

93. Corbin, Le Miasme, 301; Richard, "Washing Household Linens"; also Belting, Kaskaskia, 47.

94. RSCL 1747061001.

95. KM 48:1:10:1

96. Kathleen M. Brown, Foul Bodies, part 3. On women's "body work," see also Marla R. Miller, The Needle's Eye; and Crowston, Fabricating Women.

97. On the dichotomy between the visibility of washed artifacts and the invisibility of washerwomen, see Biow's discussion of visual and verbal sources in Renaissance Italy, in The Culture of Cleanliness, 42.

98. Smits, "The 'Squaw Drudge'"; Hauser, "The Other Half"; Thorne, "Continuity and Change."

99. This point is made in Berkin and Horowitz, Women's Voices, Women's Lives, 94–95.

100. Richard Eden, "First Voyage to Guinea," in The First Three English Books on America, ed. Edward Arber (Birmingham, 1885), 384, cited in Kathleen M. Brown, "Native Americans and Early Modern Concepts of Race," 91.

101. Vigarello, Concepts of Cleanliness, 28–38.

102. Viau, Enfants du néant et mangeurs d'âmes, 164.

103. Brooks, Captives and Cousins, 1–40; Rushforth, "Savage Bonds," 15–47.

104. Bonnefoy, "Journal of Antoine Bonnefoy," 246. See also Claude Charles Le Roy de la Potherie, "Histoire de l'Amérique septentrionale," in Blair, Indian Tribes, 2:36–43; as well as Rushforth, "Savage Bonds," 19; on stripping as a component of captivity rituals, see, for example, Castro, "Stripped," esp. 119–22; Little, Abraham in Arms, esp. chap. 2; Richter, The Ordeal of the Longhouse, 50–74; Viau, Enfants du néant, 137–60; Sophie White, "Massacre, Mardi Gras and Torture."

105. Bushman and Bushman, "Early History of Cleanliness," 1214–15.

106. See Kan, Memory Eternal, 79–84, for an example of using a red shirt instead of a white one, a concession to Tlingit taste and religious symbolism.

107. Letter from Marie de l'Incarnation, September 4, 1640, in Oury, Correspondance, 112.

108. Podruchny, "Baptizing Novices."

109. "Relation du voyage de la Louisiane ou Nouv.lle France fait par le Sr. Caillot en l'année 1730," HNOC Ms 2005.11, 37–49, analyzed in Sophie White, "Massacre, Mardi Gras and Torture." See also the forthcoming editon of Erin Greenwald.

110. Vigarello, Concepts of Cleanliness, 47–48.

111. "Relation du voyage," HNOC Ms. 2005.11, 42–43.

112. Podruchny, "Baptizing Novices," 182; see also Podruchny, *Making the Voyageur World*, chap. 3.

113. On the ways that water is imbued with ritualistic and spiritual meanings, especially in the Christian tradition, see, for example, Strang, *The Meaning of Water*, chap. 5.

114. Le Page du Pratz, *The History of Louisiana*, 308; also 333.

115. *JR*, 67:313.

116. ANOM, ser. DFC, Louisiane 3, translation from "The Talon Interrogations: A Rare Perspective," in Weddle, *La Salle, the Mississippi, and the Gulf*, 209–24, 231; for their tattooing, see 238. On tattooing, see Balvay, "Tattooing and Its Role"; Sayre, *Les Sauvages Américains*, 145–214; Havard, *Empires et métissages*, 603–4; also Caplan, *Written on the Body*.

117. Joseph Jouvekcy, S.J., "Concerning the Country and Manners of the Canadians, or The Savages of New France" [1610–13] in *JR*, 1:279.

118. Shoemaker, *A Strange Likeness*, 130–34. But see Amerigo Vespucci's description of the skin color of the Indians he encountered in 1497: "their flesh is of a colour the verges into red like a lion's mane: and I believe that if they went clothed, they would be as white as we," http://www.fordham.edu/halsall/mod/1497vespucci-america.html.

119. "Relation du voyage," HNOC Ms 2005.11, 117.

120. Delâge, "L'influence des Amérindiens," 126.

121. Pargellis, "An Account of the Indians in Virginia," 230.

122. Williams, *Adair's History of the American Indians*, 4, discussed in Fischer, "The Imperial Gaze," 8.

123. Gourdeau, *Les Délices de nos coeurs*, 63–67; Oury, *Correspondance*, 97.

124. Translated from Charlevoix, *Journal d'un voyage*, 6:15. The original text uses the term "friction," which I have translated as "rub" to convey the medicinal meaning of the original French definition of either (dry) rubbing the body, or rubbing a medicinal substance into the body. This medicinal meaning is consistent with the ubiquitous descriptions of Indians rubbing grease onto their skin, as outlined in this chapter. See *Dictionnaires d'Autrefois, The Project for American and French Research on the Treasury of the French Language*; "Friction," *Oxford-Hachette French Dictionary*.

125. Phrase from Kupperman, "Presentment of Civility," see 193; see also Kupperman, "Fear of Hot Climates" and *Indians and English*, 41–76.

126. See Sleeper-Smith, "Washing Away Race."

127. RSCL 1748052601.

128. On Indians' disinclination to launder clothing, see Axtell, *Beyond 1492*, 138; see also Viau, *Enfants du néant*, 164–65.

129. Sayre, *Les Sauvages Américains*, 148.

130. Translation from Charlevoix, *Journal of a Voyage*, 1:145.

131. Sonenscher, *The Hatters of Eighteenth-Century France*, 39; Carlos and Lewis, *Commerce by a Frozen Sea*, chap. 1; also Allaire, *Pelleteries, manchons et chapeaux de castor*. For prices, see KM 23:1:30:1; ANOM, C13A, vol. 11, fol. 154.

132. Adriaen van der Donck, *A Description of the New Netherlands*, trans. Jeremiah Johnson, ed. Thomas F. O'Donnell (Syracuse, N.Y.: Syracuse University Press, 1968), 113, cited in Sayre, *Les Sauvages Americains*, 148.

133. Pellegrin, "Chemises et chiffons"; Furetière, *Dictionnaire universel*.

134. Gourdeau, *Les Délices*, 63–67.

135. KM 30:5:17:1, 40:12:4:3; 40:11:22:1, 47:1:29:1, 47:2:15:1, 48:1:18:1, 48:1:20:1, 63:6:19:1. On missionaries, see ANOM, C13A 10:72 n.d. On the presence of soap among the belongings of traders and merchants, see KM 47:9:5:2, 47:9:30:1.

Chapter 6. "We Are All *Sauvages*"

1. Shannon, "Dressing for Success on the Mohawk Frontier"; Deloria, *Playing Indian*; Little, " 'Shoot That Rogue.' " On European perceptions of Indian dress, see Sayre, *Les Sauvages Americains*, 144–79.

2. Phillips and Idiens, "A Casket of Savage Curiosities."

3. These samples, taken from the KM, date from 1720 to 1767. Also included in this sample are two Illinois successions archived in the RSCL, and the succession of an Illinois *habitant* who died on his way from Illinois to New Orleans in the NONA. See Sophie White, "Trading Identities," 81–82.

4. See KM 25:3:15:1; 28:8:6:1.

5. La Salle, *Relation of the Discoveries and Voyages*, 232–33.

6. For biographical and genealogical information on Marigny, see Woods and Nolan, *Sacramental Records of the Roman Catholic Church of the Archdiocese of New Orleans*, 1:35, 74, 2:83; *DLB*, 2:117; Brasseaux, *France's Forgotten Legion*. Some additional information is provided in Wilson, "Ignace François Broutin," in *The Architecture of Colonial Louisiana*, 247. Mandeville had at least two children with his Indian slave; see Spear, *Race, Sex, and Social Order*, 40 and n. 119.

7. See Wilson, "Ignace François Broutin."

8. "Abstracts of the Records of the Superior Council," *Louisiana Historical Quarterly* 17 (1934): 184–85 (original not located). Judgment was rendered in Marigny's favor in July 1747 and Broutin complied with the Superior Council order in October 1747, *Louisiana Historical Quarterly* 18 (1935): 703–4 (original not located); RSCL 1747102501. There is no record of Marigny legally contesting Broutin's accounting, although the expenditure account showed that Marigny's expenses during his tutelage had depleted—indeed far outstripped—the inheritance. The expected inheritance was 3,375 livres, against total expenses of 9,134 livres, leaving an excess payment by Broutin of 5,759 livres.

9. D'Aleyrac, *Aventures militaires*, 32.

10. KM 55:3:17:1.

11. J.-C. B., *Voyage au Canada fait depuis l'an 1751 jusqu'en l'an 1761* (reprint Paris: Aubier, 1978), 67.

12. On the trope of the naked Indian, see for example Scott Manning Stevens, "New World Contacts."

13. Translation adapted from Ekberg and Foley's edition of Finiels, *An Account of Upper Louisiana*, 114–15.

14. See Ekberg, *Colonial Ste. Genevieve*, 172–73, for data on the British and French provenance of many of the goods sold in Spanish Ste. Genevieve.

15. Cited in Morris S. Arnold, *Colonial Arkansas, 1686–1804*, 112–13.

16. Cited in Havard, *Empires et métissages*, 602.

17. "Relation du voyage de la Louisiane ou Nouv.lle France fait par le Sr. Caillot en l'année 1730," HNOC MS 2005.11, p. 149.

18. "Journal of Antoine Bonnefoy," 253.

19. Charlevoix, *Histoire et description generale de la Nouvelle-France* 3:416–17; see also Back, "Notes on Clothing."

20. RSCL 1747102501, fol. 1r.

21. "Suplement au Memoire sur les Moyens d'Introduire en Espagne et aux Indes les Etoffes de Rouen Soye et Cotton, fil et Coton et tout Coton pour accompagner la Carte d'Echantillons. Et Sur Ceux par lesques l'on peut en france faire une Consommation considerable des Cotons des Isles, et du Micissipy," n.d., Maurepas Papers, Joseph Downs Manuscript Collection, Winterthur Museum, no. 62 x 14.4. On dress and climate, see Sophie White, "'This Gown . . . Was Much Admired.'"

22. KM 40:12:12:1.

23. "Relation de Joutel: Voyage de M. de La Salle dans l'Amérique (1685)," in Margry, *Mémoires et documents*, 3:222–23.

24. Dumont, "Mémoire," NL Ayer Ms 257, 115.

25. Ibid., 165.

26. "Relation de Henri Joutel," in Margry, *Mémoires et documents*, 3:91.

27. See the definition of *grandes culottes* in a 1765 New Orleans document: "the breeches that he was wearing were large breeches that reached down to his feet" (RSCL 1765091602).

28. For example, in 1750 local administrators in Louisiana requested 2,500 men's trade shirts from the French government for the annual trade with Choctaw Indians; see ANOM, C13A, vol. 33, fol. 228; also RSCL 1737041702, 1737081405, 1742110101, 1765102802. Savary shows that as early as the seventeenth century, ready-made shirts ("des chemises toutes faites") were common staples of trade on the Guinea Coast (*Le Parfait Negociant* . . . , 2:248); see also Lemire's *Dress, Culture, Commerce*.

29. The original term was *cadet à l'aiguillette*, referring to the ornamental braid worn by these cadets of rank who served without pay; see Brasseaux, *Forgotten Legions*, "Glossary," n.p. The translation as "gentleman cadet" is that of Villiers du Terrage, *Les Dernieres années de la Louisiane française*, 51n, cited in *MPA* 4:201 n. 2. Marigny remained in the colony except for a two-year stint in France beginning in September 1745, and again from 1764 to 1765. On his military progression through the ranks, see Brasseaux, *Forgotten Legions*, n.p. Marigny achieved the rank of full ensign rank in 1746, followed by final promotion to the rank of lieutenant in 1752.

30. On the matchcoat, see Becker, "Match Coats and the Military"; also Gail DeBuse Potter, "The Matchcoat."

31. On New France precedents for its inclusion among gifts to Indians, see Back, "Clothing and Marks of Honor Given to Indians." In an oft-repeated association of the health and well-being of slaves with an adequate supply of clothing, it was this garment that was explicitly linked by officials to the survival of Africans in the climate of the colony. Governor Perier and Commissaire-Ordonnateur La Chaise to the Minister of the Marine, April 9, 1728, ANOM, C13A 11:27; see also ANOM C13A 11:305, January 30,1729; and ANOM B 43:808–9, March 31, 1728.

32. Contemporary commentators noted that soldiers in Canada were issued with *capots* when they went on campaign; see Kalm, *Travels in North America*, 1:367; and d'Aleyrac, *Aventures militaires*, 32. That the *capot* was not identified with dress of men in the maritime region of New France is apparent from Monique La Grenade's study of Louisbourg; see "Le Costume civil à Louisbourg au XVIIIe siècle," 97–98.

33. Chartrand, "Winter Costume of Soldiers," 157; Pontchartrain to Lusançay, September 16, 1714, ANOM, B 36:258; see also Rochefort, ser. IE 137, 461–65 [1743]; Bienville and Salmon to Minister, May 12, 1733, ANOM C13A 16:47; C13A 18:33 April 1, 1734; Lorient, ser. IP 279, liasse 38:44 and Lorient, ser. IP 3, p. 14v; and ANOM, C13A 31:218, July 1747.

34. See D'Orgon (in Natchez) to Vaudreuil, October 7, 1752, VP LO 399; Chartrand, "Winter Costume," esp. 156–59; Back, "Le Capot canadien"; Roche, *The Culture of Clothing*, 220.

35. The regularity with which the *capot* was inventoried in succession records of common soldiers who died in the colony (often in lieu of any other regimental coat) highlights its ubiquity in the wardrobes of military personnel; see RSCL 1745030403 and 1762040402; KM 26:5:4:4.

36. Robin, *Voyages dans l'interieur de la Louisiane*, 2:103; Perrin du Lac, *Voyage dans les deux Louisianes*, 410–11.

37. Vrignaud, *Vêture et parure en France*; Roche, *Culture des apparences*, 211–44. On the relationship between uniforms worn in France and Louisiana, see White, "Trading Identities," chap. 3; Chartrand, "The Troops of French Louisiana."

38. See RSCL 1740012701, 1740030202 respectively.

39. Scarlet coats were owned by Alphonse de la Buissonniere, commandant at Illinois, and Sieur de Granpré (KM 40:12:12:1 and RSCL 1763070602 respectively). In addition, Grandpré owned another military uniform with embroidered waistcoat. Commandant de la Buissonniere, for his part, owned elaborate horse trappings and two gold-laced hats adorned with a feather. The officer de Coustillas had retained only the more valuable remains of his hat, in the form of a "bord dor de chapeau à la Mousquetaire"; see RSCL 1739030201. Military accoutrements were itemized in RSCL 1740012701 and 1739030201; see also Norall, *Bourgmont*, 75.

40. KM 40:12:12:1 and RSCL 1738122301.

41. See Portré-Bobinski, *Colonial Natchitoches*. The commandant had married a Spanish colonial woman whose wardrobe contained Spanish-style garments including a patterned black silk mantilla; see NP 1758/4/24. It is possible, given the ties between the posts of (French) Natchitoches and (Spanish) Los Adayes that some of these elaborate surtouts were intended for trade with the Spanish. On these interactions, see Sophie White, "Geographies of Slave Consumption"; and Loren, "Colonial Dress at the Spanish Presidio of Los Adaes." On St. Denis, see *DLB*, 1:449.

42. KM 25:3:15:1, 28:8:6:1; quotation from RSCL 1725021501.

43. Vrignaud, *Vêture et parure*, 32.

44. For one study of permanent cultural cross-dressing, achieved progressively, see Mackie, "Cultural Cross-Dressing." In this literary study of the British West Indies, Mackie describes cultural cross-dressing as a crucial step in the English colonist's progressive "ethnocultural transformation" or creolization. Mackie's emphasis here is on metropolitan English perceptions of cultural cross-dressing and its impact on England's "cultural-symbolic map."

45. "Journal du voyage que le Sr Roussel natif de Versailles a fait dudit Versailles a La Louisiane, et de son retour de la Louisiane a Versailles," in Memoranda on French Colonies in America, including Canada, Louisiana, and the Carribbean [1702–50], NL Ayer Ms 293, 513; NL Ayer Ms 257, 36; Balvay, "Tattooing and Its Role"; Sayre, *Les Sauvages Americains*, 145–214; Havard, *Empires et métissages*, 603–4; see also Caplan, *Written on the Body*.

46. See Aubert, "'The Blood of France'"; also Kupperman, "Fear of Hot Climates," and *Indians and English*, chap. 1, "Reading Indian Bodies," 41–76; Shoemaker, *A Strange Likeness*, 125–40.

47. *JR*, 67:313.

48. Douthwaite, *The Wild Girl, Natural Man, and the Monster*, esp. chap. 1.

49. A fuller analysis is provided in Sophie White, "Massacre, *Mardi Gras*, and Torture in Early New Orleans." Erin Greenwald is preparing an edition of the Caillot manuscript.

50. See Giraud, *History of French Louisiana*, 5:390 n. 8 (on the population of Natchez), 398 (on disparities in the estimates of the dead); see also Balvay, *La Révolte*, 229 and Milne, "Rising Suns."

51. This near obsession with dress and stripped bodies was also found in captivity narratives; see Castro, "Stripped."

52. "Relation du voyage," HNOC Ms 2005.11, 144, 164, 148; NL Ayer Ms 257, 233, 235. A fuller description of the ransom objects is found in Anonymous, "Relation de la Louisianne" [ca. 1735], NL Ayer Ms 530, 62–63.

53. Dumont "Mémoire," 244; Le Page du Pratz, *Histoire*, vol. 3, chap. 17; also Balvay, *La Révolte*, 134–35; and Sayre, *Indian Chief*, 230–31.

54. "Relation du voyage," HNOC Ms 2005.11, 154–63. On masquerade costumes in the eighteenth century, see Ribeiro, *The Dress Worn at Masquerades*.

55. NL Ayer Ms 530, 54.

56. NL Ayer Ms 257, 240.

57. "Relation du voyage," HNOC Ms 2005.11, 151.

58. Zitomersky, "Urbanization in French Colonial Louisiana."

59. Sophie White, "This Gown"; Baillardel and Prioult, *Le Chevalier de Pradel*, 184, 189–90, 235.

60. In 1748, a master shoemaker of Kaskaskia, La Chapelle, was summoned to appear before the judge to testify in a case stemming from an insult to a woman's honor. The insult had taken place as this woman and her husband were taking a walk around the prairie ("un tour de prairie"); see KM 48:3:1:3. On the prevalence of verbal assaults and injuries to honor in Canada, see Lachance, "Une Étude de mentalité."

61. See RSCL 1763041502 for a further example of children taught by dancing and school masters. A dancing master from New Orleans, Babi, was even present at the German Coast, where he perished in 1748 from an Indian attack, suggesting that at least some of the inhabitants of this agricultural settlement outside New Orleans were not immune from social yearnings (Vaudreuil to Maurepas, November 16, 1748, VP LO 153).

62. Two useful surveys on this topic are Annas, "The Elegant Art of Movement"; and Haugland, "The Art of Natural Good Breeding."

63. For my identifications of the uniforms, see Sophie White, "Trading Identities," 106.

64. The two sets of matching *siamoise* breeches and waistcoats were purchased for 30 livres; the two sets of gingham breeches and waistcoats cost 68 livres; the price of the three-piece suit of drab came to 210.15 livres. On the use of filigree for dispensing perfume onto clothing, see Welch, "Scented Buttons and Perfumed Gloves."

65. In this, their dress can be contrasted with the sartorial elections of professional, long-term voyageurs. See Podruchny, "Baptizing Novices," for the degrees of professionalism in the occupation of voyageur, and some of the ways that these were marked, for example by ritual "baptism."

66. Etienne de Carheil to Louis Hector de Callières, August 30, 1702, *JR*, 65:219–21.

Epilogue

1. KM 25:6:1:1; 25:8:12:1; 25:8:12:2; 25:8:13:1; 25:8:27:2, 25:8:28:1; 25:8:29:1.

2. Sophie White, "'Wearing Three or Four Handkerchiefs" and "Geographies of Slave Consumption."

3. "Lettres patentes en forme d'édit concernant les esclaves des isles de France et de Bourbon, Décembre 1723," ser. 0A 96 (1723), National Archives of Mauritius at Coromandel. See also

"Ordonnance ou Code Noir: Lettres patentes en forme d'édit concernant les esclaves des isles de France et de Bourbon, Décembre 1723," *Le Fonds de Publication des Archives de Maurice* 17 (2000); Rivière, *Codes Noirs et autres documents concernant l'esclavage.* My thanks to Guillaume Aubert for first bringing his research on this link between the two codes to my attention; and see also Aubert, " 'To Establish One Law and Definite Rules' " and for an Atlantic perspective, Aubert, "Kinship, Blood."

4. Ly-Tio-Fane Pineo, *Île de France, 1715–1746,* 82.

5. See Ekberg and Pregaldin, "Marie Rouensa-8cate8a," 157; also Belting, *Kaskaskia,* 102–3.

6. Belting, *Kaskaskia,* 14; and Morrissey, "Bottomlands and Borderlands," 235–36.

7. KM 25:9:12:1.

8. KM 25:6:13:1 and 25:6:20:1.

9. "Journal of Diron D'Artaguiette," 76.

10. KM 25:6:13:1. As noted by Ekberg, there is no record of their marriage in the Kaskaskia parish register, so this wife must not have been baptized and the union not sanctified; "Marie Rouensa-8canic8e," 214.

11. KM 28:11:13:1; see also Ekberg, "Marie Rouensa-8canic8e," 217.

12. Father Tartarin [1738], ANOM, C13A 23:241–44.

13. See KM 39:3:9:3, René Roy's petition that he be paid for looking after the late Michel Accault during his illness.

14. *PFFA* 2:234.

15. A "René de Couagne *fils*" was present at Michilimackinac in 1756; see *PFFA* 1:122.

16. Tartarin [1738], ANOM, C13A 23: 241v.

BIBLIOGRAPHY

Manuscript Sources

U.S.A.

Chicago Historical Society, Chicago. Kaskaskia and Fort de Chartres Collection.

Eugene P. Watson Memorial Library, Northwestern State University of Louisiana. Cloutier and Melrose Collections.

Historic New Orleans Collection, New Orleans. Papers Relating to Colonial Louisiana.

Howard-Tilton Memorial Library, Tulane University. Favrot Family Papers and Rosemonde E. and Emile Kuntz Collection, French Colonial Period.

Huntington Library, San Marino, California. Loudoun Collection: The Personal and Private Records of Pierre de Rigaud de Vaudreuil, Royal Governor of the French Province of Louisiana, 1743–1753.

Louisiana State Museum, New Orleans. Records of the Superior Council of Louisiana.

Missouri Historical Society Collections, St. Louis.

Natchitoches Parish, Louisiana. Natchitoches Archives. Microfilm copy in Family History Library of the Church of Jesus Christ of Latter Day Saints.

Newberry Library, Chicago. Ayer Collection.

Notarial Archives Research Center, New Orleans. New Orleans Notarial Archives.

Randolph County Courthouse, Chester, Illinois. Kaskaskia Manuscripts, 1714–16.

St. Charles Parish, Hahnville, Louisiana. Original Acts, 1740–1803. Microfilm in Louisiana State Museum, New Orleans.

St. Landry Parish Opelousas, Louisiana, Colonial Records, 1764–1789. Microfilm in Louisiana State Museum, New Orleans.

St. Martin Parish, St. Martinville, Louisiana. Original Acts, 1760–1803. Microfilm in Louisiana State Museum, New Orleans.

Ste. Genevieve Archives, Ste. Genevieve, Missouri. Microfilm copy in State Historical Society of Missouri, St. Louis.

Ursuline Convent Archives, Parish of Orleans, New Orleans. Microfilm of select archives available at the Historic New Orleans Collection.

Western Michigan University Regional Archives, Kalamazoo, Michigan. French Michilimackinac Research Project Collection. Microfilm of Business and Fur Trade Records of Montreal Merchants, 1712–1806.

FRANCE

Archives de France. Marine. Microfilm available in Manuscripts Division of Library of Congress. Series:

    B1 Délibérations du Conseil de Marine.

    3JJ Documents Scientifiques, vol. 276, Louisiane, 1678–1881

    4JJ Voyages à la Louisiane et à la Floride

Archives de l'arrondissement maritime de Lorient, Lorient.

    Archives de la Compagnie des Indes, Series 1P, 2P

Archives Départementales de la Gironde

Archives Nationales d'Outre-mer, Aix-en-Provence. Microfilm available in Manuscripts Division of Library of Congress

Series:

    A Louisiane, Édits, Arrêts, et Ordonnances, 1712–54, vols. 22–23

    B Louisiane, Correspondance au Départ

    C11A   Louisiane, Correspondance à l'Arrivéé, Canada

    C13A   Louisiane, Correspondance Reçue, 1697–1807, vols. 1–54

    C13B   Louisiane, Correspondance Reçue, Supplement, 1699–1803, vol. 1

    C13C   Louisiane, Correspondance Reçue, Supplement, 1673–1782, vols. 1–5

    D2c   Louisiane, Troupes des Colonies, 1684–1803, vols. 50–52, 54, 59

    D2d   Louisiane, Personnel Militaire et Civil des Colonies, 1744–1765, vol. 10

    DFC 9 Louisiane, Dépôt des Fortifications, 1698–An 10

    F2a   Louisiane, Compagnies de Commerce, 1620–xviiie Siècle, vols. 10–11

    F3   Louisiane, Collection Moreau de Saint Méry, 1680–1806, vols. 24–25, 241–43

    G1   Louisiane, Dépôt des Papiers publics des Colonies, 1706–1873, vols. 412, 464–65

    NIII   Cartes de la Louisiane

    T   Sequestre, 1667–1799, vols. 508, 1725

Archives du Port de Rochefort

    Series IE, IL, IA

Bibliothèque de l'Arsenal, Bibliothèque Nationale de France, Paris

CANADA

Archives of the Seminary of Quebec, Quebec.

Archives of the Monastery of the Ursulines, Quebec.

Archives of the Ursulines of Quebec, Quebec.

ENGLAND

Public Record Office, Kew, High Court of the Admiralty, Series 65, 30, 32

Published and Secondary Sources

Adams, Diane L. *Lead Seals from Fort Michilimackinac, 1715–1781*. Archaeological Completion Report 14. Mackinac Island, Mich.: Mackinac State Historic Parks, 1989.

Albala, Ken. *Food in Early Modern Europe*. Westport, Conn.: Greenwood, 2003.

Allain, Mathé. "French Emigration Policies: Louisiana, 1699–1715." *Proceedings of the Fourth*

Meeting of the French Colonial Historical Society, ed. Alf Andrew Heggoy and James J. Cooke, 39–46. Washington, D.C.: University Press of America, 1979.

———. "L'Immigration française en Louisiane, 1718–1721." *Revue d'Histoire de l'Amérique Française* 28 (1974–75): 555–64.

——— *"Not Worth a Straw": French Colonial Policy and the Early Years of Louisiana.* Lafayette: University of Southwestern Louisiana, 1988.

Allain, Mathé and Vincent H. Cassidy. "Blanpain: Trader Among the Attakapas." *Attakapas Gazette* 3, 4 (1968): 32–38.

Allaire, Bernard. *Pelleteries, manchons et chapeaux de castor: Les Fourrures nord-américaines à Paris, 1500–1632.* Paris: Septentrion, 1999.

Allaire, Gratien. "Fur Trade Engagés, 1701–1745." In *Rendezvous: Selected Papers of the Fourth North American Fur Trade Conference, 1981,* ed. Thomas C. Buckley. St. Paul, Minn.: The Conference, 1984. 15–26.

———. "Les Engagements pour la traite des fourrures: Évaluation de la documentation." *Revue d'Histoire de l'Amérique Française* 34, 1 (1980): 3–26.

———. "Officiers et marchands: Les sociétés de commerce des fourrures, 1715–1760." *Revue d'Histoire de l'Amérique Française* 40, 3 (1987): 409–29.

Allemagne, Henry-René. *La Toile imprimée et les indiennes de traite . . .* Paris: Gründ, 1942.

Alvord, Clarence Walworth. *The Illinois Country, 1673–1818.* Centennial History of Illinois 1. Springfield: Illinois Centennial Commission, 1920.

Alvord, Clarence Walworth and Clarence Edwin Carter, eds. *The Critical Period, 1763–1765.* Collections of the Illinois State Historical Library 10, British Ser. 1. Springfield: Trustees of the Illinois State Historical Library, 1915.

Anderson, Dean L. "Documentary and Archaeological Perspectives on European Trade Goods in the Western Great Lakes Region." Ph.D. dissertation, Michigan State University, 1992.

———. "The Flow of European Trade Goods into the Western Great Lakes Region, 1715–1760." In *The Fur Trade Revisited: Selected Papers of the Sixth North American Fur Trade Conference, Mackinac Island, Michigan, 1991,* ed. Jennifer S. H. Brown, W. J. Eccles, and Donald P. Heldman. East Lansing: Michigan State University Press, 1994. 93–115.

Anderson, Karen L. *Chain Her by One Foot: The Subjugation of Native Women in Seventeenth-Century New France.* New York: Routledge, 1993.

Annaert, Philippe. *Les Collèges au féminin: Les Ursulines; enseignement et vie consacrée aux XVIIe et XVIIIe siècles.* Namur, Belgium: Vie Consacrée, 1992.

Annas, Alicia M. "The Elegant Art of Movement." In *An Elegant Art: Fashion and Fantasy in the Eighteenth Century,* ed. Edward Maeder. Los Angeles: Los Angeles County Museum of Art, 1983. 35–60.

Arnold, J. Barto, III. "The Texas Historical Commission's Underwater Archaeological Survey and Preliminary Report on the *Belle,* La Salle's Shipwreck of 1686." *Historical Archaeology* 30, 4 (1996): 66–87.

Arnold, Morris S. *Colonial Arkansas, 1686–1804: A Social and Cultural History.* Fayetteville: University of Arkansas Press, 1985.

———. "Eighteenth-Century Arkansas Illustrated." *Arkansas Historical Quarterly* 53, 2 (1994): 119–36.

———. *Unequal Laws unto a Savage Race: European Legal Traditions in Arkansas, 1686–1836.* Fayetteville: University of Arkansas Press, 1985.

Astorquia, Madeleine. *Guide des sources de l'histoire des États-unis dans les archives françaises.* Paris: France-Expansion, 1976.

Aubert, Guillaume. "'The Blood of France': Race and Purity of Blood in the French Atlantic World." *William and Mary Quarterly* 61, 3 (2004): 439–78.

———. "'Français, Nègres et Sauvages': Constructing Race in Colonial Louisiana." Ph.D. dissertation, Tulane University, 2002.

———. "Kinship, Blood, and the Emergence of the Racialized Nation in the French Atlantic World, 1600–1789." In *Blood and Kinship: Matter for Metaphor from Ancient Rome to the Present,* ed. Christopher H. Johnson, Bernhard Jussen, David Warren Sabean, and Simon Teuscher. New York: Berghahn, 2013.

———. "'To Establish One Law and Definite Rules': Race, Religion, and the Transatlantic Origins of the Louisiana Code Noir." Paper presented at the workshop on Louisiana and the Atlantic World in the Eighteenth and Nineteenth Centuries, École des Hautes Études en Sciences Sociales, Paris, and Tulane University, New Orleans, April 2008.

Audet, Bernard. *Le Costume paysan dans la région de Québec au XVIIe siècle.* Québec: Leméac, 1980.

Augeron, Mickaël and Robert S. DuPlessis. *Fleuves, rivières et colonies: La France et ses empires (xviiᵉ–xxᵉ siècle); Waterways and Colonies: France and Its Empires (17th–20th Centuries).* Paris: Indes Savantes, 2010.

Auslander, Leora. "Beyond Words." *American Historical Review* 110 (2005): 1015–45.

Axtell, James. *Beyond 1492: Encounters in Colonial North America.* New York: Oxford University Press, 1992.

———. *The European and the Indian: Essays in the Ethnohistory of Colonial North America.* New York: Oxford University Press, 1981.

———. *The Indians' New South: Cultural Change in the Colonial Southeast.* Baton Rouge: Louisiana State University Press, 1997.

———. *Natives and Newcomers: The Cultural Origins of North America.* Oxford: Oxford University Press, 2001.

Baade, Hans W. "Marriage Contracts in French and Spanish Louisiana: A Study in 'Notarial' Jurisprudence." *Tulane Law Review* 53 (1978): 1–92.

Back, Francis. "Le Capot canadien: Ses origines et son évolution aux XVIIe et XVIIIe siècles." *Folklore Canadien* 10, 1–2 (1988): 99–128.

———. "The Dress of the First Voyageurs, 1650–1715." *Museum of the Fur Trade Quarterly* 36, 2 (2000).

———. "Notes on the Clothing and Marks of Honor Given to Indians During the French Regime, 1682–1757." *Military Collector and Historian* 40, 1 (1988).

Back, Francis, and Luce Vermette. "Sources pour l'histoire du costume au Québec." *Folklore Canadien* 10, 1–2 (1988).

Baclawski, Karen. *The Guide to Historic Costume.* New York: Drama Book Publishers, 1995.

Baillardel, A., and A. Prioult. *Le Chevalier de Pradel: Vie d'un colon français en Louisiane au XVIIIe siècle d'après sa correspondance et celle de sa famille.* Paris: Maisonneuve, 1928.

Baker, Vaughan. "*Cherchez les Femmes*: Some Glimpses of Women in Early Eighteenth-Century Louisiana." *Louisiana History* 31, 1 (1990): 21–37.

Baker, Vaughan, Amos Simpson, and Mathé Allain. "*Le Mari est Seigneur*: Marital Laws Governing Women in French Louisiana." In *Louisiana's Legal Heritage,* ed. Edward F. Haas. Pensacola, Fla.: Perdido Bay Press for Louisiana State Museum, 1983. 7–18.

Balesi, Charles John. *Time of the French in the Heart of North America, 1673–1818*. Chicago: Alliance Française Chicago, 1992.

Balvay, Arnaud. *La Révolte des Natchez*. Paris: Félin, 2008.

———. "Tattooing and Its Role in French-Native American Relations in the Eighteenth Century." *French Colonial History* 9 (2008): 1–14.

Banks, Kenneth J. *Chasing Empire Across the Sea: Communications and the State in the French Atlantic, 1713–1763*. Montreal: McGill-Queen's University Press, 2002.

Barr, Juliana. "From Captives to Slaves: Commodifying Indian Women in the Borderlands." *Journal of American History* 92, 1 (2005): 19–46.

———. *Peace Came in the Form of a Woman: Indians and Spaniards in the Texas Borderlands*. Chapel Hill: University of North Carolina Press, 2007.

Barron, Bill, comp. *The Vaudreuil Papers: A Calendar and Index of the Personal and Private Records of Pierre de Rigaud de Vaudreuil, Royal Governor of the French Province of Louisiana, 1743–1753*. New Orleans: Polyanthos, 1975.

Bartram, William. *Travels and Other Writings*. Ed. Thomas P. Slaughter. New York: Library of America, 1996.

Baumgarten, Linda. *Costume Close-Up: Clothing Construction and Pattern, 1750–1790*. Williamsburg, Va.: Colonial Williamsburg Foundation, 1999.

———. *What Clothes Reveal: The Language of Clothing in Colonial and Federal America*. New Haven, Conn.: Yale University Press, 2002.

Bauxar, J. Joseph. "History of the Illinois Area." In *Handbook of North American Indians*, ed. William C. Sturtevant, vol. 15, *Northeast*, ed. Bruce G. Trigger. Washington, D.C.: Smithsonian Institution, 1978. 594–601.

Beaudoin-Ross, Jacqueline. "À la canadienne: Some Aspects of 19th Century Habitant Dress." *Dress* 6 (1980): 71–82.

———. "'À la canadienne' Once More: Some Insights into Quebec Rural Female Dress." *Dress* 7 (1980): 69–81.

———. *Form and Fashion: Nineteenth-Century Montreal Dress*. Montreal: McCord Museum of Canadian History, 1992.

Beauregard, Marthe. *La Population des forts français d'Amérique (XVIIIe siècle): Répertoire des baptêmes, mariages et sépultures célèbres dans les forts et les établissements français en Amérique du nord au XVIIIe*. Montréal: Bergeron, 1982.

Bécart de Granville, Charles. *Les Raretés des Indes: "Codex canadiensis"; Album manuscrit de la fin du XVIIe siècle contenant 180 desssins concernant les indigènes, leurs coutumes, tatouages, la faune et la flore de la Nouvelle France, plus deux cartes*. Facsimile. Montréal: Bouton d'Or, 1974.

Becker, Marshall Joseph. "Match Coats and the Military: Mass-Produced Clothing for Native Americans as Parallel Markets in the Seventeenth Century." *Textile History* 41 (2010): 153–81.

Beers, Henry Putnam. *French and Spanish Records of Louisiana: A Bibliographic Guide to Archival and Manuscript Sources*. Baton Rouge: Louisiana State University Press, 1989.

———. *The French in North America: A Bibliographical Guide to French Archives, Reproductions, and Research Missions*. Baton Rouge: Louisiana State University Press, 1957.

Bell, David. "Recent Works on Early Modern French National Identity." *Journal of Early Modern History* 68 (1996): 84–113.

Belmessous, Saliha. "Assimilation and Racialism in Seventeenth- and Eighteenth-Century French Colonial Policy." *American Historical Review* 110, 2 (2005): 322–49.

———. "D'un préjugé culturel à un préjugé racial: La politique indigène de la France au Canada." Ph.D. dissertation, A.N.R.T., Université de Lille III, 1999.

———. "Être français en Nouvelle-France: Identité française et identité coloniale aux dix-septième et dix-huitième siècles." *French Historical Studies* 27, 3 (2004): 507–40.

Belting, Natalia Maree. *Kaskaskia Under the French Regime.* 1948. Reprint New Orleans: Polyanthos, 1975.

Bénard de la Harpe, Jean-Baptiste. *Historical Journal of the Establishment of the French in Louisiana.* Trans. Virginia Koenig and Joan Cain, ed. Glenn R. Conrad. Lafayette: Center for Louisiana Studies, University of Southwestern Louisiana, 1971, reprint 1985.

Benes, Peter, ed. *Early American Probate Inventories.* Dublin Seminar for New England Folklife Annual Proceedings, 1987. Boston: Boston University, 1989.

———. *Families and Children:* Dublin Seminar for New England Folklife Annual Proceeding, 1985. Boston: Boston University, 1987.

Berinstain, Valérie. "Les Toiles de l'Inde et la Compagnie des Indes (XVII–XVIIIe siècles)." *Cahiers de la Compagnie des Indes* 2 (1997).

Berinstain, Valérie, Dominique Cardon, and Thierry-Nicolas C. Tchakaloff. *Indiennes et palampores à l'Ile Bourbon au XVIIIe siècle.* Saint-Louis, La Réunion: MFMC, 1994.

Berkhofer, Robert F. *The White Man's Indian: Images of the American Indian from Columbus to the Present.* New York: Vintage, 1978.

Berkin, Carol, and Leslie Horowitz, eds. *Women's Voices, Women's Lives: Documents in Early American History.* Boston: Northeastern University Press, 1998.

Berlin, Ira. *Many Thousands Gone: The First Two Centuries of Slavery in North America.* Cambridge, Mass.: Belknap Press of Harvard University Press, 2000.

Berlo, Janet Catherine and Ruth B. Phillips. *Native North American Art.* New York: Oxford University Press, 1998.

Bernard, Jean Frédéric. *Relations de la Louisiane, et du fleuve Mississippi: Où l'on voit l'état de ce grand païs les avantages qu'il peut produire.* Amsterdam: Bernard, 1720.

Biehn, Michel. *En jupon piqué et robe d'indienne: Costumes provençaux.* Marseille: Laffitte, 1987.

Bilodeau, Christopher. "'They Honor Our Lord Among Themselves in Their Own Way': Colonial Christianity and the Illinois Indians." *American Indian Quarterly* 25, 3 (2001): 352–77.

Biow, Douglas. *The Culture of Cleanliness in Renaissance Italy.* Ithaca, N.Y.: Cornell University Press, 2006.

Blair, Emma Helen, ed. and trans. *The Indian Tribes of the Upper Mississippi Valley and Region of the Great Lakes: As Described by Nicolas Perrot, French Commandant in the Northwest; Bacqueville de la Potherie, French Royal Commissioner to Canada; Morrell Marston, American Army Officer; and Thomas Forsyth, United States Agent at Fort Armstrong.* 2 vols. in 1. Lincoln: University of Nebraska Press, 1996.

Blume, Herbert. *The German Coast During the Colonial Era, 1722–1803: Evolution of a Distinct Cultural Landscape in the Lower Mississippi Delta During the Colonial Era.* Trans. Helen C. Merrill. Destrehan, La.: German-Acadian Coast Historical and Genealogical Society, 1990.

Bohaker, Heidi. "Contesting the Middle Ground: The Dynamic Tradition of Indigenous Kinship Networks and Cross-Cultural Alliances in North America's Eastern Great Lakes Region, 1600–1700." Paper presented at International Seminar on the History of the Atlantic World, 1500–1825, Indigenous Cultures, Harvard University, August 2004.

———. "*Nindoodemag*: The Significance of Algonquian Kinship Networks in the Eastern Great Lakes Region, 1600–1701." *William and Mary Quarterly* 63, 1 (2006): 23–52.

Bond, Bradley G. *French Colonial Louisiana and the Atlantic World*. Baton Rouge: Louisiana State University Press, 2005.

Bonnefoy, Antoine. "Journal of Antoine Bonnefoy." In *Travels in the American Colonies*, ed. Newton Mereness. New York: Macmillan, 1916. 239–58.

Bossu, Jean Bernard. *New Travels in North America*. Ed. and trans. Samuel Dorris Dickinson. Natchitoches, La.: Northwestern State University Press, 1982.

———. *Nouveaux voyages aux Indes occidentales*. 2 vols. Paris: Le Jay, 1768.

———. *Nouveaux voyages dans l'Amérique septentrionale*. Amsterdam: Changuion, 1777.

Boulle, Pierre. *Race et esclavage dans la France d'ancien régime*. Paris: Perrin, 2007.

Boulanger, Patrick. *Mémoires du savon de Marseille*. Marguerittes, France: Équinoxe, 1994.

Bourdieu, Pierre. *Distinction: A Social Critique of the Judgement of Taste*. Trans. Richard Nice. New York: Routledge, 1984.

Boyle, Susan C. "Did She Generally Decide? Women in Ste. Genevieve, 1750–1805." *William and Mary Quarterly* 3rd ser. 44 (1987): 775–89.

Brain, Jeffrey P. *Tunica Archaeology*. Papers of the Peabody Museum of Archaeology and Ethnology 78. Cambridge, Mass.: Peabody Museum of Archaeology and Ethnology, Harvard University, 1988.

———. *Tunica Treasure*. Papers of the Peabody Museum of Archaeology and Ethnology 71. Cambridge, Mass.: Peabody Museum of Archaeology and Ethnology, Harvard University, 1979.

Brandão, José António and Michael Shakir Nassaney. "A Capsule Social and Material History of Fort St. Joseph and Its Inhabitants (1691–1763)." *French Colonial History* 7 (2006): 61–75.

———. "Suffering for Jesus: Penitential Practices at Fort St. Joseph (Niles, Michigan) During the French Regime." *Catholic Historical Review* 94 (2008): 476–99.

Brasseaux, Carl A. *The Founding of New Acadia: The Beginnings of Acadian Life in Louisiana, 1765–1803*. Baton Rouge: Louisiana State University Press, 1987.

———. *France's Forgotten Legion: Service Records of French Military and Administrative Personnel Stationed in the Mississippi Valley and Gulf Coast Region, 1699–1799*. Baton Rouge: Louisiana State University Press, 2000.

———. "The Image of Louisiana and the Failure of Voluntary French Emigration, 1683–1731." *Proceedings of the Fourth Meeting of the French Colonial Historical Society*, ed. Alf Andrew Heggoy and James J. Cooke. Washington, D.C.: University Press of America, 1979. 47–56.

Brasseaux, Carl A. and Glenn R. Conrad. *A Bibliography of Scholarly Literature on Colonial Louisiana and New France*. Lafayette: University of Southwestern Louisiana, 1992.

Brasser, Ted J. "Notes on a Recently Discovered Indian Shirt from New France." *American Indian Art Magazine* 24 (1999): 46–55.

Braund, Kathryn. *Deerskins & Duffels: The Creek Indian Trade with Anglo-America, 1685–1815*. Lincoln: University of Nebraska Press, 1993.

Breen, T. H. *The Marketplace Revolution: How Consumer Politics Shaped American Independence*. Oxford: Oxford University Press, 2004.

Brewer, John and Roy Porter, eds. *Consumption and the World of Goods*. London: Routledge, 1993.

Brewer, John and Frank Trentmann, eds. *Consuming Cultures, Global Perspectives: Historical Trajectories, Transnational Exchanges*. New York: Berg, 2006.

Briggs, Winstanley. "Le Pays des Illinois." *William and Mary Quarterly* 3rd ser. 47, 1 (1990): 30–56.

Brooks, James F. *Captives and Cousins: Slavery, Kinship, and Community in the Southwest Borderlands.* Chapel Hill: University of North Carolina Press, 2002.

———. "'This Evil Extends Especially . . . to the Feminine Sex': Negotiating Captivity in the New Mexico Borderlands." *Feminist Studies* 22, 2 (1996): 279–309.

Brown, Jennifer S. H., W. J. Eccles, and Donald P. Heldman, eds. *The Fur Trade Revisited: Selected Papers of the Sixth North American Fur Trade Conference, Mackinac Island, Michigan.* East Lansing: Michigan State University Press, 1994.

Brown, Jennifer S. H. and Jacqueline Peterson, eds. *The New Peoples: Being and Becoming Métis in North America.* Lincoln: University of Nebraska Press, 1985.

Brown, Kathleen M. "The Anglo-Algonquian Gender Frontier." In *Negotiators of Change: Historical Perspectives on Native American Women,* ed. Nancy Shoemaker. New York: Routledge, 1995. 26–48.

———. "Beyond the Great Debates: Gender and Race in Early America." *Reviews in American History* 26, 1 (1998): 96–123.

———. "'Changed . . . into the Fashion of Man': The Politics of Sexual Difference in a Seventeenth-Century Anglo-American Settlement." *Journal of the History of Sexuality* 6, 2 (1995): 171–93.

———. *Foul Bodies: Cleanliness in Early America.* New Haven, Conn.: Yale University Press, 2009.

———. "The Historical Body, Our Humanity, and the Cost of Modernity." *William and Mary Quarterly* 3rd ser. 68, 4 (2011): 690–93.

———. "Native Americans and Early Modern Concepts of Race." In *Empire and Others: British Encounters with Indigenous Peoples, 1600–1850,* ed. Martin Daunton and Rick Halpern, 79–100. Philadelphia: University of Pennsylvania Press, 1999. 79–100.

Brown, Margaret Kimball. "Allons Cowboys!" *Journal of the Illinois State Historical Society* 76, 4 (1983): 273–82.

———. *Cultural Transformations Among the Illinois: An Application of a Systems Model.* Publications of the Museum, Anthropological Series 1, 3. East Lansing: Michigan State University, 1979.

———. "An Eighteenth Century Trade Coat." *Plains Anthropologist* 16 (1971): 128–33.

———. *History as They Lived It: A Social History of Prairie du Rocher, Illinois.* Tucson, Ariz.: Patrice Press, 2005.

———. *The Voyageur in the Illinois Country: The Fur Trade's Professional Boatman in Mid-America Based on Unpublished Documents from Illinois' Kaskaskia Manuscripts and Related Sources.* Extended Publication Series 3. Naperville, Ill.: Center for French Colonial Studies, 2002.

———. "The Waterman Site: A Michigamia Village." 1991. Manuscript on file, Illinois State Museum.

Brown, Margaret and Lawrie Cena Dean. *The French Colony in the Mid-Mississippi Valley.* Carbondale, Ill.: American Kestrel Books, 1995.

———, eds. *The Village of Chartres in Colonial Illinois, 1720–1765.* New Orleans: Polyanthos, 1977.

Brubaker, Rogers, and Frederick Cooper. "Beyond 'Identity.'" *Theory and Society* 29, 1 (2000): 1–47.

Bruneau, Marguerite. *Histoire du costume populaire en Normandie.* 2 vols. Rouen: Cercle d'Action et d'Études Normandes, 1986.

Bruns, Mrs. Thomas. *Louisiana Portraits.* New Orleans: National Society of the Colonial Dames of America in the State of Louisiana, 1975.

Bruseth, James E., and Toni S. Turner. *From a Watery Grave: The Discovery and Excavation of La Salle's Shipwreck, "La Belle."* College Station: Texas A&M University Press, 2007.

Buck, Anne. *Clothes and the Child: A Handbook of Children's Dress in England, 1500–1900*. Bedford: R. Bean, 1996.

———. *Dress in Eighteenth-Century England*. New York: Holmes & Meier, 1979.

Buckridge, Steeve O. *The Language of Dress: Resistance and Accommodation in Jamaica, 1760–1890*. Kingston, Jamaica: University of the West Indies Press, 2004.

Buisseret, David, Daniel H. Usner, Mary L. Galvin, Richard Cullen Rath, and J. L. Dillard. *Creolization in the Americas*, ed. David Buisseret and Steven G. Reinhardt. College Station: Texas A&M University Press, 2000.

Burke, Timothy. *Lifebuoy Men, Lux Women: Commodification, Consumption, and Cleanliness in Modern Zimbabwe*. Durham, N.C.: Duke University Press, 1996.

Burnham, Dorothy K. *Cut My Cote*. Toronto: Royal Ontario Museum, 1973.

———. *To Please the Caribou: Painted Caribou-Skin Coats Worn by the Naskapi, Montagnais, and Cree Hunters of the Quebec-Labrador Peninsula*. Seattle: University of Washington Press, 1992.

———. *Warp & Weft: A Textile Terminology*. London: Royal Ontario Museum, 1980.

Burnston, Sharon Ann. *Fitting & Proper: 18th Century Clothing from the Collection of the Chester County Historical Society*. Texarcana, Tex.: Scurlock, 2000.

Burton, Clarence. *Cadillac's Village, or Detroit Under Cadillac: With List of Property Owners, and a History of the Settlement, 1701 to 1710*. Detroit: Detroit Society for Genealogical Research, 1999.

Burton, H. Sophie. "'To Establish a Stock Farm for the Raising of Mules, Horses, Horned Cattle, Sheep, and Hogs': The Role of Spanish Bourbon Louisiana in the Establishment of Vacheries Along the Louisiana-Texas Borderland, 1766–1803." *Southwestern Historical Quarterly* 109, 1 (2005): 99–132.

Burton, H. Sophie and Todd F. Smith. *Colonial Natchitoches: A Creole Community on the Louisiana-Texas Frontier*. College Station: Texas A&M University Press, 2008.

Buser, Thomas. "Jerome Nadal and Early Jesuit Art in Rome." *Art Bulletin* 58, 3 (1976): 424–33.

Bushman, Richard L. and Claudia L. Bushman. "The Early History of Cleanliness in America." *Journal of American History* 74 (1988): 1213–38.

Bushnell, David I., Jr. *Drawings by A. De Batz in Louisiana, 1732–1735 (with Six Plates)*. Smithsonian Miscellaneous Collections 80, 5. Washington, D.C.: Smithsonian Institution, 1927.

Butler, Alban. *Butler's Lives of the Saints*. Concise ed., rev. and updated. Ed. Michael Walsh. San Francisco: HarperSanFrancisco, 1991.

Butler, Judith. *Gender Trouble: Feminism and the Subversion of Identity*. New York: Routledge, 1990.

Butler, Ruth Lapham, trans. *Journal of Paul du Ru (February 1 to May 8, 1700): Missionary Priest of Louisiana*. Chicago: Caxton Club, 1934.

Caldwell, Norman W. *The French in the Mississippi Valley, 1740–1750*. Urbana: University of Illinois Press, 1941.

Callender, Charles. "Illinois." In *Handbook of North American Indians*, ed. William C. Sturtevant, vol. 15, *Northeast*, ed. Bruce G. Trigger. Washington, D.C.: Smithsonian Institution, 1978. 673–80.

Calloway, Colin G. *New Worlds for All: Indians, Europeans, and the Remaking of Early America*. Baltimore: Johns Hopkins University Press, 1997.

Calvert, Karin. "The Function of Fashion in Eighteenth-Century America." *William and Mary Quarterly* 3rd ser. 39, 1 (1982): 87–113.

Cangany, Catherine. "'Altogether Preferable to Shoes': The Business of Moccasins in French Colonial Towns." Paper presented at the Annual Meeting of the French Colonial Historical Society, Quebec City, May 2008.

Caplan, Jane, ed. *Written on the Body: The Tattoo in European and American History*. Princeton, N.J.: Princeton University Press, 2000.

Carlos, Ann M. and Frank D. Lewis. *Commerce by a Frozen Sea: Native Americans and the European Fur Trade*. Philadelphia: University of Pennsylvania Press, 2010.

Caron, Peter. "'Of a Nation Which the Others Do Not Understand': Bambara Slaves and African Ethnicity in Colonial Louisiana, 1718–60." *Slavery & Abolition* 18 (1997): 98–121.

Carr, Lois and Lorena Walsh. "Forum: Toward a History of the Standard of Living in Colonial America." *William and Mary Quarterly* 45, 1 (January 1988): 135–59.

Carson, Cary, Ronald Hoffman, and Peter J. Albert, eds. *Of Consuming Interests: The Style of Life in the Eighteenth Century*. Charlottesville: University Press of Virginia, 1994.

Castro, Wendy Lucas. "Stripped: Clothing and Identity in Colonial Captivity Narratives." *Early American Studies* 6, 1 (2008): 104–36.

Chaplin, Joyce E. *Subject Matter: Technology, the Body, and Science on the Anglo-American Frontier, 1500–1676*. Cambridge, Mass.: Harvard University Press, 2003.

Charlevoix, Pierre-François-Xavier de. *Histoire et description générale de la Nouvelle-France*. Paris: Rolin Fils, 1744.

———. *Journal d'un voyage fait par ordre du roi dans l'Amérique Septentrionale: Adressé à Madame la Duchesse de Lesdiguières*. Vols. 5 and 6. Paris: Rolin Fils, 1744.

———. *Journal of a Voyage to North America*. Trans. Louise Phelps Kellogg. 2 vols. Chicago: Caxton Club, 1923.

Chartrand, René. "The Troops of French Louisiana, 1699–1769." *Military Collector and Historian* 25, 2 (1973): 58–65.

———. "The Winter Costume of Soldiers in Canada." *Canadian Folklore* 10 (1988): 155–80.

Chauchetière, Père Claude, S.J. *Annual Narrative of the Mission of the Sault from Its Foundation Until the Year 1686*. Bristol, Pa.: Evolution Publishing, 2006.

———. *Narration de la Mission du Sault depuis sa fondation jusqu'en 1686*. Ed. Hélène Avisseau. 2 vols. Bordeaux: Archives Départementales de la Gironde, 1984.

Choquette, Leslie. *Frenchmen into Peasants: Modernity and Tradition in the Peopling of French Canada*. Cambridge, Mass.: Harvard University Press, 1997.

Clark, Emily. "'By All the Conduct of Their Lives': A Laywomen's Confraternity in New Orleans, 1730–1744." *William and Mary Quarterly* 54, 4 (1997): 769–94.

———. *Masterless Mistresses: The New Orleans Ursulines and the Development of a New World Society, 1727–1834*. Chapel Hill, N.C.: Omohundro Institute of Early American History and Culture, 2007.

———. "Moving from Periphery to Centre: The Non-British in Colonial North America." *Historical Journal* 42, 3 (September 1999): 903–10.

———. "A New World Community: The New Orleans Ursulines and Colonial Society, 1727–1803." Ph.D. dissertation, Tulane University, 1998.

———. "Peculiar Professionals: The Financial Strategies of the New Orleans Ursulines." In *Neither Lady Nor Slave: Working Women of the Old South*, ed. Susanna Delfino and Michele Gillespie. Chapel Hill: University of North Carolina Press, 2002. 198–220.

———. *Voices from an Early American Convent: Marie Madeleine Hachard and the New Orleans Ursulines, 1727–1760*. Baton Rouge: Louisiana State University Press, 2007.

Clark, Emily with Virginia M. Gould. "The Feminine Face of Afro-Catholicism in New Orleans, 1727–1852." *William and Mary Quarterly* 3rd ser. 59 (2002): 409–48.

Clark, John G. *La Rochelle and the Atlantic Economy During the Eighteenth Century*. Baltimore: Johns Hopkins University Press, 1981.

———. *New Orleans, 1718–1812: An Economic History*. Baton Rouge: Louisiana State University Press, 1970.

Cleary, Patricia. *Elizabeth Murray: A Woman's Pursuit of Independence in Eighteenth Century America*. Amherst: University of Massachusetts Press, 2000.

Codignola, Luca. "The Holy See and the Conversion of the Indians in French and British North America, 1486–1760." In *America in European Consciousness, 1493–1750*, ed. Karen Ordahl Kupperman. Chapel Hill: University of North Carolina Press, 1995. 195–242.

Coffin, Judith G. "Gender and the Guild Order: The Garment Trades in Eighteenth-Century Paris." *Journal of Economic History* 54, 4 (1994): 768–93.

Collard, Eileen. *Early Clothing in Southern Ontario*. Burlington, Ont.: Mississauga Press, 1969.

Colpitts, George. "'Animated like Us by Commercial Interests': Commercial Ethnology and Fur Trade Descriptions in New France, 1660–1760." *Canadian Historical Review* 83, 3 (2002): 305–37.

Colten, Craig E. "Meaning of Water in the American South: Transatlantic Encounters." *Atlantic Studies* 5 (2008): 203–22.

Conrad, Glenn R., ed. *A Dictionary of Louisiana Biography*. 2 vols. New Orleans: Louisiana Historical Society, 1988.

———. "*Émigration forcée*: A French Attempt to Populate Louisiana 1716–1720." In *Proceedings of the Fourth Meeting of the French Colonial Historical Society*, ed. Alf Andrew Heggoy and James J. Cooke,. Washington, D.C.: University Press of America, 1979. 57–66.

———. *The First Families of Louisiana*. 2 vols. Baton Rouge: Claitor's, 1970.

———. *The French Experience in Louisiana*. Lafayette: Center for Louisiana Studies, University of Southwestern Louisiana, 1995.

Conrad, Lawrence A. "An Early Eighteenth Century Reference to 'Putting a Woman on the Prairies' Among the Central Algonquians and Its Implications for Moore's Explanation of the Practice Among the Cheyennes." *Plains Anthropologist* 28, 100 (1983): 141–42.

Cooke, Sarah E. and Rachel B. Ramadhyani, eds. *Indians and a Changing Frontier: The Art of George Winter*. Indianapolis: Indiana Historical Society, 1993.

Corbin, Alain. *Le Miasme et la jonquille*. 1982. Reprint Paris: Flammarion, 1986.

Costa, David J. "An Overview of the Illinois Language." In *Kaskaskia Illinois-to-French Dictionary*, ed. Carl Masthay. St. Louis: Masthay, 2002. 2–5.

Crawford, Joanna. "Clothing Distributions and Social Relations c. 1350–1500." In *Clothing Culture, 1350–1650*, ed. Catherine Richardson. Aldershot: Ashgate, 2004. 153–64.

Croizat, Yassana C. "'Living Dolls': François Ier Dresses His Women." *Renaissance Quarterly* 60, 1 (Spring 2007): 94–130.

Crowston, Clare Haru. *Fabricating Women: The Seamstresses of Old Regime France, 1675–1791*. Durham, N.C.: Duke University Press, 2001.

Cruzat, Heloise H. "Records of the Superior Council of Louisiana, LXII." *Louisiana Historical Quarterly* 18, 1 (1935): 161–92.

Cummins, Light Townsend and Glen Jeansonne, eds. *A Guide to the History of Louisiana*. Westport, Conn.: Greenwood, 1982.

d'Aleyrac, Jean-Baptiste. *Aventures militaires au XVIIIe siècle*. Ed. Charles Coste. Paris: Berger-Levrault, 1935.

d'Allaire, Micheline. *Les Dots des religieuses au Canada français, 1639–1800*. Québec: Hurtubise, 1986.

———. *L'Hôpital-général de Québec, 1692–1794*. Montréal: Fides, 1971.

Dalrymple, Margaret Fisher, ed. *The Merchant of Manchac: The Letterbooks of John Fitzpatrick, 1768–1790*. Baton Rouge: Louisiana State University Press, 1978.

Daniels, Bruce. "Probate Court Inventories and Colonial American History: Historiography, Problems, and Results." *Social History* 9, 18 (1976): 387–405.

Daniels, Christine and Michael V. Kennedy, eds. *Negotiated Empires: Centers and Peripheries in the Americas, 1500–1820*. New York: Routledge.

Davis, Natalie Zemon. "Iroquois Women, European Women." In *Women, "Race," and Writing in the Early Modern Period*, ed. Margo Hendricks and Patricia Parker. New York: Routledge, 1994. 243–61.

———. *Women on the Margins: Three Seventeenth-Century Lives*. Cambridge, Mass.: Belknap Press of Harvard University Press, 1997.

Dawdy, Shannon Lee. *Building the Devil's Empire: French Colonial New Orleans*. Chicago: University of Chicago Press, 2008.

———. "'A Wild Taste': Food and Colonialism in Eighteenth-Century Louisiana." *Ethnohistory* 57 (2010): 389–414.

Dawson, Joyce Taylor. "An Analysis of Liturgical Textiles at Sainte-Marie Among the Hurons." *Material History Bulletin* 24 (1986): 1–12.

Dechêne, Louise. *Habitants and Merchants in Seventeenth-Century Montreal*. Montreal: McGill-Queen's University Press, 1992.

de Garsault, François-Antoine. *L'Art du tailleur, contenant le tailleur d'habits d'hommes, les culottes de peau, le tailleur de corps de femmes et enfants, la couturière, et la marchande de modes*. Paris: L. F. Delatour, 1769.

Delâge, Denys. "L'Influence des Amérindiens sur les Canadiens et les Français au temps de la Nouvelle-France." *Lekton* 2, 2 (1992): 103–91.

Delâge, Denys and Paul-André Dubois. "L'Eau, les Amérindiens et les Franco-Canadiens: Mythes et réalités en Amérique du Nord au XVIIe et XVIIIe siècles." Paper presented at 1997 biennial conference of the Associazione Italiana di Studi Canadasi, Sienna, July 1997.

Delanglez, Jean. "The French Jesuits in Lower Louisiana, 1700–1763." Ph.D. dissertation, Catholic University of America, 1935.

———. "A Louisiana Post-Historian: Dumont *dit* Montigny." *Mid-America: An Historical Review* 19 (1937): 31.

Deloria, Philip J. *Playing Indian*. New Haven, Conn.: Yale University Press, 1999.

Delpierre, Madeleine. *Dress in France in the Eighteenth Century*. New Haven, Conn.: Yale University Press, 1997.

Demos, John. *The Unredeemed Captive: A Family Story from Early America*. New York: Vintage, 1995.

Denissen, Christian. *Genealogy of the French Families of the Detroit River Region, Revision, 1701–1936*. Detroit: Detroit Society for Genealogical Research, 1987.

Derounian-Stodola, Kathryn Zabelle, ed. *Women's Indian Captivity Narratives*. New York: Penguin, 1998.

Desbarats, Catherine. "The Cost of Early Canada's Native Alliances: Reality and Scarcity's Rhetoric." *William and Mary Quarterly* 52, 4 (1995): 609–30.

Deslandres, Dominique. *Croire et faire croire: Les missions françaises au XVIIe siècle (1600–1650).* Paris: Fayard, 2003.

———. "L'Éducation des Amérindiennes d'après la correspondance de Marie Guyart de l'Incarnation." *Studies in Religion* 16 (1987): 91–110.

———. "In the Shadow of the Cloister: Representations of Female Holiness in New France." In *Colonial Saints: Discovering the Holy in the Americas, 1500–1800,* ed. Allan Greer and Jodi Bilinkoff. New York: Routledge: 2003. 129–52.

———. "Un projet éducatif au XVIIe siècle: Marie de l'Incarnation et la femme amérindienne." *Rechereches Amérindiennes au Québec* 13 (1983): 277–85.

Detroit Institute of Arts. *The French in America, 1520–1880.* Detroit: Detroit Institute of Arts, 1951.

Devens, Carol. *Countering Colonization: Native American Women and Great Lakes Missions, 1630–1900.* Berkeley: University of California Press, 1992.

De Ville, Winston. *The Ste. Catherine Colonists, 1719–1720: Early Settlers of Natchez and Pointe Coupée in the French Province of Louisiana.* Ville Platte, La.: Smith Books, 1991.

Dickason, Olive Patricia. *The Myth of the Savage and the Beginnings of French Colonialism in the Americas.* Edmonton: University of Alberta Press, 1984.

Diderot, Denis and Jean d'Alembert, eds. *L'Encyclopédie, ou Dictionnaire raisonné des sciences, des arts et des métiers.* 35 vols. University of Chicago: ARTFL Encyclopédie Project (Winter 2008 ed.), ed. Robert Morrissey.

Diron d'Artaguiette, Bernard. "Journal of Diron d'Artaguiette." In *Travels in the American Colonies,* ed. Newton Dennison Mereness. New York: Macmillan, 1916. 15–92.

Douglas, Mary. *Purity and Danger: An Analysis of Concept of Pollution and Taboo.* 1966. Reprint with a new preface by the author. London: Routledge, 2002.

Douthwaite, Julia. *The Wild Girl, Natural Man, and the Monster: Dangerous Experiments in the Age of Enlightenment.* Chicago: University of Chicago Press, 2002.

Douville, Raymond. "Jacques Largillier dit 'Le Castor,' coureur des bois et "Frère Donné.'" *Cahiers des Dix* 29 (1964): 47–69.

Dubé, Alexandre. "Les Biens publics: Culture politique de la Louisiane française 1730–1770." Ph.D dissertation, McGill University, 2009.

Dumont de Montigny, Jean-François-Benjamin. *Mémoires historiques sur la Louisiane.* 2 vols. Paris: C.J.B. Bauche, 1753.

———. *Regards sur le monde atlantique, 1715–1747.* Sillery, Quebec: Septentrion, 2008.

DuPlessis, Robert S. "Circulation des textiles et des valeurs dans la Nouvelle-France aux XVIIe et XVIIIe siècles." In *Échanges et cultures textiles dans l'Europe pré-industrielle,* ed. Jacques Bottin and Nicole Pellegrin. Revue du Nord. Hors série, Collection Histoire 12. Villeneuve-d'Ascq: Université Charles-de-Gaulle-Lille III, 1996. 73–78.

———. "Circulation et appropriation des mouchoirs chez les colons et aborigènes de la Nouvelle-France aux XVIIe et XVIIIe siècles." In *Le Mouchoir dans tous ses états: Actes du colloque international,* ed. Jean-Joseph Chevalier and Elisabeth Loir-Mongazon. Cholet: Association des Amis du Musée du Textile Choletais, 2000. 165–71.

———. "Cloth and the Emergence of the Atlantic Economy." In *The Atlantic Economy During the Seventeenth and Eighteenth Centuries: Organization, Operation, Practice, and Personnel,* ed. Peter A. Coclanis. Columbia: University of South Carolina Press, 2005. 72–94.

———. "Cotton Consumption in the Seventeenth- and Eighteenth-Century Altantic World." In *The*

Spinning World: A Global History of Cotton Textiles, 1200–1850, ed. Giorgio Riello and Prasannan Parthasarathi. Oxford: Oxford University Press, 2009.

———. "Transatlantic Textiles: European Linens in the Cloth Culture of Colonial North America." In *The European Linen Industry in Historical Perspective*, ed. Brenda Collins and Philip Ollerenshaw. Pasold Series in Textile History. Oxford: Oxford University Press, 2003.

———. "Was There a Consumer Revolution in Eighteenth-Century New France?" *French Colonial History* 1 (2002): 143–59.

DuVal, Kathleen. "Indian Intermarriage and Metissage in Colonial Louisiana." *William and Mary Quarterly* 65, 2 (2008): 267–304.

———. *The Native Ground: Indians and Colonists in the Heart of the Continent*. Philadelphia: University of Pennsylvania Press, 2007.

Eagan, Geoff, Michael Cowell, and Hero Granger-Taylor. *Lead Cloth Seals and Related Items in the British Museum*. Occasional Paper 93. London: Department of Medieval and Later Antiquities, British Museum, 1994.

Ebbs, Tracy. "Subjected and Productive Bodies: The Educational Vision of the Ursulines in Early Colonial New Orleans." Ph.D. dissertation, University of Pennsylvania, 1996.

Eccles, W. J. *The Canadian Frontier, 1534–1760*. Hinsdale, Ill.: Dryden Press, 1969.

Edict du roy povr l'establissement de la Compagnie de la Nouuelle France auec l'arrest de verification de la Cour des Aydes de Roüen. Paris: S. Cramoisy, 1633. Boston: Massachusetts Historical Society, 1929.

Édits, ordonnances royaux, déclarations et arrêts du Conseil d'État du Roi concernant le Canada. 3 vols. Québec: E.R. Fréchette, 1854–56.

Edmunds, David R. and Joseph L. Peyser. *The Fox Wars: The Mesquakie Challenge to New France*. Norman: Oklahoma University Press, 1993.

Edwards, Jay D. "The Origins of Creole Architecture." *Winterthur Portfolio* 49, 2/3 (1994): 155–89.

Ekberg, Carl J. "Agriculture, *Mentalités*, and Violence on the Illinois Frontier." *Illinois Historical Journal* 88, 2 (1995): 101–16.

———. "Black Slavery in Illinois, 1720–1765." *Western Illinois Regional Studies* 12, 1 (1989): 5–19.

———. "Black Slaves in the Illinois Country, 1721–1765." *Proceedings of the Annual Meeting of the French Colonial Historical Society* 11 (1987): 265–77.

———. *Colonial Ste. Genevieve: An Adventure on the Mississippi Frontier*. Gerald, Mo.: Patrice Press, 1985.

———. "The Flour Trade in French Colonial Louisiana." *Louisiana History* 37 (2006): 261–82.

———. *François Vallé and His World*. Columbia: University of Missouri Press, 2002.

———. *A French Aristocrat in the American West: The Shattered Dreams of De Lassus de Luzières*. Columbia: University of Missouri Press, 2010.

———. *French Roots in the Illinois Country: The Mississippi Frontier in Colonial Times*. Urbana: University of Illinois Press, 1998.

———. "Marie Rouensa-8canic8e and the Foundations of French Illinois." In *Native Women's History in Eastern North America Before 1900*, ed. Rebecca Kugel and Lucy Eldersveld Murphy. Lincoln: University of Nebraska Press, 2007. 203–33.

———. *Stealing Indian Women: Native Slavery in the Illinois Country*. Urbana: University of Illinois Press, 2007.

———. "Terrisse de Ternan: Epistoler and Soldier." *Louisiana History* 23, 4 (1982): 400–408.

Ekberg, Carl J. with Anton J. Pregaldin. "Marie Rouensa-8cate8a and the Foundations of French Illinois." *Illinois Historical Journal* 84 (1991): 146–60.

Ellis, Richard N., and Charlie R. Steen, eds. "An Indian Delegation in France, 1725." *Journal of the Illinois State Historical Society* 67, 4 (1974): 385–405.

Esarey, Duane. "Seasonal Occupation Patterns in Illinois History: A Case Study in the Lower Illinois River Valley." *Illinois Archaeology* 9 (1987): 164–219.

Etheridge, Robbie, and Sherri M. Shuck Hall, eds. *Mapping the Mississippian Shatter Zone: The Colonial Indian Slave Trade and Regional Instability in the American South.* Lincoln: University of Nebraska Press, 2009.

Faribault-Beauregard, Marthe, ed. *La Population des forts français d'Amérique (XVIIIe siècle): Repertoire des baptêmes, marriages et sépultures célébrés dans les forts et les établissements français en Amérique du Nord au XVIIIe siècle,* 2 vols. Montréal: Bergeron, 1982–84.

———. *La Vie aux Illinois au XVIIIe siècle: Souvenirs inédits de Marie-Anne Cerré.* Montréal: Archiv-Histo, 1987.

Faye, Stanley. "The Arkansas Post of Louisiana: French Domination." *Louisiana Historical Quarterly* 26 (1943): 633–721.

Feest, Christian F. *Native Arts of North America.* London: Thames and Hudson, 1992.

———, ed. *Premières nations, collections royales: Les Indiens des forêts et des prairies d'Amérique du Nord.* Paris: Musée du Quai Branly, 2007.

Finiels, Nicolas de. *An Account of Upper Louisiana.* Ed. Carl J. Ekberg and William E. Foley, trans. Carl J. Ekberg. Columbia: University of Missouri Press, 1989.

"First Visit of Nebraska Indians to Paris in 1725." *Nebraska History* 6 (1923): 33–38.

Fischer, Kirsten. "The Imperial Gaze: Native American, African American, and Colonial Women in European Eyes." In *A Companion to American Women's History,* ed. Nancy A. Hewitt, 3–19. Oxford: Blackwell, 2005.

———. *Suspect Relations: Sex, Race, and Resistance in Colonial North Carolina.* Ithaca, N.Y.: Cornell University Press, 2001.

Fivel, Sharon. "Creole Dress in St. Louis." Paper given at Missouri Historical Society, August 1989.

Foley, William E. and David C. Rice. *The First Chouteaus: River Barons of Early St. Louis.* Urbana: University of Illinois Press, 1983.

Folmer, Henri. "Étienne Veniard de Bourgmond in the Missouri Country." *Missouri Historical Review* 36, 3 (1942): 279–98.

Foret, Michael James. "French Colonial Indian Policy in Louisiana, 1699–1763." In *Proceedings of the Eighth Annual Meeting of the French Colonial Historical Society, 1982,* ed. E. P. Fitzgerald. Lanham, Md.: University Press of America.

———. "Red over White: Indians, Deserters, and French Colonial Louisiana." In *Proceedings of the Seventeenth Meeting of the French Colonial Historical Society, Chicago, May 1991,* ed. Patricia Galloway. Lanham, Md.: University Press of America, 1993.

Foster, Helen Bradley. *New Raiments of Self: African American Clothing in the Antebellum South.* New York: Berg, 1997.

Foster, William C., ed. *The La Salle Expedition on the Mississippi River: A Lost Manuscript of Nicolas de La Salle, 1682.* Austin: Texas State Historical Association, 2003.

———. *The La Salle Expedition to Texas: The Journal of Henri Joutel, 1684–1687.* Austin: Texas State Historical Association, 1998.

Fowler, Don D. "Images of American Indians, 1492–1892." *Halcyon* 11 (1991): 75–100.

Franke, Judith A. *French Peoria and the Illinois Country, 1673–1846.* Illinois State Museum Popular Science Series 12. Springfield: Illinois State Museum Society, 1995.

French, Benjamin Franklin, ed. *Historical Collections of Louisiana, Embracing Translations of Many Rare and Valuable Documents.* 7 vols. New York: Wiley and Putman, 1846–53.

———. *Historical Memoirs of Louisiana: From the First Settlement of the Colony to the Departure of Governer O'Reilly in 1770.* New York: Lamport, Blakeman, and Law, 1853.

Friederici, Georg. *Scalping and Torture: Warfare Practices Among North American Indians.* Ohsweken, Ont.: Iroqrafts, 1985.

Furetière, Antoine de. *Dictionnaire universel, contenant generalement tous les mots français tant vieux que modernes et les termes des sciences et des arts.* Rotterdam-La Haye: Leers, 1690.

Gagnon, François-Marc. *La Conversion par l'image: Un aspect de la mission des jésuites auprès des Indiens du Canada au XVIIe siècle.* Montréal: Bellarmin, 1975.

———. *Premiers peintres de la Nouvelle-France.* Vol. 2. Québec: Ministère des Affaires Culturelles, 1976.

Galloway, Patricia. *Choctaw Genesis 1500–1700.* Lincoln: University of Nebraska Press, 1995.

———. *La Salle and His Legacy: Frenchmen and Indians in the Lower Mississippi Valley.* Jackson: University Press of Mississippi, 1982.

Gaudio, Michael. *Engraving the Savage: The New World and Techniques of Civilization.* Minneapolis: University of Minnesota Press, 2008.

Gilman, Carolyn. *Where Two Worlds Meet: The Great Lakes Fur Trade.* St. Paul: Minnesota Historical Society, 1982.

Giraud, Marcel. *Histoire de la Louisiane française (1698–1723).* 4 vols. Paris: PUF, 1953–74.

———. *A History of French Louisiana.* 5 vols. Baton Rouge: Louisiana State University Press, 1974–93.

Glassie, Henry. "Meaningful Things and Appropriate Myths: The Artifact's Place in American Studies." *Prospects* 3 (1977): 1–49.

Godbeer, Richard. "Eroticizing the Middle Ground: Anglo-Indian Sexual Relations Along the Eighteenth-Century Frontier." In *Sex, Love, Race: Crossing Boundaries in North America History*, ed. Martha Hodes. New York: New York University Press, 1999. 91–111.

———. *Sexual Revolution in Early America.* Baltimore: Johns Hopkins University Press, 2004.

Good, Mary Elizabeth. *Guébert Site: An 18th Century Historic Kaskaskia Indian Village in Randolph County, Illinois.* Wood River, Ill.: Central States Archaeological Societies, 1972.

Goodman, Dena, and Kathryn Norberg, eds. *Furnishing the Eighteenth Century: What Furniture Can Tell Us About the European and American Past.* Oxford: Routledge, 2006.

Gourdeau, Claire. *Les Délices de nos coeurs: Marie de l'Incarnation et ses pensionnaires amérindiennes, 1639–1672.* Sillery, Québec: Septentrion, 1994.

Gousse, Suzanne and André Gousse. *Lexique illustré du costume en Nouvelle-France, 1740–1760.* Chambly, Québec: Fleur de Lyse, 1995.

Greer, Allan. "Colonial Saints: Gender, Race, and Hagiography in New France." *William and Mary Quarterly* 57, 2 (2000): 323–48.

———, ed. *The Jesuit Relations: Natives and Missionaries in Seventeenth-Century North America.* Boston: Bedford/St. Martin's, 2000.

———. *Mohawk Saint: Catherine Tekakwitha and the Jesuits.* New York: Oxford University Press, 2005.

——. *Peasant, Lord, and Merchant: Rural Society in Three Quebec Parishes, 1740–1840.* Toronto: University of Toronto Press, 1985.

——. *The People of New France.* Toronto: University of Toronto Press, 1997.

Grégoire, Vincent. "L'Éducation des filles au Couvent des Ursulines de Québec à l'époque de Marie de l'Incarnation (1639–1672)." *Seventeenth-Century French Studies* 17 (1995): 87–98.

Gringhuis, Dirk. "Indian Costume at Mackinac: Seventeenth and Eighteenth Century." *Mackinac History: An Informal Series of Illustrated Vignettes* 2, 1 (1972).

Gums, Bonnie L. *Archaeology at French Colonial Cahokia.* Springfield: Illinois Historic Preservation Agency, 1988.

Gums, Bonnie L. and Charles O. Witty. "A Glimpse of Village Life at Nouvelle Chartres." *Illinois Archeology* 12, 1 (2000).

Haefeli, Evan and Kevin Sweeney. *Captive Histories: English, French, and Native Narratives of the 1704 Deerfield Raid.* Amherst: University of Massachusetts Press, 2006.

——. *Captors and Captives: The 1704 French and Indian Raid on Deerfield.* Amherst: University of Massachusetts Press, 2003.

Hall, Gwendolyn Midlo. *Africans in Colonial Louisiana: The Development of Afro-Creole Culture in the Eighteenth Century.* Baton Rouge: Louisiana State University Press, 1995.

Hamilton, Peter Joseph. *The Founding of Mobile, 1702–1718.* Mobile: Commercial Print Co., 1911.

Hanger, Kimberly S. *Bounded Lives, Bounded Places: Free Black Society in Colonial New Orleans, 1769–1803.* Durham, N.C.: Duke University Press, 1997.

Hanson, James. "Point Blankets." *Museum of the Fur Trade Quarterly* 33, 3 (1997): 6.

Hardcastle, David. "The Military Organization of French Colonial Louisiana." In *The Military Presence on the Gulf Coast,* ed. William S. Coker. Proceedings of the Gulf Coast History and Humanities Conference 7. Pensacola, Fla.: Gulf Coast History and Humanities Conference, 1978.

——. "Swiss Mercenary Soldiers in the Service of France in Louisiana." In *Proceedings of the Fourth Meeting of the French Colonial Historical Society,* ed. Alf Andrew Heggoy and James J. Cooke. Washington, D.C.: University Press of America, 1979. 82–91.

Hardy, James D., Jr. "The Transportation of Convicts to Colonial Louisiana." *Louisiana History* 7 (1966): 115–24.

Hardy, Jean-Pierre and David-Thierry Ruddel, *Les Apprentis artisans à Québec 1660–1815.* Montreal: Presses de l'Université de Montréal, 1977.

Hardy, Meredith D. "Living on the Edge: Foodways and Early Expressions of Creole Culture on the French Colonial Gulf Coast Frontier." In Kelly and Hardy, eds., *French Colonial Archaeology,* 152–88.

Hart, Avril and Susan North. *Historical Fashion in Detail: The 17th and 18th Centuries.* London: V&A, 2009.

Harter, John Burton and Mary Louise Tucker. *The Louisiana Portrait Gallery.* Vol. 1, *To 1870.* Baton Rouge: Louisiana State Museum, 1979.

Hatley, Thomas M., Gregory A. Waselkov, and Peter H. Wood. *Powhatan's Mantle: Indians in the Colonial Southeast.* Lincoln: University of Nebraska Press, 1989.

Haudrière, Philippe. *La Compagnie française des Indes au XVIIIème siècle (1719–1795).* Paris: Librairie de l'Inde, 1989.

Haugland, H. Kristina. "The Art of Natural Good Breeding: Dress and Deportment in Eighteenth-Century England." In *Dressing 'Em Up: 18th Century Costume & Custom.* 44th Washington Antiques Show. Washington, D.C., 1999. 67–74.

Haulman, Katherine. "Fashion and the Culture Wars of Revolutionary Philadelphia." *William and Mary Quarterly* 3rd ser. 62 (2005): 625–62.

Hauser, Raymond. "The Berdache and the Illinois Indian Tribe During the Last Half of the Seventeenth Century." *Ethnohistory* 37, 1 (1990): 45–65.

——. "The Fox Raid of 1752: Defensive Warfare and the Decline of the Illinois Indian Tribe." *Journal of the Illinois State Historical Society* 86, 4 (1993): 210–24.

——. "The Illinois Indian Tribe: From Autonomy and Self-Sufficiency to Dependency and Depopulation." *Journal of the Illinois State Historical Society* 69, 2 (1976): 127–38.

——. "The Other Half: Women and the Illinois Indian Tribe." *Illinois Heritage* 1, 1 (1997): 6–10.

——. "Warfare and the Illinois Indian Tribe During the Seventeenth Century: An Exercise in Ethnohistory." *Old Northwest Journal of Regional Life and Letters* 10, 4 (1984–85): 367–88.

Havard, Gilles. *Empire et métissages: Indiens et français dans le Pays d'en Haut, 1660–1715.* Sillery Québec: Septentrion, 2003.

——. "'Les forcer à devenir cytoyens': État, sauvages et citoyenneté en Nouvelle-France (XVIIe–XVIIIe siècle). *Annales* 64 (2009): 985–1018.

——. "Le Rire des jésuites: Archéologie du mimétisme dans la rencontre franco-amérindienne (XVIIe–XVIIIe siècle)." *Annales HSS* 62 (2007): 539–74.

Havard, Gilles and Cécile Vidal. *Histoire de l'Amérique française.* Paris: Flammarion, 2003.

——. "Making New France New Again: French Historians Rediscover Their American Past." *Common-Place* 7, 4 (2007). http://www.common-place.org/vol-07/no-04/harvard/.

Heaney, Jane Frances. *A Century of Pioneering: A History of the Ursuline Nuns in New Orleans, 1727–1827.* New Orleans: Ursuline Sisters of New Orleans, 1993.

Heerman, M. Scott. "That 'A'cursed Illinois Venture": Slavery and Revolution in Atlantic Illinois." *Journal of Illinois History* 13 (2010): 107–28.

Hennepin, Father Louis. *Description de la Louisiane nouvellement découverte au sud-ouest de la Nouvelle-France, par ordre du roy: Avec la carte du pays; les moeurs et la manière de vivre des sauvages, dediée à Sa Majesté.* Paris, 1683.

——. *A New Discovery of a Vast Country in America.* 2 vols. Chicago: McClurg, 1903.

Higginbotham, Jay. *Old Mobile: Fort Louis de la Louisiane, 1702–1711.* Mobile: Museum of the City of Mobile, 1977. Reprint Tuscaloosa: University of Alabama Press, 1991.

Hinderaker, Eric. *Elusive Empires: Constructing Colonialism in the Ohio Valley, 1673–1800.* New York: Cambridge University Press, 1999.

Hodson, Christopher. "Weird Science: Identity in the Atlantic World." *William and Mary Quarterly* 3rd ser. 68, 4 (2011): 227–32.

Hoffmann, John, ed. *A Guide to the History of Illinois.* New York: Greenwood, 1991.

Holden, Jack et al. *Furnishing Louisiana: Creole and Acadian Furniture, 1735–1835.* New Orleans: Historic New Orleans Collection, 2010.

Hood, Adrienne D. *The Weaver's Craft: Cloth, Commerce, and Industry in Early Pennsylvania.* Philadelphia: University of Pennsylvania Press, 2003.

Horse Capture, George P., Anne Vitart, Michel Waldberg, and R. Richard West. *Robes of Splendor: Native North American Painted Buffalo Hides.* New York: New Press, 1993.

Hotz, Gottfried. *The Segesser Hide Paintings: Masterpieces Depicting Spanish Colonial New Mexico.* Santa Fe: Museum of New Mexico Press, 1991.

Hudson, Nicholas. "From 'Nation' to 'Race': The Origin of Racial Classification in Eighteenth-Century Thought." *Eighteenth-Century Studies* 29 (1996): 247–64.

Hurtado, Albert L. "When Strangers Met: Sex and Gender on Three Frontiers." *Frontiers* 17, 3 (1996): 52–75.

Hutchins, Thomas. *A Topographical Description of Virginia, Pennsylvania, Maryland, and North Carolina*. 1778. Reprint Cleveland: Burrows Brothers, 1904.

Ingersoll, Thomas N. "Free Blacks in a Slave Society: New Orleans, 1718–1812." *William and Mary Quarterly* 3rd ser. 48 (1991): 173–200.

———. *Mammon and Manon in Early New Orleans: The First Slave Society in the Deep South, 1718–1819*. Knoxville: University of Tennessee Press, 1999.

———. "Slave Codes and Judicial Practice in New Orleans, 1718–1807." *Law and History Review* 13 (1995): 23–62.

Jacquin, Philippe. *Les Indiens blancs: Français et indiens en Amérique du Nord (XVIe–XVIIe siecle)*. Paris: Payot, 1987.

Jaenen, Cornelius J. "The Frenchification and Evangelization of the Amerindians in Seventeenth Century New France." *Canadian Catholic Historical Association Study Sessions* 35 (1968): 57–71.

———. *Friend and Foe: Aspects of French-Amerindian Cultural Contact in the Sixteenth and Seventeenth Centuries*. New York: Columbia University Press, 1976.

———. "Miscegenation in Eighteenth Century New France." In *New Dimensions in Ethnohistory: Papers of the Second Laurier Conference on Ethnohistory and Ethnology*, ed. Barry Gough and Laird Christie. Hull: Canadian Museum of Civilization, 1991. 79–115.

Jelks, Edward B., Carl J. Ekberg, and Terrance J. Martin. *Excavations at the Laurens Site: Probable Location of Fort de Chartres I*. Studies in Illinois Archaeology 5. Springfield: Illinois Historic Preservation Agency, 1989.

Jenner, Mark. "Bathing and Baptism: Sir John Floyer and the Politics of Cold Bathing." In *Refiguring Revolutions: Aesthetics and Politics from the English Revolution to the Romantic Revolution*, ed. Kevin Sharpe and Steven N. Zwicker. Berkeley: University of California Press, 1998. 197–216.

Jennings, Francis. *The Ambiguous Iroquois Empire: The Covenant Chain Confederation of Indian Tribes with English Colonies from Its Beginnings to the Lancaster Treaty of 1744*. New York: Norton, 1984.

Johnson, Jerah. "Colonial New Orleans: A Fragment of the Eighteenth-Century French Ethos." In *Creole New Orleans: Race and Americanization*, ed. Arnold R. Hirsch and Joseph Logsdon. Baton Rouge: Louisiana State University Press, 1992. 12–54.

———. "*La Coutume de Paris*: Louisiana's First Law." *Louisiana History* 30 (1989): 145–55.

Jonah, Anne Marie Lane. "Unequal Transitions: Two Métis Women in Eighteenth-Century Île Royale." *French Colonial History* 11 (2010): 109–29.

Jones, Jennifer M. "Repackaging Rousseau: Femininity and Fashion in Old Regime France." *French Historical Studies* 18, 4 (1994): 939–67.

———. *Sexing la Mode: Gender, Fashion, and Commercial Culture in Old Regime France*. New York: Berg, 2004.

Jouanna, Arlette. *L'Idée de race en France au XVIème siècle et au début du XVIIème siècle (1498–1614)*. 3 vols. Lille: Atelier de Reproduction des Thèses, Université Lille III, 1976.

Jumonville, Florence M., comp. *Bibliography of New Orleans Imprints, 1764–1864*. New Orleans: Historic New Orleans Collection, 1989.

Juratic, Sabine and Nicole Pellegrin. "Femmes, villes et travail en France dans la deuxième moitié du XVIIIᵉ siècle." *Histoire, Économie, Société* 13, 3 (1994): 477–500.

Kalm, Pehr. *Peter Kalm's Travels in North America: The America of 1750.* Ed. Adolph Benson. 2 vols. New York: Dover, 1966.

Kaplan, Steven L. "L'Apprentissage au XVIIIe siècle: Le cas de Paris," *Revue d'Histoire Moderne et Contemporaine* 40, 3 (Juillet–Septembre 1993): 436–79

———. "The Luxury Guilds in Paris in the Eighteenth Century," *Francia* 9 (1981): 257–98.

Kan, Sergei. *Memory Eternal: Tlingit Culture and Russian Orthodox Christianity Through Two Centuries.* Seattle: University of Washington Press, 1999.

Keene, David J. "Beyond the Fur Trade: The Eighteenth Century Colonial Economy of French North America as Seen from Fort de Chartres in the Illinois Country." Ph.D. dissertation, University of Wisconsin-Madison, 2002.

Kellogg, Louise Phelps, ed. *Early Narratives of the Northwest, 1634–1699.* New York: Scribner's, 1917.

Kelly, Kenneth G. and Meredith D. Hardy. *French Colonial Archaeology in the Southeast and Caribbean.* Gainesville: University Press of Florida, 2011.

Kenny, Laurence J., S.J. "The First American Nun in This Country." *Illinois Catholic Historical Review* 1 (1918): 495–99.

Kent, Timothy J. *Ft. Pontchartrain at Detroit: A Guide to the Daily Lives of Fur Trade and Military Personnel, Settlers, and Missionaries at French Posts.* Detroit: Wayne State University Press, 2002.

Kidwell, Claudia. "Making Choices: The Real and Pictorial Dresses of Margaret Marston Philipse Ogilvie (1728–1807)." In *Dressing 'Em Up: 18th Century Costume & Custom.* 44th Washington Antiques Show. Washington, D.C., 1999, 86–93.

———. "Short Gowns." *Dress* 4 (1978): 30–65.

Knowles, Nathaniel. *The Torture of Captives.* New York: Garland, 1977.

Krakovitch, Odile. *Arrêts, déclarations, édits et ordonnances concernant les colonies.* Paris: Archives Nationales, 1993.

Küchler, Susanne and Daniel Miller. *Clothing as Material Culture.* New York: Berg, 2005.

Kupperman, Karen Ordahl. "Fear of Hot Climates in the Anglo-American Colonial Experience." *William and Mary Quarterly* 3rd ser. 41 (1984): 213–40.

———. *Indians and English: Facing Off in Early America.* Ithaca, N.Y.: Cornell University Press, 2000.

———. "Presentment of Civility: English Reading of American Self-Presentation in the Early Years of Colonization." *William and Mary Quarterly* 3rd ser. 54 (1997): 193–228.

Lachance, André. "Une étude de mentalité: Les injures verbales au Canada au XVIIIe siècle (1712–1748)." *Revue d'Histoire de l'Amérique française* 31, 2 (1977): 229–38.

Lagarde, Francois. *The French in Texas: History, Migration, Culture.* Austin: University of Texas Press, 2003.

La Grenade, Monique. "Le Costume civil à Louisburg au XVIIIe siècle." Master's thesis, University of Montreal, 1974.

Lamontagne, Roland. *Textiles et documents Maurepas.* Montreal: Leméac, 1970.

Lande, Lawrence M. *The Development of the Voyageur Contract (1686–1821).* Montreal: Lawrence Lande Foundation for Canadian Historical Research, 1989.

Lallement, Jérôme. *Constitutions et règlements des premiéres Ursulines de Quebec.* 1647. Ed. Gabrielle Lapointe. Québec: s.n., 1974.

Laqueur, Thomas Walker. *Making Sex: Body and Gender from the Greeks to Freud.* Cambridge, Mass.: Harvard University Press, 1992.

La Salle, Robert Cavelier de. *Relation of the Discoveries and Voyages of Cavelier de La Salle from 1679 to 1681: The Official Narrative.* Trans. Melville Best Anderson. Chicago: Caxton Club, 1901.

Lazarus, Keo Felker. *Coif, Cape and Canoe: A Study of Women's Dress at an Early French Outpost.* Lafayette, Ind.: Tippecanoe County Historical Association, 1971.

Leavelle, Tracy Neal. "'Bad Things' and 'Good Hearts': Mediation, Meaning, and the Language of Illinois Christianity." *Church History* 76, 2 (2007): 363–94.

———. *The Catholic Calumet: Colonial Conversions in French and Indian North America* Philadelphia: University of Pennsylvania Press, 2011.

———. "Geographies of Encounter: Religion and Contested Spaces in Colonial North America." *American Quarterly* 56, 4 (2004): 913–43.

———. "Religion, Encounter, and Community in French and Indian North America." Ph.D. dissertation, Arizona State University, 2001.

———. "Why Were Illinois Women Attracted to Catholicism, 1665–1750?" Edited and annotated documentary sources, *Women and Social Movements in the United States, 1600–2000* 11 (June 2007). womhist.alexanderstreet.com/issueV11N2.htm

Lefrançois, Thierry, ed. *La Traite de la fourrure: Les français et la découverte de l'Amérique du Nord.* Thonon-les-Bains, Haute-Savoie:'Albaron, 1992.

Le Glaunec, Jean-Pierre. "'Un nègre nommé Lubin ne connaissant pas Sa Nation': Africans and 'Africanization' in Saint Charles Parish, Louisiana, 1780–1812." Paper presented at workshop on "Louisiana and the Atlantic World in the Eighteenth and Nineteenth-Centuries," École des Hautes Études en Sciences Sociales, Paris, and Tulane University, New Orleans, April 2008.

Legrand, A. and Felix Marec. *Archives de l'Arrondissement maritime de Lorient: Inventaire des archives de la Compagnie des Indes (sous-série 1P).* Paris: Imprimerie de la Marine, 1978.

Lemann, Susan Gibbs. "The Problems of Founding a Viable Colony: The Military in Early French Louisiana." In *Proceedings of the Sixth and Seventh Annual Meetings of the French Colonial Historical Society, 1980–1981,* ed. James J. Cooke. Washington, D.C.: University Press of America, 1982.

Lemire, Beverly. *Dress, Culture, Commerce: The English Clothing Trade Before the Factory, 1660–1800.* New York: Palgrave Macmillan, 1997.

———. *Fashion's Favourite: The Cotton Trade and the Consumer in Britain, 1660–1800.* New York: Oxford University Press, 1991.

———. "The Theft of Clothes and Popular Consumerism in Early Modern England." *Journal of Social History* 24, 2 (1990): 255–76.

———. "Transforming Consumer Custom: Linen, Cotton, and the English Market 1600–1800." In *The European Linen Industry in Historical Perspective,* ed. Brenda Collins and Philip Ollerenshaw. Oxford: Oxford University Press, 2004. 187–207.

Le Page du Pratz, Antoine Simon. *Histoire de la Louisiane: Contenant la découverte de ce vaste pays; sa description géographique; un voyage dans les terres; l'histoire naturelle; les moeurs, coûtumes & religion des naturels, avec leurs origines; deux voyages dans le nord du nouveau Mexique, dont un jusqu'à la mer du sud; ornée de deux cartes & de 40 planches en taille douce.* 3 vols. Paris: De Bure, l'aîné, 1758.

———. *The History of Louisiana.* 1774. Facsimile reprint. Ed. Joseph G. Tregle. Baton Rouge: Louisiana State University Press, 1975.

Lepore, Jill. *Encounters in the New World: A History in Documents.* New York: Oxford University Press, 2002.

Lescarbot, Marc. *The History of New France.* 1618. Ed. and trans. W. L. Grant. 3 vols. Toronto: Champlain Society, 1907–14.

Lespagnol, André. "Des toiles bretonnes aux toiles 'Bretagne': Conditions et facteurs d'émergence d'un 'produit-phare' sur les marchés ibériques." In *Échanges et cultures textiles dans L'Europe pré-industrielle*, ed. Jacques Bottin and Nicole Pellegrin. Villeneuve-d'Ascq,: Université Charles-de-Gaulle-Lille III, 1996. 179–92.

Lessard, Renald, Jacques Mathieu, and Lina Gouger. "Peuplement colonisateur au pays des Illinois." In *Proceedings of the Twelfth Meeting of the French Colonial Historical Society, Ste. Genevieve, May 1986*, ed. Philip P. Boucher and Serge Courville. Lanham, Md.: University Press of America, 1988. 577–68.

Lewis, Jan Ellen, "Cleanliness and Culture." *William and Mary Quarterly* 3rd ser. 68, 4 (2011): 671–78.

———. "Cleanliness and Culture: Further Thoughts." *William and Mary Quarterly* 3rd ser. 68, 4 (2011): 694–96.

Lindman, Janet Moore and Michele Lise Tarter, eds. *A Centre of Wonders: The Body in Early America*. Ithaca, N.Y.: Cornell University Press, 2001.

Little, Ann M. *Abraham in Arms: War and Gender in Colonial New England*. Philadelphia: University of Pennsylvania Press, 2007.

———. "Bodies, Geographies, and the Environment." *William and Mary Quarterly* 3rd ser. 68, 4 (2011): 679–85

———. "L'Étrangère: Leadership and Identity Politics in an Eighteenth-Century Ursuline Convent." Paper presented at the Western Society for French History annual conference, Quebec, November 7, 2008.

———. "'Shoot That Rogue, for He Hath an Englishman's Coat On!': Cultural Cross-Dressing on the New England Frontier, 1620–1760." *New England Quarterly* 74, 2 (2001): 238–73.

———. "Where the Boys Were." *William and Mary Quarterly* 3rd ser. 68, 4 (2011): 697–98.

Loren, Diana DiPaolo. *The Archaeology of Clothing and Bodily Adornment in Colonial America*. Gainesville: University Press of Florida, 2010.

———. "Beyond the Visual: Considering the Archaeology of Colonial Sounds." *International Journal of Historical Archaeology* 12, 4 (2008): 360–69.

———. "Colonial Dress at the Spanish Presidio of Los Adaes." *Southern Studies* 7, 1 (1996): 45–64.

———. "The Intersections of Colonial Policy and Colonial Practice: Creolization on the Eighteenth-Century Louisiana/Texas Frontier." *Historical Archaeology* 34, 3 (2000): 85–98.

———. "Refashioning a Body Politic in Colonial Louisiana." *Cambridge Archaeological Journal* 13 (2003): 231–37.

———. "Threads: Collecting Cloth in the North American French Colonies." *Archaeologies* 4, 1 (2008): 50–66.

Lubbers, Klaus. "Colonial Images of Native Americans: The Problem of Authenticity." *American Studies* 37, 2 (1992): 189–205.

Lux-Sterritt, Laurence. *Redefining Female Religious Life: French Ursulines and English Ladies in Seventeenth-Century Catholicism*. Aldershot: Ashgate, 2006.

Ly-Tio-Fane Pineo, Huguette. *Île de France, 1715–1746: L'émergence de Port Louis*. 2 vols. Moka, Mauritius: Mahatma Gandhi Institute, 1993.

Mackie, Erin Skye. "Cultural Cross-Dressing: The Colorful Case of the Caribbean Creole." In *The*

Clothes That Wear Us: Essays on Dressings and Transgressing in Eighteenth-Century Culture, ed. Jessica Munns and Penny Richards. Newark: University of Delaware Press, 1999. 250–70.

Maduell, Charles R., ed. *The Census Tables for the French Colony of Louisiana from 1699 Through 1732.* Baltimore: Genealogical Publishing, 1972.

Mahé, John A. and Rosanne McCaffrey, eds. *Encyclopædia of New Orleans Artists, 1718–1918.* New Orleans: Historic New Orleans Collection, 1987.

Main, Gloria L. "Notes and Documents: Probate Records as a Source for Early American History." *William and Mary Quarterly* 32, 1 (January 1975): 89–99.

Mainfort, Robert C., Jr. *Indian Social Dynamics in the Period of European Contact: Fletcher Site Cemetery, Bay County, Michigan.* East Lansing: Michigan State University, 1979.

Mandell, Daniel R. "The Saga of Sarah Muckamugg: Indian and African American Intermarriage in Colonial New England." In *Sex, Love, Race: Crossing Boundaries in North American History*, ed. Martha Hodes. New York: New York University Press, 1999. 72–90.

Margry, Pierre, ed. *Découvertes et établissements des français dans l'ouest et dans le sud de l'Amérique septentrionale, 1614–1754: Mémoires et documents originaux recueillis et pub.* 5 vols. Paris: D. Jouaust, 1876–86.

———. *Relations et mémoires inédits pour servir à l'histoire de la France dans les pays d'outre-mer.* Paris: Challamel Aîné, 1867.

Marrero, Karen. "A Tale of Three Marguerites: Women's Lives and Roles in Detroit and New France." Paper presented at the Women of New France series of the Fort St. Joseph Archaeological Project, Niles, Michigan, July 2010.

Marschner, Joanna. "Baths and Bathing at the Early Georgian Court." *Furniture History: The Journal of the Furniture History Society* 31 (1995): 23–28.

Martin, Ann Smart. *Buying into the World of Goods: Early Consumers in Backcountry Virginia.* Baltimore: Johns Hopkins University Press, 2008.

———. "Material Things and Cultural Meanings: Notes on the Study of Early American Material Culture." *William and Mary Quarterly* 53, 1 (January 1996): 5–12.

———. "The Role of Pewter as Missing Artifact: Consumer Attitudes Toward Tablewares in Late 18th Century Virginia." *Historical Archaeology* 23, 2 (1989): 1–27.

Martin, Ann Smart and J. Ritchie Garrison, eds. *American Material Culture: The Shape of the Field.* Winterthur, Del.: Winterthur Museum, 1997.

Massicote, É. Z. "Le Costume des voyageurs et des coureurs de bois." *Bulletin des Recherches Historiques* 48, 8 (1942): 235–40.

Masthay, Carl, ed. *Kaskaskia Illinois-to-French Dictionary.* St. Louis: Carl Masthay, 2002.

Maynard, Margaret. *Fashioned from Penury: Dress as Cultural Practice in Colonial Australia.* Cambridge: Cambridge University Press, 1994.

Mazrim, Robert. "Recent Research at the French Village of Peoria." *Illinois Heritage* 7, 1 (2003): 12–15.

———. "Rethinking the Dawn of History: The Schedule, Signature, and Agency of European Goods in Protohistoric Illinois." *Midcontinental Journal of Archaeology*, 32, 2 (2007): 145–200.

McCafferty, Michael. *Native American Place Names of Indiana.* Urbana: University of Illinois Press, 2008.

———. "Correction: Etymology of *Missouri*." *American Speech*, 79, 1 (2004): 32.

McClintock, Anne. *Imperial Leather: Race, Gender, and Sexuality in the Imperial Contest.* London: Routledge, 1995.

McDermott, John Francis, ed. *The French in the Mississippi Valley*. Urbana: University of Illinois Press, 1965.

——. *Frenchmen and French Ways in the Mississippi Valley*. Urbana: University of Illinois Press, 1969.

——. *Glossary of Mississippi Valley French, 1673–1850*. St. Louis, 1941.

——. *Old Cahokia: A Narrative and Documents Illustrating the First Century of its History*. St. Louis: St. Louis Historical Documents Foundation, 1949.

McGowan, James T. "Creation of a Slave Society: Louisiana Plantations in the Eighteenth Century." Ph.D. dissertation, University of Rochester, 1976.

McMillen, Margot Ford and Heather Roberson. "Ignon Ouaconisen, or 'Françoise of the Missouri Nation.'" Chap. 1 in *Called to Courage: Four Women in Missouri History*. Columbia: University of Missouri Press, 2002.

Melzer, Sara E. "The French Relation and Its 'Hidden' Colonial History." In *A Companion to the Literatures of Colonial America*, ed. Susan Castillo and Ivy Schweitzer. Malden, Mass.: Blackwell, 2005. 220–40.

——. "L'Histoire oubliée de la colonisation française: Universaliser la 'Francité.'" *Dalhousie French Studies* 65 (Winter 2003): 36–44.

——. "Le Nouveau Monde et la querelle des Anciens et des Modernes dans de Furetière." *Littératures Classiques* 47 (Winter 2003): 133–48.

——. "The Magic of French Culture: Transforming 'Savages' into French Catholics in Seventeenth-Century France." In *The Meanings of Magic: From the Bible to Buffalo Bill*, ed. Amy Wygant. New York: Berghahn, 2006. 136–60.

——. "Myths of Mixture in *Phèdre* and the Sun King's Assimilation Policy in the New World." *Esprit Créateur* 38, 2 (Summer 1998): 72–81.

——. "The *Relation de voyage*: A Forgotten Genre of 17th-Century France." In *Relations and Relationships in Seventeenth-Century French Literature*, ed. Jennifer R. Perlmutter, 33–52. Tübingen: Narr, 2006.

——. "The Underside of France's Civilizing Mission: Assimilationist Politics in 'New France.'" In *Classical Unities: Place, Time, Action*, ed. Erec R. Koch. Tübingen: Narr, 2002. 151–64.

Melzer, Sara E. and Kathryn Norberg, eds. *From the Royal to the Republican Body: Incorporating the Political in Seventeenth- and Eighteenth-Century France*. Berkeley: University of California Press, 1998.

Menier, Marie-Antoinette et al., comps. *Inventaire des archives coloniales: Correspondance à l'arrivée en provenance de la Louisiane*. 2 vols. Paris: Archives Nationales, 1976–83.

Mereness, Newton Dennison, ed. *Travels in the American Colonies*. New York: Macmillan, 1916.

Merrell, James Hart. *Into the American Woods: Negotiators on the Pennsylvania Frontier*. New York: Norton, 1991.

Merritt, Jane T. *At the Crossroads: Indians and Empires on a Mid-Atlantic Frontier, 1700–1763*. Chapel Hill: University of North Carolina Press, 2003.

Meyer, Jean. *La Noblesse bretonne au XVIIIe siècle*. Bibliothèque Générale de l'École Pratique des Hautes Études. Paris: S.E.V.P.E.N., 1966.

Mézin, Louis. "Nouvelles acquisitions du Musée de la Compagnie des Indes: Nouvelles présentations." *Cahiers de la Compagnie des Indes* 2 (1997).

Miller, Christopher L. and George R. Hamell. "A New Perspective on Indian-White Contact: Cultural Symbols and Colonial Trade." *Journal of American History* 73, 2 (September 1986): 315–20.

Miller, J. Jefferson. *Eighteenth-Century Ceramics from Fort Michilimackinac: A Study in Historical Archeology.* Washington, D.C.: Smithsonian Institution Press, 1970.

Miller, Marla R. *The Needle's Eye: Women and Work in the Age of Revolution.* Amherst: University of Massachusetts Press, 2006.

Mills, Donna. *The First Families of Louisiana: An Index to Glenn R. Conrad's 2-Volume Series of 1970.* Tuscaloosa Ala.: Mills Historical Press, 1992.

Mills, Elizabeth Shown. *Chauvin dit Charleville.* State College: Mississippi State University, 1976.

Mills, Gary B. "The Chauvin Brothers: Early Colonists of Louisiana." *Louisiana History* 15, 2 (1974): 117–32.

Milne, George Edward. "Rising Suns, Fallen Forts, and Impudent Immigrants: Race, Power, and War in the Lower Mississippi Valley." Ph.D. dissertation, University of Oklahoma, 2006.

Montgomery, Florence M. *Textiles in America, 1650–1870.* New York: Norton, 1984.

Moogk, Peter N. "Reluctant Exiles: Emigrants from France in Canada Before 1760." *William and Mary Quarterly* 46, 3 (1989): 463–505.

Morgan, M. J. *Land of Big Rivers: French and Indian Illinois, 1699–1778.* Carbondale: Southern Illinois University Press, 2010.

Morris, Christopher. "Impenetrable but Easy: The French Transformation of the Lower Mississippi Valley and the Founding of New Orleans." In *Transforming New Orleans and Its Environs: Centuries of Change,* ed. Craig E. Colten. Pittsburgh: University of Pittsburgh Press, 2000. 22–42

Morrissey, Robert Michael. "Bottomlands and Borderlands: Empires and Identities in the Illinois Country, 1673–1785." Ph.D. dissertation, Yale University, 2006.

——. "Facebook Kaskaskia: Kinship and Social Networks in a French-Illinois Borderland, 1695–1735." Paper presented at 126th Annual Meeting of the American Historical Association, Chicago, January 5–8, 2012.

——. "'I Speak It Well': Language, Cultural Understanding, and the End of a Missionary Middle Ground in Illinois Country, 1673–1712." *Early American Studies* 9 (2011): 618–48.

Moussette, Marcel. "An Encounter in the Baroque Age: French and Amerindians in North America." *Historical Archaeology* 37, 4 (2003): 29–39.

Murphy, Lucy Eldersveld. *A Gathering of Rivers: Indians, Métis, and Mining in the Western Great Lakes, 1737–1832.* Lincoln: University of Nebraska Press, 2000.

Murphy, Lucy Eldersveld and Wendy Haman Venet, eds. *Midwestern Women: Work, Community, and Leadership at the Crossroads.* Bloomington: Indiana University Press, 1997.

Nadal, Gerónimo [Jerome]. *Evangelicae historiae imagines, ex ordine evangeliorum quae toto anno in missae sacrificio recitantur, in ordinem temporis vitae Christi digestae.* Antwerp: [Martin Nutius], 1593.

——, ed. *The Illustrated Spiritual Exercises.* English preface by Richard W. Rousseau. Scranton, Pa.: University of Scranton Press, 2001.

Náñez Falcón, Guillermo, ed. *The Favrot Family Papers: A Documentary Chronicle of Early Louisiana.* New Orleans: Howard Tilton Memorial Library, Tulane University, 1988.

Nassaney, Michael Shakir and José António Brandão. "Archaeological Evidence of Economic Activities at an Eighteenth-Century Frontier Outpost in the Western Great Lakes." *Historical Archaeology* 41, 4 (2007): 3–19.

Neitzel, Robert. *Archeology of the Fatherland Site: The Grand Village of the Natchez.* New York: American Museum of Natural History, 1965.

———. *The Grand Village of the Natchez Revisited: Excavations at the Fatherland Site, Adams County, Mississippi, 1972.* Jackson: Mississippi Deptartment of Archives and History, 1983.

Newman, Simon P. "Wearing Their Hearts on Their Sleeves: Reading the Tattoos of Early American Seafarers." In *American Bodies: Cultural Histories of the Physique*, ed. Tim Armstrong. New York: New York University Press, 1996.

Noble, Vergil E., Jr. "Eighteenth-Century Ceramics from Fort de Chartres III." *Illinois Archaeology* 9 (1997): 36–78.

Noel, Jan. "Caste and Clientage in an Eighteenth-Century Quebec Convent." *Canadian Historical Review* 82, 3 (2001): 465–90.

Nolan, Charles E. *A Southern Catholic Heritage.* Vol. 1, *Colonial Period, 1704–1813.* New Orleans: Archdiocese of New Orleans, 1976.

———. *Sacramental Records of the Roman Catholic Church of the Archdiocese of New Orleans,* 12 vols. New Orleans: Archdiocese of New Orleans, 1987–1997.

Norall, Frank. *Bourgmont, Explorer of the Missouri, 1698–1725.* Lincoln: University of Nebraska Press, 1988.

Norberg, Kathryn. "Bodies in European and American Historiography." *William and Mary Quarterly* 3rd ser. 68, 4 (2011): 686–89.

———. "Cleanliness and Rights." *William and Mary Quarterly* 3rd ser. 68, 4 (2011): 699–700.

North, Susan and Jenny Tiramani. *Seventeenth-Century Women's Dress Patterns.* London: V&A, 2011.

Olivier-Martin, François. *Histoire de la coutume de la prévôté et vicomté de Paris.* 2 vols. Paris: Leroux, 1922–30.

O'Neill, Charles Edwards. *Church and State in French Colonial Louisiana: Policy and Politics to 1732.* New Haven, Conn.: Yale University Press, 1966.

Oury, Don Guy, ed. *Correspondance: Marie de l'Incarnation.* Solesmes, France: Abbaye Saint-Pierre, 1971.

Oszuscik, Philippe. "The French Creole Cottage and Its Caribbean Connection." In *French and Germans in the Mississippi Valley: Landscape and Cultural Traditions*, ed. Michael Roark. Cape Girardeau: Center for Regional History and Cultural Heritage, Southeast Missouri State University, 1988. 61–78.

Palm, Mary Borgias. *The Jesuit Missions of the Illinois Country, 1673–1763.* Cleveland, 1933.

Paradis, Andrée. "L'Avènement d'un costume canadien d'après les documents du fonds Madeleine-Doyon-Ferland." *Cap-aux-Diamants* 4, 2 (1988): 11–14.

Parent, France and Geneviève Postolec. "Quand Thémis rencontre Clio: Les femmes et le droit en Nouvelle-France." *Les Cahiers de Droit* 36 (1995): 293–318.

Paresys, Isabelle. "The Dressed Body: The Molding of Identities in Sixteenth-Century France." In *Cultural Exchange in Early Modern Europe*, ed. Robert Muchembled. 4 vols. Cambridge: Cambridge University Press, 2007. 6: 227–57.

Pargellis, Stanley. "An Account of the Indians in Virginia." *William and Mary Quarterly* 3rd ser. 16 (1959): 228–43.

Pastoureau, Michel. *Blue: The History of a Color.* Princeton, N.J.: Princeton University Press, 2001.

———. *The Devil's Cloth: A History of Stripes.* Trans. Jody Gladding. New York: Washington Square Press, 2003.

Peabody, Sue. *"There Are No Slaves in France": The Political Culture of Race and Slavery in the Ancien Régime.* New York: Oxford University Press, 1996.

Pease, Theodore Calvin. *Illinois on the Eve of the Seven Years' War, 1747–1755.* Collections of the Illinois State Historical Library French Series 3. Springfield: State Historical Library, 1940.

Pellegrin, Nicole. "Chemises et chiffons: Le vieux et le neuf en Poitou et Limousin, XVIIIe–XIXe siècles," *Ethnologie Française* 16, 3 (1986): 282–94.

———. "Le Goût du bleu: Histoires à suivre." In *Histoires du jeans de 1750 à 1994.* Paris: Palais Galliera, 1994. 43–52.

———. *Les Vêtements de la liberté: Abécédaire des pratiques vestimentaires en France de 1780 à 1800.* Aix-en-Provence: Alinea, 1989.

Pénicaut, André. *Fleur de Lys and Calumet: Being the Pénicaut Narrative of French Adventure in Louisiana.* Trans. and ed. Richebourg Gaillard McWilliams. 1953. Reprint Tuscaloosa: University of Alabama Press, 1988.

Perez, Stanis, ed. *Journal de santé de Louis XIV écrit par Vallot, Daquin et Fagon.* Grenoble: Jérôme Millon, 2004.

Perrin du Lac, M. *Voyage dans les deux Louisianes, et chez les nations sauvages du Missouri . . . en 1801, 1802 et 1803.* Lyon: Bruysset aîné et Buynand, 1805.

Perrot, Nicolas. *Mémoire sur les moeurs, coustumes et religion des sauvages de l'Amérique septentrionale.* Paris, 1864.

Pestana, Carla Gardina and Sharon V. Salinger, eds. *Inequality in Early America.* Hanover, N.H.: Dartmouth College, 1999.

Peterson, Charles E. *Colonial St. Louis: Building a Creole Capital.* St. Louis: Missouri Historical Society, 1949.

——— "Early Ste. Genevieve and Its Architecture." *Missouri Historical Review* 35 (1941): 207–32.

———. "Notes on Old Cahokia: Part Three, American Domination (1778–1790)." *Journal of the Illinois State Historical Society* 42, 3 (1949): 319–43.

Peterson, Jacqueline. "Many Roads to Red River: Métis Genesis in the Great Lakes Region, 1680–1815." In *The New Peoples: Being and Becoming Métis in North America*, ed. Jacqueline Peterson and Jennifer S. H. Brown, 37–72. St. Paul: Minnesota Historical Society Press, 2001.

———. "Prelude to Red River: A Social Portrait of the Great Lakes Metis." *Ethnohistory* 25, 1 (1978): 41–67.

———. "Women Dreaming: The Religiopsychology of Indian-White Marriages and the Rise of Metis Culture." In *Sexual Borderlands: Constructing an American Sexual Past*, ed. Kathleen Kennedy and Sharon Ullman: Ohio State University Press, 2003. 27–44.

Peyser, Joseph L. "The Fall and Rise of Thérèse Catin: A Portrait from Indiana's French and Canadian History." *Indiana Magazine of History* 91, 4 (1995): 361–79.

———. *Jacques Legardeur de Saint-Pierre: Officer, Gentleman, Entrepreneur.* East Lansing: Michigan State University Press, 1996.

Phillips, Ruth B. *Trading Identities: The Souvenir in Native North American Art from the Northeast, 1700–1900.* Seattle: University of Washington Press, 1998.

Phillips, Ruth B. and Dale Idiens. " 'A Casket of Savage Curiosities': Eighteenth-Century Objects from North-eastern North America in the Farquharson Collection." *Journal of the History of Collections* 6 (1994): 21–33.

Piponnier, Françoise. "Linge de maison et linge de corps au Moyen Âge d'après les inventaires bourguignons." *Ethnologie Française* 16 (1986).

Plane, Ann Marie. *Colonial Intimacies: Indian Marriage in Early New England.* Ithaca, N.Y.: Cornell University Press, 2000.

Podruchny, Carolyn. "Baptizing Novices: Ritual Moments Among French Canadian Voyageurs in the Montreal Fur Trade, 1780–1821." *Canadian Historical Review* 83, 2 (2002): 165–95.

———. *Making the Voyageur World: Travelers and Traders in the North American Fur Trade*. Lincoln: University of Nebraska Press, 2006.

Pommereu, Marie-Augustine. *Les Chroniques de l'ordre des Ursulines*. Paris: Henault, 1673.

Portré-Bobinski, Germaine. *Colonial Natchitoches*. 2nd ed. 1966.

———. "French Civilization and Culture in Natchitoches." Ph.D.dissertation, George Peabody College for Teachers, 1940.

———. *Sixain, Selected Sections: Louisiana in Colonial Days, Natchitoches, the Oldest Town in Louisiana*. 1965.

Potter, Gail DeBuse. "The Matchcoat." In *Rethinking the Fur Trade: Cultures of Exchange in the Atlantic World*, ed. Susan Sleeper-Smith. Lincoln: University of Nebraska Press, 2009.

Pritchard, James S. *In Search of Empire: The French in the Americas, 1670–1730*. New York: Cambridge University Press, 2004.

Prude, Jonathan. "To Look upon the 'Lower Sort': Runaway Ads and the Appearance of Unfree Laborers in America, 1750–1800." *Journal of American History* 78 (June 1991): 124–59.

Quimby, George Irving. *Indian Culture and European Trade Goods: The Archaeology of the Historic Period in the Western Great Lakes Region*. Madison: University of Wisconsin Press, 1966.

Rapley, Elizabeth. *The Dévotes: Women and Church in Seventeenth-Century France*. Montreal: McGill-Queen's University Press, 1990.

———. *A Social History of the Cloister: Daily Life in the Teaching Monasteries of the Old Regime*. London: McGill-Queen's University Press, 2001.

Règlemens des religieuses ursulines de la congrégation de Paris. 3 vols. Paris: L. Josse, 1705.

"Relation de l'arrivée en France de quatre Sauvages de Missicipi, de leur sejour, & des audiences qu'ils ont euës du Roi, des Princes du Sang, de la Compagnie des Indes, avec les complimens qu'ils ont faits, les honneurs & les presens qu'ils ont reçûs, &c." *Mercure de France* 1 (December 1725): 2827–59. Facsimile ed. Geneva: Slatkine.

Ribeiro, Aileen. *The Art of Dress: Fashion in England and France 1750–1820*. New Haven, Conn.: Yale University Press, 1995.

———. *Dress and Morality*. New York: Holmes & Meier, 1986.

———. *Dress in Eighteenth-Century Europe, 1751–1789*. Rev. ed. New Haven, Conn.: Yale University Press, 2002.

———. *The Dress Worn at Masquerades in England, 1730 to 1790, and Its Relation to Fancy Dress in Portraiture*. London: Garland, 1984.

———. *Fashion and Fiction: Dress in Art and Literature in Stuart England*. New Haven, Conn.: Yale University Press, 2005.

———. *Fashion in the French Revolution*. New York: Holmes & Meier, 1988.

———. "Re-Fashioning Art: Some Visual Approaches to the Study of the History of Dress." *Fashion Theory* 2, 4 (1998): 315–25.

Ribeiro, Aileen and Valerie Cumming. *The Visual History of Costume*. London: Batsford, 1989.

Richard, Maureen. "Washing Household Linens and Linen Clothing in 1627 Plymouth." *Annual Proceedings, Dublin Seminar for New England Folklife* 26 (2001): 10–21.

Richter, Daniel K., *Before the Revolution: America's Ancient Pasts*. Cambridge, Mass.: Harvard University Press, 2011

——. *Facing East from Indian Country: A Native History of Early America*. Cambridge, Mass.: Harvard University Press, 2003.

——. *The Ordeal of the Longhouse: The Peoples of the Iroquois League in the Era of European Colonization*. Chapel Hill: University of North Carolina Press for Institute of Early American History and Culture, 1992.

Rioux, Jean-Roch; Louis Hennepin. *Dictionary of Canadian Biography Online*. http://www.biographi .ca/EN/ShowBio.asp?Biold=34963&query=accaul.

Rivière, Marc Serge. *Codes Noirs et autres documents concernant l'esclavage (1671-1762)*. Beau Bassin, Mauritius: Osman, 2009.

Roberts, David. "Sieur de La Salle's Fateful Landfall." *Smithsonian* 28, 1 (April 1997): 40-52.

Robin, C.-C. *Voyages dans l'interieur de la Louisiane, de la Floride occidentatle et dans les Iles de la Martinique et de Saint-Dominique pendant les années 1802, 1803, 1804, 1805 et 1806*. 3 vols. Paris: F. Buisson, 1807.

Roche, Daniel. *La Culture des apparences: Une histoire du vêtement, XVIIe–XVIIIe siècle*. Paris: Fayard, 1989.

——. *The Culture of Clothing: Dress and Fashion in the Ancien Régime*. Trans. Jean Birrell. 1994. Reprint New York: Cambridge University Press, 1999.

Roediger, David R. *The Wages of Whiteness: Race and the Making of the American Working Class*. London: Verso, 1991.

Rose, Clare. *Children's Clothes Since 1750*. London: Batsford, 1989.

Rothstein, Natalie, ed. *Barbara Johnson's Album of Fashions and Fabrics (1746-1823)*. London: Thames and Hudson, 1987.

——. *Silk Designs of the Eighteenth Century in the Collection of the Victoria and Albert Museum, London: With a Complete Catalogue*. Boston: Little, Brown, 1990.

Rowland, Dunbar, A. G. Sanders, and Patricia Galloway, eds. and trans. *Mississippi Provincial Archives: French Dominion*. 5 vols. Jackson: Press of the Mississippi Department of Archives and History, 1927-1984.

Rowlandson, Mary. *Captivity and Restoration*. Scotts Valley, Calif.: CreateSpace, 2009.

Roy, Pierre-Georges. *À travers l'histoire des Ursulines de Québec*. Lévis, Québec, 1939.

——, ed. *Rapport de l'archiviste de la Province de Québec pour 1930-1931*. Québec: Rédempti Paradis, 1931.

Ruddel, David-Thiery. "Consumer Trends, Clothing, Textiles, and Equipment in the Montreal Area, 1792-1835." *Material History Bulletin* 32 (1990): 45-64.

——. "Domestic Textile Production in Colonial Quebec, 1608-1840." *Material History Bulletin* 31 (1990): 39-49.

Rushforth, Brett. "'A Little Flesh We Offer You': The Origins of Indian Slavery in New France." *William and Mary Quarterly* 3rd. ser. 60 (2003): 777-803

——. "Savage Bonds: Indian Slavery and Alliance in New France." Ph.D. dissertation, University of California at Davis, 2003.

——. "Slavery, the Fox Wars, and the Limits of Alliance." *William and Mary Quarterly* 3rd. ser. 63 (2006): 53-80.

Rushforth, Brett and Paul W. Mapp. *Colonial North America and the Atlantic World: A History in Documents*. Upper Saddle River, N.J.: Pearson Prentice Hall, 2009.

Rushton, Pauline. *18th Century Costume in the National Museums and Galleries on Merseyside* Liverpool: National Museums Liverpool, 1999.

Saadani, Khalil. "Colonialisme et stratégie: Le rôle des forces militaires en Louisiane, 1731–1743."
    In *France in the New World, Proceedings of the 22nd Annual Meeting of the French Colonial
    Historical Society*, ed. David Buisseret. East Lansing: Michigan State University Press, 1998.
    203–24.

Sahlins, Peter. "Fictions of a Catholic France: The Naturalization of Foreigners, 1685–1787." *Repre-
    sentations* 47 (1994): 85–100.

Sala-Molins, Louis. *Le Code noir, ou Le calvaire de Canaan*. Paris: Quadrige, 2005.

Sanderson, Elizabeth C. "Nearly New: The Second-Hand Clothing Trade in Eighteenth Century
    Edinburgh." *Costume* 31 (1997): 38–48.

———. *Women and Work in Eighteenth-Century Edinburgh*. New York: St. Martin's, 1996.

Savary des Brûlons, Jacques. *Dictionnaire universel de commerce*. 3 vols. Geneva: Cramer & Phi-
    libert, 1742.

———. *Le Parfait Négociant.* . . . Paris: J. Guignard, 1679.

Sayre, Gordon M. "Natchez Ethnohistory Revisited: New Manuscript Sources from Le Page du
    Pratz and Dumont de Montigny." *Louisiana History* 50, 4 (2009): 407–36.

———. "Plotting the Natchez Massacre: Le Page du Pratz, Dumont de Montigny, Chateaubriand."
    Early American Literature 37 (2002): 381–413.

———. *Les Sauvages Américains: Representations of Native Americans in French and English Colo-
    nial Literature*. Chapel Hill: University of North Carolina Press, 1997.

Schenck, Theresa M. "The Cadottes: Five Generations of Fur Traders on Lake Superior." In *The Fur
    Trade Revisited*, East Lansing: Michigan State University Press, 1994. 189–98.

Schlarman, J. H. *From Quebec to New Orleans*. Belleville, Ill.: Buechler, 1929.

Schlereth, Thomas J., ed. *Material Culture: A Research Guide*. Lawrence: University of Kansas Press,
    1985.

———. *Material Culture Studies in America*. Walnut Creek, Calif.: AltaMira Press, 1999.

Scott, Katie and Deborah Cherry, eds. *Between Luxury and the Everyday: Decorative Arts in
    Eighteenth-Century France*. Oxford: Blackwell, 2005.

Seck, Ibrahima. "The Relationships Between St. Louis of Senegal, Its Hinterlands, and Colonial
    Louisiana." In *French Colonial Louisiana and the Atlantic World*, ed. Bradley Bond. Baton
    Rouge: Louisiana State University Press, 2005. 265–90

Séguin, Robert-Lionel. *La Civilisation traditionelle de l'habitant aux XVIIe et XVIIIe siècles*. Mon-
    treal: Fides, 1967.

Severa, Joan. *Dressed for the Photographer: Ordinary Americans and Fashion, 1840–1900*. Kent,
    Ohio: Kent State University Press, 1995.

Shackelford, Alan G. "Navigating the Opportunities of New Worlds: The Land of the Illinois in Pre-
    history, Protohistory, and History." Paper presented at International Seminar on the History of
    the Atlantic World, 1500–1825, Harvard University, August 2004.

Shammas, Carole. *The Pre-Industrial Consumer in England and America*. New York: Clarendon,
    1990.

Shannon, Timothy J. "Dressing for Success on the Mohawk Frontier: Hendrick, William Johnson,
    and the Indian Fashion." *William and Mary Quarterly* 3rd ser. 53, 1 (January 1996): 13–42.

———. *Indians and Colonists at the Crossroads of Empire: The Albany Congress of 1754*. Ithaca, N.Y.:
    Cornell University Press, 2002.

Shea, John Gilmary. *Discovery and Exploration of the Mississippi Valley: With the Original Narra-
    tives of Marquette, Allouez, Membré, Hennepin, and Anastase Douay*. New York: Redfield, 1853.

———, ed. *Early Voyages Up and Down the Mississippi, by Cavelier, St. Cosme, Le Sueur, Gravier, and Guignas*. Albany, N.Y.: Joel Munsell, 1861.

Shoemaker, Nancy. "Body Language: The Body as a Source of Sameness and Difference in Eighteenth-Century American Indian Diplomacy East of the Mississippi." In *A Centre of Wonders: The Body in Early America*, ed. Janet Moore Lindman and Michele Lise Tarter, 211–22. Ithaca, N.Y.: Cornell University Press, 2001.

———."Kateri Tekakwitha's Tortuous Path to Sainthood." In *Negotiators of Change: Historical Perspectives on Native American Women*, ed. Nancy Shoemaker. New York: Routledge, 1995. 49–71.

———. *A Strange Likeness: Becoming Red and White in Eighteenth-Century North America*. New York: Oxford University Press, 2004.

Simmons, David A. "Excavations at the Laurens Site: Probable Location of Fort de Chartres I." *Old Northwest* 14 (1988).

Skinner, Claiborne A. "Marie Rouensa and the Jesuits: Conversion, Gender, and Power." In *Indian Women and French Men*, ed. Colin Galloway and Barry O'Connell. Amherst: University of Massachusetts Press.

———. "The Sinews of Empire: The *Voyageurs* and the Carrying Trade of the Pays d'en Haut." Ph.D. dissertation, University of Illinois at Chicago, 1991.

———. "'[A]n Unpleasant Transaction on This Frontier': Challenging Female Autonomy and Authority at Michilimackinac." *Journal of the Early Republic* 25, 3 (2005): 417–43.

———. *The Upper Country: French Enterprise in the Colonial Great Lakes*. Baltimore: Johns Hopkins University Press, 2008.

Sleeper-Smith, Susan. *Indian Women and French Men: Rethinking Cultural Encounter in the Western Great Lakes*. Amherst: University of Massachusetts Press, 2001.

———, ed. *Rethinking the Fur Trade: Cultures of Exchange in the Atlantic World*. Lincoln: University of Nebraska Press, 2009.

———. "Washing Away Race: The Lost Child; or, The Child Claimed by Two Mothers." Paper presented at the Annual Meeting of the American Studies Association, Albuquerque, N.M., October 2008.

———. "Women, Kin, and Catholicism: New Perspectives on the Fur Trade." *Ethnohistory* 40, 2 (2000): 423–52.

Smith, Virginia. *Clean: A History of Personal Hygiene and Purity*. Oxford: Oxford University Press, 2007.

Smits, David D. "'Abominable Mixture': Toward the Repudiation of Anglo-Indian Intermarriage in Seventeenth-Century Virginia." *Virginia Magazine of History and Biography* 95 (1987): 157–92.

———. "The 'Squaw Drudge': A Prime Index of Savagism." *Ethnohistory* 29, 4 (1982): 281–306.

———. "'We Are Not to Grow Wild': Seventeenth-Century New England's Repudiation of Anglo-Indian Intermarriage." *American Indian Culture and Research Journal* 11, 4 (1987): 1–32.

Snyder, Christina. "Conquered Enemies, Adopted Kin, and Owned People: The Creek Indians and Their Captives." *Southern Historical Association* 73 (2007).

———. *Slavery in Indian Country: The Changing Face of Captivity in Early America*. Cambridge, Mass.: Harvard University Press, 2010.

Sommerville, Suzanne Boivin. *All Sources Are Not Created Equal: The Couc/Montour Family of Nouvelle France and the English Colonies*. CD-ROM. Royal Oak, Mich.: French-Canadian Heritage Society of Michigan, 2009.

Sonenscher, Michael. *The Hatters of Eighteenth-Century France.* Berkeley: University of California Press, 1987.

Spear, Jennifer. "Colonial Intimacies: Legislating Sex in French Louisiana." *William and Mary Quarterly* 60, 1 (2003): 75–98.

———. *Race, Sex, and Social Order in Early New Orleans.* Baltimore: Johns Hopkins University Press, 2009.

———. " 'They Need Wives': Métissage and the Regulation of Sexuality in French Louisiana, 1699–1730." In *Sex, Love, Race: Crossing Boundaries in North American History,* ed. Martha Hodes, 35–59. New York: New York University Press, 1999.

Starna, William A. and Ralph Watkins. "Northern Iroquoian Slavery." *Ethnohistory* 38, 1 (1991): 34–57.

Stavenow-Hidemark, Elisabet, ed. *1700–tals textil: Anders Berchs samling i Nordiska museet.* Stockholm: Nordiska museets förlag, 1990.

St. Charles, Mother. "The First American Born Nun." *Illinois Catholic Historical Review* 1 (1918): 173–75.

Steele, Valerie. *The Corset: A Cultural History.* New Haven, Conn.: Yale University Press, 2001.

Stevens, Paul L. *Louis Lorimier in the American Revolution, 1777–1782: A Mémoire by an Ohio Indian Trader and British Partisan, the Role of One French-Canadian in the American Revolution.* Naperville, Ill.: Center for French Colonial Studies, 1997.

Stevens, Scott Manning. "New World Contacts and the Trope of the 'Naked Savage.' " In *Sensible Flesh: On Touch in Early Modern Culture,* ed. Elizabeth D. Harvey. Philadelphia: University of Pennsylvania Press, 2003. 125–40.

St. George, Robert Blair, ed. *Material Life in America, 1600–1860.* Boston: Northeastern University Press, 1988.

Stoler, Ann Laura, ed. *Haunted by Empire: Geographies of Intimacy in North American History.* Durham, N.C.: Duke University Press, 2006.

———. *Race and the Education of Desire: Foucault's History of Sexuality and the Colonial Order of Things.* Durham, N.C.: Duke University Press, 1995.

Stols, Eddy. "L'Âge d'or du déshabillé: Échanges et cultures vestimentaires au Brésil colonial du XVIIIe siècle." In *Échanges et cultures textiles dans l'Europe pré-industrielle,* ed. Jacques Bottin and Nicole Pellegrin. Villeneuve-d'Ascq: Université Charles-de-Gaulle-Lille III, 1996. 277–94.

Strang, Veronica. *The Meaning of Water.* Oxford: Berg, 2004.

Styles, John. "Dress in History: Reflections on a Contested Terrain." *Fashion Theory* 2, 4 (1998).

———. *The Dress of the People: Everyday Fashion in Eighteenth-Century England.* New Haven, Conn.: Yale University Press, 2007.

———. *Threads of Feeling: The London Foundling Hospital's Textile Tokens, 1740–1770.* London: Foundling Museum, 2010.

Styles, John and Amanda Vickery, eds. *Gender, Taste, and Material Culture in Britain and North America, 1700–1830.* New Haven, Conn.: Yale Center for British Art, 2006.

Surrey, Nancy Miller. *The Commerce of Louisiana During the French Regime, 1699–1763.* New York: Columbia University Press, 1916.

Tanguay, L'Abbé Cyprien. "Les Canadiens en Louisiane." In *À travers les registres: Notes recueillies par l'Abbé Cyprien Tanguay.* Montreal: Librairie Saint-Joseph, Cadieux & Derome, 1886.

———. *Dictionnaire généalogique des familles canadiennes.* 7 vols. Montréal: E. Senécal, 1871–90.

Tanner, Helen Hornbeck. "The Career of Joseph La France, Coureur de Bois in the Upper Great

Lakes." In *The Fur Trade Revisited*, ed. Jennifer S. H. Brown, W. J. Eccles, and Donald P. Heldman. East Lansing: University of Michigan Press, 1994. 171–87.

Taylor, Lou. *Mourning Dress: A Costume and Social History*. London: Allen & Unwin, 1983.

Thépaut-Cabasset, Corinne. *L'Esprit des modes au Grand Siècle*. Paris: CTHS, 2010.

Thomas, Daniel H. *Fort Toulouse: The French Outpost at the Alabamas on the Coosa*. Tuscaloosa: University of Alabama Press, 1989.

Thomas, Keith. "Cleanliness and Godliness in Early Modern England." In *Religion, Culture and Society in Early Modern Britain: Essays in Honour of Patrick Collinson*, ed. Anthony Fletcher and Peter Roberts. Cambridge: Cambridge University Press, 1994.

Thorne, Tanis C. "For the Good of Her People: Continuity and Change for Native Women of the Midwest, 1650–1850." In *Midwestern Women: Work, Community, and Leadership at the Crossroads*, ed. Lucy Eldersveld Murphy and Wendy Hamand Venet. Bloomington: Indiana University Press, 1997. 95–120.

———. *The Many Hands of My Relations: French and Indians on the Lower Missouri*. Columbia: University of Missouri Press, 1996.

Thurman, Melburn D. *Building a House in 18th Century Ste. Genevieve*. Ste. Genevieve, Mo.: Pendragon's Press, 1984.

Thwaites, Reuben Gold, ed. *The Jesuit Relations and Allied Documents: Travels and Explorations of the Jesuit Missionaries in New France, 1610–1791*. 73 vols. Cleveland: Burrows Bros., 1896–1901.

Tobin, Beth Fawkes. *Picturing Imperial Power: Colonial Subjects in Eighteenth-Century British Painting*. Durham, N.C.: Duke University Press, 1999.

Todhunter, Andrew. "Diving into the Wreck." *Preservation* 48, 4 (1996): 60–65.

Tongiorgi, Fabio, ed. *Per una storia della moda pronta: Problemi e ricerche*. Florence: Edifir, 1991.

Tonti, Henri de. *Dernières découvertes dans l'Amérique septentrionale de M. de La Salle*. Paris: Jean Guignard, 1697.

Tranchepain de St. Augustin, Marie. *Relation du voyage des premières Ursulines à la Nouvelle Orleans et de leur établissement en cette ville*. 1859.

Trexler, Richard C. *Sex and Conquest: Gendered Violence, Political Order, and the European Conquest of the Americas*. Ithaca, N.Y.: Cornell University Press, 1995.

Trigger, Bruce D. *Natives and Newcomers: Canada's "Heroic Age" Reconsidered*. Montreal: McGill-Queen's University Press, 1985.

———. *Understanding Early Civilizations: A Comparative Study*. New York: Cambridge University Press, 2003.

Trudel, Marcel. *L'Esclavage au Canada français: Histoire et conditions de l'esclave*. Quebec: Presses Universitaires Laval, 1960.

Turgeon, Christine. *Art, foi et culture*. Québec: Musée des Ursulines de Québec, 2004.

———. *Le Fil de l'art: Les broderies des Ursulines de Québec*. Québec: Musée du Québec, 2002.

Turgeon, Laurier. "French Beads in France and Northeastern North America During the Sixteenth Century." *Historical Archaeology* 35, 4 (2001): 58–82.

———. "The Tale of the Kettle: Odyssey of an Intercultural Object." *Ethnohistory* 44 (1997): 1–29

Ulrich, Laurel Thatcher. *The Age of Homespun: Objects and Stories in the Creation of an American Myth*. New York: Knopf, 2001.

———. "Cloth, Clothing, and Early American Social History." *Dress* 18 (1991): 39–48.

———. "Of Pens and Needles: Sources in Early American Women's History." *Journal of American History* 77 (1990): 200–207.

Ungerer, Catherine. "Les Valeurs urbaines du propre: Blanchissage et hygiene à Paris au XVIIIe siècle." *Ethnologie Française* 16, 3 (1986): 295–98.

Usner, Daniel H., Jr. *American Indians in the Lower Mississippi Valley: Social and Economic Histories*. Lincoln: University of Nebraska Press, 1998.

———. "Between Creoles and Yankees: The Discursive Representation of Colonial Louisiana in American History." In *French Colonial Louisiana and the Atlantic World*, ed. Bradley G. Bond. Baton Rouge: Louisiana State University Press, 2005. 1–21.

———. "From African Captivity to American Slavery: The Introduction of Black Laborers to Colonial Louisiana." *Louisiana History* 20 (1979): 25–48.

———. "The Frontier Exchange Economy of the Lower Mississippi Valley in the Eighteenth Century." *William and Mary Quarterly* 44 (1987): 165–92.

———. *Indians, Settlers, and Slaves in a Frontier Exchange Economy: The Lower Mississippi Valley Before 1783*. Chapel Hill: University of North Carolina Press, 1992.

Vallot, Antoine, Antoine Daquin, and Guy-Crescent Fagon. *Journal de sante de Louis XIV*. Ed. Stanis Perez. Grenoble: J. Millon, 2004.

Van Kirk, Sylvia. *Many Tender Ties: Women in Fur-Trade Society, 1670–1870*. Norman: University of Oklahoma Press, 1983.

Vernin, Alexandre. "Savons et savonneries à Nyons au XVIIe siècle" *Provence Historique* 51 (2001): 177–91.

Viau, Roland. *Enfants du néant et mangeurs d'âmes: Guerre, culture et societé en Iroquoisie ancienne*. Montreal: Boréal, 1997.

Vickery, Amanda. *The Gentleman's Daughter: Women's Lives in Georgian England*. New Haven, Conn.: Yale University Press, 1998.

———. "Women and the World of Goods: A Lancashire Consumer and Her Possessions, 1751–1781." In *Consumption and the World of Goods*, ed. John Brewer and Roy Porter. London: Routledge, 1993. 274–305.

Vidal, Cécile. "Africains et européens au pays des Illinois durant la periode française (1699–1765)." *French Colonial History* 3 (2003): 51–68.

———. "Francilé et situation coloniale: Nation, empire et race en Louisiane française (1699–1769)." *Annales, HSS* 64, 5 (2009): 1019–50.

———. "French Louisiana and Saint-Domingue: 'The Dependent Servant of an Island Master—in Short, the Colony of a Colony'?" Paper presented at workshop on "Louisiana and the Atlantic World in the Eighteenth and Nineteenth Centuries," École des Hautes Études en Sciences Sociales, Paris, and Tulane University, New Orleans, April 2008.

———. "Les Implantations françaises au pays des Illinois au XVIIIème siècle." Ph.D. dissertation, E.H.E.S.S., 1995.

———. "La Louisiane: L'émigration en provenance du Centre-Ouest français." In *Champlain, ou Les portes du Nouveau-Monde: Cinq siècles d'échanges entre le Centre-Ouest français et l'Amerique du Nord, XVIe–XXe siècles*, ed. Mickaël Augeron and Dominique Guillemet. La Crèche: Geste, 2004.

———. "Le Pays des Illinois, six villages français au cœur de l'Amérique du Nord, 1699–1765." In *De Québec à l'Amérique française, histoire et mémoire: Textes choisis du deuxième colloque de la Commission franco-québécoise sur les lieux de mémoire communs*, ed. Thomas Wien, Cécile Vidal, and Yves Frénette. Québec: Presses de l'Université Laval, 2006. 125–38.

———. "Private and State Violence Against African Slaves in Lower Louisiana During the French Period, 1699–1769." In *New World Orders: Violence, Sanction, and Authority in the Colonial*

Americas, ed. John Smolenski and Thomas J. Humphrey. Early American Studies Philadelphia: University of Pennsylvania Press, 2005. 92–110.

Vigarello, Georges. *Concepts of Cleanliness: Changing Attitudes in France Since the Middle Ages.* Trans. Jean Birrell. Cambridge: Cambridge University Press, 1988.

Villiers du Terrage, Marc. *Les Dernières années de la Louisiane française.* Paris: Guilmoto, 1904.

———. "Établissement de la Province de la Louisiane." *Journal de la Société des Américanistes* 23 (1931).

Vincent, Susan. *Dressing the Elite: Clothes in Early Modern England.* New York: Berg, 2003.

Vrignaud, Gilberte. *Vêture et parure en France au dix-huitième siècle.* Paris: Messene, 1995.

Waldstreicher, David. "Reading the Runaways: Self-Fashioning, Print Culture, and Confidence in Slavery in the Eighteenth-Century Mid-Atlantic." *William and Mary Quarterly* 3rd ser. 56, 2 (April 1999): 243–72.

Walthall, John. "Aboriginal Pottery in the Eighteenth-Century Illini." In *Calumet and Fleur-de-Lys: Archaeology of Indian and French Contact in the Midcontinent,* ed. John A. Walthall and Thomas E. Emerson. Washington, D.C.: Smithsonian Institution Press, 1992. 155–76.

———. Faïence in French Colonial Illinois." *Historical Archaeology* 25, 1 (1991): 80–105.

———, ed. *French Colonial Archaeology: The Illinois Country and the Western Great Lakes.* Urbana: University of Illinois Press, 1991.

Walthall, John A. and Thomas E. Emerson. *Calumet and Fleur-de-Lys: Archaeology of Indian and French Contact in the Midcontinent.* Washington, D.C.: Smithsonian Institution Press, 1992.

Warkentin, Germaine. "Aristotle in New France: Louis Nicolas and the Making of the *Codex canadensis.*" *French Colonial History* 11 (2010): 71–107.

Warkentin, Germaine and Carolyn Podruchny, eds. *Decentering the Renaissance: Canada and Europe in Multidisciplinary Perspective, 1500–1700.* Toronto: University of Toronto Press, 2001.

Waselkov, Gregory A. *The Archaeology of French Colonial North America: English-French Edition.* Guides to the Historical Archaeological Literature 5. Tucson, Ariz.: Society for Historical Archaeology, 1997.

———. "Archaeology of Old Mobile, 1702." *Gulf Coast Historical Review* 6 (1990–91).

———. "French Colonial Trade in the Upper Creek Country." In *Calumet and Fleur-de-Lys: Archaeology of Indian and French Contact in the Midcontinent,* ed. John A. Walthall and Thomas E. Emerson. Washington, D.C.: Smithsonian Institution Press, 1992. 35–53.

Waselkov, Gregory A., Peter H. Wood, and Tom Hatley, eds. *Powhatan's Mantle: Indians in the Colonial Southeast.* Lincoln: University of Nebraska Press, 2006.

Waugh, Norah. *The Cut of Men's Clothes, 1600–1900.* London: Faber and Faber, 1964.

———. *The Cut of Women's Clothes, 1600–1930.* New York: Theatre Arts Books, 1985.

Way, Peter. "The Cutting Edge of Culture: British Soldiers Encounter Native Americans in the French and Indian War." In *Empire and Others: British Encounters with Indigenous Peoples, 1600–1850,* ed. Martin Daunton and Rick Halpern. Philadelphia: University of Pennsylvania Press, 1999.

Weatherill, Lorna. "Consumer Behaviour, Textiles and Dress in the Late Seventeenth and Early Eighteenth Centuries." *Textile History* 22 (1991): 297–310.

Weber, Caroline. *Queen of Fashion: What Marie Antoinette Wore to the Revolution.* New York: Henry Holt, 2006.

Weber, David J. *Barbaros: Spaniards and Their Savages in the Age of Enlightenment.* New Haven, Conn.: Yale University Press.

———. *The Spanish Frontier in North America*. New Haven, Conn.: Yale University Press, 1992.

Weber, Henry. *La Compagnie française des Indes, 1604–1875*. Paris: Librairie Nouvelle de Droit et de Jurisprudence, 1904.

Webster, Mildred. *French St. Joseph: La poste de la Rivière St. Joseph 1690–1780*. St. Joseph, Mich.: Webster, 1990.

Weddle, Robert S., Mary Christine Morkovsky, and Patricia Galloway, eds. *La Salle, the Mississippi, and the Gulf: Three Primary Documents*. College Station: Texas A&M University Press, 1987.

Weigert, Roger-Armand. *Textiles en Europe sous Louis XV: Les plus beaux spécimens de la collection Richelieu*. Fribourg: Office du Livre, 1964.

Welch, Evelyn. "Art on the Edge: Hair and Hands in Renaissance Italy." *Renaissance Studies* 23 (2009): 241–68.

———. "Scented Buttons and Perfumed Gloves: Smelling Things in Renaissance Italy." In *Ornamentalism: The Art of Renaissance Accessories*, ed. Bella Mirabella. Ann Arbor: University of Michigan Press, 2011.

———. *Shopping in the Renaissance*. New Haven, Conn.: Yale University Press, 2005.

White, Bruce M. "The Woman Who Married a Beaver: Trade Patterns and Gender Roles in the Ojibwa Fur Trade." *Ethnohistory* 46, 1 (1999): 109.

White, Luise. "Sex, Soap, and Colonial Studies." *Journal of British Studies* 38 (1999): 478–86.

White, Richard. *The Middle Ground: Indians, Empires, and Republics in the Great Lakes Region, 1650–1815*. New York: Cambridge University Press, 1991.

White, Shane and Graham J. White. *Stylin': African American Expressive Culture from Its Beginnings to the Zoot Suit*. Ithaca, N.Y.: Cornell University Press, 1998.

White, Sophie. "'A Baser Commerce': Retailing, Class, and Gender in French Colonial New Orleans." *William and Mary Quarterly* 3rd ser. 63, 3 (2006): 517–50.

———. "A Certain Article of Furniture: Women and Marriage in the Illinois Country." Paper presented at the Women of New France series of the Fort St. Joseph Archaeological Project, Niles, Michigan, August 2010.

———. "Cultures of Consumption in French Colonial Louisiana: Slaves' Informal Economies in an Atlantic Context." Paper presented at the two-part Workshop on Colonial Louisiana and the Atlantic World in the Eighteenth-Century, École des Hautes Études en Sciences Sociales, Paris, November 9–10, 2007, and Tulane University, April 4–5 2008.

———. "Dress in French Colonial Louisiana, 1699–1769: The Evidence from Notarial Sources." *Dress* 24 (1997): 69–75.

———. "Geographies of Slave Consumption: French Colonial Louisiana and a World of Things." *Winterthur Portfolio* 44 (Fall 2011): 229–48.

———. "Marie Rouensa-8canic8e: Amérindienne Catholique Illinoise." In *Les Femmes dans le bassin des Caraïbes*, ed. Dominique Rogers. Paris: Karthala, forthcoming.

———. "Massacre, *Mardi Gras*, and Torture in Early New Orleans." *William and Mary Quarterly* 3rd ser. 70, 1 (2013), forthcoming.

———. "'This Gown . . . was Much Admired and Caused Much Jealousy': Fashion and the Forging of Identities in French Colonial Louisiana." In *George Washington's South*, ed. Tamara Harvey and Greg O'Brien. Gainesville: University Press of Florida, 2004. 86–118.

———. "'To ensure that he not give himself over to the Indians': Cleanliness, Frenchification, and Whiteness." *Journal of Early American History* 2 (2012): 111–49.

———. "Trading Identities: Cultures of Consumption in French Colonial Louisiana, 1699–1769." Ph.D. dissertation, Courtauld Institute of Art, University of London, 2000.

———. "'Wearing Three or Four Handkerchiefs Around His Neck, and Elsewhere About Him': Slaves' Constructions of Masculinity and Ethnicity in French Colonial New Orleans." *Gender & History* 15, 3 (2003): 528–49.

———. "Widow's Weeds: Masking Loss in French Colonial Louisiana." Paper presented at 34th Annual Meeting of the Costume Society of America, New Orleans, May 20–25, 2008.

Williams, Samuel Cole, ed. *Adair's History of the American Indians*. Ann Arbor, Mich.: Argonaut Press, 1966.

Wilson, Samuel, Jr. *The Architecture of Colonial Louisiana: Collected Essays of Samuel Wilson, Jr. F.A.I.A.* Ed. Jean M. Farnsworth and Ann M. Masson. Lafayette: Center for Louisiana Studies, University of Southwestern Louisiana, 1987.

———. "Louisiana Drawings by Alexandre de Batz." *Journal of the Society of Architectural Historians* 22 (1963): 75–89.

Woods, Rev. Mgr. Earl C. and Charles E. Nolan, eds. *Sacramental Records of the Roman Catholic Church of the Archdiocese of New Orleans*. 10 vols. New Orleans: Archdiocese of New Orleans, 1987–95.

Zitomersky, Joseph. "The Form and Function of French-Native American Relations in Early Eighteenth-Century French Colonial Louisiana." In *Proceedings of the Fifteenth Meeting of the French Colonial Historical Society Martinique and Guadeloupe, May 1989*, ed. Patricia Galloway and Philip P. Boucher. Lanham, Md.: University Press of America, 1992.

———. *French Americans-Native Americans in Eighteenth-Century French Colonial Louisiana: The Population Geography of the Illinois Indians, 1670s-1760s: The Form and Function of French-Native Settlement Relations in Eighteenth Century Louisiana*. Lund: Lund University Press, 1994.

———. "In the Middle and on the Margin: Greater French Louisiana in History and in Professional Historical Memory." In *Le Citoyen dans "l'empire du milieu": Perspectives comparatistes*, ed. Claude Feral. Special issue, *Alizés* (March 2001): 201–64.

———. "Urbanization in French Colonial Louisiana (1706-1766)." *Annales de Démographie Historique* (1974): 261–78.

Zoltvany, Yves F. "Esquisse de la coutume de Paris." *Revue d'Histoire de l'Amérique Française* 25 (1971): 365–84.

INDEX

ACKNOWLEDGMENTS

I am so glad to be in the position to give thanks to the many people and institutions that paved the way for this book.

Given the logistics of conducting research throughout the U.S., Canada,
and Europe, I am deeply indebted for funding received from the Huntington
Library, the Newberry Library, the Louisiana Historical Association, the Pasold Research Fund, the Joseph L. Peyser Endowment for the Study of New
France, and the Costume Society of America. I am also grateful to the University of Notre Dame, and especially to the Institute for Scholarship in the
Liberal Arts (ISLA) in the College of Arts and Letters, for its unflinching
and generous support of innumerable research trips and microfilm purchases
over the last six years. In addition, both ISLA and the Pasold Research Fund
provided generous publication subvention grants to help defray the costs of
color illustrations in the book. A timely year-long fellowship from the National Endowment for the Humanities in 2010-11 provided the proverbial
cherry on the cake, and allowed me to complete my manuscript.

This research was facilitated by the patient assistance of the archivists
and staff members who oversee the major collections of material pertaining
to French colonial Louisiana. I am grateful to the archivists at the Archives
of the Ursuline Convent of New Orleans, the Chicago History Museum, the
Historic New Orleans Collection, the Huntington Library, the Illinois State
Archives in Springfield, the Manuscripts Division at the Library of Congress,
the Louisiana Historical Center at Louisiana State Museum, the Newberry
Library, the Parish of Orleans Notarial Archives (now the Notarial Archives
Research Center), the State Historical Society of Missouri in St. Louis, the
Tilton Memorial Library at Tulane University and the Western Michigan
University Regional Archives in the U.S.; the Archives of the Arrondisse-
ment Maritime de Lorient, the Archives départementales de la Gironde in
Bordeaux, the Archives nationales d'outre-mer, the Bibliothèque de l'Arsenal,
and the Bibliothèque nationale de France, in France; the Archives of the

Monastery of the Ursulines in Quebec, the Archives of the Seminary of Quebec, in Canada; and the Public Record Office at Kew, in England. My thanks also to the microfilm division of the Family History Centers of the Church of the Latter Day Saints (Urbana, Illinois and South Bend, Indiana branches); and the Interlibrary Loan, Microtext, and Rare Books and Special Collections divisions of the University of Notre Dame Libraries. My special appreciation goes to Dr. John Hoffmann of the Illinois Historical Survey at the University of Illinois at Urbana-Champaign, for directing me towards the Illinois Country when I first embarked on my study of Louisiana.

A book on material culture owes much to the kindness and generosity of curators. I owe thanks to the curatorial staff at the Detroit Institute of Art; the Historic New Orleans Collection; Louisiana State Museum (Costume and Art departments); the Missouri Historical Society; the Peabody Museum of Archaeology and Ethnology at Harvard University; and the Winterthur Museum. At the musée du Quai Branly in Paris, Fabienne de Pierrebourg was especially generous; at the Archives of the Monastery of the Ursulines in Quebec, Christine Cheyrou was unstinting in her help; while Michael Nassaney and Joe Brandão introduced me to the archaeological finds at Fort St. Joseph (Niles, Michigan). At the Colonial Williamsburg Foundation, Linda Baumgarten made available the holdings of the costume collection; at the Los Angeles County Museum of Art, Kimberly Chrisman and Clarissa Esguerra did the same. At the Victoria and Albert Museum, my good friend Susan North always made me feel like I was a part of that special institution, and never once balked at my requests to have her pull out yet another eighteenth-century garment for me to examine. I would also like to recognize Aileen Ribeiro, to whom I owe my foundation in dress history.

Working on Louisiana, I am part of a special coterie of scholars of French America characterized by their generosity (whether in giving feedback, sharing documents, new findings or suggestions for potential avenues of research), as well as their conviviality. My special thanks to Guillaume Aubert, Emily Clark, Alexandre Dubé, Robert S. DuPlessis, Carl Ekberg, Brett Rushforth, Susan Sleeper-Smith and Cécile Vidal. Along the way, I also benefited from exchanges with Joe Brandão, Margaret Kimball Brown, Shannon Lee Dawdy, Denis Delâge, Sylvia Frey, Erin Greenwald, Gilles Havard, Thomas N. Ingersoll, Jean-Pierre Le Glaunec, Robert M. Morrissey, Gordon M. Sayre, Claiborne Skinner, Jennifer Spears, Thomas Wien, and Joseph Zitomersky. I owe a particular debt to Cecile Vidal, Carl Ekberg and Dominique Deslandres for commenting on draft chapters, and to Guillaume Aubert and Emily

Clark for reading the entire manuscript. Emily Clark also directed me to Ursuline Sister Ste. Marthe, who now anchors one of my chapters.

An earlier version of Chapter 5 was published in the *Journal of Early American History* 2, 2 (2012) and is reprinted here with permission.

At the University of Pennsylvania Press, Bob Lockhart was a joy to work with—and I will forever be in his debt for granting me forty-eight images, including thirty-three in color. At the McNeil Center, I owe thanks to Dan Richter to whom I first pitched my book, while Kathleen M. Brown was quite simply a dream while Adrienne Hood and Ann M. Little proved to be perfect readers. At Notre Dame, Lisa Harteker helped at a crucial juncture, and Margaret Meserve, Robert Goulding, Sara Maurer, Emily Osborne, Annie Coleman, and Heidi Ardizzone commented on various chapters. This book is so much richer for their input and I for their friendship.

My parents laid the foundations for my conviction that historic textiles and dress matter; my sister Sarah was the first to open my eyes to the legacies of colonialism in our homeland of Mauritius, a former French colony. Above all, this book is dedicated to my beloved Charlie (who read *every* single draft of this book) and to our wonderful daughters, Cleome and Josephine. Long may we travel together around the world.

Printed in the USA
CPSIA information can be obtained
at www.ICGtesting.com
JSHW010339030924
69182JS00010B/514